The Economics of Mic

The Economics of Microfinance

Second Edition

Beatriz Armendáriz and Jonathan Morduch

PHI Learning Private Limited
Delhi-110092
2013

This Indian Reprint—₹ 425.00
(Original U.S. Edition—₹ 1701.00)

THE ECONOMICS OF MICROFINANCE, 2nd ed.
by Beatriz Armendáriz and Jonathan Morduch

ISBN-978-81-203-4271-2

Original edition published by the MIT Press, Cambridge, MA, U.S.A.

Reprinted in India by special arrangement with MIT Press, Cambridge, MA, U.S.A. Not for sale or shipment outside India, Bangladesh, Burma, Nepal, Sri Lanka, Bhutan, Pakistan and the Maldives.

Published by Asoke K. Ghosh, PHI Learning Private Limited, Rimjhim House, 111, Patparganj Industrial Estate, Delhi-110092 and Printed by Glorious Printer, Delhi-110092.

A Georges-Antoine, Mikhaela y Eduardo. Con amor.
To Amy, Leon, Joseph, and Samuel

Contents

Preface to the Second Edition

When we started writing this book in 1998, the idea of microfinance was already gaining ground. But it did not fully burst onto the global scene until around the time that the first edition of *The Economics of Microfinance* was published in 2005. The year 2005 marked the United Nations International Year of Microcredit, a worldwide celebration that engaged banks, governments, philanthropists and the media. Kofi Annan, then Secretary-General of the United Nations, lauded the social promise of microfinance as "an integral part of our collective effort to meet the Millennium Development Goals" (United Nations 2003). In November 2005, *The Economist* devoted a special supplement to microfinance with a decidedly commercial slant. Newspapers, blogs, and television shows started to cover microfinance with greater frequency. The UN year was followed by the announcement in Oslo that the 2006 Nobel Peace Prize would go to Muhammad Yunus and Grameen Bank, the most visible microfinance pioneers. The Nobel Prize brought even more media attention, investment, and research.

Microfinance itself has also been transforming. When we started writing the first edition, the most comprehensive global count of microfinance customers totaled 13 million customers. By the time the first edition went to press, the count had reached 67 million. By the end of 2007, the number had swelled to 155 million, with $5.4 billion invested in the sector in that year. By the time you read this, the number of customers may well exceed 200 million. Many are women: the most recent count shows that women made up 71 percent of the 155 million customers at the end of 2007 (Daley-Harris 2009).

The expansion of scale and investment has brought new ideas and new debates. Like the first edition of this book, the second edition aims to provide an honest reckoning rather than a pure celebration. Most in the microfinance sector have embraced the pursuit of profit, but not with identical degrees of ease and enthusiasm. If there is one unresolved tension that animates those who spend their days working on microfinance, it entails how to navigate the trade-offs between maximizing social impact and building strong, large financial institutions. It is a healthy tension, but an inescapable one.

New to this edition is a chapter on commercialization. We take up tensions and debates directly, define financial terms, and give an empirical assessment of the full financial landscape so far.

The past six years have also seen an outpouring of work on savings and insurance, much of it framed within the emerging academic field of behavioral economics. The first edition strongly pointed in the direction in which the work proceeded, and we're pleased to describe new ideas and evidence. Chapter 6, on savings and insurance, is thus considerably bulked up.

Chapter 9, on impact evaluations, has also grown. When we wrote the chapter for the first edition, we had to conclude that more evaluations should be done—and we awaited them. As we go to press for the second edition, we can happily report on a handful of excellent new studies. Perhaps more important, we can report on a set of newly refined evaluation tools based on randomized control trials. The new results show mixed impacts of microfinance. Microfinance advocates may be disappointed by the lack of stronger results so far, but the evidence should be taken as a prompt to return to basic assumptions with an eye toward improved solutions.

Apart from these large changes, we have taken the chance to update data and describe new studies in nearly every chapter. Chapter 7 on gender and microfinance has been particularly revised, reflecting the importance of women among microfinance customers—and as agents of social change in their families and communities.

As with the first edition, familiarity with economics will help, and we use mathematical notation where it clarifies arguments, but the main points can be understood without the math. We have especially tried to make the book engaging for undergraduates and graduate students in economics and public policy (and have fully updated the exercises at the end of each chapter; as before some are written for advanced economics students with a desire for analytical challenge).

We were pleased to find that microfinance practitioners and policy-makers found useful discussion in the first edition. In response, the second edition is even more focused on drawing analytical lessons that extend outside the bounds of classrooms and seminar rooms.

Beatriz Armendáriz
Jonathan Morduch

Preface to the First Edition

Microfinance is one of those small ideas that turn out to have enormous implications. When Muhammad Yunus, an economics professor at a Bangladesh university, started making small loans to local villagers in the 1970s, it was unclear where the idea would go. Around the world, scores of state-run banks had already tried to provide loans to poor households, and they left a legacy of inefficiency, corruption, and millions of dollars of squandered subsidies. Economic theory also provided ample cautions against lending to low-income households that lack collateral to secure their loans. But Yunus vowed to one day make profits—and he argued that his poor clients would pay back the loans reliably. Today, Muhammad Yunus is recognized as a visionary in a movement that has spread globally, claiming over 65 million customers at the end of 2002. They are served by microfinance institutions that are providing small loans without collateral, collecting deposits, and, increasingly, selling insurance, all to customers who had been written off by commercial banks as being unprofitable. Advocates see the changes as a revolution in thinking about poverty reduction and social change, and not just a banking movement.

The movement has grown through cross-pollination. Muhammad Yunus's Grameen Bank has now been replicated on five continents. Approaches started in Latin America have found their way to the streets of El Paso and New York City; experiments in Bolivia have given birth to institutions in Uganda and Azerbaijan; and policymakers in the world's two most populous countries, India and China, are now developing their own homegrown microfinance versions. Recognizing the energy and activity, the United Nations designated 2005 as the International Year of Microcredit.

This book is about the ideas that have driven the movement. It is also about lessons that the movement holds for economics and, more specifically, for thinking about why poor people stay poor—questions that, at some level, go back to Adam Smith's inquiry into the wealth and poverty of nations. Microfinance successes force economists to rethink assumptions about how poor households save and build assets, and how institutions can overcome market failures. In telling the story, we draw on new developments in economic theories of contracts and incentives, and we also point to unanswered questions and ways to reframe old debates.

There is a great deal already written on microfinance, both by practitioners and academic economists, but the two literatures have for the most part grown up separately and arguments have seldom been put into serious conversation with each other. Both literatures contain valuable insights, and both have their limits; one of our aims in this book is to bridge conversations, to synthesize and juxtapose, and to identify what we know and what we need to know. In this way, this book is both retrospective and prospective.

Combining lessons from the classroom and the field is natural for us. Armendáriz, apart from contributing to the theory of banking in her academic role, founded the Grameen Trust Chiapas in Mexico in 1996, the first replication of the Grameen Bank in Mexico. While writing this book, she devoted much time to the Chiapas project as it went through major reorganizational changes. At the same time, Morduch was carrying out research in Bangladesh, advising projects at Bank Rakyat Indonesia, and analyzing financial data he had helped collect in Chinese villages.

We have been thinking about this book since 1998, when Morduch was visiting Princeton University and Armendáriz was visiting the Massachusetts Institute of Technology. Our common concern at the time was that our respective field experiences in Asia and Latin America did not seem to accord well with the growing theoretical literature, with its focus on group lending contracts to the exclusion of most else. Broader ideas were needed to create workable microfinance institutions in sparsely populated areas, in urban areas, and in the Eastern European countries that were making the transition from Communism to capitalism. Even in the densely populated rural and semi-rural areas where microfinance had first taken root, we saw a variety of mechanisms that were already at work and that economists had so far ignored. This prompted us to undertake our first joint project, "Microfinance Beyond Group Lending" (Armendáriz and Morduch 2000).

   Although we had written drafts of the opening chapters in 1998, good intentions were displaced by other research projects and travel. Two events made us return to the book. One was a grant from the ESRC to Armendáriz, and another was Morduch's research leave at the University of Tokyo in 2001–2002. We then resumed writing the book and started rethinking what we had learned.

   The result is a book on the economics of microfinance that we hope will be useful for students, researchers, and practitioners. We hope that, in different ways for different readers, the book will challenge received wisdom and provoke richer understandings of economic institutions.

Beatriz Armendáriz
Harvard University and
University College London

Jonathan Morduch
New York University

Acknowledgments

The chance to write a second edition is dangerous. If starting to write a book is hard, finishing a book is harder. Writing the second edition was made more exciting and more complicated by the fact that so much new thinking and evidence has emerged in the six years between completing the first edition and completing this one. We have incurred many debts in staying on top of the latest developments.

In writing the book, our views have been shaped and challenged by many colleagues, including Patricia Armendáriz, Abhijit Banerjee, Tim Besley, Patrick Bolton, François Bourguignon, Anne Case, Maria Leonor Chaingneau, Daryl Collins, Jonathan Conning, Robert Cull, Angus Deaton, Asli Demirgüç-Kunt, Mathias Dewatripont, Esther Duflo, Bill Easterly, Maitreesh Ghatak, Xavier Giné, Christian Gollier, Claudio González-Vega, Charles Goodhart, Denis Gromb, Marek Hudon, Dean Karlan, Michael Kremer, Marc Labie, Jean-Jacques Laffont, Valerie Lechene, Julio Luna, Malgosia Madajewicz, Maria Maher, David McKenzie, Lamiya Morshed, Sendhil Mullainathan, Mark Pitt, Jean Tirole, Robert Townsend, Ashok Rai, Shamika Ravi, Debraj Ray, David Roodman, Ariane Szafarz, Lucy White, and Jacob Yaron.

We also thank the many policy analysts and practitioners who have taken time to share their views and experience. Armendáriz gratefully acknowledges collaboration from the Board of Grameen Trust Chiapas and, in particular, from Rubén Armendáriz Guerra, Maricela Gamboa, Karina López-Sánchez, Francisco and Virginia Millán, and Regis Ernesto Figueroa. She is particularly grateful to the members of the Grameen Crédit Agricole Microfinance Foundation, and, especially, to Raphaël Appert, René Carron, Yves Coutourier, Agnès de Cleremont Tonnerre, Luc Démazure, Huzzat Latifee, Daniel

Lebèque, M. Shahjahan, Jean-Luc Perron, and Muhammad Yunus. She is particularly grateful to Jean-Luc Perron and Emmanuel de Lutzel for their intellectual and logistical support. Beatriz Armendáriz thanks Alissa Fishbane, Dean Karlan, and Sendhil Mullainathan for great insights and support in developing a randomized control trial in southern Mexico; Neka Eza's hard work in supervising the surveys was incredibly helpful.

Morduch thanks especially Vikram Akula, Daryl Collins, Carlos Danel, Frank DeGiovanni, Asif Dowla, Chris Dunford, Syed Hashemi, Don Johnston, Elizabeth Littlefield, Imran Matin, Nachiket Mor, Lynne Patterson, Beth Rhyne, Marguerite Robinson, Jay Rosengard, Stuart Rutherford, and Tony Sheldon.

Fortunately, we were able to work with a group of talented and energetic individuals. We are particularly indebted to Catherine Burns for her active participation as researcher, writer, and editor on the second edition. Caitlin Weaver ably managed research assistants at the Financial Access Initiative, and Jonathan Bauchet helped overhaul the new chapter on impact evaluation.

Syed Hashemi, Stuart Rutherford, Mark Schreiner, Richard Rosenberg, and five anonymous reviewers provided detailed comments on an early version of the first edition, and their suggestions greatly improved the manuscript. Dale Adams, Marc Labie, Shamika Ravi, and Adel Varghese gave specific comments which shaped parts of the second edition.

Minh Phuong Bui wrote a set of exercises that accompanied the first edition, and we appreciate her useful feedback overall. Sarah Tsien provided research assistance on the first edition. Emily Wang gave helpful feedback on the first edition, and drafted challenging exercises for chapter 8 of this second edition. Stimulating conversations with Katherine Prescott and Annabel Vanroose are gratefully acknowledged. Alex Kaufman provided exceedingly useful comments and ideas for a new set of exercises, and José Ignacio Cuesta reviewed and re-drafted the exercises for the second edition. Beatriz Armendáriz is particularly grateful to Alex and José Ignacio who were there, by her side, at all times, reading every chapter and delivering most useful comments and suggestions for challenging exercises.

Jane Macdonald, our editor at the MIT Press, proposed the second edition and confidently steered the process to completion. We also thank John Covell at MIT for supporting the project.

Morduch gratefully acknowledges financial support from the Ford Foundation and from the Gates Foundation and AIG through the Financial Access Initiative. (The views expressed here, and any errors, are attributable to the authors only.)

Last, we thank our families. Beatriz Armendáriz thanks George-Antoine Capitani for his intellectual and moral support while writing the second edition. Jonathan Morduch thanks Amy Borovoy for her intellectual partnership.

1   Rethinking Banking

1.1 Introduction

In March 1978, seven years after Bangladesh won its war for independence, a small group of young men joined together to make a secret
pledge. They vowed to create a new and dynamic organization dedicated to fighting rural poverty. Some saw Bangladesh's plight as hope-
less, as the country struggled in a world increasingly divided between
haves and have-nots. Thirty years later, however, the organization
started by the young men serves nearly six million villagers in
Bangladesh and is celebrated by global business leaders. The Association for Social Advancement (now best known by its acronym, ASA)
targets Bangladesh's poorest villagers, many of them women, offering
tools to create better lives. ASA found success by applying fundamental lessons from economics and management, coupled with important
(and not obvious) new insights. In the process, ASA is expanding
financial markets and creating fresh ways to think about business strategies, economics, and social change.[1]

The hurdles have been high and ASA's leaders have had to rethink
their plans more than once. While ASA started with a commitment to
fomenting political transformation, its course shifted radically. Today
ASA is squarely a bank for the poor, headquartered in a new office
tower in Bangladesh's capital. In this, ASA stands as part of a global
"microfinance" movement dedicated to expanding access to small-scale
loans, savings accounts, insurance, and broader financial services in
poor and low-income communities. Their bet is that access to microfinance can offer powerful ways for the poor to unlock their productive
potential by growing small businesses. Increasingly, the focus is also on
helping customers save for the future and create more stable lives. In

doing so, ASA and institutions like it are challenging decades of thinking about markets and social policy in low-income communities.

ASA's customers borrow on average around $120 per loan, and repay the loans over the better part of a year. Traditional commercial banks avoid this population. First, the loans are so small that profits are typically hard to find, and, second, lending seems risky since the borrowers are too poor to offer much in the way of collateral. But at the end of 2008 ASA reported loan recovery rates of 99.6 percent, and their reported revenues have fully covered costs in every year since 1993.

For many observers, microfinance is nothing short of a revolution or a paradigm shift (Robinson 2001). Innovators are profiled in leading newspapers and business magazines (in December 2007, ASA topped *Forbes* magazine's global ranking of microfinance providers), and the 2006 Nobel Peace Prize, awarded to the microfinance pioneers Muhammad Yunus and Grameen Bank, signals the ways in which microfinance has shaken up the world of international development. One of the most striking elements is that the pioneering models grew out of experiments in low-income countries like Bolivia and Bangladesh—rather than from adaptations of standard banking models in richer countries.

Entrepreneurs, academics, social activists, and development experts from around the world have been attracted by the lessons about retail banking through microfinance, as well as by the promise that banks like ASA hold for getting much-needed resources to underserved populations.[2] Scores of doctoral dissertations, master's theses, and academic studies have now been written on microfinance. Some focus on the nontraditional contracts used to compensate for risks and to address information problems faced by the microlenders. Others focus on microfinance as a way to better understand the nature of markets in low-income economies—with possible lessons for how to supply insurance, water, and electricity through markets rather than through inefficient state-owned companies. Still others focus on the ways that microfinance promises to reduce poverty, fight gender inequality, and strengthen communities. This book provides a critical guide to some of the most important new ideas.

The ideas give reasons for hope. Banks and NGOs like ASA are flourishing at a time when the effectiveness of foreign aid to ease the burdens of the world's poor faces fundamental questions (e.g., Boone 1996; Easterly 2006). Governments around the world routinely face criticism for at times being corrupt, bloated, and uninterested in reform. Against this background, banks and NGOs like ASA offer the promise of innovative, cost-effective paths to poverty reduction and social change.

ASA is not the only microlender flourishing in rural Bangladesh. ASA's leadership could learn from the experiences of Grameen Bank and from BRAC (formerly the Bangladesh Rural Advancement Committee). When we looked at the figures at the end of 2003, Grameen claimed 3.1 million members, BRAC claimed 3.9 million, and ASA claimed 2.3 million, nearly all of whom had been written off by commercial banks as being "unbankable." Just four years later, at the end of 2007, the 3 biggest microlenders in Bangladesh claimed over 20 million customers: Grameen counted 7.4 million members, BRAC counted another 7.4 million, and ASA counted 5.4 million.[3] Even accounting for the fact that people may belong to more than one microlending program at a time, both the absolute and relative figures show the potential for rapid growth and scale.

The institutions anchor a movement that is global and growing. Microfinance programs have created new opportunities in contexts as diverse as villages along the Amazon, inner-city Los Angeles, the Paris outskirts, and war-ravaged Bosnia. Programs are well-established in Bolivia, Bangladesh, and Indonesia, and momentum is gaining in Mexico and India. Table 1.1 shows the results of a survey conducted by the Microcredit Summit Campaign. By the end of 2007, the campaign had reports of 154.8 million microfinance clients served worldwide by over 3,350 microfinance institutions. Of these clients, 106.6 million were reported as being in the bottom half of those living below their nation's poverty line or were living in households earning under $1 per day per person (defined as "the poorest"; Daley-Harris 2009). Between 1997 and 2007, the numbers grew on average by about 30 percent per year, and the movement's leaders expect continued expansion as credit unions, commercial banks, and others enter the market.

Microfinance presents a series of exciting possibilities for extending markets, reducing poverty, and fostering social change. But it also presents a series of puzzles, many of which have not yet been widely discussed. One aim of this book is to describe the innovations that have created the movement. Another aim is to address and clarify the puzzles, debates, and assumptions that guide discussions but that are too often overlooked. Debates include whether the poorest are best

Table 1.1
Growth of microfinance coverage as reported to the Microcredit Summit Campaign, 1997–2007

End of year	Total number of institutions	Total number of clients reached (millions)	Number of "poorest" clients reported (millions)
1997	655	16.5	9.0
1998	705	18.7	10.7
1999	964	21.8	13.0
2000	1,477	38.2	21.6
2001	2,033	57.3	29.5
2002	2,334	67.8	41.6
2003	2,577	81.3	55.0
2004	2,814	99.7	72.7
2005	3,056	135.2	96.2
2006	3,244	138.7	96.2
2007	3,352	154.8	106.6

Source: Daley-Harris 2009.

served by loans or by better ways to save, whether subsidies are a help or a hindrance, whether providing credit without training and other complements is enough, and which aspects of lending mechanisms have driven successful performances. Many of the insights from the microfinance experience can be seen fruitfully through the lens of recent innovations in economics (especially the economics of information, contract theory, and behavioral economics). Other microfinance insights point to areas where new research is needed, especially around possibilities and constraints for saving by the poor and for estimating social impacts.

Another aim of the book is to tackle the myths that have made their way into conversations on microfinance. The first myth is that microfinance is essentially about providing loans. In chapter 6 we show that providing better ways for low-income households to save and insure can be as important. But we take issue with the argument that, for the poorest, saving is *more* important. The second myth is that the secret to the high repayment rates on loans is tied closely to the use of the group lending contracts made famous by Bangladesh's Grameen Bank and Bolivia's BancoSol. (Grameen's original approach is described in section 1.4 and in chapter 4.) Group lending has indeed been a critical innovation, but we note emerging tensions, and in chapter 5 we describe a series of innovations in contracts and banking practices that go beyond group lending. We believe that the future of microfinance lies with these less-heralded innovations—including the focus on female customers (discussed in greater detail in chapter 7) and the improved management practices described in chapter 11.

The third myth is that microfinance has a clear record of social impacts and has been shown to be a major tool for poverty reduction and gender empowerment. We believe that microfinance can make a real difference in the lives of those served (otherwise we would not have written this book), but microfinance is neither a panacea nor a magic bullet, and it cannot be expected to work everywhere or for everyone. Relatively few rigorous studies of impacts have been completed, and the evidence on statistical impacts has been mixed so far. There is not yet a widely acclaimed study that robustly shows strong impacts, but many studies suggest the possibility. Better impact studies can help resolve debates, and we review recent results using randomized control trials. Chapter 9 describes approaches and challenges to be confronted in pushing ahead.

The final myth is that most microlenders today are both serving the poor and making profits. We show in chapters 8 and 10 that profitability has been elusive for many institutions, and we describe why good banking practices matter—and how subsidies can be deployed strategically to move microfinance forward.

Unlike most discussions of microfinance oriented toward practitioners, we do not begin by describing new microfinance institutions.[4] We will have much to say about recent innovations later, but our approach begins instead with the nature of poverty and the markets and institutions that currently serve poor households. By beginning with households, communities, and markets, we develop analytical tools and insights that can then be used to think about the new institutions, as well as to think about directions that go beyond current approaches.

1.2 Why Doesn't Capital Naturally Flow to the Poor?

From the viewpoint of basic economics, the need for microfinance is somewhat surprising. One of the first lessons in introductory economics is the principle of diminishing marginal returns to capital, which says that enterprises with relatively little capital should be able to earn higher returns to their investments than enterprises with a great deal of capital. Poorer enterprises should thus be able to pay banks higher interest rates than richer enterprises. Money should flow from rich depositors to poor entrepreneurs.

The "diminishing returns principle" is derived from the assumed concavity of production functions, as illustrated in figure 1.1. Concavity is a product of the plausible assumption that when an enterprise invests more (i.e., uses more capital), it should expect to produce more output, but each additional unit of capital will bring smaller and smaller incremental ("marginal") gains. When a tailor buys his first $100 sewing machine, production can rise quickly relative to the output when using only a needle and thread. The next $100 investment, say for a set of electric scissors, will also bring gains, but the incremental increase is not likely to be as great as that generated by the sewing machine. After all, if buying the scissors added more to output than the sewing machine, the wise tailor would have bought the scissors first. The size of the incremental gains matter since the marginal return to capital determines the borrowers' ability to pay.[5] As figure 1.1 shows, concavity implies that the poor entrepreneur has a higher marginal return to capital (and thus a higher ability to repay lenders) than a richer entrepreneur.

Figure 1.1
Marginal returns to capital with a concave production function. The poorer entrepreneur has a greater return on his next unit of capital and is willing to pay higher interest rates than the richer entrepreneur.

On a larger scale, if this basic tool of introductory economics is correct, global investors have got it all wrong. Instead of investing more money in New York, London, and Tokyo, wise investors should direct their funds toward India, Kenya, Bolivia, and other low-income countries where capital is relatively scarce. Money should move from North to South, not out of altruism but in pursuit of profit. The Nobel-winning economist Robert Lucas Jr. has measured the extent of the expected difference in returns across countries (assuming that marginal returns to capital depend just on the amount of capital relative to other productive inputs). Based on his estimates of marginal returns to capital, Lucas (1990) finds that borrowers in India should be willing to pay fifty-eight times as much for capital as borrowers in the United States. Money should thus flow from New York to New Delhi.[6]

The logic can be pushed even further. Not only should funds move from the United States to India, but also, by the same argument, capital should naturally flow from rich to poor borrowers *within* any given country. Money should flow from Wall Street to Harlem and to the poor mountain communities of Appalachia, from New Delhi to villages throughout India. The principle of diminishing marginal returns says that a simple cobbler working on the streets or a woman selling flowers in a market stall should be able to offer investors higher returns than General Motors or IBM or the Tata Group can—and banks and investors should respond accordingly.

Lucas's ultimate aim is to point to a puzzle: given that investors are basically prudent and self-interested, how has introductory economics got it wrong? Why are investments in fact far more likely to flow from poor to rich countries, and not in the other direction? Why do large corporations have a far easier time obtaining financing from banks than self-employed cobblers and flower sellers?

The first place to start in sorting out the puzzle is with risk. Investing in Kenya, India, or Bolivia is for many a far riskier prospect than investing in U.S. or European equities, especially for global investors without the time and resources to keep up-to-date on shifting local conditions. The same is true of lending to cobblers and flower sellers versus lending to large, regulated corporations. But why can't cobblers and flower sellers in the hinterlands offer such high returns to investors that their risk is well compensated for?

One school argues that poor borrowers can pay high interest rates in principle but that government-imposed interest rate restrictions prevent banks from charging the interest rates required to draw capital from North to South and from cities to villages.[7] If this is so, the challenge for microfinance is wholly political. Advocates should just convince governments to remove usury laws and other restrictions on banks, then sit back and watch the banks flood into poor regions. That is easier said than done of course, especially since usury laws (i.e., laws that put upper limits on the interest rates that lenders can charge) have long histories and strong constituencies.

Reality is both more complicated and more interesting. Even if usury laws could be removed, providing banks with added freedom to serve the poor and cover costs is not the only answer. Indeed, as we show in chapter 2, raising interest rates can undermine institutions by weakening incentives for borrowers. Once (lack of) information is brought into the picture (together with the lack of collateral), we can more fully explain why lenders have such a hard time serving the poor, even households with seemingly high returns. The important factors are the bank's incomplete information about poor borrowers and the poor borrowers' lack of collateral to offer as security to banks.

The first problem—adverse selection—occurs when banks cannot easily determine which customers are likely to be more risky than others. Banks would like to charge riskier customers more than safer customers in order to compensate for the added probability of default. But the bank does not know who is who, and raising average interest rates for everyone often drives safer customers out of the credit market. The second problem, moral hazard, arises because banks are unable to ensure that customers are making the full effort required for their investment projects to be successful. Moral hazard also arises when customers try to abscond with the bank's money. Both problems are made worse by the difficulty of enforcing contracts in regions with weak judicial systems.

These problems could potentially be eliminated if banks had cheap ways to gather and evaluate information on their clients and to enforce contracts. But banks typically face relatively high transactions costs when working in poor communities since handling many small transactions is far more expensive than servicing one large transaction for a richer borrower. Another potential solution would be available if borrowers had marketable assets to offer as collateral. If that were so, banks could lend without risk, knowing that problem loans were covered by assets. But the starting point for microfinance is that new ways of delivering loans are needed precisely because borrowers are too poor to have much in the way of marketable assets. In this sense, for generations poverty has reproduced poverty—and microfinance is seen as a way to break the vicious circle by reducing transactions costs and overcoming information problems.[8]

1.3 Good Intentions Gone Awry: The Failures of State-Owned Development Banks

The lack of banks does not mean that poor individuals are unable to borrow. They do—but from informal sources such as moneylenders, neighbors, relatives, and local traders. Such lenders often have the rich information (and effective means of enforcing contracts) that banks lack. Their resources, however, are limited. Microfinance presents itself as the latest solution to the age-old challenge of finding a way to combine the banks' resources with the local informational and cost advantages of neighbors and moneylenders. Like traditional banks, microfinance institutions can bring in resources from outside the community. Microfinance is not the first attempt to do this, but it is by far the most successful.

The success of microfinance depends in part on studiously avoiding the mistakes of the past. As low-income countries attempted to develop their agricultural sectors after World War II, rural finance emerged as a large concern then too. Large state agricultural banks were given the responsibility for allocating funds, with the hope that providing subsidized credit would induce farmers to irrigate, apply fertilizers, and adopt new crop varieties and technologies (e.g., Reserve Bank of India 1954). The hope was to increase land productivity, increase labor demand, and thereby to increase agricultural wages.

Heavy subsidies were also deployed to compensate the banks for entering into markets where they feared taking huge losses due to high transactions costs and inherent risks. The subsidies were also used to keep interest rates low for poor borrowers. In the Philippines, for example, interest rates charged to borrowers were capped at 16 percent before a reform in 1981, while inflation rates were around 20 percent annually (David 1984). The negative real interest rates created excess demand for loans, adding pressure to allocate loans to politically favored residents, rather than to target groups. Meanwhile, the interest rates offered to rural depositors were only about 6 percent per year, so inflation eroded the purchasing power of savings at a rate of about 14 percent per year. Not surprisingly, such policies turned out disastrously. David (1984, 222) concludes that in the Philippines "credit subsidies through low interest rates worsen income distribution because only a few, typically well-off farmers, receive the bulk of the cheap credit. When interest rates are not allowed to reflect costs of financial intermediation, wealth and political power replace profitability as the basis of allocating credit." Rather than delivering greater financial credit, the policies have been blamed for creating financial repression (McKinnon 1973).[9]

India's Integrated Rural Development Program (IRDP) is, to many, a too perfect example of inefficient subsidized credit. The program allocated credit according to "social targets" that in principle pushed 30 percent of loans toward socially excluded groups (as signified by being a member of a "scheduled" tribe or caste) and 30 percent toward women. Achieving social goals became as important as achieving efficiency. Under the system, capital was allocated according to a series of nested planning exercises, with village plans aggregating to block plans aggregating to district plans aggregating to state plans. Subsidies between 1979 and 1989, a period of rapid IRDP growth, amounted to $6 billion (roughly 25 percent to 50 percent of loan volume made to weak sectors). Those resources did not generate good institutional performance. According to Pulley (1989), IRDP repayment rates fell below 60 percent, and just 11 percent of borrowers took out a second loan after the first (which is particularly striking given the importance accorded to repeat lending by microfinance practitioners). In 2000, the IRDP loan recovery rate fell to just 31 percent (Meyer 2002).[10] As institutional performance dramatically weakened, the IRDP failed to be a reliable and meaningful source of services for the poor.

In the late 1970s and early 1980s, the Rural Finance Program at Ohio State University launched a devastating critique of government-led development banks like the IRDP and the Philippine programs.[11] Its starting point was that credit is not like fertilizer or seeds. Instead, Ohio School critics argued, credit should be thought of as a fungible tool of financial intermediation (with many uses) and not as a specific input into particular production processes. Thus one problem, according to such criticisms, came from mistakenly believing that credit could be "directed" to particular ends favored by policymakers (e.g., expanding the use of high-yielding crop varieties). And that, coupled with cheap credit policies, created havoc in rural financial markets and ultimately undermined attempts to reduce poverty (Adams, Graham, and von Pischke 1984). The story hinges on a failure to adequately account for the incentive effects and politics associated with subsidies. Subsidizing banks, it was argued, made those banks flabby by creating monopolies and removing market tests.

Thus, critics of the subsidized state banks argue that poor households would often have been better off *without* the subsidies. This is in part because, first, subsidized banks pushed out informal credit suppliers on which the poor rely. Second, the market rate of interest is a rationing mechanism—those who are willing to pay for credit are only those with projects that are most worthy. But with subsidies driving interest rates well below market rates of interest, the rationing mechanism broke down. Credit was no longer allocated to the most productive recipients, but instead was often allocated on the basis of politics or social concerns. Good projects thus went unfunded. Third, bankers' incentives to collect savings deposits were diminished by the steady flow of capital from the government, so poor households were left with relatively unattractive and inefficient ways to save. Fourth, the fact that the banks were state banks led to pressure to forgive loans just before elections, to privilege the powerful with access to cheap funds meant for the poor, and to remove incentives for management to build tight, efficient institutions. Braverman and Guasch (1986) conclude that government credit programs in Africa, the Middle East, Latin America, South Asia, and Southeast Asia have, with a few exceptions, ended up with default rates between 40 percent and 95 percent. And at such rates, borrowers can be excused for seeing the credit programs as providing grants rather than loans. The misallocation of resources happened so regularly that González-Vega (1984) dubs it the "iron law of interest rate restrictions."

Critics hold that these kinds of subsidies undermined the poor, although the evidence from India at least provides a more nuanced picture. Empirical work by Burgess and Pande (2005), for example, shows net positive average impacts on the poor in India.[12] Similarly, Binswanger and Khandker (1995) find that between 1972–1973 and 1980–1981 the state banks in India increased nonfarm growth, employment, and rural wages. Still, the Indian programs have been clearly inefficient, and a great deal of money that was originally targeted to the poor ended up being wasted or going into the "wrong" hands. As a result, Binswanger and Khandker find only modest impacts on agricultural output and none on agricultural employment, and they conclude that the costs of the government programs were so high that they nearly swamped the economic benefits. More than any positive historical precedent, it is the repudiation of these negative legacies that has driven the microfinance movement to look to the private sector for inspiration.

1.4   Grameen Bank and the Beginnings of Microfinance

The roots of microfinance can be found in many places, but the best-known story is that of Muhammad Yunus and the founding of Bangladesh's Grameen Bank. We briefly tell the story now and return to Grameen's experience in later chapters.[13]

In the middle of the 1970s, Bangladesh was starting down the long road to build a new nation. The challenges were great: independence from Pakistan had been won in December 1971 after a fierce war, and two years later widespread flooding brought on a famine that killed tens of thousands (Sen 1981). Government surveys found over 80 percent of the population living in poverty in 1973–1974 (Bangladesh Bureau of Statistics 1992).

Muhammad Yunus, an economist trained at Vanderbilt University, was teaching at Chittagong University in southeast Bangladesh. The famine, though, brought him disillusionment with his career as an economics professor. In 1976, Yunus started a series of experiments lending to poor households in the nearby village of Jobra. Even the little money he could lend from his own pocket was enough for villagers to run simple business activities like rice husking and bamboo weaving. Yunus found that borrowers were not only profiting greatly by access to the loans but that they were also repaying reliably, even though the villagers could offer no collateral. Realizing that he could only go so far with his own resources, in 1976 Yunus convinced the Bangladesh Bank (the central bank of Bangladesh) to help him set up a special branch that catered to the poor of Jobra. That soon spawned another trial project, this time in Tangail in North-Central Bangladesh. Assured that the successes were not region-specific flukes, Grameen went nation-wide. One innovation that allowed Grameen to grow explosively was group lending, a mechanism that essentially allows the poor borrowers to act as guarantors for each other. With group lending in place, the bank could quickly grow village by village as funding permitted. And funding—supplied in the early years by the International Fund for Agriculture and Development, the Ford Foundation, and the governments of Bangladesh, Sweden, Norway, and the Netherlands—permitted rapid growth indeed. As figure 1.2 shows, the bank grew by 40 percent per year at its peak. By 1991 the Grameen

Figure 1.2
Growth in Grameen Bank membership, 1976–2007. *Source*: Grameen Bank Historical Data
Series, available at www.grameeninfo.org.

bank had over one million members in Bangladesh, and by June 2008
the number had swollen to 7.5 million. Today, replications exist in
thirty countries, from East Timor to Bosnia.[14] Group lending programs
also operate in thirty of the fifty states in the United States.[15]

Grameen's "classic" group lending contract works very differently
from a standard banking contract for small business. In a standard
relationship, the borrower gives the bank collateral as security, gets a
loan from the bank, invests the capital to generate a return, and finally
pays the loan back with interest. If borrowers cannot repay, their collateral is seized. But Grameen clients are most often too poor to be able
to offer collateral; instead, the classic Grameen contract takes advantage of clients' close ties within their communities. To take advantage
of those relationships, the loan contract involves groups of customers,
not individuals acting on their own. The groups form voluntarily, and,
while loans are made to individuals within groups, all members are
expected to support the others when difficulties arise.

The groups consist of five borrowers each; loans go first to two
members, then to another two, and then to the fifth group member. In
this "classic" contract, the cycle of lending continues as long as loans
are being repaid. But, according to the rules, if one member defaults
and fellow group members do not pay off her debt, all in the group are
denied subsequent loans.[16] This feature gives customers important
incentives to repay promptly, to monitor their neighbors, and to select
responsible partners when forming groups (Fugelsang and Chandler
1993). Moreover, the five-member group is part of a "center" composed
of eight groups. Repayments are made in public, that is, before the forty

members of the center, in weekly installments. Group lending thus takes advantage of local information, peer support, and, if needed, peer pressure. The mechanisms rely on informal relationships between neighbors that facilitate borrowing for households lacking collateral (Besley and Coate 1995; Armendáriz 1999a). The program thus combines the scale advantages of a standard bank with mechanisms long used in traditional modes of informal finance.

The "joint liability" condition is the most celebrated feature of the classic Grameen contract, and it is why microfinance is so closely associated with the idea of group lending. Economic theorists have been intrigued by Grameen's contracts, and there has been an outpouring of research, beginning with Stiglitz (1990) and Varian (1990), on how joint liability works.[17] Throughout the 1990s, however, we have witnessed a growing diversity of approaches that go well beyond group lending with joint liability. As we argue in chapter 5, although Grameen Bank's "joint liability" contract gets much attention, there are other, often overlooked, features of the lending relationship that make the Grameen model different from the textbook bank example. In particular, Grameen creates "dynamic incentives" and generates information by starting with very small loans and gradually increasing loan size as customers demonstrate reliability. In addition, the bank uses an unusual repayment schedule: repayments usually begin just a week after the initial loan has been disbursed and continue weekly after that. This makes the contract look much closer to a consumer loan than a business loan, and it changes the nature of the risk that the bank is taking on— and the service that the bank is providing. Beyond these economic mechanisms, Grameen has found that not only does having a customer base that is 95 percent female improve social impacts, but it may also reduce the financial risk for the bank, an issue to which we return in chapters 5 and 7. While traditional banks have historically lent nearly exclusively to men, married women make up the bulk of Grameen borrowers and they are often more reliable customers than their husbands (Khandker 1998).

Disentangling how the various mechanisms work matters, since what works in Bangladesh may work less well in Brazil or Uganda. Even in rural Bangladesh a variety of approaches are being employed. ASA, for example, started with group lending in 1991, with twenty-person groups (rather than five-person groups) and a highly standardized process. In the beginning, ASA's members took loans in the same amount as one another and thus repaid the same each week, and also saved the same amount. But ASA's program has become far more flexible, one outcome of which has been to reduce reliance on the joint liability contract. ASA's repayment rates have not suffered at all.[18] In other countries different methods are used, including the use of collateral—but often on more flexible terms than a standard bank would use. In general, the use of "individual lending" (as opposed to group lending) methods is gaining ground. As of 2001, even Grameen Bank joined the pack moving away from the joint liability contract. We unpack these mechanisms and models in chapters 4 and 5.

1.5 A Microfinance Revolution? From "Microcredit" to "Microfinance"

One of the most important departures has involved the shift from "microcredit"—which refers specifically to small loans—to "microfinance." The broader term embraces efforts to collect savings from low-income households, to provide insurance ("microinsurance"), and, in some places (BRAC in Bangladesh has pioneered here), to also help in distributing and marketing clients' output. Robinson (2001) provides a rich description of a "microfinance revolution" that is just beginning.[19]

While the words *microcredit* and *microfinance* are often used interchangeably, they have different resonances and are loosely attached to contrasting beliefs about the state of rural finance and the nature of poverty. The small difference in language signals, for some, a big difference in opinion.[20] Microcredit was coined initially to refer to institutions like the Grameen Bank that were focusing on getting loans to the very poor. The focus was explicitly on poverty reduction and social change, and the key players were NGOs. The push to "microfinance" came with recognition that households can benefit from access to financial services more broadly defined (at first the focus was mainly on savings) and not just credit for microenterprises. With the change in language has come a change in orientation, toward "less poor" households and toward the establishment of commercially oriented, fully regulated financial entities.

The push to embrace savings is a welcome one, because it recognizes the pent-up demand for secure places to save, and in that context, the shift from microcredit to microfinance should not be contentious. Debate arises, though, with the relatively new (and wrongheaded in our belief) argument that in fact the poorest customers need savings facilities *only*—that making loans to the poorest is a bad bet.[21] (So much for the principle of diminishing returns to capital!)

Our argument against the primacy of saving for the poorest is both theoretical and empirical. Saving is hard for the poorest but not impossible, and credit usually provides the surest way to quickly obtain large sums of money when needed quickly. Empirical evidence shows that households, rich and poor, often borrow *and* save simultaneously, an idea underscored by new work in behavioral economics and the financial stories detailed by Collins, Morduch, Rutherford et al. (2009). Typically, major outlays are financed by a combination of drawing down savings, selling assets, and borrowing. The ability to borrow in a pinch can be especially critical in keeping savings strategies from becoming derailed. Thus, in practice, borrowing and saving are often complementary activities, not substitutes.

The debate on credit versus saving drags up the legacy of the "exploitative moneylender" on one side and the legacy of the subsidized state banks on the other. In the process it also brings out tensions that run through academic work on household consumption patterns in rural areas. Those who see informal moneylenders as exploitative are sensitive to the powerlessness of poor borrowers (e.g., Bhaduri 1973, 1977). But, as Basu (1997) argues, the question then becomes: Why do the poor remain powerless? If only borrowers could tuck away a bit of money at regular intervals, eventually they would accumulate enough to get out from under the clutches of the moneylender.[22] Bhaduri's response is that the very poor are so close to subsistence that saving is impossible—all extra resources need to go into consumption.[23] Loans, not savings, are thus essential.

Against this is the argument that, to the contrary, even the very poor can save in quantity if only given the chance. The fact that they have not been saving, it is argued, is due to "mistaken" beliefs along the line of Bhaduri (1973) and the fact that subsidized state banks never made a serious effort to collect saving deposits, leading some to wrongly infer that the lack of savings is due to inability, not lack of opportunity (Adams, Graham, and von Pischke 1984). Moreover, Adams and von Pischke (1992) argue that very poor households can seldom productively use loans. Exactly counter to Bhaduri, they argue that savings facilities (and not loans) are thus critical for the poorest. Only the "less poor" should thus be the target of microlending.[24] The precepts that were the basis of the early microfinance movement have thus been turned on their head.

In chapter 6, we attempt to steer between these two poles of rhetoric. Our view is that the very poor can profit from having better ways to both save and borrow, and in chapter 6 we describe new data that unveils the financial lives of poor households. We also discuss insights into saving from behavioral economics, the emerging field at the intersection of economics and psychology. A growing body of research into decision-making reveals that people, rich and poor, consistently save less than they would like to. The problem is not simply impatience and a lack of "future orientation." Instead, new explanations point to limits to complex decision making and weak internal self-control mechanisms on the part of individuals. The theory translates into innovative practice and products. Field studies, for example, show the power of mechanisms like structured savings accounts that require regular deposits toward a fixed goal. Having the right mechanisms can make the difference between saving a little and saving a lot.

In chapter 6, we also consider new initiatives to provide "micro-insurance." Like credit markets, insurance markets are plagued by information problems, high per-unit transactions costs, and a host of contract enforcement difficulties. These problems are magnified in rural areas (where the majority of the poor live) because of the high incidence of risk from floods, droughts, crop loss, and infectious disease. This makes common types of losses particularly difficult to insure against through traditional, local measures. But in chapter 6 we describe innovations in insurance provision that show the potential to match the successes of microfinance to date.

1.6 Rethinking Subsidies

We began the chapter by describing two simple ideas that have inspired the microfinance movement and challenged decades of thinking: first, that poor households can profit from greater access to banks, and, second, that institutions can profit while serving poor customers. Microfinance presents itself as a new market-based strategy for poverty reduction, free of the heavy subsidies that brought down large state banks. In a world in search of easy answers, this "win-win" combination has been a true winner itself. The international Microcredit Summits, first held in 1997, have been graced by heads of state and royalty, and the 2006 Nobel Peace Prize has generated even greater attention for the movement. As foreign aid budgets have been slashed, microfinance so far remains a relatively protected initiative, and foreign investment has grown rapidly through 2008.

Somewhat paradoxically, though, the movement continues to be driven by hundreds of millions of dollars of subsidies, and those subsidies beget many questions. The hope for many is that microfinance programs will use the subsidies in their early start-up phases only, and, as scale economies and experience drive costs down, programs will eventually be able to operate without subsidies. Once free of subsidies, it is argued, the programs can grow without the tether of support (be it from governments or donors). To do this, sustainability-minded advocates argue that programs will need to mobilize capital by taking savings deposits or by issuing bonds, or institutions must become so profitable that they can obtain funds from commercial sources, competing in the marketplace with businesses like computer makers, global retailers, and large, well-established banks.

In the latter regard, Latin America's largest microlender, Banco Compartamos, an affiliate of ACCION International, has led the way, first through large bond issues (starting with a 100-million-peso bond— approximately $10 million—in July 2002) and later with a major public stock offering. As ACCION's president, María Otero, remarked in 2002, "This sale is an exciting first for an ACCION partner and an important benchmark in microfinance. ACCION is committed to the growth of financially self-sufficient microlenders who need not depend on donor funding to fight poverty." Banco Compartamos has grown quickly, serving over one million clients across Mexico by 2008, and aiding clients in informal businesses like food vending, handicraft production, and small-scale trade.[25]

Its entrance into commercial banking is part of a larger trend of commercialization in microfinance, which is the topic of chapter 8. With some micro lenders transforming from nonprofit to regulated institutions and banks redefining their operations to include lending to the poor, the microfinance industry has become more business-like, and more complex. New players have entered the field, including Microfinance Investment Vehicles (MIVs), private funds that invest in microfinance institutions. MIVs have grown at a remarkable rate—their assets increased by 78 percent between the end of 2006 and 2007 (CGAP 2008b)—although the increases are apt to level off with time.

Access to commercial funding gives microfinance institutions freedom from reliance on donor support, but at a price. In general, commercial sources of funding are accessible only to lenders that have demonstrated that they can turn a profit, and often lenders achieve profitability by raising their interest rates on loans or serving better-off customers able to take larger, more profitable loans. That issue—the transfer of costs to poor borrowers and "mission drift"—is the basis for an at times heated disagreement around the commercialization of microfinance. Banco Compartamos has found itself in the middle of this debate. On the one hand, it reaches more clients than any other micro lender in Latin America. On the other, to win the (Mexico) A+ rating granted by Standard and Poor's rating agency and to get attention for its public offering, it covered a relatively inefficient administrative structure by charging borrowers effective interest rates above 100 percent per year, putting its charges close to the range of moneylenders upon which microfinance was meant to improve.[26]

If, as we saw in figure 1.1, the returns to capital function is steeply concave, typical poor borrowers may be able to routinely pay interest rates above 100 percent and still have surplus left over. The fact that Banco Compartamos does not suffer from a lack of clients suggests that there are low-income customers in Mexico willing and able to pay high fees. Microlenders elsewhere, though, have balked at charging high rates and managed to keep them much lower (and Banco Compartamos has reduced its fees in recent years). One global survey shows that after adjusting for inflation, median average interest rates are 25 percent for nongovernmental organizations (NGOs), 20 percent for nonbank financial institutions, and just 13 percent for banks (Cull, Demirgüç-Kunt, and Morduch 2009b). These charges are not low, but they are in line with the costs of handling small transactions.

Why balk at high rates? Ethical considerations aside, let us return to the principle of diminishing marginal returns to capital. Can all poorer borrowers really pay higher interest rates than richer households? An unspoken assumption made in figure 1.1 is that everything but capital is held constant; the analysis implicitly assumed that education levels, business savvy, commercial contacts, and access to other inputs are the same for rich and poor. If this is untrue (and it is hard to imagine it would be true), it is easy to see that entrepreneurs with less capital could have lower marginal returns than richer households. We illustrate this point in figure 1.3. In this case, a poor individual would not be able to routinely pay very high interest rates. Some might, of course, but a considerable group would plausibly be screened out by high rates.

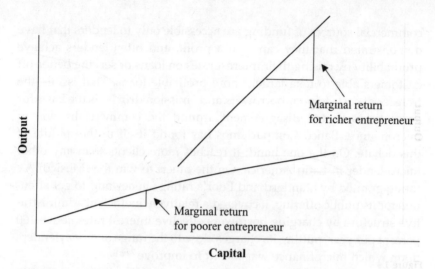

Marginal return
for richer entrepreneur

Marginal return
for poorer entrepreneur

Capital

Figure 1.3
Marginal returns to capital for entrepreneurs with differing complementary inputs.
Poorer entrepreneurs have lower marginal returns despite having less capital.

Even if we imagine, though, for the moment that both rich and poor were alike in these noncapital characteristics, the principle of diminishing marginal returns to capital may still not hold; this is because the production function may not be so "conveniently" concave. Figure 1.4, for example, shows a scenario where the production technology exhibits increasing returns to scale over a relevant range. Here, there may be larger profits per dollar invested by the larger-scale entrepreneur relative to the returns generated by the entrepreneur with less capital.

Here, again, poorer households cannot pay for credit at high prices. This case has the feature that, without adequate financing, poorer entrepreneurs may never be able to achieve the required scale to compete with better-endowed entrepreneurs, yielding a credit-related poverty trap.[27] The challenge taken up in Bangladesh and Indonesia has been to charge relatively low rates of interest (around 15–25 percent per year after inflation adjustments), while continuing to serve very poor clients and covering costs.[28]

The programs in Bangladesh and Indonesia have also been strategic in their use of subsidies. Like other microfinance lenders, Banco Compartamos received large start-up subsidies, as have most major microfinance institutions. Typical arguments for early subsidization

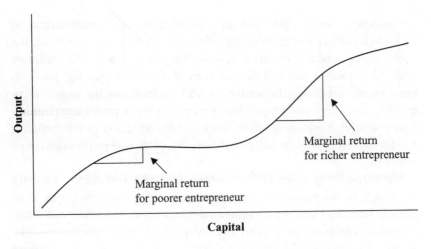

Figure 1.4
Marginal returns to capital with a production function that allows for scale economies (while everything else is the same). As in figure 1.3, poorer entrepreneurs have lower marginal returns despite having less capital.

echo "infant industry" arguments for protection found in the international trade literature. And, as found in such writings, there is fear that some of the "infants" will soon be getting a little long in the tooth. The Grameen Bank, for example, was still taking advantage of subsidies twenty-five years after its start.

A different question is whether the anti-subsidy position is the right one—or, more precisely, whether it is the right position for all programs. Again, there is a parallel with trade theory. The strongly anti-protectionist sentiments that had characterized trade theory for decades (Bhagwati 1988) have given way to more nuanced approaches to globalization, with mainstream economists identifying cases that justify extended protection in the name of economic and social development (e.g., Krugman 1994; Rodrik 1997). So, too, with microfinance: Serious arguments are accumulating that suggest a role for ongoing subsidies if thoughtfully deployed. Of course, that is a big "if," and chapter 10 provides a guide through the thicket.

Sorting out the stories requires taking apart the "win-win" vision put forward by advocates within the donor community, and recognizing the great diversity of programs jostling under the microfinance tent. ASA's story, with which we started the chapter, provides a pointed contrast to many other programs. In 1978 Shafiqual Choudhury and his collaborators started ASA as a small grassroots organization to provide legal aid and training in villages, with the hope of raising the social consciousness of rural households. But in 1991, Choudhury and ASA took a very different turn. Instead of placing hope in consciousness-raising, the leaders of ASA decided that the way to most quickly raise the well-being of the rural poor was by providing banking services, and banking services only. ASA's stripped-down banking model makes profits in large part because of its self-imposed narrow mandate.

But other institutions started where ASA did and took a broader approach to microfinance. They can also count successes, but their bottom lines include improvements in health and education outcomes in addition to financial metrics. Like ASA, charitable organizations like BRAC, Catholic Relief Services, CARE, and Freedom from Hunger have become major microlenders, with missions that also include working to improve health conditions, empower women, and meet the sort of aims articulated as the United Nations' Millennium Development Goals (Littlefield, Morduch, and Hashemi 2003). Latin America's *Pro Mujer* is a case in point. Pro Mujer adds education sessions on health topics to weekly bank meetings for customers; it also provides pap screens for cervical cancer and other basic health services. Freedom from Hunger's affiliates provide health education as well, and their evaluations show positive impacts (relative to control groups) on breastfeeding practices, treatment of diarrhea in children, and rates of completed immunizations (Dunford 2001). Bangladesh's BRAC is perhaps the most fully realized "integrated" provider, offering financial services along with schools, legal training, productive inputs, and help with marketing and business planning. If you are in Dhaka these days, for example, you can buy Aarong brand chocolate milk, which is produced by a BRAC dairy marketing affiliate. A different BRAC subsidiary produces Aarong brand textiles made by poor weavers, and still another subsidiary runs craft shops that sell the goods of microfinance clients.

The microfinance movement is thus populated by diverse institutions, some large and many small, some urban and some rural, some more focused on social change and others more focused on financial development. If the programs that are focusing on social change are cost-effectively achieving their goals, should we be concerned that part of their operation is subsidized? Should we be concerned that, to achieve financial success, Banco Compartamos has had to charge very high interest rates—and that, while a study found that roughly 20 percent of its borrowers were poorer on average than their neighbors, most of its clients are less poor than their neighbors (Zeller, Wollni, and Shaban 2003)?[29] Can cross-subsidization from "richer" customers to "poorer" be sustainable over the long term? It is not clear that there is only one correct answer to each of these questions—and, as we show, answers posed as simple, "universal" truths turn out to rest on strings of assumptions that need disentangling.

We focus on one important strand of these entangled assumptions in chapter 10. There, we describe the possibility for designing "smart subsidies." Doing so will mean making sure that institutions offer quality services that are better than those already available, while also paying close attention to the complicated incentives and constraints of institutions and their staffs. The debate continues as to whether this is possible and, if so, even desirable. Introducing a stronger economic frame will sharpen understandings, and in chapter 10 we analyze concepts behind the trade-offs between lending practices that maximize the depth of outreach (i.e., that serve a greater number of poorer clients) and those that aim to maximize the extent of outreach (those that serve more—but less poor—clients). The book closes by turning to a critical practical issue for microlenders: how to give staff members the appropriate incentives to carry out their economic and social missions. In chapter 11 we draw lessons from agency theory and behavioral economics to describe and challenge conventional wisdom on good management practices.

1.7 Summary and Conclusions

This chapter has set the scene for considering microfinance. We began by asking why "microfinance" is needed in the first place. Why don't existing markets take care of the problems already? Why doesn't capital today flow naturally from richer to poorer countries, and from more affluent individuals to poorer individuals? As described in greater detail in chapter 2, the problems largely hinge on market failures that stem from poor information, high transactions costs, and difficulties enforcing contracts.

Microfinance presents itself as an answer to these problems. It challenges long-held assumptions about what poor households can and cannot achieve and, more broadly, shows the potential for innovative contracts and institutions to improve conditions in low-income communities. Microfinance is a clear improvement over the development banks that emerged in the 1960s, but the implicit "promise" to achieve complete financial self-reliance in short order has been far from fulfilled. And we question whether it should have been a promise in the first place. We have described institutions like Mexico's Banco Compartamos that have pioneered the path toward commercialization by charging very high interest rates. We have described Bangladesh's ASA, which has kept a close eye on cost efficiency (and thus has managed to keep interest rates relatively low) and has approached financial self-sufficiency while keeping social objectives in clear view. And we have also described institutions like Bangladesh's BRAC that work with expanded mandates to provide schools, clinics, and marketing services along with financial services. They too may have a role. Can poverty be most effectively reduced by providing financial services alone? Or can the integrated provision of "complementary" services deliver important added benefits at reasonable costs?

Bold visions have taken the movement this far, and strong, clear ideas are needed to carry the movement forward. Reaching 175 million people (as practitioners hope to do by 2015) is impressive, but as the leaders of the movement are quick to point out, this is just a minority of those who lack access to efficient and reliable financial services at affordable interest rates. Global estimates of the number of unbanked and under-banked adults range between 1 and 2 billion people.

In looking to the future, we will try to dispel microfinance "myths" and revisit ongoing debates in microfinance (particularly about how it works, which customers can be profitably served, and what is the appropriate role for subsidies). In the next chapters we set out ideas that will help evaluate experiences to date, frame debates, and point to new directions and challenges.

1.8 Exercises

1. Microfinance has spread very quickly in low-income countries. However, poor households in relatively high-income countries also lack access to financial services at reasonable prices. Why do financial access and constraints differ between low and high-income countries?

2. Consider an American investor based in New York City. She is attempting to diversify her portfolio across countries. Explain why investing in Kenya or Bolivia might seem riskier than investing in her own country. Contrast this scenario with the choice that a commercial bank manager faces when deciding to lend to high and low-income individuals within her own country.

3. Recall the concept of marginal returns to capital. When the shape of the production function is "conveniently" concave, how does this concept factor into a commercial bank manager's decision about what interest rates to charge a poor entrepreneur and a rich entrepreneur? Give two plausible scenarios where the standard prediction of interest rates for rich and poor entrepreneurs doesn't apply. Based on these two examples, explain why the marginal return to capital might be high for a rich entrepreneur and low for a poor entrepreneur.

4. Take the example of a poor individual who does not have any collateral, and therefore cannot obtain a loan from a standard commercial bank. What is the link between financial exclusion and moral hazard in this particular scenario? Draw a graph showing how credit markets can be inefficient when a potential borrower lacks assets that can be used as collateral to gain access to loans from standard commercial banks.

5. The principle of diminishing returns to capital might not always hold in reality. Explain why this may be the case, based on this principle's main assumptions. How is a violation of the principle of diminishing returns related to the existence of poverty traps?

6. Consider a typical Solow-model framework for a representative entrepreneur. Her production function is given by $y = A(k)k^\alpha$. Her savings rate is s, and capital, k, depreciates at rate δ. $A(k)$ is a productivity parameter given by:

$$\begin{cases} A = A_1 & if \quad k \le k' \\ A = A_2 & if \quad k > k', \end{cases}$$

where $A_1 \ll A_2$ and $A_1 < k^{1-\alpha}\dfrac{\delta}{s} < A_2$. Departing from the idea that the intensive use of capital is associated with high levels of productivity, show that there are two steady states for this particular entrepreneur. Explain why, in the initial stages of this scenario, poor potential entrepreneurs can get caught in a poverty trap. How might credit markets help release poor entrepreneurs from poverty traps?

7. An entrepreneur has an idea for a profitable project, but she is unsure about where to carry it out. She could implement it in Russia, where there is a possibility of political turmoil with a probability of 0.5. If there is no political turmoil, the entrepreneur's project obtains a return of 200 euros; if there is political turmoil, the entrepreneur gets nothing. The same project could also take place in Belgium, where the entrepreneur can obtain a return of 110 euros with certainty. The entrepreneur is risk neutral. Suppose that the project would cost the same to undertake in either country, and that the entrepreneur's only motivation is to maximize expected profits. In which of the two countries should she invest? Briefly explain your answer.

8. As discussed in section 1.3, state-owned rural credit initiatives generally have failed to achieve their objectives. Consider such an institution, and assume that credit supply is inelastic, and that the institution lends at subsidized interest rates. Briefly discuss potential negative consequences of subsidized credit on: (a) the efficiency of credit allocation, and (b) repayment rates. (You may wish to use a graph to sharpen your discussion.)

9. Suppose you live in a low-income community, and that the government wants to help you by granting you the right to borrow $120 at a subsidized annual interest rate of 6 percent. Explain which of the following two strategies you would choose and why: (i) invest the $120 in your family business to obtain an annual net return of 15 percent while incurring a cost of $16, or (ii) deposit the money in a local commercial bank with an annual interest rate of 2.5 percent. What does this simple numerical exercise reveal about the design of government interventions to assist poor individuals' businesses?

10. A bank is subsidized by the government. For each $1,000 loan it extends, it receives a subsidy of $200. The bank's manager is considering extending a $1,000 loan to two potential borrowers. Borrower A promises to give the bank 50 percent of the profit she earns from investing the loan, while borrower B promises only 10 percent of her profit. However, A can generate a gross return of $1,200 with probability 0.8 or get zero with probability of 0.2, but B can generate a gross return of $1,100 with certainty.
a. Which of the two projects is more socially efficient and why?
b. Which of the potential borrowers will the manager choose to finance if he aims to maximize expected profits and why?

c. Compare your answers to questions (a) and (b) and briefly explain what this simple numerical exercise reveals about government intervention in credit markets.

11. A microfinance institution charges interest rates that approach those charged by informal moneylenders. Why might the institution provide social benefits, even though the interest rate it charges is high relative to those charged by commercial banks? What sort of information do you need to assess whether the pricing strategy of this particular institution is socially optimal?

2   Why Intervene in Credit Markets?

2.1   Introduction

Policymakers throughout the world have actively tried to improve financial markets in poor regions, but often with disappointing results. As highlighted in section 1.3, good intentions repeatedly went awry as state-owned development banks mismanaged resources and interest rate restrictions prevented banks from operating viably in poor areas. Against this background, microfinance emerged as an especially promising way to rethink banking for the poor.

Assessing the successes and failures of the early experiences—and, more important, thinking about newer ideas and innovations—requires clear understandings of the aims for intervening. Policymakers and practitioners often skip this beginning step in the hurry to get new programs started. But, as we show, the result is that debates remain unresolved about issues as basic as whether existing credit markets deserve any interventions at all. We believe that appropriately designed interventions can often help, and this chapter describes why. More generally, we aim to clarify principles to use when considering why and when microfinance works—and why and when it fails to achieve its promise. To help answer these questions, sections 2.3 and 2.4 describe common sources of financial market failure.

When markets fail, hardworking entrepreneurs cannot obtain all of the capital needed to run their businesses. As a result, they may turn to wage labor, stay in traditional farming, or take other paths that are less desirable and less profitable. Paulson and Townsend (2004) seek to understand who becomes an entrepreneur and why. Using a survey of 2,880 rural and semi-urban households in central and northeastern Thailand, Paulson and Townsend find strong interests in entrepreneurship. In particular, the authors report that one-third of households in their survey stated that they would like to change occupations. Of the households who would like to change occupations, most would like to open a business. Many of these households report that they do not start businesses because they do not have the necessary funds. Among entrepreneurial households, 54 percent report that their business would be more profitable if they could expand it. When asked why they do not undertake this profitable opportunity, 56 percent of households report that they do not have enough money to do so. Both the formation of new businesses and the way that existing businesses are run appears to be affected by financial constraints.

The costs of those financial constraints are suggested by the finding that the average annual income of business owners in the sample is three times higher than that of non–business owners. Business owners may, of course, also have more relevant skills than non–business owners. If that is so, the comparison overstates the advantage that an average person would gain by switching from farming to business. But the Thai data set is rich with measures for talent, and Paulson and Townsend find that, even after accounting for entrepreneurial ability, poorer households are less likely to start new businesses. They thus argue that the income difference is not explained away by a talent difference, leaving credit rationing as the chief candidate. In principle, microlenders like Thailand's Bank of Agriculture and Agricultural Cooperatives (BAAC) can, as a result, play a pivotal role in expanding opportunities for poor but talented households.

Studies that directly measure financial constraints thus give one impetus for the microfinance movement.[1] For others, merely knowing the high interest rates charged by moneylenders is enough to bring calls that "something must be done!" We argue, though, that just seeing high informal-sector interest rates is insufficient. Instead, determining whether there is an important niche for microfinance requires understanding how markets work and how the informal sector fills gaps—and how and where markets and the informal sector come up short. This chapter describes rationales for intervention, common sources of market failure, and some simple possibilities (short of microfinance) to improve matters.

Section 2.2 considers economies without microfinance. In particular, we describe evidence on moneylenders and what they do. Since an important rationale for microfinance is that it improves on the status quo, we first assess the existing landscape of informal credit. Are moneylenders really exploitative? Will squeezing them out make matters better or worse? Why might it seem that microfinance can do better?

We focus both on the efficiency of outcomes and on their implications for the fair distribution of resources. Sections 2.3 and 2.4 turn to problems faced by commercial banks that hope to lend in low-income communities. This is the other part of the existing financial landscape, although the scene is notable often for the absence of commercial banking rather than its presence. The basic analytics of adverse selection (section 2.3) and moral hazard (section 2.4) provide two important cases in which formal-sector commercial lenders face difficulties serving low-income communities. We employ both algebra and numerical examples to make the points, and we return to the same analytical structures in chapters 4 to explain how microfinance can help. The main arguments should be clear without the math, but we use the analytics to make several less obvious points.

Both adverse selection and moral hazard create situations in which raising interest rates can exacerbate incentive problems in lending. This, in turn, can reduce profits for banks working in poor communities, imposing a major bind on commercial banks trying to expand access. Without added measures to retain good incentives—such as those provided by microfinance contracts—commercial banks will understandably avoid places where collateral is scarce and operating costs are high. Before getting to microfinance contracts, sections 2.5 and 2.6 describe prospects for potentially profitable alliances between informal-sector moneylenders and formal-sector commercial banks.

2.2 Rationales for Intervention

It is easy to see why moneylenders are viewed as being exploitative: their clients are typically poor and have few other options to get capital, while interest rates are typically well above those found in the formal banking sector. Moneylenders are routinely characterized as exploitative monopolists who systematically squeeze the poor. The poor, for their part, are seen as vulnerable, driven to pay usurious rates out of desperation. The enmity is long-standing. In ancient Babylon, Hammurabi's Code tolerated moneylenders and allowed interest charges, but ancient Greeks and Romans—including Plato and Aristotle—inveighed against moneylenders and the very act of charging interest on loans (Vermeersch 1912). The Qur'an carries clear injunctions against charging interest, while the Old Testament is ambivalent.

The New Testament is generally mute on the topic, although canonical laws in the Middle Ages took strong stands against moneylending (with an exception made for Jews). In ancient India, moneylenders were tolerated, but the early Hindu scriptures prescribe set interest rates that should be charged according to a borrower's caste, ranging from 2 percent per year for Brahmins to 60 percent for traders (Reddy 1999).[2]

High interest rates continue to worry observers today. Singh (1968), for example, surveys seven moneylenders in a village close to Amritsar in the Punjab region of India, finding annualized interest rates from 134 to 159 percent—rates that were far higher than commercial bank interest rates. In Thailand, Siamwalla, Pinthong, Poapongsakorn et al. (1990) find typical informal sector annualized rates of 60 percent (compared to 12–14 percent from BAAC). Siamwalla et al. also report rates that are as high as 120 percent in Thailand's remote areas. In the market town of Chambar in Pakistan, Aleem (1990) finds interest rates varying from 18 to 200 percent, with an average of just under 70 percent per year; in contrast, local banks in the region charged 12 percent per year. In Ghana, Malawi, Nigeria, and Tanzania, Steel, Aryeetey, and Hettige et al. (1997) find moneylender interest rates at least 50 percentage points higher than formal sector rates.

In present-day low-income communities, moneylenders remain an important part of the financial landscape, with just as much debate about their roles.[3] One of the hopes for microfinance is that it will facilitate the start of new businesses and the adoption of new practices. Moneylenders, though, have been accused of doing the opposite. For example, Bhaduri (1973) pins India's technological stagnation in agriculture at the feet of moneylenders who double as landlords. He argues that, in the latter role, moneylender-landlords discourage the adoption of new agricultural technologies that would improve the lot of poor farmers since, ultimately, it would make farmers richer and reduce the demand for loans. By keeping farmers perpetually in debt, Bhaduri argues, moneylenders strengthen their bargaining power in order to tighten the squeeze.[4] According to this view, exploitation is possible since moneylenders have local monopoly power; that power is "protected" because potential competitors lack the necessary information and connections to break into local markets. This kind of argument is commonly heard, and undermining the "exploitative moneylender" became a central goal of credit market strategies in India and other developing countries (e.g., RBI, cited in Bell 1990).

But things are not so simple. Getting rid of moneylenders could actually make matters worse for villagers if the moneylenders provide valuable and unique services or financial products. After all, moneylenders can charge high interest rates because at least some villagers are willing to pay them. Moreover, the high interest rates may largely reflect the high costs of doing business (i.e., the costs associated with screening the borrowers, monitoring the use of loans, and enforcing repayments). Those costs may not be small, particularly when potential borrowers do not offer seizable collateral, and when legal enforcement mechanisms are weak. Braverman and Guasch (1989), for example, estimate that the administrative costs of handling small loans range from 15 to 40 percent of loan size.[5]

So how and when can credit market interventions be justified? Economists focus on two features of markets above all else—their efficiency and their effects on the distribution of resources. The first issue relates to "how large the pie is" and the second to "how the pie is sliced." Understanding both and making judgments about interventions requires a clear reckoning of cost structures and the nature of markets; the mere presence of moneylenders is not evidence enough.

2.2.1 Efficiency

Let's consider production loans; villagers, say, want to borrow to buy sewing machines to start small tailoring businesses.[6] Maximizing efficiency does not imply that everyone in a village should have access to credit. Instead, only the most productive villagers should get access; those with mediocre prospects should be excluded (at least if efficiency is the sole criterion). Specifically, all villagers should be given the chance to buy sewing machines if (and only if) their expected returns are greater than the cost of capital.

Imagine that it costs 20 cents per year for a bank to acquire each dollar of capital (say, the bank has to pay 10 cents per dollar per year in interest to depositors and then cover 10 cents per dollar per year in administrative costs); then loans should be given to all borrowers who can take the capital and earn more than 20 cents per dollar.[7] In this way, the total amount of funds generated in the economy expands; the size of the pie increases. In contrast, lending the money to someone who can only generate a return of 15 percent makes the pie smaller.

The ideas can be extended easily to accommodate risk. So far we have assumed that borrowers' returns to investing are given with certainty. But more typically returns may be sometimes high, sometimes low, and most often somewhere in between. In the preceding scenario, we would want to lend only to those individuals with *expected* returns greater than 20 cents per dollar. If, for example, prospective borrowers earn 40 cents per dollar 75 percent percent of the time and zero the remaining 25 percent of the time, their expected returns are 30 cents per dollar (75% · $0.40 + 25% · $0), and they should be funded since capital costs are just 20 cents per dollar. This is ex ante efficiency, capturing the fact that judgments are made before knowing the actual outcomes of investments. If the individual only made positive profits half the time, it would still be ex ante efficient to lend to them (50% · $0.40 + 50% · $0 = $0.20). But if hypothetical success rates were any lower than 50 percent, it is no longer ex ante efficient to lend to them since capital costs are higher than expected returns.

No matter whether monopolists are exploitative or not, it can be inefficient to have them around. In the case of credit markets, monopolists can charge interest rates well above their marginal cost of capital (which we will assume is still 20 cents per dollar per year). So rather than charging an interest rate of 20 percent (as a competitive bank would charge), moneylenders might restrict the quantity lent and charge all borrowers, say, one dollar for each dollar that is lent (a 100 percent annual interest rate); the remaining 80 cents per dollar goes into the moneylender's pocket. When this is the case, only the exceedingly productive villagers can afford to borrow to finance their investments; a wide range of otherwise worthy investment projects will go unfunded.[8] The pie shrinks relative to how large it could potentially be in the absence of monopolistic practices.

Do high interest rates imply monopoly and inefficiency? Merely seeing interest rates of 100 percent does not imply that moneylenders are monopolists; the rates may instead genuinely reflect how costly it is for moneylenders to acquire capital, to transact business, monitor clients, and accommodate risk. When default rates are high, moneylenders may have to charge a lot merely to stay afloat. If this is the case, and if the moneylender is the only possible source of capital, the cause of efficiency will be furthered by only lending to the most productive villagers.

Adams (1984) argues that this is indeed the case: rural credit markets are far more competitive than typically imagined, and he cites studies that show that moneylenders are charging rates in accord with their transactions costs and risks. If Adams is right and the market is truly competitive, microfinance providers will do little to improve access to credit, unless they can figure out a way to cut costs relative to moneylenders. Even worse, if microfinance providers are inappropriately subsidized, they may squeeze out moneylenders, worsening overall access to financial services for poor households: good intentions will have had perverse consequences (Adams and von Pischke 1992). So sorting out the debate about moneylenders and market structure matters to whether supporting microfinance improves efficiency.

Bottomley (1975) uses a much-cited hypothetical example to argue that moneylender rates are plausibly competitive, and Basu (1997) gives a comparison of two moneylenders in this spirit. Imagine one moneylender in the city and one in the countryside. Assuming away transactions costs and capital costs for now, the forces of competition will push the expected returns of the two moneylenders to be equal in a competitive setting. The first moneylender charges 10 percent per year to her urban customers who are so reliable that the chance of default is nil; the moneylender's expected net return is thus 10 percent. The second moneylender expects that half of his customers will default. His expected net return is [(1 + interest rate) · (1 − probability of default) − 1]. In order to do as well as the first moneylender, the second must charge at least 120 percent per year since $(1 + 120\%) \cdot (1 - 50\%) - 1 = 10\%$. Thus, if default rates are high, moneylender interest rates don't look usurious after all. (Looked at a different way, the example shows that default rates have to be 50 percent in order to explain interest rates of 120 percent in this setting.)

This stylized example relies on the assumption that moneylenders can recover nothing at all from those who default, and it ignores opportunity costs and transactions costs. To resolve debates, we need data. A broad range of careful case studies show that typical default rates are nowhere close to 50 percent, but transactions costs and opportunity costs are high. Singh's (1968) study found, for example, that in 1 of 45 transactions, a moneylender lost the full principle, but in every other case it was recovered. In 29 of the cases some part of the interest was not recovered, but this could explain only 23–43 percentage points of the overall interest rates charged. In Pakistan, Aleem (1990) similarly finds that loans and interest are not always paid on time, but the cost is typically a matter of several months of delay in retrieving funds rather than a full loss. In line with Aleem, Collins, Morduch, Rutherford et al. (2009, chapter 5) find that the stated prices of loans and the prices actually paid vary considerably—but that they are high no matter what. The researchers found many one-month consumer loans in the rural South Africa sample carrying a stated interest rate of

30 percent per month, but many of these loans were not paid by the end of the month and interest was not compounded or even extended. Calculations show that for customers who failed to repay after 3 months, the effective cost of these loans dipped close to 8 percent per month. The risk for the lender thus hinges on timeliness of repayments as much as on actual default. One survey in Ghana showed that 70 to 80 percent of informal lenders had perfect loan recovery rates in 1990 and 1991, and in Nigeria, although moneylenders had delinquency rates of 14 percent, all were confident that loans would be fully paid within three months of the due date (Steel et al. 1997). The Bottomley (1975) and Basu (1997) analyses can't fully square these data.

Singh instead argues that the high interest rates are mainly due to high opportunity costs, not to monopoly profits or high default rates. With capital so scarce, he argues, if moneylenders invested their money directly in farm enterprises they would earn net returns that average 77 percent per year. Once the costs of loan distribution are added in (14–31 percentage points), the residual left over for "monopoly profit" averages just 9 percentage points. This is far from exploitation, but much hinges on how "opportunity costs" are interpreted. The high (77 percent) annual returns that the moneylenders can expect on their own farm investments may themselves be partly due to monopoly profits (since capital is scarce in general). Moreover, if borrowers use the funds for farm investments, they must be able to earn returns that are roughly twice as high as the moneylender just to be able to pay back loans with interest rates that average 143 percent per year. It should not be surprising then that all of the borrowers in Singh's sample are borrowing to finance consumption needs (often at desperate times), not to finance production.

A larger issue concerns market structure. Adams (1984) argues that markets are competitive since there is relatively free entry by locals (if not by outside banks). A simple test of this assertion is to check whether the introduction of new funds into an area drives down interest rates (as it should if markets are truly competitive). Siamwalla et al. (1990) do this and find no evidence of falling informal-sector rates in their sample from Thailand.

Aleem (1990) suggests that the apparent confusion may derive from a conflation of "free entry" and "competition." In Chambar market in Pakistan, for example, he too finds free entry, but the market structure better resembles "monopolistic competition" rather than perfect competition.[9] In monopolistic competition, lenders operate in segmented markets, each handling a small share of the overall market. Specialization by geography or other characteristics give lenders local monopolies that allow them to make profits in the short term. At the same time, there may be free entry into the market, so lenders may have difficulty maintaining profits over the long run. To pursue this line, Aleem argues that only considering average costs misses the story. If markets are truly competitive, interest rates should be driven down to the marginal cost of lending—that is, the cost of lending an extra 100 rupees, which is typically below the average cost.

In Aleem's sample, interest rates average 79 percent and average costs (after taking into account risk, opportunity costs, and transactions costs) also average 79 percent. Aleem estimates that the cost of lending an extra 100 rupees, though, is about 48 percent, which is considerably lower than the average cost. Steel et al. (1997) also provide evidence that average costs are much higher than marginal costs in surveys of moneylenders in Ghana, Malawi, Nigeria, and Tanzania. Most of the costs incurred by the moneylenders surveyed in Africa involve the pre-screening of clients. Once that is taken care of, administrative costs of handling loans—the largest element of the marginal cost of lending— is small (equal to only 0.6%–3.2% of loan amounts). In perfectly competitive markets, interest rates should be driven down to the marginal cost, but clearly this has not happened in these cases.

The fact that marginal costs are below average costs is a hallmark of monopolistic competition, as is the fact that average costs match interest rates and that entry into the market is relatively free for insiders. In Chambar market, Aleem describes a situation in which there are too many moneylenders serving too few clients. As a result, moneylenders have difficulty covering the fixed costs of lending, and interest rates stay high because returns to scale cannot be reaped. Although there is no evidence of exploitation of a kind stressed by Bhaduri (1977), the market is inefficient and, in principle at least, interventions could yield a larger pie.

Robinson (2001, 170–171) concludes that "if much of informal moneylending can be explained by a form of monopolistic competition, then it can be argued that banks can cost-effectively gain reliable information about borrowers that is far broader in scope than the information to which informal lenders have access." The reason, she suggests, is that moneylenders only really get to know their own small segments of the market (in contrast to the claim that moneylenders have easy access to local information generally). Microfinance institutions, on the other hand, aim to serve many clients on a large scale, pushing existing barriers out of the way as they bring additional resources into local markets.

Before leaving these issues, we offer one more comment on Adams (1984). Let's accept—for the sake of argument—that it really does cost the moneylender one dollar to lend an additional dollar; the money-lender then just breaks even when charging 100 percent interest rates. He's not a greedy monopolist after all; he's merely a hardwork-ing entrepreneur just scraping by. But readers would be too quick if they then concluded that interventions will not improve efficiency: efficiency must also be judged relative to what *could be*, not just by the current state of affairs. If a microfinance institution could find new ways to lend to those same villagers and charge 25, 50, or 75 percent, efficiency is improved: more projects get funded and the hardworking moneylender goes out of business in the name of prog-ress. The promise is that microfinance can indeed do better than what exists.

2.2.2 Distribution

Considering distribution is another matter. Economists have histori-cally assumed that there is a trade-off between reaching distributional goals and efficiently allocating resources—the steady economic decline of the socialist economies is just the most dramatic recent example of the trade-off. But in a world with limited financial markets, there will not necessarily be a trade-off: spreading access to financial services can both open opportunities for the poor and increase aggregate produc-tive efficiency.[10]

One source of inequity is discrimination on the basis of race, gender, ethnicity, social class, or religion. Such discrimination manifests itself in credit markets, just as it does in labor markets. And when markets are characterized by monopoly, the "disciplining" nature of the market, imperfect as it may be, is even more restricted. Overcoming discrimi-nation will yield a more just society—and possibly a richer one if excluded individuals have worthy investment projects that are going unfunded.

In principle, then, taking resources from privileged households and using them to subsidize the financial access of excluded households can improve both equality and efficiency. As described in chapter 1, policy-makers need to be careful, though, since, as the experience of large, subsidized state banks showed, some ostensibly pro-poor credit market interventions can be so inefficient that, in the end, everyone might lose.

There may also be contexts in which concerns with efficiency and distribution run in opposite directions. To see this, let's return to the monopolist moneylender. We have assumed previously (implicitly) that moneylenders charge all borrowers the same rate of interest. Moneylenders will hold back loans in order to maximize revenues, pushing up average interest rates in the local market. The outcome is inefficient since the quantity of capital is restricted. But consider the case in which a savvy moneylender is able to perfectly adjust interest rates to each client's demand patterns.[11] In this case, the moneylender will not restrict quantities in order to prop up prices. Instead, the moneylender will lend "efficient" quantities but charge rates that extract all of the "consumer surplus" from the clients. The savvy lender will raise interest rates just to the point at which each client is indifferent between borrowing or not, and the moneylender will then reduce the price by a small notch to convince clients to borrow.

The strategy maximizes the moneylender's potential for exploitation, since all of the borrower's benefits are siphoned off. But notice that it's not "inefficient" in the strict sense. Indeed, the moneylender is most successful if all productive borrowers get ample credit—as long as the moneylender can then grab the benefits. The pie grows, but the borrowers' slices shrink. The moral is that even fully efficient informal markets can be improved by pro-poor interventions.

The emerging evidence suggests important pro-poor impacts of microfinance, and in chapter 10 we return to issues of equity and distribution in the context of subsidies. The rest of this chapter focuses on the problems that formal sector banks traditionally have when lending in poor regions, and it is efficiency that will be our first concern for now.

2.3 Agency Problems

Modern economics has made great strides in understanding the so-called agency problems that are ubiquitous in economic life. Consider a borrower and a lender. The borrower has a project, but no money to finance it; she must then turn to the lender. Here, the agency problem refers to the lender's inability to observe the borrower's characteristics (e.g., project riskiness), to observe the borrower's effort, or to observe her profits. These information problems create inefficiencies, and microfinance can be seen as one attempt to overcome them. In this case, the tension involves a "principal" (the lender) trying to do business with an "agent" (the borrower).

The information problems arise at three distinct stages. First, prior to extending a loan, the lender may have little if any reliable information about the quality of the borrower. Sometimes a bit of quick scouting around by a loan officer can yield the required information, but too often the necessary background research on borrowers is prohibitively costly. Better information can prevent the lender from mistakenly extending a loan to a "low quality" borrower without adequately accounting for the risk involved. Second, once the loan has been granted, the lender does not entirely know how the borrower will use the resources. Will the borrower work hard to ensure that the investments are successful? Or might the borrower work less hard than he or she would if the project was entirely self-financed? Third, once investment returns have been realized, the lender may not be able to verify the magnitude of the returns. It is tempting then for the borrower to claim to have had bad luck (and to ask for a reprieve in paying the loan) when in fact the investment was highly profitable, particularly in the presence of limited liability as we discuss below. Having information about the borrower's true profits would allow the lender to be able to claim full repayment and impose sanctions that could potentially prevent future misconduct by the borrower.

The absence of formal credit institutions in village economies is often attributed to these kinds of agency problems. They are accentuated when individuals cannot offer seizable collateral, transactions are costly, and when legal enforcement mechanisms are weak. In what follows we describe the problems faced by a typical commercial bank, and in chapters 4 and 5 we describe microfinance solutions.

2.3.1 Limited Liability

Traditional banks face a series of problems because they come from outside the communities in which they seek to work. Clients have no inherent loyalty to outside banks, and lenders have little information about potential clients. Traditional banks thus tend to require collateral: "no collateral, no business." Before microfinance came along, this usually just meant "no business." The problem faced by traditional banks is that, on the one hand, they lack reliable and inexpensive mechanisms to disburse and collect funds profitably in poor areas; on the other hand, they often have abundant resources to lend. De Soto (2000) has argued that the solution is to tackle the root of the problem by establishing formal titles to land and clear property rights over assets that make it easier for the poor to offer collateral.[12]

But even with clearer property rights, lenders may have difficulty seizing assets from the very poor for social and legal reasons. Steel et al. (1997, 822), for example, find that in their African surveys "it is much easier for a landlord-lender to make productive use of pledged farmland indefinitely than for a bank to seize it." Seizing assets from the poor can be particularly difficult since taking resources away from households that are already poor runs against the anti-poverty missions of many microfinance banks. It also may run into stiff community opposition. It is thus possible for very poor households to have adequate collateral—and to be willing to use it to secure loans—but for banks nevertheless to be wary of the offer.

In Peru, Field and Torero (2006) find that a massive government titling campaign had limited impact on credit expansion, possibly because the program may have actually *reduced* the banks' confidence in being able to seize assets. The argument is supported by data showing that individuals with title indicate *less* fear of losing property when in default. Field and Torero (2006) suggest that "one reason that titling programs may fail to reduce credit constraints is because they unavoidably signal to lenders that a government prioritizes housing for the poor, and hence is more likely to side with borrowers in enforcing credit contracts."

In the analysis that follows, we assume that liability is limited: borrowers cannot repay more than their current income. The task of microfinance is thus to solve the information problems or to find mechanisms that compensate for borrowers' lack of collateral—or both.

2.3.2 Adverse Selection

We first analyze the agency problem that arises before the contractual arrangements actually take place. This is the "adverse selection" problem. Stiglitz and Weiss (1981) pioneered a family of adverse selection models in which banks lack good information about the riskiness of the borrowers' projects. Banks, the argument goes, are therefore unable to discriminate against risky borrowers and interest rates become exceedingly high. Such rates in turn drive worthy borrowers out of the credit market. This is a market "imperfection" since worthy borrowers do not participate in the credit market when efficiency would suggest that they should. The extent of the imperfection is magnified by the extent of limited liability. Note that the concern here is with the *inherent* riskiness of borrowers. Some may simply be more prudent, more conservative, or better insured. Others may be risk-loving, may be poorly disciplined, or may face competing claims on their funds. When discussing moral hazard in section 2.4, we consider cases in which borrowers can take actions that affect their risk of being unable to repay loans.

We illustrate the adverse selection problem with a simple example. Consider an economy populated by individuals who seek to maximize profits. Each individual can invest $1 in a one-period project. Individuals do not have wealth of their own, so they need to borrow to carry out their investment projects. Potential borrowers are heterogeneous: they can either be inherently "safe" or "risky." A safe borrower invests $1 and obtains revenue $\underline{y}$ with certainty. A risky borrower invests $1 and obtains revenue $\bar{y}$ with probability p, where $0 < p < 1$. When they are lucky, risky borrowers earn higher profits than safe borrowers. But when risky borrowers are not successful (which happens with complementary probability $1 - p$), they earn zero and cannot repay the loan. For simplicity we assume that both types have identical *expected* returns; that is, we suppose that riskier borrowers do better than safe borrowers when lucky $(\bar{y} > \underline{y})$ but that they do just as well when returns are adjusted for risk $(p\bar{y} = \underline{y})$.[13]

Assume that the lender is a competitive bank committed to breaking even. The assumption allows us to focus on problems raised by the lack of information and collateral without having to worry about problems created by monopoly as well. Under competition, at minimum the bank tries to cover its gross cost, k, per unit lent. This gross cost includes the full cost of raising money from depositors or donor agencies: for every dollar lent, $k > \$1$ since the bank must account for the loan principal itself as well as bearing transactions costs and paying interest to depositors, donors, commercial banks, or whoever supplied the capital. Suppose that even the low-revenue gross outcome exceeds the gross cost of capital (i.e., $\underline{y} > k$ and $p\bar{y} > k$), so that investment by either borrower is efficient in expectation. We can then see that if the population was made up of *only* safe borrowers, the competitive bank will set the gross interest rate (i.e., interest plus principal) exactly equal to k because safe borrowers always repay; there is no risk, and competitive pressures drive the bank's interest rate down to its marginal costs. At this rate, the bank just breaks even and the borrower keeps a net profit of $(\underline{y} - k)$.

Things get more complicated when we consider the risky population too. When risky borrowers also apply for loans, the bank will want to charge them interest rates higher than k in order to compensate for the added risk. The complication arises when the bank cannot adequately distinguish between safe and risky borrowers beforehand. If the lender only knows that a portion q of the loan applications come from safe borrowers and that a portion $1 - q$ comes from risky borrowers, the break-even gross interest rate of the lender will increase from k to R_b.

Now we have to figure out what that rate R_b is—and what it means for the economy. The next step is for the bank hoping to just cover its costs, to figure out what gross interest rate R_b it should charge so that the *expected* return from lending to a borrower of an unknown type is exactly equal to k, the bank's gross cost of funds: $[q + (1 - q)p]$ $R_b = k$. Flipping the equation around, we find that the gross interest rate charged by the bank in order to just break even will be

$$R_b = k/[q + (1 - q)p] \tag{2.1}$$

A bit of algebra shows that the new break-even rate R_b will exceed k by an amount $A = [k(1 - q)(1 - p)]/[q + (1 - q)p]$, so we can simply write $R_b = k + A$. Now, all borrowers, whether safe or risky, must pay this higher rate since the bank is unable to tell who is who.

It's not surprising that adding risky borrowers into the pool will cause the bank to raise interest rates. The problem is that R_b may rise so high that safe borrowers are discouraged from applying for loans. That would be inefficient since, by assumption, both the risky and the safe borrowers have worthy projects and, in the best of all worlds, they should both be funded. The bottom line is that the lender's lack of information on who is safe and who is risky leads to a situation where the lender may not be able to find an interest rate that both (a) appeals to all creditworthy customers and (b) allows the bank to cover its expected costs.

The example is illustrated in figures 2.1 and 2.2. In figure 2.1, we see that at gross interest rates between $k + A$ and $\underline{y}$ the bank earns an expected profit and both safe and risky types want to borrow.

Assuming that the bank's setup costs are covered, the market is efficient, with no credit rationing. While expected profit rises between $R_b = k + A$ and $\underline{y}$, the bank will set the gross interest rate at $k + A$ since it is only trying to break even. Note that if the bank pushed interest

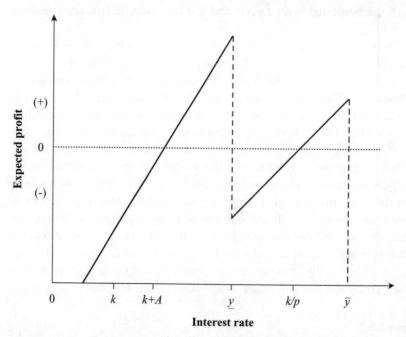

Figure 2.1
Adverse selection example (a). At gross interest rates between $k + A$ and $\underline{y}$ the bank earns a profit and both safe and risky types want to borrow. Safe types leave the market once interest rates rise above $\underline{y}$, and the bank loses money. Once gross interest rates are pushed up to k/p, the bank can again earn profit, while serving only risky borrowers. At gross interest rates above $\bar{y}$ even the risky borrowers leave the market.

rates above $\underline{y}$, it would lose all of its safe clients and immediately lose money. In that case, the prudent bank would either reduce interest rates—or raise them. If the bank raised rates, it would have to increase rates all the way to k/p, in order to cover expected costs while serving only risky borrowers. Profit again rises as the interest rate is pushed above k/p, but the market collapses when rates rise above $\bar{y}$. Above that rate, no one is willing to borrow. The example shows that raising interest rates does not necessarily increase profit in a linear way. As illustrated in figure 2.1, the peak at $\underline{y}$ may be higher than the peak at $\bar{y}$, indicating that the greatest profit is earned at the *lower* interest rates.[14]

Figure 2.2 shows a situation in which the "risky" types are riskier than before. Now the "safe" types can never be induced to enter the market: even at interest rate $\underline{y}$ the bank fails to earn a profit. If the bank raises rates up to k/p, it can finally earn profit, but it will serve only

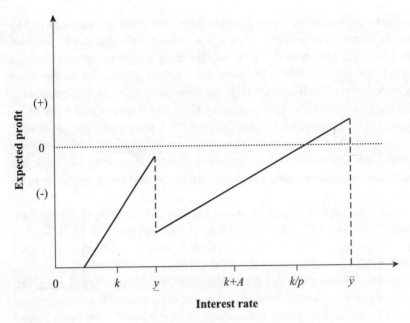

Figure 2.2
Adverse selection example (b). Here, the "risky" types are riskier than in example (a) in figure 2.1. Now the "safe" types can never be served by a bank aiming to break even (since profit is negative even at interest rate $\underline{y}$). The bank must raise gross rates to k/p to earn profit, at which price the bank will only attract risky borrowers. At gross interest rates above $\bar{y}$, the risky borrowers leave the market.

risky borrowers. The bank's information problems preclude serving the safer individuals, and the outcome is both inefficient and inequitable.

2.3.3 A Numerical Example

Let's take another look at adverse selection, this time using hypothetical data. Again, we assume that there are two types of borrowers, safe and risky, and the lender can't tell who is who. The lender, however, knows the fraction of safe types in the population. Again, all borrowers are risk neutral and neither has collateral to secure their loans.

And, again, the lender is in a competitive environment, so it simply tries to break even. The lender's net cost of capital is 40 cents per dollar lent, so it needs to get back at least that much from borrowers on average (after accounting for the probability of default).[15] A project requires $100 of investment and takes one month to complete. If the prospective borrower chooses not to borrow, he can earn a wage of $45 for the month (his "reservation wage"). In the first scenario, let's assume that safe borrowers succeed all of the time and earn gross revenues of $2 for each dollar borrowed (i.e., before paying back the loan with interest). Their expected gross revenues are thus $200, and efficiency is achieved if $200 is greater than the value of the loan to be repaid ($100) plus the net cost of capital ($40) plus the opportunity cost of the borrower's labor ($45). It is: a $15 expected social surplus that is generated. The borrower can generate enough income to pay back the bank and still have more left over than he would make working for a wage.

Risky borrowers invest in riskier projects. When they do well, they earn revenues of $222, but when they do badly (which is 10 percent of the time) they earn zero.[16] Their expected gross return is thus also $200 ($0.90 \cdot \$222$), and the expected social surplus is again $15.

Clearly, efficiency is enhanced if both safe and risky types are given loans—since both have projects that will earn more by investing than could be earned working for a wage. Will the bank offer them loans? If half the population is safe and the other half is risky, the average probability of success in the population is 0.95 ($= 0.5 \cdot 0.90 + 0.5 \cdot 1.00$), and the interest rate charged by the bank has to be at least 47.4 percent to cover capital costs and principal ($0.95 \cdot \$147.4 \approx \$140$). At a net interest rate of 47.4 percent both types will indeed borrow, since the expected net returns are better than what can be earned from working for a

Table 2.1
Numerical example: Base data

The economic environment

Lender's cost of capital	$40 per month per $100 loan
Borrowers' opportunity cost (wage)	$45 per month
Fraction of safe borrowers in the population	50%

	Gross revenue if successful	Probability of success	Expected gross revenue
Scenario 1			
Safe type	$200	100%	$200
Risky type	$222	90%	$200
Scenario 2			
Safe type	$200	100%	$200
Risky type	$267	75%	$200

wage. For the safe borrower, ($200 − $147.4) = $52.6 > $45, and for the risky borrower, $0.90 \cdot (\$222 - \$147.4) \approx \$67.1 > \$45$. The calculation reflects that neither borrower repays interest or principal when he fails. Risky borrowers clearly do better here (at least in expectation), but safe borrowers at least do better than they would working in the wage job. In effect, the safe borrowers are cross-subsidizing their risky neighbors. Still, it beats working for a wage.

The example so far shows that the mere fact that the lender is poorly informed does not necessarily create an inefficiency. Asymmetric information does have distributional consequences (the safer borrowers are the worse for it), but there is no credit rationing and thus no presumption that interventions will automatically make the pie bigger.

Now let's see what happens if we keep everything exactly the same, except we make the risky borrowers even more risky. In this second scenario, we'll assume that risky borrowers succeed only 75 percent of the time, but they earn revenues of $267 when they do well. As a result, the risky individuals again expect to gross $200 $(= 0.75 \cdot \$267)$ if they borrow. Since everything else has been kept the same, a $15 social surplus is again generated when either safe or risky individuals borrow.

But the lender's situation is now very different—it faces more risk. The average probability of success in the population is now just 0.875 $(= 0.5 \cdot 0.75 + 0.5 \cdot 1.00)$, and the interest rate charged by the lender has to rise to at least 60 percent to cover expected capital costs and principal $(0.875 \cdot \$160 = \$140)$. At an interest rate of 60 percent, the risky individual will still want to borrow since $0.75 \cdot (\$267 - \$160) \approx \$80 > \$45$. But the safe individual will depart for a wage job; for him, ($200 − $160) = $40 < \$45$.

The situation is no longer efficient, since both safe and risky individuals should still borrow, but the bank cannot charge an interest rate that works for both. If the lender could charge different types of borrowers different interest rates, the situation might improve, but the lender lacks the information with which to tell who is who.

Once the safe individuals depart, the risky individuals are the only ones left as borrowers. The lender sees what has happened and is forced to raise interest rates even further in order to cover costs (since there is no longer any cross-subsidization by the safe individuals).[17] Interest rates rise to 86.7 percent, which allows the lender to just break even and still gives the risky individuals reason to borrow (0.75[$267 − $187]) = $60 > $45, but they don't do quite as well as before.

The simple example shows that when a bank lacks information, the market may cease to be efficient.[18] Microfinance presents itself as one way to address the inefficiencies, broaden access to markets, and improve distribution as well.

2.4   Moral Hazard

Moral hazard in lending refers to situations where the bank's risk is tied to unobservable choices made by borrowers. Lenders cannot observe the borrowers' choices (about how hard to work or which projects to choose) nor the realization of project returns. As in the previous example, we assume that borrowers are protected by limited liability so they are prevented from repaying more than their current cash flows. In short, borrowers have no collateral.

2.4.1   Ex Ante Moral Hazard

Ex ante moral hazard relates to the idea that unobservable actions or efforts are taken by borrowers after the loan has been disbursed but *before* project returns are realized. These actions affect the probability of a good realization of returns.

In this section we show why the combination of limited liability and moral hazard can lead to inefficient outcomes. As in section 2.3, each individual can invest \$1 in a one-period project. Individuals do not have wealth of their own, so they need to borrow to carry out their investment projects. Suppose that once a particular borrower has obtained a loan, she can either expend effort and thereby make positive profits y with certainty, or not work at all, in which case she makes positive profits with probability $p < 1$ only. We denote by c the cost of effort for the borrower (think of a nonmonetary cost, e.g., an opportunity cost of not earning a wage on a landlord's property). Suppose also that the required gross repayment (again, principal plus interest) to be made to the lender is equal to R, where $R > k$. Again, k is the cost of a unit of capital. Because of limited liability, the amount R will only be paid by the borrower if the borrower earns profits.

Now consider the borrower's decision about whether or not to expend effort on the project. Her net return if she expends effort is $(y - R) - c$. If she doesn't work hard, the expected net return (accounting for uncertainty about the likelihood of succeeding) is $p(y - R)$. In this second case, she does not have to bear the cost c, but she only succeeds p percent of the time. Comparing the two scenarios, the borrower is likely to expend effort only if $(y - R) - c > p(y - R)$. Solving the equation yields a relationship in terms of the gross interest rate: $R < y - [c/(1 - p)]$. That is, if the gross interest rate is raised above $y - [c/(1 - p)]$, the borrower will no longer have an incentive to expend effort. Instead she will take her chances and simply hope for a good outcome. If she's unlucky, it is the bank that will suffer the consequences of the default. So, if the bank wants to reduce its risk, it will have to cap gross interest rates. Just as we saw in the case of adverse selection in section 2.3, raising interest rates does not necessarily increase profits.

Imagine now that the bank's costs of funds k are such that $y - c > k$. In other words, when the borrower expends effort (and thus bears cost c), there is still a net return that is higher than the bank's cost of capital. In a perfect world, the borrower should then be given a loan, and the borrower will expend the effort necessary for success. Borrowing is ex ante efficient, to use the economics terminology.

The problem, of course, is that the bank has no way to force the borrower to take the required effort. Here, it may be that the bank's cost of capital k, while smaller than $(y - c)$, is at the same time greater than $y - [c/(1 - p)]$. But when $k > y - [c/(1 - p)]$, the bank sets $R = k/p$. At such a high interest rate, though, the borrower's incentives militate against expending any effort. Even though the bank in this situation breaks even at $R = k/p$, the bank nevertheless decides not to lend money at all. If only the borrower could somehow commit not to shirk, the bank would make the loan. But the commitment would not be credible without collateral or some other added incentive device. This is one sense in which poverty begets poverty.

We will come back to this scenario in section 4.4.1 to show how microfinance can circumvent moral hazard in the absence of collateral. In anticipation of that discussion, we focus a bit longer on the incentive problem. If the borrower had private wealth to use as collateral, the preceding "credit rationing" problem might be avoided since the existence of collateral would relax the "limited liability constraint" described in section 2.3.1. Threatened with the possible loss of collateral, the borrower finds it more "costly" to shirk. For example, let w denote the borrower's collateral and suppose that w is less than k; then if the project fails (which happens with probability $1 - p$), the borrower loses w. The bank gets w, which is not enough to fully cover the loan loss, but which can still help with the incentive problem. The borrower's incentive constraint now becomes $(y - R) - c > p (y - R) + (1 - p)(-w)$. This says that her net return when expending effort should be greater than her expected return when shirking—which now takes into account that collateral is forfeited $(1 - p)$ percent of the time. Rearranging gives a ceiling for the largest feasible gross interest rate that the bank would charge: $R < y + w - c/(1 - p)$. Thanks to the collateral, this interest rate is higher than the previous ceiling (derived previously). If the collateral were valuable enough—namely, if $k < w$—the bank would be able to set interest rates at levels that always allow borrowing. One challenge of microfinance is to remedy the absence of collateral and use innovative mechanisms as a substitute.

2.4.2 Ex Post Moral Hazard

Another source of credit market imperfection is often referred to as "ex post moral hazard" or the "enforcement problem." The term *ex post* refers to difficulties that emerge after the loan is made and the borrower has invested. Even if those steps proceed well, the borrower may decide to "take the money and run" once project returns are realized. This kind of situation arises either when the lender does not fully observe the borrower's profits (so the borrower can falsely claim a loss and default), or, when having observed returns, the lender cannot enforce repayment by the borrower. In the extreme case where no repayment can be legally enforced ex post (e.g., because project returns are not verifiable), there is no point in making any loan unless the lender can rely on some kind of threat not to refinance a defaulting borrower.[19] However, the threat may not pack much power when potential borrowers can easily migrate and change identity; this poses yet another challenge for microlenders.

To be more explicit about the notion of ex post moral hazard, let us suppose that $1 is invested and the project is always successful, yielding revenue y with certainty. Let us also assume that (1) the borrower has private wealth w, which she can use as collateral for the loan and which the lender is allowed to confiscate in case of default, (2) the gross interest rate R to the lender is fixed so that the lender breaks even when financing the extra cost of the project (once again, the gross interest rate includes principal plus interest), and (3) default is "verified" with probability s. The question then is: When will the borrower choose to repay her loan? Her ex post payoff if she repays is $y + w - R$. Her payoff if she does not repay is $(1 - s)(y + w) + sy$. The first term captures what happens if she is able to "take the money and run"; in this case, which happens with probability $(1 - s)$, she keeps her net returns and her wealth without having to pay interest charges. The second term captures what happens when the bank catches her and seizes the collateral; in this case, which happens with probability s, she gets away with her net returns but forfeits her collateral. Therefore, the borrower will take the money and run if and only if the following enforcement (incentive) constraint is satisfied: $y + w - R > (1 - s)(y + w) + sy$. A bit of algebra shows that the constraint is satisfied if $R < sw$. In other words, where ex post moral hazard is an issue, the gross interest rate cannot exceed the borrower's collateral multiplied by the probability that it will be seized. A borrower without collateral (i.e., with $w = 0$) cannot access outside finance at all, since $s \cdot 0 = 0$. Moreover, if the probability that the bank can seize the collateral is very low, the bank will also refuse to lend. As de Soto (2000) argues, improving property rights and the court systems that enforce those rights can thus be critical to the ability of poor borrowers to get loans.

As we show in section 4.4.2, by combining peer monitoring of ex post returns with the threat of social sanctions to punish strategic defaults, microcredit relaxes the incentive constraint here and thereby increases the amount of credit available.

2.5 Empirical Evidence

The problems resulting from information asymmetries in credit markets are well established in theory. The evidence to date largely backs up the theory, though with some qualifications. Taking a global look, Cull, Demirgüç-Kunt, and Morduch (2007) analyze the financial performance of 124 microfinance institutions and find a pattern that generally lines up with the theoretical predictions derived above. The authors investigate how loan repayment rates vary with the interest rates that institutions charge borrowers. The study considers different kinds of lenders: those that make traditional loans to individuals, others that use Grameen Bank-style group contracts, and "village banks" that also use group-based methods. The researchers find that for the individual-based lenders, loan delinquency rates increase as interest rates rise. The finding is consistent with adverse selection: "safe types" choose not to borrow when the interest rate on loans rises above a threshold, leaving a disproportionate fraction of "risky types" in the pool of borrowers—exacerbating problems with loan repayment. The finding is also consistent with moral hazard: when the interest rate gets too high, borrowers lose the incentive to invest effort in their enterprises and defaults increase. In the Cull et al. dataset, the threshold interest rate is about 40 percent (after inflation). The authors don't find this type of pattern for village banks or group lenders, which, as described in chapter 4, may show the power of group-based contracts in these contexts.

The Cull et al. (2007) results suggest a challenge in studying information problems. The consequences of adverse selection and moral hazard are similar in the data (both predict rising loan default rates as interest rates rise), so they're difficult to disentangle from one another. Karlan and Zinman (2009b) describe an imaginative experimental methodology that takes us closer to separating the roles of adverse selection and moral hazard. The authors worked with a South African lender that deals in consumer credit and uses direct-mail solicitation (the lender is not a typical microfinance institution in its social orientation, though most of its customers are low-income and seek small-sized loans). For the experiment, the lender mailed offers of loans to former clients. Some recipients were chosen at random to receive letters advertising relatively high interest rates, and others were chosen at random to receive offers of lower-interest rate loans. Both rates, though, were "special" offers, in that they were lower than the lender's normal rates. When individuals showed up at the bank to take up the offer, they were given a contract with either a high or low interest rate. In a twist, some borrowers received a contract rate that was lower than the offer rate they thought they would be getting. In addition, some of the borrowers were told that the special contract rate was a one-time offer, while others were given a dynamic incentive—an offer to borrow again at the special contract rate, conditional on their timely repayment of the initial loan.

Randomizing the interest rates both before and after clients select into borrowing separates the roles of adverse selection and "repayment burden." (The authors define "repayment burden" as ex post moral hazard plus the income effect of the contract interest rate.) To test for adverse selection, Karlan and Zinman (2009b) compare the repayment rates for individuals who responded to offers for different rates but ultimately received the same contract rate. Varying the offers individuals selected into draws both high and low risk individuals. With the repayment burden (embodied by the contract rate) held constant, differences in repayment can be attributed to the borrowers' types. The authors isolate moral hazard by comparing individuals who responded to offers for the same rate, but received loans at different rates. The riskiness or type of borrowers is held constant while the repayment burden varies, allowing the authors to look for a repayment burden effect on repayment rates. Finally, the random assignment of a dynamic repayment incentive allows the authors to identify pure moral hazard. If individuals who expect to receive a low rate in the future default less often than individuals who expect to receive a high rate in the future, we expect that moral hazard is present and the dynamic incentive has done its job by mitigating it.

Karlan and Zinman (2009b) find weak evidence of adverse selection and a repayment burden effect, but fairly robust evidence of moral hazard. They observe a sharp increase in repayment when only the incentive to repay is changed, suggesting that borrowers' choices, not their types, are responsible for the improvement in repayment. We will return to a more detailed discussion of moral hazard and dynamic incentives in chapter 5.

The Karlan-Zinman results are consistent with those of de Mel, McKenzie, and Woodruff (2008). In this study, the authors investigate returns to investment in Sri Lankan microenterprises. The researchers examine what happens when a random sample of micro-entrepreneurs receive cash infusions designed to help their businesses. The authors are able to quantify the effect of additional capital on business profits, and then identify the correlation between this effect and a measure of risk aversion. They find that whether entrepreneurs are risk-averse or risk-loving has little impact on returns to capital, suggesting that attitudes about risk may not be as important for determining profits as the theory of adverse selection assumes.

We close this section with a recent counter-example. Klonner and Rai (2008) show that adverse selection appears to drive behavior in a set of financial institutions in India. The institutions are chit funds, a formalized, commercialized version of rotating savings and credit associations (ROSCAs), which we analyze in greater detail in chapter 3. Klonner and Rai examine the impact of a 1993 decision by the Supreme Court of India to put a ceiling on the prices that customers could pay for funds from chit funds—and a 2002 reversal of the decision. In line with the theory of adverse selection, as prices rose, the pool of customers got riskier. At this point, the general case tilts against the empirical importance of adverse selection relative to moral hazard in putting up barriers to banking, but as Klonner and Rai show, the general case may be immaterial in specific settings.

2.6   Linking to Local Markets: A Potential Solution

Before getting to the next chapter, we consider one potential solution to some of the problems outlined so far. Agency theory explains a mismatch of resources and abilities. On one side, banks have funds to lend, but they lack adequate information and cost-effective ways of enforcing contracts. On the other side, moneylenders, traders, and others who live and work in poor communities have the opposite problem: they have quite good information and enforcement mechanisms, but they lack adequate resources. This section tackles the question: Why don't banks and moneylenders join forces? The prominent microfinance models involve wholly new institutions like Bangladesh's ASA or Bolivia's BancoSol that compete head-on with local lenders, but why go to all the trouble? Why don't banks simply hire moneylenders to be their agents? Why not just pay moneylenders (or other local actors) to disburse loans and collect payments for a fee?

Consider the *susu* collectors of West Africa described by Aryeetey and Steel (1995). In Ghana, *susu* collectors visit clients daily, collecting fixed installments ranging from 25¢ to $2.50. Most of the money they collect (on average $218 daily) is deposited in interest-bearing bank accounts, and a small amount is directly lent to clients as advances on savings.[20] *Susu* collectors are thus already positioned between poor clients and commercial banks.

Although 60 percent of clients typically request advances, collectors say they can only give credit to 13 percent of their clients (Steel and Aryeetey 1994). Why not then employ *susu* collectors as loan officers for banks? The idea has special appeal since *susu* collectors are trusted and knowledgeable about their clients' financial situations, while lacking the baggage of moneylenders. Moreover, Aryeetey and Steel estimate that *susu* collectors who are already engaged with the potential borrowers would only face marginal costs of 3 percent of the loan amounts if they expanded lending. The idea has promise, but, as we show, the bank can end up circumventing one agency problem only to be faced with another even more difficult problem: how to get the collectors to honestly and reliably carry out the bank's wishes.

A simpler idea is to create a link to local lenders indirectly. The problem identified earlier is that local lenders lack resources. So, instead of directly hiring local agents, a bank could simply make funds available to moneylenders and other small-scale intermediaries with the expectation that the increase in supply leads to more lending to poor households and lower interest rates. The aim is to relax the local lenders' resource constraints but to stop short of a formal contractual linkage. This "trickle-down" approach is also promising, but new work shows that increasing the supply of credit may do more than just increase available capital; it may also change the dynamics of the market in unintended ways, possibly *raising* interest rates and ultimately hurting poor borrowers.

Although the discussion here carries cautionary messages, the ideas will continue to prove seductive due to their simplicity. As described in what follows, policymakers in India, one of the world's largest markets for microfinance, have put much of their hope in linking banks and local agents. In an interesting twist, links are being made with "self-help groups" of poor women, most often organized by NGOs. By March 2007, 2.9 million self-help groups were providing services to 41 million members (NABARD 2007).[21]

2.6.1 Employing Well-Informed Local Agents

Consider a bank that hires a moneylender as an agent.[22] When lending his own money, the moneylender has a strong reputation for getting loans repaid. But will the moneylender be as vigilant when acting as the bank's agent? What is to keep the moneylender from colluding with borrowers, pocketing the loan, and falsely telling the bank that the borrowers had bad luck and cannot repay? Since the bank is hiring the moneylender because the bank lacks reliable information on local conditions, how can the bank then keep tabs on the moneylender?

The bank can do better than simply paying the moneylender a fixed wage. The moneylender's incentives can be aligned with those of the bank by paying moneylenders a bonus based on loan repayments. As Fuentes (1996) shows, the bonus should be a smaller part of the money-lender's compensation when the probability that a borrower will repay is relatively sensitive to the moneylender's effort. Since the money-lender doesn't need to do so much to achieve repayments, there is less need to provide strong incentives. But when repayment probabilities are less sensitive to effort (i.e., when moneylenders have to work hard to achieve the desired outcome), bonuses should be a bigger part of the compensation package.

The plan is simple to implement if the bank knows how sensitive borrowers are to the efforts of moneylenders. If the bank has concerns beyond just getting its money back, things get more complicated. If, for example, the bank also cares about *who* is borrowing (perhaps there is a preference for lending to women or to the very poor), there will be need for additional monitoring of the moneylender. A similar concern arises if the bank worries about the moneylender's tactics (e.g., it may be against extreme strong-arm strategies).[23] *Quis custodiet ipsos custodes?* Who will guard the guards? If the bank has to closely monitor the agent, the advantages of linking with the moneylender are undermined.

This concern explains why moneylenders are not usually the target when creating linkages.[24] In the example of the Indian self-help groups, linking to NGO-sponsored groups of women mitigated many fears of government planners. All the same, NGOs have their own agendas and costs, making them imperfect conduits when the goal is simply to expand basic financial services. We return to these issues in chapter 11, where we address managerial incentives in microfinance.

2.6.2 Indirect Links to Local Markets

A different way to expand financial services is by increasing supply. Basic microeconomic theory suggests that increasing the supply of capital will alleviate credit constraints and reduce interest rates for poor borrowers. Subsidizing the capital infusion should, in principle, create even stronger downward pressure on interest rates. But when local markets are imperfectly competitive and information is costly to acquire (as discussed in section 2.2), the prediction is not so simple. Hoff and Stiglitz (1998) start with the observation that a massive and prolonged injection of funds in the Thai and Indian rural banking systems lowered the interest rates charged by neither commercial banks nor rural moneylenders.

Hoff and Stiglitz (1998) and Bose (1998) seek to explain the puzzle. They illustrate cases in which the entry of a subsidized program worsens the terms and availability of loans offered by moneylenders in the informal sector. The negative impacts occur because the subsidized funds can change borrowers' incentives, reduce optimal scale for moneylenders, and siphon off the best borrowers, leaving moneylenders with a riskier pool of clients and higher enforcement costs than before.

Hoff and Stiglitz tell three stories. In the first, the injection of new funds into the market increases the number of moneylenders in the market. The new moneylenders compete for clients with established moneylenders, and each lender ends up with a small number of clients. Marginal costs thus rise, raising interest rates for borrowers. In the second story, the incentives of borrowers are adversely affected by the new funds. Borrowers know that if they fail to repay their given lender, there are now more alternative lenders to turn to; incentives to work hard to avoid difficulties are thus weakened. The third story involves inherent borrower quality. Consider a market with borrowers of varying reliability. In the benchmark case, borrowers who have established reputations for reliability are favored by moneylenders. As before, once the banks make more funds available, a larger number of potential moneylenders can enter the market. With more lenders in the market and less attachment of lenders and borrowers, the establishment of borrower reputations weakens. With less reliance on reputation-building as an enforcement device, moneylenders must put more effort into other forms of enforcement; since that is costly, interest rates again rise. Hoff and Stiglitz (1998) conclude that the new entry increases excess capacity among moneylenders and raises unit costs. The subsidy is not passed onto the small farmer. Instead, the subsidy is swallowed up by the reduced efficiency of the informal sector.

Bose (1998) tells a related story with a similar bottom line. In his model, new entrants must lend to lower-than-average-quality borrowers, since the highest-quality borrowers are already in relationships with established moneylenders. Serving lower-quality borrowers increases the average default rate and raises the risk premium that must be charged. Floro and Ray (1997) provide another scenario drawing on experiences in the Philippines. Their focus is on trader-lenders who, again, are in a monopolistically competitive market. In their model, the moneylenders in a region want to collude to keep interest rates high, and collusion is enhanced by the threat of a "credit war." When the credit war occurs, lenders rapidly expand credit, which drives down interest rates and undercuts the profitability of the deviating lenders. The scarcity of resources keeps this impulse in check, which in turn renders collusion more difficult. But with the injection of funds, the possibility of a viable credit war increases, and, with that threat, collusion gets easier. With stronger collusive possibilities, interest rates rise and poor borrowers are the worse for it.

2.7 Summary and Conclusions

There are good and bad reasons for intervening in financial markets. If the markets are already working relatively well, interventions won't make much of a dent—or, worse, they might undermine the quality and extent of services provided by the market. Merely seeing high interest rates charged by moneylenders is not sufficient grounds for intervention. Instead, interventions (like creating a microfinance institution) should be based on clear understandings of how the efficiency and equity of outcomes will change. This requires evaluation of possible market failures.

The analyses of moral hazard and adverse selection provide two tools for analyzing market imperfections. Both are based on problems posed by informational asymmetries—the borrowers have better information on their creditworthiness and risk-taking than does the bank. In the case of moral hazard, inefficiencies arise when the bank cannot deter borrowers from taking excessive risks that raise the probability of default. The problem is that by defaulting, borrowers avoid facing the full consequences of their actions. Inefficiencies due to adverse selection arise when banks cannot adequately distinguish safer borrowers from riskier borrowers. When that happens, all borrowers are charged the same interest rates, and safer borrowers end up effectively cross-subsidizing riskier borrowers. If the problem is acute enough, safer borrowers will refuse to borrow at the going interest rate, leaving the bank saddled with a riskier-than-average pool of customers. Both adverse selection and moral hazard show serious constraints faced by banks in low-income communities—posed especially by the lack of collateral. In these cases, if the bank raises its interest rates as a response to perceived risks, it may end up exacerbating incentive problems to such a degree that profits fall rather than rise. Commercial banks will understandably be reluctant to enter markets where collateral is scarce and transactions costs are high.

Both adverse selection and moral hazard could be solved if borrowers could credibly offer collateral to secure their loans. But the starting point here is that borrowers don't have adequate collateral. As a result, it would seem that for the bank to do better, it would need a way to get more information—but an important assumption is that commercial lenders face high costs in getting more information.

The microfinance innovations described in chapters 4 and 5 provide innovative ways around these problems. One of the notable aspects of these microfinance approaches is that improvements are possible even when lenders do not actually acquire more information. Instead, the contracts harness local information and give borrowers incentives to use their own information on their peers to the advantage of the bank. It is not that the older analyses of information problems were incorrect, it is just that they failed to consider new ideas to circumvent information problems.

The discussion in this chapter also helps to explain why microfinance has mainly been carried out by new institutions, rather than by trying to engage, coopt, and otherwise influence existing local lenders. In large part, the logic follows that of the modern theory of the firm, which seeks to explain why firms exist, rather than using independent contractors—from accountants to secretaries—to make all transactions (e.g., Hart 1995). Even though, as Fuentes (1996) suggests, incentive contracts in principle can be devised to facilitate hiring local lenders as agents for banks, practical implementation is a challenge. The chosen task of most microlenders has thus been to find cheap, simple mechanisms that improve *on* the informal sector—rather than trying to improve the informal sector itself.

Finally, the discussion of moral hazard and adverse selection provides important perspective on arguments about setting interest rates. In *Undermining Rural Development with Cheap Credit*, Adams, Graham, and von Pischke (1984) drive home the argument that interest rates that are too low can undermine microfinance for political reasons. In a related argument, policy-makers often argue that interest rates should be raised as high as is needed to fully cover costs, otherwise programs will not be financially sustainable (e.g., Consultative Group to Assist the Poorest 1996). This has been a hard-fought debate, and we agree that prudently raising interest rates can be a key to microfinance success. But the analysis in this chapter warns us that there can also be problems posed by interest rates that are too high. The previous analyses of moral hazard and adverse selection show how raising interest rates too high can undermine the quality of an institution's loan portfolio and reduce profitability. As with charging interest rates that are too low, good intentions can again go awry when raising interest rates. The challenge for microfinance is to couple smart interest rate policies with new ways of doing business to ensure good incentives for customers. We return to the discussion of interest rates (from the perspective of maximizing social welfare) in chapter 10.

2.8 Exercises

1. If being a moneylender is as profitable as many observers claim it is, give two reasons why moneylenders in low-income countries do not appear to operate in a competitive environment.

2. Moneylenders are known to charge exceedingly high interest rates.

a. Provide three alternative explanations as to why this might be the case.

b. Briefly assess the efficiency and equity of informal credit markets in light of your explanations.

3. It is quite common for households in poor communities to rely on loans from their families and neighbors. Such loans often carry very low interest rates, sometimes as low as zero percent.

a. Why are family and friends willing to lend money at such low rates in credit markets where households are typically credit-constrained?

b. How can one reconcile the idea of loans with zero percent interest with the existence of moneylenders charging rates above 100 percent per year?

4. Think of moneylenders as credit agents operating in a monopolistic environment.

a. Why is the fact that moneylenders' marginal costs are below their average costs considered to be a hallmark of monopolistic competition?

b. Explain the social inefficiencies in this scenario.

5. Free entry by businesses into a market is generally taken to imply that the market is perfectly competitive. Why might seeing free entry into local credit markets not be sufficient to determine whether the market is competitive?

6. Consider the framework used by Ghatak (2000). Assume a one-period economy with a population normalized to one. Each entrepreneur in this economy owns one unit of labor and has a risky project that needs one unit of labor and one unit of capital to be completed. The project can either succeed or fail, yielding return of R_i in case of success, and "zero" in case of failure, where subscript i stands for the type of the entrepreneur (i.e., risky or safe). There is a proportion θ of risky entrepreneurs and a proportion $(1 - \theta)$ of safe entrepreneurs, whose projects have, respectively, probabilities of success given by p_r and p_s with $0 < p_r < p_s < 1$. For simplicity, assume that $p_r R_r = p_s R_s = \bar{R}$, and that every entrepreneur has a reservation payoff of $\bar{u}$. There is a bank in this economy that lends funds at a cost $\rho > 1$ per unit of capital, in pursuit of a break-even objective. All the bank knows about the entrepreneurs is the proportion of risky and safe entrepreneurs, and their respective probabilities of success. Assume that there are no enforcement costs for debt repayments, and thus that there aren't any ex post moral hazard problems here.

a. What condition is required for a project to be carried out and to be socially efficient?

b. Assume that the condition you spelled out in (a) holds. Now suppose that there is complete information, so the bank can perfectly distinguish between the entrepreneurs' types (i.e., the bank knows whether each loan applicant is risky or safe). Find the complete information optimal contract, and interpret it briefly.

c. What type of entrepreneurs invest under complete information contracts, and why?

d. Now suppose that the bank cannot distinguish the types of loan applicants. Find the optimal incomplete information contract, and contrast your result with that of a complete information scenario.

e. Again, which types of individuals invest under incomplete information contracts? What is the threshold level of $\bar{R}$ where safe borrowers will exit the credit market, or switch from wanting to borrow to not wanting to borrow? Comment on what would happen if $\bar{R}$ is lower than that threshold.

f. How much would safe entrepreneurs be willing to pay in order to show the bank that they are indeed safe, so that they are charged an interest rate r_s? What is a necessary condition for this to be possible (pertaining to risky entrepreneurs' incentives)? Contrast this with the incomplete information scenario as per (d) above.

g. Explain the relevance of this exercise for the particular case of microfinance institutions.

7. Consider an economy with risk neutral entrepreneurs, a competitive bank that wants to break even, and two types of potential borrowers. Starting a project costs $100, and it takes one period for the project to yield a positive return, which only happens if the project succeeds. If the project fails, the return is zero. Projects managed by both types of entrepreneurs are risky and can only be carried out if they receive loans from the bank. If entrepreneurs' projects in this economy are not financed by the bank, they can work as day laborers and earn a positive wage. The break-even bank aims to cover its gross cost $K = \$145$ per $100 loan. Assume that all potential entrepreneurs in this economy, if and when they gain access to loans from the bank, are protected by limited liability. Additional relevant information about the borrowers and their projects is contained in the following table:

Entrepreneur Type	Proportion	Probability of Success	Gross Revenue if Successful	Outside Wages
1	0.6	0.9	$230	$52
2	0.4	0.5	$420	$55

a. Is it socially efficient for both types of entrepreneurs to access loans in this economy? Briefly explain your answer.

b. Suppose that the bank can observe entrepreneurs' types. What will be the interest rate that the bank will charge to each type? Briefly explain whether potential entrepreneurs will actually decide to carry out their investments at such interest rates.

c. If the bank is unable to distinguish between type 1 and type 2 borrowers, which of the two types will be credit rationed?

d. Briefly explain the relevance of this exercise to the case of microfinance institutions.

8. Consider an economy that is similar to the one in the previous exercise, but there are three types of entrepreneurs. The projects in this scenario are also risky and yield a positive return only when they succeed. The cost of starting-up a project is $150, which only a competitive bank can deliver via a loan of an equivalent amount. The gross cost of raising capital for the bank is $204 per each $150 loan. Additional relevant information about the entrepreneurs and their projects is contained in the following table:

Entrepreneur Type	Proportion	Probability of Success	Gross Revenue if Successful	Outside Wages
1	1/3	0.9	$300	$55
2	1/3	0.75	$333.33	$40
3	1/3	0.5	$500	$40

All relevant information is public, except for entrepreneurs' types, which is private information to each entrepreneur—that is, the break-even bank cannot distinguish the type of entrepreneurs it faces when deciding whether or not to lend. Compute the prevailing interest rate in this economy, and briefly comment on the relevance of this exercise for the case of microfinance institutions facing a continuum of entrepreneurs' types.

9. Moral hazard is a problem because poor borrowers lack collateral. If they had collateral, it could be taken away, providing a punishment to shirkers.
a. Can lenders circumvent moral hazard if they are given the right to harshly punish borrowers that have put insufficient effort by, say, throwing them into a "debtors' prison?"
b. Would you expect borrowers to take this risk?
c. In what way could this particular strategy be considered an improvement over the status quo, characterized by credit rationing and limited financial access?
d. Why is such a debtors' prison strategy likely to raise major problems in terms of incentives for microfinance institutions, and why would it challenge common perceptions on fairness and equity?

10. A microfinance institution aims to break even. Its manager cannot distinguish between entrepreneurs of different types, but she knows that the population of potential borrowers contains entrepreneurs who are safe with probability 0.5 and risky with probability 0.5. Safe entrepreneurs contract $100 loans and obtain $200 from investing with probability 1. Risky entrepreneurs contract $100 loans and obtain $222 from investing with probability 0.9, and zero with probability 0.1. If the cost of raising capital for the institution is $40 per loan, then the institution will charge an interest rate of 40 percent and break even without subsidies. In plain and clear language, explain why this is the case.

11. Consider an economy with risk neutral individuals. There is a borrower who wants to run a project with a required investment of $100. If the borrower puts enough effort into her project, she will succeed with probability 0.9 and get a gross revenue of $y = \$150$. Otherwise, she fails and gets nothing. But if the borrower's effort level is low, the probability that she will obtain the gross revenue $y = \$150$ is only 0.75. Effort is costly for the borrower, costing $c = \$18$. The bank's gross cost of lending is $115. Assume that the lender just wants to break even, and that the borrower cannot repay more than her current income.
a. Show that investment in this case is socially efficient only if the borrower puts forth an "adequate" level of effort.
b. Compute the threshold interest rate (the maximum rate) that the lender can charge to induce an adequate effort level from the borrower.
c. Will the borrower be able to obtain the required funds from the lender? (Assume that the opportunity cost for the borrower is zero.)

d. Briefly explain the main insights gained from this ex ante moral hazard exercise for the particular case of microfinance institutions.

12. Assume that borrowers are not very poor, in that they have some collateral, but they are nevertheless suffering from financial exclusion. Now consider the case of two borrowers with different levels of collateral. Borrower 1 has $w = \$20$ as collateral, Borrower 2 has no collateral at all. Borrower 1 is as productive as Borrower 2, so if they can undertake an investment project that requires $100, both can produce the same gross return $y = \$190$ with certainty, assuming both borrowers put in sufficient levels of effort, which cost $c = \$30$ to each of them. If the borrowers do not work hard enough, the probability of success falls to 0.5. The gross cost of capital lent is $K = \$140$ per each \$100 loan.
a. Show that if the lender can observe the effort made by each borrower, it is socially efficient to lend money to both borrowers.
b. If, on the other hand, the borrowers' behavior cannot be observed, then, show that only the one with collateral can borrow. (Note that the collateral here cannot be invested in production.)
c. Comment on the main lesson drawn from this exercise with respect to the use of collateral to facilitate credit access.

13. Consider the case of two borrowers who are equally productive. Borrower 1 is considered to be "rich" as she has cash equivalent to $A = \$50$ in her pocket. Borrower 2 is considered to be "poor" as she has zero cash in her pocket. Both borrowers are interested in a project that requires an initial investment of \$100. If they put forth a sufficient level of effort, they can both get a gross return $y = \$300$ with certainty. Otherwise, both borrowers succeed with probability 0.25. The cost of exerting effort for both borrowers is $c = \$145$. The necessary funds for financing the project may come either from borrowing or from the potential investors' own pockets. The gross cost of lending capital per dollar for a competitive bank is $k = \$1.50$.
a. Show that only the rich borrower can invest and comment on the efficiency of this result.
b. Comment on what this exercise reveals, given the asymmetric value of financial access at different levels of wealth.

14. Consider a project that needs a fixed investment $I = \$100$ and yields a gross return $y > I$ with certainty. A risk-neutral borrower wants to invest in this project, but she only has private wealth $w = \$58$ that can be used for investment. She has the option to go to a risk neutral and competitive bank in order to borrow the rest of the money that she needs to carry out her investment project, $(I - w)$. Once the project has yielded a positive return, the borrower can either run away with the money or repay her debt. The lender can observe the result of this particular investor's project with probability $s = 0.7$. If the borrower refuses to repay the money and the bank observes that the project has been successful, the bank can seize w. Explain whether you would expect the bank to be repaid in this ex post moral hazard scenario and why. (For the sake of simplicity, you can assume that the cost of raising capital for the bank is zero per each dollar lent.)

15. Consider a project that needs a fixed investment, I, and which yields a gross return of $y > I$ with probability p, and a gross return of zero with probability $(1 - p)$. A risk-neutral borrower who has private wealth w is willing to borrow $(I - w)$ in order to invest in the project. The lender knows y and p, but can only observe the final return with probability q. If the borrower refuses to repay and the lender knows that the return on her project is y, the lender can seize w. Suppose that the lender's cost of capital is zero, that it is competitive, and that it only wants to recuperate the expected value $(I - w)$ attached to the loan. Compute the threshold w^* below which the lender is unwilling to finance the project, and comment on how your result relates to microfinance institutions facing unbanked but wealthy potential clients.

16. If banks lack local knowledge and loan repayment enforcement is limited, why can't they overcome all sorts of problems by simply hiring local, knowledgeable individuals as their agents?

17. Comment on the merits of the following statement: "A borrower is always better off if she is able to hide her earnings from the bank."

18. Suppose that there are two types of potential borrowers, each one making up half of the population. When they receive a loan of $100, risky borrowers will get a return of $150 with probability 0.5, and a return of zero with probability 0.5. Safe borrowers are not completely safe: they get $150 with probability 0.9, but still get zero with probability 0.1. Suppose that both types have zero wealth, and have an outside option in the labor market worth $10. Both borrowers are risk neutral.

a. Suppose there is a bank that can differentiate between the borrowers' types. For simplicity, assume that the bank's gross cost of capital is $k = 1$—in other words, the bank's cost of lending $100 is $100. Assuming the bank faces perfect competition, which of the two borrower types will it lend to?

b. Now suppose the bank cannot differentiate between types. Which of the borrower types will it lend to?

c. Suppose that there is another lending option in this community: a moneylender. This moneylender offers loans with a new feature: if you do not pay back your debt to the moneylender, he will smash your kneecaps. The value to the borrower of smashed kneecaps is –$200. The value to the moneylender is zero. In all other ways, the moneylender is identical to the bank. Would the moneylender be willing to lend in the first place, and would anyone enter into such a dangerous contract with the moneylender? Briefly explain your answers.

d. Assuming that neither banks nor moneylenders can distinguish between borrowers' types, are borrowers better off or worse off when kneecapping contracts are available? Explain why and what kind of problem, if any, smashing kneecaps solves.

e. Briefly explain how things might change if borrowers had some positive wealth.

f. This is a typical adverse selection exercise. Briefly explain how the reasoning would differ or stay the same if this had been an exercise focusing on moral hazard.

3   Roots of Microfinance: ROSCAs and Credit Cooperatives

3.1   Introduction

Even without microfinance, poor households' lack of collateral does not mean a complete lack of access to financial intermediation. To the contrary, poor households typically have multiple credit sources in village economies, as well as informal ways to save and insure. In a 1990 survey carried out in rural Indonesia, for example, Mosley (1996a) reports that as many as 70 percent of the households interviewed borrowed from informal lenders, a figure in line with studies of informal economies elsewhere.

An intensive view of informal finance is obtained in the "financial diaries" of poor households in Bangladesh, India, and South Africa collected by Stuart Rutherford, Orlanda Ruthven, and Daryl Collins (described in Collins et al. 2009). The households in the studies were visited every two weeks over a year, and all financial transactions were recorded, whether informal, semi-formal, or formal.[1] Morduch and Rutherford (2003, 5) summarize the activities found in Bangladesh: "On average the Bangladeshi households push or pull through financial services and devices each year a sum of money ($839) equivalent to two-thirds of their annual cash income. In the Bangladesh case, households enter a fresh financial arrangement—with a moneylender, money guard, savings club, or formal provider, among others—on average every two weeks. In Bangladesh, a sample of just forty-two households were found to have used, between them, thirty-three types of service or device during the year: no household used less than four, and a third of them used more than ten." Collins et al. (2009) argue that the households have active financial lives because of their poverty, not despite it.

The devices that are used are typically diverse and overlapping. At one end of the cost spectrum are loans among family, relatives, and friends. Because these loans are often made reciprocally (you lend to me now and, in return, I'll lend to you at a time when you particularly need some cash), they often do not carry interest charges and are part of broader informal insurance relationships (Ray 1998). At the other end are moneylenders, with long-standing, if not always accurate, reputations as loan sharks. Rotating savings and credit associations (ROSCAs), savings clubs, and credit cooperatives are in the middle. The premise of microfinance is that these mechanisms are far from perfect, constrained by local resources, and, in the case of money-lenders, often very costly. Still, understanding informal mechanisms can provide guidance about how to design workable microfinance contracts.

Like many microfinance models, both ROSCAs and credit coopera-tives involve groups. But ROSCAs, which are simpler, are built on informal understandings among friends and acquaintances, while cooperatives typically have a formal constitution and a degree of legal status.[2] Understanding the way these two institutions function thus paves the way for understanding group lending in microfinance (i.e., how groups can help to reduce costs, mobilize funds, improve monitor-ing, and deploy informal community-based enforcement mechanisms). They also foreshadow limits to group lending in microfinance.

Understanding how ROSCAs hold together sheds light on savings constraints as well. While ROSCAs and credit cooperatives are com-monly seen as ways to compensate for the credit market problems described in the last chapter, newer work suggests that they are just as valuable in providing simple ways to save. Indeed, their internal logic may hinge critically on the fact that ROSCAs can provide more effec-tive ways to save than are typically available to low-income house-holds. We introduce ROSCAs in section 3.2 and describe ways that they overcome credit market problems. We then explain why ROSCAs don't fall apart, and, in answering that, we confront savings constraints. (Chapter 6 picks up this theme and describes savings and savings constraints more broadly.)

In turning to nineteenth-century European credit cooperatives in section 3.3, we turn to an early antecedent for microfinance—a con-certed attempt to attack poverty in the countryside by creating new financial institutions aimed at low-income families without collateral. The discussion of credit cooperatives shows how these formalized group-based mechanisms have helped overcome the troubles that tra-ditional banks face when lending to poor borrowers. In particular, cooperatives can induce helpful "peer monitoring" among members. These lessons have become part of modern microfinance, and we continue the discussion of related contractual innovations in chapters 4 and 5.

3.2 ROSCAs

One way to avoid the steep costs charged by moneylenders is to borrow from neighbors and friends, but while interest rates may be low (or even zero), social costs and obligations can be considerable. ROSCAs provide an alternative solution, based on pooling resources with a broad group of neighbors and friends. ROSCAs do this in a systematic way, and they can be found nearly universally, from the *tontines* of rural Cameroon to the *hui* organized in Taipei, and the *tanda* and the *polla* of Mexico and Chile, respectively.[3] A few examples illustrate just how important they can be. In the survey which serves as the basis for table 3.1, for example, roughly 40 percent of households with steady access to microfinance through Bank Rakyat Indonesia also participate in ROSCAs. Bouman (1977) reports that ROSCAs in Ethiopia comprised 8–10 percent of GDP in the early 1970s, and 20 percent of all bank deposits in Kerala State, India. Bouman (1995) reports that at least half the rural residents in Cameroon, Côte d'Ivoire, Congo, Liberia, Togo, and Nigeria participated in ROSCAs. Levenson and Besley (1996) find that between 1977 and 1991 roughly one-fifth of the Taiwanese population participated in

Table 3.1
ROSCA Participation in Indonesia

Quintile	Ever a member (%)	Median income per capita per month of participants (rupiah)	Median size of pot (rupiah)	Ratio of median income to median pot (%)	Daily, weekly, or biweekly pots	Monthly or quarterly pots	Other
Bottom	33	40,260	3,000	7.5	38	49	12
Second	44	75,000	3,000	4.0	45	41	14
Third	60	134,150	3,500	2.6	45	52	3
Fourth	71	241,667	5,000	2.1	26	70	4
Fifth	63	600,000	10,000	1.7	24	71	5

Source: Survey of 1,066 households collected by BRI in fall 2000. Calculations are by Jonathan Morduch. The poverty line averaged 90,901 rupiah per capita per month, and at the end of 1999 the exchange rate was 7,855 rupiah per U.S. dollar.

ROSCAs in any given year, and, to their surprise, the data show robustly that participation increased with income.[4]

ROSCAs tend to have simple structures. The basic element is a group of individuals who agree to regularly contribute money to a common "pot" that is allocated to one member of the group each period. Twenty people, say, may agree to contribute $15 each for twenty months, generating a monthly pot of $300. At monthly intervals the group meets to collect dues and allocate the proceeds, with past recipients excluded from getting the pot again until every member has had a turn with the $300 pot (unless it is a "bidding" ROSCA; more on that later). ROSCAs thus successfully take the bits of surplus funds that come into households and translate those bits into a large chunk that can be used to fund a major purchase.

The simplicity has advantages. The life of a ROSCA has a clear beginning and end, accounting is straightforward (one only has to keep track of who has received the pot already and who is in line to do so), and storage of funds is not required since money goes straight from one person's pocket into another's. ROSCAs come in a number of variations, and each has implications for what the ROSCA offers, how it stays together, and who is attracted to join. The main variants involve the way groups determine who gets the pot. The order of receipt may be predetermined and unchanging from cycle to cycle, the order may be chosen randomly at the beginning of each cycle, or, in a third twist, members may be allowed to bid for a given pot, rather than simply waiting their turn (e.g., this is the main form found in Taiwan; see Levenson and Besley 1996, and Calomiris and Rajaraman 1998).[5]

Like moneylenders, ROSCAs are very much local institutions. In Bangladesh, for example, ROSCAs are known as *loteri samities*, and among the ninety-five *samities* investigated by Rutherford (1997), 70 percent were made up of people in the same neighborhood, with the others based on a shared workplace. ROSCA memberships ranged from five members to over one hundred, and the pots ranged from about $25 to $400. The larger ROSCAs in Bangladesh provided enough capital for members to make investments like the purchase of a rickshaw, freeing drivers from having to pay high rental rates. About two-thirds of the ROSCAs had daily collections in amounts as small as 5–25 cents (with less frequent disbursements), and about one-quarter collected payments monthly, which was especially popular with garment workers receiving monthly paychecks.

Gugerty (2007) reports on seventy ROSCAs in western Kenya, close to the Uganda border. Most of the ROSCAs formed as groups of friends and neighbors, and, on average, participants report that other members visit their homes fourteen times per month (for reasons other than a ROSCA meeting). The area is rural, mainly dependent on small-scale subsistence farming, some cash crops (cotton, tobacco, and sugarcane), and local market trade. The average daily agricultural wage is less than $1, so it is noteworthy that the average pot is about $25, usually disbursed monthly (with an average individual contribution of $2). The typical ROSCA cycle lasts for about one year. The pot is roughly one-quarter of average monthly household expenditures, which is adequate to pay primary school fees, or to buy two bags of maize, two iron roofing sheets, or a mattress or blanket (Gugerty 2007).

Related patterns emerge in a survey collected by Bank Rakyat Indonesia (BRI), shown in table 3.1. The survey covers over one thousand households from across the country, and nearly half of the households turned out to include current ROSCA members (with another 7 percent including individuals previously in ROSCAs). As in Taiwan, the probability of having participated rises with income—although the median size of the pots fails to keep up with income so that ROSCAs become increasingly less important as households get richer. As in Bangladesh, richer households favor less frequent collections: the top two richest quintiles strongly favor monthly or quarterly pots, while poorer groups tend to favor daily, weekly, or biweekly pots. (We will draw out the implications of this result in section 5.3, where we describe the relatively unheralded, but critically important, microfinance innovation of weekly and monthly loan repayment schedules).

3.2.1 The Simple Analytics of ROSCAs

To see how ROSCAs work, we give an example of a case where the order in which individuals obtain the pot is predetermined. We follow it in section 3.2.2 with a discussion of why the ROSCA doesn't fall apart. We begin with a group of individuals who voluntarily commit to putting resources into a common pot at regular intervals. At each meeting, every participant adds her share to the pot. The order of who gets the pot is decided at the first meeting by picking names from a hat.

To see one appeal of ROSCAs (and continuing our previous example), suppose that there are twenty individuals who each wish to acquire a sewing machine that costs $300.[6] (Instead of a sewing machine, the desired good may be a radio or a piece of farm equipment—what really matters is that it is *indivisible*; that is, there is no value in just half a radio or two-thirds of a sewing machine—you need to obtain the whole thing.) As a result, each individual has to wait until she has the $300 fully in hand before making the purchase, and the sooner she can buy it, the better off she is.

Each participant earns $50 each month, but once the sewing machine has been purchased the owner can earn extra income of $20 each month. Everyone needs at minimum $35 to meet basic subsistence needs, so that prior to the purchase of the sewing machine, there is at most only $15 per month left over for saving. If the individual does not join the ROSCA, she can save up the $15 per month and be able to buy the sewing machine after twenty months (assuming, for simplicity, that savings generate no interest.) Her pattern of consumption will thus be $35 per month for twenty months and then $50 + $20 = $70 per month thereafter. Owning the sewing machine allows her to double her consumption!

Now let us consider an individual who joins a ROSCA with twenty neighbors, each of whom is willing and able to contribute $15 each month; her order of receiving the pot is a number between 1 and 20. Before ranks are determined she can a priori end up with any rank with equal probability 1/20, but on average she will be the tenth recipient. If she is indeed the tenth recipient, she will consume $35 for nine periods and get the pot in the tenth. At that point, she can consume $35 + $20 = $55 for the remaining ten periods, at which time the ROSCA cycle has been completed and her obligations are over. From then on, she earns $50 + $20 = $70 each month. By speeding up the expected date of purchasing the sewing machine, the ROSCA is a better bet than saving on one's own. In fact, it's better for everyone except the last person to get the pot, and the last person is no worse off than they would have been when saving up on their own.

Anderson, Baland, and Moene (2009) call this the "early pot motive" for ROSCA participation, but as we describe in section 3.2.2, there are other explanations, including two quite different explanations based on savings motives. One is the "household conflict motive" favored by Anderson, Baland, and Moene (2009); in this explanation, participants—who are often women—seek to get money out of the household and away from their husbands. The other is the "commitment to savings" motive argued by Gugerty (hinging on the fact that ROSCAs present a clear, public, disciplined way to accumulate funds).

3.2.2 Enforcing Agreements and Facilitating Saving

The existence of ROSCAs can make everyone better off in principle, but how do they work in practice? The ROSCA model that we have just described hinges on three crucial assumptions: first, that all individuals wish to buy an indivisible durable good; second, that they are impatient to do so; and, third, that ROSCA participation is enforced in that all individuals who win the pot earlier keep on turning up and contributing to the pot until every participant has their chance to purchase the durable good.

If the good was not indivisible, participants could start buying pieces of it and reap the returns immediately. Instead, indivisibility means that without a ROSCA, individuals are forced to save until they have payment in full.[7] The role of indivisibility is in line with evidence from two very different contexts. Besley and Levenson (1996), for example, use data for Taiwan to show that ROSCA participants are indeed more likely than others to buy durables like microwave ovens, videocassette recorders, and air conditioners, even after controlling for income and for the endogeneity of participation. In the slums of Nairobi, Anderson and Baland (2002) similarly find that ROSCA participation is associated with making lumpy purchases (in this case, school fees, clothing, rent, and medical costs).

These results are only suggestive. Gugerty (2007) counters that in western Kenya, it is not uncommon to use the pot for more than one item, the most expensive of which takes up no more than two-thirds of the pot on average. Moreover, the expenditures generally favored by ROSCA participants are often divisible. School fees, for example, can be paid in installments; food can be purchased in small quantities; and household items like cups or plates can be purchased individually. Of course, making bulk purchases may cut costs, and the early pot motive for ROSCAs then survives. But Gugerty also shows evidence that in fact most participants do not put an especially high value on getting an early pot; instead, for example, getting the pot during the harvest season is often a bigger prize.

The assumption of impatience also matters to the early pot story; otherwise, households would be content to save up on their own. Assuming impatience is common, economists routinely assume some degree of impatience (i.e., that a given amount of money today is

valued by individuals more than the same amount tomorrow). In practice, though, we suggest that the constraint may not be impatience so
much as the absence of an effective way to save, an argument in line
with Gugerty's evidence from Kenya and developed formally by Karna
Basu (2008a).

To see this, we need to first turn to enforcement issues. In our simple
description of the model, we have emphasized the benefits of ROSCA
participation versus those of going solo. But enforcement issues arise
once the order of who gets the pot is determined. Consider the participant who is very last in line. Why should she stay in the agreement
when, after all, she is at least as well off saving up on her own? The
ROSCA will not help her get the durable good sooner than she could
on her own. In fact, the ROSCA could impose costs since it forces her
to save in fixed, regular increments each period when she might instead
prefer flexibility in deciding how to accumulate. If the last person
refuses to stay in, the whole arrangement unravels since someone
always has to be last. One reason why this may work is that in fact
ROSCA members do not have better ways to save. The absence of well-
established savings institutions for small savings may thus be a key to
making ROSCAs work.

The incentive problem with regard to the first participants who win
the pot may be even worse. What prevents them from taking the
pot and then refusing to make contributions in later periods? The participants who get the pot first are de facto borrowing from the
other members of the ROSCA; and they therefore must turn up at
subsequent meetings to repay their debt obligations, just like any
borrower. Rutherford (2000, 34) notes that the risk of early absconders
is the most commonly heard worry of people when presented with the
idea of a ROSCA. To work, ROSCAs must rely on potential penalties
for not honoring one's obligations.

One possible sanction is to refuse the absconders access to future
cycles of the ROSCA, but, as Anderson, Baland, and Moene (2009)
argue, this is insufficient; the sanction will not work since the absconder
could simply save up on his own and do just as well. Again consider
the example of a twenty-member ROSCA with $15 contributions and
a $300 pot. Also assume that the order of who gets the pot is unchanged
from cycle to cycle—and that once one twenty-period cycle ends,
another immediately starts up. Would exclusion from subsequent
cycles help the enforcement problem? If the individual stays in the
ROSCA, she would have to contribute $15 to the pot for the next nine-

teen periods until the round ends. In the following period, a new round of the ROSCA commences. Since we have assumed that this individual is again first in line to get the pot, she will make her $15 contribution and again get the allotted $300. Then, again, she is obligated to pay $15 for another nineteen periods, and so forth.

The enforcement problem arises because the individual could do better by reneging. After the first period of the first round, she absconds with a "free" $300, and then, rather than making good on her obligations, she could simply save $15 on her own each period for twenty periods. Twenty periods later, she would have another $300 in hand, just as she would if she had stayed true to the ROSCA rules. Not only that, but she would be able to save flexibly, freed from the rigidity of the ROSCA contribution schedule. The ROSCA will thus fall apart if it is true that, as a ROSCA member in Nairobi said: "You cannot trust people in matters of money. People tend to cheat" (Anderson, Baland, and Moene 2009). The financial diaries reported in Collins et al. (2009) give many examples of intensive ROSCA use in Bangladesh, India, and South Africa—but also tragic stories of failed ROSCAs.

Can the way that the ROSCA is designed affect the ease of enforcement? Specifically, what if we drop the assumption that the order of who gets the pot is unchanged from cycle to cycle? Imagine, instead, that the order was chosen by random lottery at the start of each twenty-period cycle.[8] This would only make the incentive problem worse for the first in line. Rather than staying true and getting the second pot in twenty more periods under the fixed order, she would not expect to get the pot for another thirty periods (since the average lottery number in the next round would be 10). The advantages to reneging are then much greater.

Why then, do we often see assignment by random lottery? First, it seems fairer. Second, it provides the best incentives for the last person in line. She may be number 20 this time, but next time she can expect to be number 10 on average. There is thus a conflict between "fairness" and providing the right incentives for the first in line. One solution used in Kenya is to use a fixed order and to put people known as being most untrustworthy at the end of the line; this is perceived to be most fair (except by those deemed untrustworthy!) and helps address incentive problems (Anderson, Baland, and Moene 2009). To facilitate this, ROSCA managers devote considerable energy to ex ante screening of prospective members. Even if members are poorly acquainted beforehand, requiring recommendations from existing members helps, and reputations can be allowed to accumulate over time (such that one's order of getting the pot moves forward after maintaining a clean record).

Other ways to keep ROSCAs together include banning problem participants from access to other relationships like trade credit, credit cooperatives, or access to material inputs. ROSCA participants in Kenya also report sometimes using force to obtain goods to be resold from members who fall behind in their obligations (Anderson, Baland, and Moene 2009). Social sanctions may be employed as well, such that those who renege are ostracized within the village or excluded from social and religious events (e.g., Ardener 1964).

Orlanda Ruthven's study of slum-dwellers in Delhi reveals these tensions clearly:

The dearth of the "right" kind of people to join a RoSCA was a key issue for Delhi respondents. Nasir . . . enjoyed well-run RoSCAs, but two of his neighbors said they didn't have sufficiently trusting relations with anyone in their neighborhood, or even in Delhi, to depend on them to pay their dues. A respondent from another slum said he'd been trying to join a RoSCA for some time and couldn't find one that would have him as a member. Finally, he met a manager of a RoSCA, who told him he could join only if he agreed to take the prize last. Two of his neighbors were excellent RoSCA members, but they had to travel all the way across Delhi to the meetings each month. Neither felt they would find anything suitable closer to home. (Collins et al. 2009, 125)

Imperfect alternative means to save can also explain why ROSCAs stay together. We have assumed up to this point that people who are not in ROSCAs have no constraints in saving; this is why it made sense to argue that absconders would be just as well off without the ROSCA (and often better off). But Rutherford (1997) finds that, when asked, the most commonly cited reason that slum dwellers in Dhaka joined a ROSCA was in fact to save, particularly given their difficulties in saving at home.[9] Daryl Collins's work on ROSCAs and savings clubs in South Africa yields a similar view. She describes a woman who was part of the financial diaries study:

At the time we knew her, Nomsa was in two different sorts of [saving] clubs . . . Nomsa's membership in the club poses a puzzle. After all, she has an account at the bank in her own name, and is used to transacting there. Why would Nomsa not bank this money for herself, avoiding the bother of the club (she has to attend its meetings) and its undoubted risks (what if the money is stolen from the secretary's house?)? Many South African diary households belonged to clubs of this sort, and their most common answer to this question was that club membership was the surest way to discipline themselves to save for a particular event. "You feel compelled to contribute your payment. If you don't do that, [it] is like you are letting your friends down. So it is better because you make your payment no matter what." (Collins et al. 2009, 113–114)

Anderson and Baland (2002) find, similarly, that women favor ROSCAs since participation helps them get money out of the house (and away from husbands). In this case, the tension is provided by a need for "spousal control" rather than self-control.[10] Nearly all ROSCA participants in their Nairobi sample are women, and this is common globally. Anderson and Baland find an interesting "inverted-U" shaped pattern in their data: women who have little autonomy from their husbands are unlikely to join ROSCAs, as are women with great autonomy (since they do not need the protections that ROSCAs afford). Participation is greatest in the middle, by women who have some autonomy and are looking for additional levers to facilitate household management. We will come back to this issue in chapter 7 on gender.

As far as saving goes, ROSCAs have an important advantage that is missing from other informal mechanisms: the beauty is that ROSCAS do not require a physical place to store money since on the same day that funds are collected, they are distributed again. The public nature and precommitment associated with ROSCA participation also serves as a device to foster discipline and encourage saving in ways that may be otherwise impossible. These advantages follow a logic given by new work in behavioral economics in which commitment devices are superior when self-control is weak (e.g., Thaler 1994; see also section 6.6). Participating in a ROSCA thus provides a secure, structured way to save that would otherwise be missing. Even households that are not particularly impatient may join a ROSCA simply for the help it provides with saving (Basu 2008a).

Gugerty's (2007) analysis of a detailed survey of 1,066 ROSCA members in western Kenya pushes the commitment to saving argument for why individuals form ROSCAs. As one ROSCA participant responded in her survey, "You can't save alone—it is easy to misuse money." Another remarked, "Saving money at home can make you extravagant in using it." And another said, "It is difficult to keep money at home as demands are high." Gugerty analyzes the responses of 308 ROSCA members to the question "What is the most important reason you joined this ROSCA?" She finds that 37 percent reported that it was "difficult to save at home because money got used up in small household needs." Another 22 percent reported that it was "difficult to save alone, that they 'got the strength to save' by sitting with others." And just 10 percent reported that they joined "as a response to household conflict, fear of theft, or demands by kin."[11]

ROSCAs are so widely observed, and seen in such varying circumstances, that there cannot be one rationale for their existence that universally trumps all others. We see truths in each of the explanations considered here: the early pot motive, the household conflict motive, and the commitment to saving motive. But we have highlighted the latter explanations because they remain underappreciated, and because—as we discuss in chapters 5 and 6—they suggest important angles on microfinance.

3.2.3 Limits to ROSCAs

The ubiquity of ROSCAs attests to their usefulness, but they have limits as well. First, neither the size of the pot nor the size of contributions is flexible within the life of a given ROSCA. Creating a bigger pot can be done by making the contributions larger (which may be difficult for some members) or by recruiting more members. Adding members, though, can lead to management problems and lengthens the life of the ROSCA (and thus lengthens the average time that members must wait to get their next chance at the pot).

Second, and perhaps more important, ROSCAs put locally held funds to good use, but they do not provide a regular way to mobilize funds from outside a given group. So, from the point of view of microfinance, ROSCAs show an interesting precedent for using groups to allocate resources (foreshadowing the practice of group lending), but they fail to present an effective way to move resources across independent communities or to easily expand in size.

One partial way to address the first problem is through a "bidding ROSCA." Here, rather than allocating the pot by a predetermined order, the pot is allocated each period to whoever is willing to pay the most for it. The rest of the participants pocket the proceeds. For those who primarily wish to save, the bidding ROSCA provides a return to saving not available under the other forms—and members do not need to take the pot at a prescribed moment. For those bidding on the pot, the ROSCA provides access to money when it is needed, albeit at a cost. In this way, the bidding ROSCA can help mitigate risk in difficult times (for more on ROSCAs and risk, see Calomiris and Rajaraman 1998).

One problem with this arrangement stems from the information problems discussed in the previous chapter. We expect that risky participants are willing to pay more for the pot than safer participants, so the earliest pots go to the riskiest borrowers. Since risky borrowers are also more likely to default (i.e., stop making contributions), participants who receive the pot later in the cycle may end up getting less from the ROSCA than they put into it. If this is the case, bidding ROSCAs could be a less efficient scheme than random ROSCAs. Research by Klonner and Rai (2008) on bidding ROSCAs in India, mentioned already in section 2.5, backs up these predictions. The authors find that default rates are higher for early borrowers. Since default rates are a proxy for riskiness, this suggests that risky borrowers do, in fact, have a higher willingness to pay. They also examine the effect of a policy shock on defaults, in this case a 1993 Supreme Court decision that put a 30 percent ceiling on ROSCA bids. A bid ceiling makes bidding ROSCAs more like random ROSCAs: multiple participants make the maximum allowable bid, and the person who gets the pot is randomly selected from among the high bidders. Klonner and Rai (2008) examine default patterns before and after the Indian government imposed the ceiling and find that defaults by early bidders were much less pronounced after the ceiling was enforced.

Another time when there may be multiple bidders seeking the pot is during downturns. A bidding war ensues, leading to a result that may be economically efficient but not necessarily equitable since needy, poorer households will easily get outbid. In this light, credit cooperatives present themselves as a more flexible institutional solution—and we turn to this next.

3.3 Credit Cooperatives

ROSCAs show a way to formalize and systematize the use of groups to allocate resources in poor communities, but their simplicity can also be a disadvantage. As described in section 3.2, many use ROSCAs largely as a way to save, rather than as a means to borrow. At the cost of a bit of complexity, the ROSCA structure can be modified to allow some participants to mainly save and others to mainly borrow—and for more than one person to borrow at a time. In this way, the ROSCA transforms into an ASCA (accumulating savings and credit association) as described by Bouman (1995), Rutherford (2000), and Collins et al.

(2009). An ASCA in its most formalized mode is essentially a credit cooperative (or credit union as they are more often called in the Americas—we will use the terms interchangeably). A chief advantage is that savers are no longer required to borrow, and the size of loans can vary with need. A cost is that funds must now be stored, and bookkeeping and management become more complex.

In moving in this direction, we get a step closer to modern microfinance. Indeed, the cooperatives share some of the features of the "village banks" promoted by microfinance NGOs like FINCA, Pro Mujer, and Freedom from Hunger, and credit cooperatives are playing an increasing role in today's microfinance landscape. In 2007, the World Council of Credit Unions (2007) counted 49,134 credit unions serving 177 million members worldwide. Over half of these were operating in Africa and Asia, accounting for 24 percent and 41 percent of the total, respectively. The roots of credit cooperatives, however, are much older. Not unlike the modern microfinance "revolution," a century before microfinance became a global movement, Friedrich Raiffeissen, a village mayor, had spearheaded a similar drive in the German countryside; his aim was to spread new group-based ways to provide financial services to the poor (Banerjee, Besley, and Guinnane 1994; Guinnane 2002; Ghatak and Guinnane 1999). Typical loans in Raiffeisen's cooperatives had ten-year durations and were made for farm investments. Raiffeisen's credit cooperative movement built on a broader movement that started in the 1850s, and by the turn of the century it had spread to Ireland, France, Italy, and Japan (and later to Korea, Taiwan, Canada, the United States, and parts of Latin America; see Adams 1995). In France, the cooperative movement gained traction in 1885, when Louis Milcent created a cooperative bank that would become one of France's largest banks, Crédit Agricole.[12] In Germany, there were over 15,000 institutions operating in 1910, serving 2.5 million people and accounting for 9 percent of the German banking market (Guinnane 2002, 89, table 3); by the early 1900s, nearly one-third of rural households were cooperative members (Adams 1995).

The British too were intrigued, and they fostered credit cooperatives in India, creating a precedent for modern microfinance in South Asia.[13] In the 1890s the government of Madras in South India, then under British rule, looked to the German experiences for solutions in addressing poverty in India, and in 1904 the Cooperative Credit Societies Act established cooperatives along Raiffeisen's basic model. By 1912, over four hundred thousand Indians belonged to the new credit cooperatives, and by 1946 membership exceeded nine million (Bedi, cited in Woolcock 1998). The cooperatives took hold in the state of Bengal, the eastern part of which became East Pakistan at independence in 1947 and is now Bangladesh. The credit cooperatives eventually lost steam in Bangladesh, but the notion of group lending had established itself.[14]

The credit cooperatives function like ROSCAs in that they gather funds from those in a community who are able to save, and those funds are allocated to those who want to invest (or consume) in a lump sum. Unlike ROSCAs, however, credit cooperatives share the following features: First, members do not have to wait their turn in order to borrow, nor do they need to bid for a loan. Second, participants, be they savers or borrowers, are all shareholders in the cooperative. Key decisions about the prevailing interest rates, the maximum loan size, and changes to the constitutional chart of the credit cooperative are taken democratically by all members, on a one-share-one vote basis. Like ROSCA participants, they share a common bond—that is, they live in the same neighborhood, attend the same church, and/or work nearby—and thus social sanctions are available for enforcing contracts (on top of the possibility that a defaulting borrower loses her shares in the credit cooperative). In the subsections that follow we analyze how these various features contribute to the success of credit cooperatives and, in particular, to mobilizing savings, inducing peer monitoring, and addressing risk.

3.3.1 Credit Cooperatives and Savings
In a study of German rural cooperatives during the period 1850–1914, Prinz (2002) analyzes the emergence of credit associations on the Raiffeisen model. The main features of the Raiffeisen model were (a) members should belong to the same local parish; (b) there was unlimited liability in that defaulting members would lose their current assets, as well as suffering social costs;[15] (c) low-income individuals could not be discriminated against and should be given the equal rights when becoming members of the cooperative; (d) the cooperative was not merely a financial intermediary in that it performed other functions such as facilitating the purchase of inputs of production for its members; and, (e) the cooperatives would extend both short-term and long-term loans.

Although Prinz does not have direct evidence on savings, he argues that such savings by participant members were most likely long-term savings since interest rates were stable, remaining fairly constant (at around 4 percent) for the entire period from 1897 to 1911. This interest rate stability is quite remarkable, the argument goes, especially for credit cooperatives operating in rural areas, and the natural explanation is that members' savings were stable too.

How were members' savings sustained and stable over time in these rural settings? Prinz emphasizes the importance of what he calls "face-to-face" relations and trust-building ties among villagers. Over time, such ties became so strong that even with the advent of strong competition at the turn of century, the Raiffeisen cooperatives continued to enjoy stable levels of savings. In Prinz's words: "Whereas villagers in the 1860s often had no choice but to deposit their saving in the Raiffeisen cooperatives, their grandsons and granddaughters definitely had. It appears that villagers, after leaving their initial suspicion behind, came to regard the Raiffeisen cooperative more and more as an extension of their own businesses" (2002, 15). We formalize this feature of the Raiffeisen cooperatives in appendix 3B. In particular, we show that members of a cooperative will be keen to invest all of their savings in the cooperative when social sanctions are sufficiently high and/or when the opportunity cost of investing elsewhere is high. The reason is that in those cases, the incidence of default falls sharply through the combination of social commitment, unlimited liability, and interest rate stability. And savings are in turn encouraged by a lower probability of default on loans.

3.3.2 Credit Cooperatives and Peer Monitoring

Also inspired by Raiffeisen's cooperatives experience, Banerjee, Besley, and Guinnane (1994) develop a model of credit cooperatives that emphasizes peer monitoring among members. The model yields insights into why a borrower's peers have incentives to monitor and enforce contracts. The insights have been applied to group lending in microfinance as well.

Consider a cooperative with only two members (it's not a realistic assumption but it allows us to show some critical features in a simple way). One of the two has a new investment opportunity and needs to finance it. The borrower's project is risky: the borrower achieves gross income y with probability p, and zero with probability $(1 - p)$, where p is the probability of success. Undertaking the opportunity requires a cost F that can be financed in part by borrowing from an outside lender.

So the project will depend on securing funds from an outside lender and a lender inside the cooperative.

Suppose first that the two cooperative members have zero wealth. Then the loan contract between the borrower and outside lender is simply a standard debt contract that specifies an amount b lent and a gross interest rate R, with $R \cdot b < y$ whenever the project succeeds. This simply says that the outside lender cannot charge a gross interest rate that is greater than the borrower's income—in the case in which the borrower makes profits. When the project fails, the borrower is protected by limited liability and does not repay.

Now consider how a well-designed credit cooperative can improve matters. Consider the case in which the borrower's fellow cooperative member (the "insider") has funds to lend the borrower, making up the difference between the full project cost F and b, the amount that the outsider is willing to lend. Thus one role of the insider is simply to lend an amount $F - b$ to the borrower. The second role of the insider is to act as a guarantor, possibly offering collateral that would secure the loan from the outsider. We'll show why offering the collateral might make sense here, even if the loan goes to the insider's partner. The third role that the insider plays is as a monitor, taking actions to encourage the borrower to work hard and increase the chances for success. A borrower who shirks suffers penalties or social sanctions imposed by his peers, and the chance of being caught shirking increases with monitoring effort.

The questions are: What will determine how much the insider monitors her peer? What will be the effect of offering collateral? How high an interest rate will the insider charge the peer for the "inside loan"?

To simplify matters, we assume that effort by the borrower translates one-for-one into a higher chance of doing well—so we can use one symbol, p, to denote both effort and the probability of success. The question is: How is p determined? The probability that the borrower will succeed is a function of how hard the borrower works. That, in turn, is a function of how much the insider monitors. To capture these elements, the cost of effort is assumed to take the particular form $(1/2)(1/m)\,p^2$, where m denotes the monitoring intensity provided by the insider. The function shows that the cost of effort *decreases* with the extent of monitoring, m. One way to think about this is to consider the relationship the other way round: the cost of shirking *increases* with the extent of monitoring, since more monitoring means that the borrower is more likely to get caught and punished. The role of p^2 in the cost function means that the cost of effort rises less than proportionally with added effort (since p, which is a probability, must be less than one).

The timing of decisions is as follows. First, the borrower contracts loans with both the inside and the outside lenders. We assume perfect competition among potential outside lenders, so that the contract will guarantee that the outside lender expects to get back the market rate of interest r plus compensation for risk. Second, the inside lender chooses how much to monitor the borrower (picks m). Third, the borrower decides how much effort p to invest in her project. Fourth, project revenues are realized.

Given the sequencing, the borrower chooses effort conditional on knowing how much the insider is going to monitor her. So, for a given monitoring intensity m by the insider, the borrower chooses effort, p, to maximize her expected returns net of costs:

$$p(y - Rb) - (1/2)(1/m)p^2. \tag{3.1}$$

It turns out that the optimal level of effort, p, equals $m(y - Rb)$.[16] We immediately see that a higher monitoring intensity m increases p, as described previously. This is because a higher monitoring intensity m lowers the borrower's marginal cost of effort, leading to higher borrower effort and a higher probability of success. We have taken the interest rate R as given, but we know that it must be higher than the market rate available on alternative, safe investments (like government bonds). This is because the outsider must bear some risk of default.[17]

The problem is that the inside lender has no incentive to invest in peer monitoring. So, what guarantees that m will in fact be positive? To see, we have to modify our assumptions slightly. Suppose that the inside cooperative member has private wealth w that she can use as collateral for the loan contract between the borrower and the outside lender. That is, the insider promises w to the outside lender in case the gross interest rate R is not repaid by the borrower. Furthermore, assume that w is sufficiently large so that the outside lender is always repaid in full.[18] Now, the outside lender faces no risk in making this loan, so he no longer requires a risk premium. Given the assumption of perfect competition, R will then fall to equal r, the market return on safe investments. The falling interest rate, in turn, implies that the borrower's effort rises, since p now equals $m(y - rb)$, which is larger than before.

Clearly, the willingness of the insider to put up collateral is helpful for the borrower. But why should the insider do so? If the project fails, the inside lender loses w. The insider can be compensated by getting a return—effectively an interest rate—in the case that the project is successful. If the insider has strong bargaining power, she will be able to obtain most of the residual return $(y - rb)$, which remains after the borrower has repaid the outside lender. So, the insider under this scenario now has an incentive to put up collateral.

Moreover, the insider now also has an incentive to invest in monitoring in order to increase the probability of success.[19] The monitoring effort, m, that the insider applies in order to elicit higher repayments from the borrower should increase in the amount of collateral w—since more collateral means more to lose when the borrower shirks. Increases in the interest rate charged by the outside lender, however, is apt to have a negative effect on monitoring. This is because the outside lender is paid in priority, so when the interest rate that the outsider receives rises, any additional monitoring that the inside lender applies will increasingly accrue to the outsider.

The model shows ways in which groups can function to increase lending. Here, the insider acts as a guarantor and a monitor, with the incentive given by the fact that the insider is a lender too. In the case of microfinance, fellow group members also act as guarantors and monitors. But in that case, their motivation is fueled by the promise of future access to credit if all group members repay loans.

The Banerjee, Besley, and Guinnane (1994) model is important in demonstrating how monitoring can come about as a function of institutional design. The optimality of monitoring is another matter. We close by noting that it is entirely possible here that insiders will monitor too much and punish borrowers too often relative to outcomes that would emerge if a benevolent social planner were making decisions.

3.4 Summary and Conclusions

In this chapter we have analyzed ROSCAs and credit cooperatives, two precursors to modern microfinance institutions. Credit cooperatives (or credit unions) are also playing an increasingly active role in the microfinance market today.

In the model we described, ROSCAs can help credit-constrained individuals purchase indivisible goods through a simple sharing arrangement. The idea is beautifully simple, but not very flexible. The approach can be made more complicated, but it will remain limited to intermediating local resources only.

While ROSCAs are commonly cited as indigenous ways that communities use to overcome credit constraints, the closer one looks, the more that ROSCAs seem notable as devices for saving. Indeed we showed that, in principle, one very common form of ROSCA will fall apart if it does not offer a way to save that is more attractive than alternative mechanisms. Given the variety of ROSCAs observed in practice, there is no single explanation of their use that will be universally valid, but recent evidence has stressed the savings side in particular (e.g., Collins et al. 2009; Gugerty 2007; Basu 2008a). The discussion of ROSCAs thus leads toward the broader discussion of savings in chapter 6—as well as providing insight that applies as well to the discussion of group lending in chapter 5.

Credit cooperatives are another way to mobilize local resources, and in section 3.3.1 we cited evidence showing that the German credit cooperatives of the nineteenth century also functioned as important ways to save. The model of the German credit cooperatives in section 3.3.2 turned instead to the nature of the institutional design of cooperatives. The design of cooperatives encourages peer monitoring and guaranteeing the loans of one's neighbors. The level of peer monitoring is not necessarily optimal from a social standpoint, however—which is a lesson that carries over to group lending in microfinance. The analysis raises the question as to whether the 98 percent (plus) loan repayment rates boasted by microlenders might ever be too *high* from a social standpoint. Are too many resources being put into monitoring and enforcement? Are borrowers ever pressured to be too risk-averse rather than seeking the greater profits that can come with risk taking? These are questions that have so far received little attention from the microfinance community.

The discussion of credit cooperatives also introduces practical complications. While the cooperatives add flexibility to what can be achieved through ROSCAs, cooperatives are much more challenging to run. Indeed, in order to borrow, participants must commit to helping run the institution.[20] This is surely appealing for some, but most microfinance programs instead pursue a more traditional bank-client relationship. As Adams (1995, 11) concludes, based on his survey of the modern credit union experience in Latin America:

Most credit unions in low-income countries are fragile. They typically have thin capital bases, often lack access to funds to meet liquidity shortfalls, have difficulties diversifying their risks, are easily crippled by inflation, and are quickly damaged when their members have economic reverses. Credit unions also face dilemmas as they grow: they lose their informational advantages, they are forced to rely on paid rather than voluntary managers, and they must increasingly count on formal sanctions to enforce contracts . . . Principal-agent problems, transaction costs, and prudential regulation also become increasingly important as credit unions grow.

What does modern microfinance add? As we will see in greater detail in the next chapter, microfinance not only is a device for pooling risk and cross-subsidizing borrowers in order to improve efficiency, but it also increases borrowers' access to outside sources of finance and institutes a professional management structure from the start. Microfinance institutions typically borrow (or otherwise obtain funds) from outside the locality (and often outside the country) to fund borrowers' needs, whereas both ROSCAs and credit unions rely mainly on local savings. A pressing question, taken up in the next chapter, is how to attract outside finance when lending to poor borrowers without collateral.

Appendix 3A: A Simple Model of a Random ROSCA

This appendix shows a rationale for ROSCAs using a mathematical approach that builds on the intuition provided in section 3.2.1. The discussion is directed to readers who are already familiar with the academic economics literature and who are comfortable with using calculus to solve constrained maximization problems.

Consider the following stripped-down version of the model of ROSCAs by Besley, Coate, and Loury (1993). Suppose that there are n individuals who wish to acquire a durable and indivisible good that costs B. These individuals contribute to put resources to a common "pot" that is allocated to one of the members of the group at regular time intervals. At each meeting, every participant adds her share to the pot, and the pot is allocated to one of the members of the group; the order is determined at the first meeting.

Each individual has additive preferences over durable and nondurable consumption: $v(c)$ without the durable good, and $v(c) + \theta$ with it. Suppose that each individual earns an amount y each period, and that she lives for T periods. For simplicity, we suppose that individuals have linear utility $v(c) = c$ whenever $c \geq \underline{c}$, where $\underline{c}$ is the subsistence level of consumption so that $v(c) = -\infty$ if $c < \underline{c}$. If the individual does not join the ROSCA, she would be solving the following problem:

$$\underset{t}{Max}\,(T-t)(y+\theta)+tc \tag{3A.1}$$

subject to the following subsistence constraint:

$$c \geq \underline{c}$$

and the budget constraint:

$$t(y-c) \geq B$$

where t is the acquisition date for the durable item, and c is the consumption flow during the accumulation phase. The first term in the maximand refers to the time interval after the durable good has been acquired. The second term refers to the time interval prior to the purchase of the durable good. The budget constraint reminds us that the adequate savings must be accumulated prior to the purchase at date t in order to afford the durable good.

The optimal solution is for the individual to minimize her consumption of the nondurable good in order to cut the time until the purchase of the durable good: that is, to consume $c = \underline{c}$ each period and save $(y - \underline{c})$. After t^*, she can enjoy consumption of her entire income flow (i.e., consume $c = y$) while enjoying the benefits of the durable good as well.

From this we can write the corresponding utility for the individual in "autarky," that is, when she decides not to participate in a ROSCA:

$$U_A = (T-t^*)(y+\theta)+t^*\underline{c} = \left(T-\frac{B}{y-\underline{c}}\right)(y+\theta)+\frac{B}{y-\underline{c}}\underline{c} \tag{3A.2}$$

The first term captures the utility from consuming $y + \theta$ from the date of the durable's purchase until the final period; and the second term captures the utility from consuming $\underline{c}$ until enough is saved up to buy the durable.

Now, consider an individual who joins a ROSCA; her order of receiving the pot is i, which is a number between 1 and n. Before ranks are determined she can a priori end up with any rank i with equal probability $1/n$. If she gets the pot at time $(i/n)t$, her lifetime utility will be

$$u_i = \left(\frac{i}{n}\right)tc + \left[t-\left(\frac{i}{n}\right)t\right](c-\theta)+(T-t)(y+\theta) \tag{3A.3}$$

where the first term refers to the individual's utility before getting the pot, the second term refers to her utility once she has received the pot and thereby acquired the indivisible good but before fulfilling her repayment obligation vis-à-vis the other members of the ROSCA, and the third term refers to her utility once all individuals have purchased the indivisible good so that no further repayment and savings are required.

The corresponding ex ante expected utility (for an individual who does not yet know when she will access the pot), is given by

$$U_R = \frac{1}{n} \sum_{i=1}^{n} u_i \qquad\qquad (3A.4)$$

or, equivalently,

$$U_R = \left(\frac{n+1}{2n}\right) tc + \left(1 - \frac{n+1}{2n}\right) t(c+\theta) + (T-t)(y+\theta) \qquad (3A.5)$$

where, as before, t is determined as the time where there is enough accumulated savings for each individual to cover the cost of purchasing the indivisible good, that is,

$$t(y-c) = B \qquad\qquad (3A.6)$$

This equation also implies that there are enough funds in the pot at each meeting date to purchase one unit of the indivisible good. Using the fact that once again individuals will minimize their initial consumption of the nondurable good in order to speed up the purchase of the durable good, the maximized lifetime utility of an individual joining a ROSCA, is equal to

$$U_R = \frac{B}{y-c} c + \left(1 - \frac{n+1}{2n}\right) \frac{B}{y-c} \theta + \left(T - \frac{B}{y-c}\right)(y+\theta) \qquad (3A.7)$$

Comparing U_R to U_A, we see that $U_R > U_A$. That is, ROSCA participation provides higher utility to each ROSCA member. The reason is that membership lowers the utility cost of saving up to acquire one unit of the indivisible good. Even if the same saving pattern is maintained as in the absence of a ROSCA, participating in a ROSCA gives each member the possibility of obtaining the pot early.

Appendix 3B: Credit Cooperatives and Savings: A Simple Model

In this appendix we show more formally how credit cooperatives can capture and mobilize long-term savings. As in appendix 3A, the discussion is directed to readers who are already familiar with the academic economics literature and who are comfortable with using calculus to solve constrained maximization problems. In order to keep the notation consistent with that found in the academic literature, readers should note that we use a different set of symbols here than we do in the main body of the text.

Consider the following stylized model. Suppose that there is a continuum of mass 1 of savers-borrowers in a credit cooperative. Each member has the same initial wealth w that she can invest either in the cooperative or in another bank. Investing inside the cooperative yields a gross interest rate θ, and investing elsewhere involves an opportunity cost δ per unit invested. For simplicity we assume here that the members of the credit cooperative are risk-neutral, and that δ is just a switching cost from the local cooperative to a bank located in the city.[21] Each member has access to a project that yields a return R in case it succeeds and zero if it fails. Success in turn occurs with probability e, where $e \in [\varepsilon, 1]$ and the multiplicative function Ce denotes the borrower's effort cost. Whenever failure occurs, the borrower is forced to default, in which case she loses the wealth that she has invested as savings in the credit cooperative, and, also incurs a nonmonetary cost H of being excluded from the community. Finally, the interest rate r is set so as to enable the cooperative as a whole to purchase capital goods for all the members (which here we take to be exogenously given).

The timing of decisions within the period is as follows: first, borrowers decide how much wealth to invest inside the cooperative. Then, given how much wealth they have invested in the cooperative, borrowers invest in effort.

We reason by backward induction, first taking as given the share of wealth w_i invested inside the cooperative by an individual borrower. The borrower will choose her effort e to

$$\max_{e \in [\varepsilon, 1]} \{e(R + \theta w_i - r) + (1 - e)(-H) - Ce\} \qquad (3B.1)$$

so that, by the first-order conditions:

$$e(w_i) = 1 \text{ if } R + \theta w_i - r + H > C \text{ or } e(w_i) = \varepsilon \text{ otherwise} \qquad (3B.2)$$

We thus see that the probability of default is reduced (here, to zero) the more savings the borrower has invested in the cooperative and the higher the non-monetary sanction H.

Now, moving back one step, a borrower will choose how much wealth w_i to invest in the cooperative, in order to

$$\max_{w_i \leq w} \left\{ \begin{array}{l} e(w_i)(R + \theta w_i - r) + (1 - e(w_i))(-H) - Ce(w_i) \\ + (\theta - \delta)(w - w_i) \end{array} \right\} \quad (3B.3)$$

This very simple model delivers several conclusions: first, given the following "no-default" condition:

$$R + \theta w - r + H > C, \quad (3B.4)$$

namely, in equilibrium all borrowers will invest all their wealth inside the cooperative. Indeed, once she has invested her own wealth, a borrower will find it optimal to invest maximum effort

$$e(w_i) = 1 \quad (3B.5)$$

by virtue of the no-default condition, so that each unit invested inside the cooperative yields an expected gross interest rate equal to θ whereas each unit invested outside yields $\theta - \delta$. The no-default condition in turn is more likely to be satisfied when H is large, hence the importance of social sanctions and/or unlimited liability.

It is worth pointing out that in the case where the no-default condition holds, together with the following "commitment" condition:

$$R - r + H < C, \quad (3B.6)$$

investing all her wealth in the cooperative acts as a commitment device for the borrower. That is, without such investment the borrower would find it optimal ex post to minimize effort, whereas investing all her wealth inside the cooperative increases the borrower's cost of defaulting on her loan, to the extent that it becomes optimal for her to invest maximum effort in her project in order to avoid costly default. This, in turn, allows the borrower to minimize the probability of bankruptcy and thereby to take advantage of the better conditions offered by the cooperative in terms of (risk-adjusted) interest rates on savings.

Finally, if the no-default condition does not hold, borrowers will always minimize effort, that is, choose $e = \varepsilon$, which in turn implies that she will default with probability $(1 - \varepsilon)$ and therefore will lose her internal savings also with probability $(1 - \varepsilon)$. Then, whenever

$$\theta\varepsilon < \theta - \delta, \quad (3B.7)$$

the borrower chooses to invest all her savings outside the credit cooperative.

Overall, sufficiently high social sanctions H and/or a high opportunity cost δ of investing elsewhere will encourage internal savings by the members of a credit cooperative. This, in turn, can explain the success of Raffeisen-style associations in mobilizing long-term savings through their unique combination of social commitment, unlimited liability (defaulting members would lose everything) and interest rate stability.

3.7 Exercises

1. Evaluate the following statement: "Enforcement is a major issue in Rotating Savings and Credit Associations (ROSCAs), yet ROSCAs do not easily fall apart in practice." Explain why.

2. Consider again the problem described in appendix 3A, and show that the expected utility of a participating member of a ROSCA is increasing with the number of members n. What problems may arise from having too many participants in a ROSCA?

3. Consider a village with n symmetric risk neutral borrowers who each live for T periods. At each period, one borrower can earn an amount y, and the level of subsistence consumption is c, with $y > c$. Each borrower has an additive preference for durable and nondurable consumption, as specified in the model in appendix 3A. Assume that if a borrower wants to save on her own in order to buy the durable good, the maximum amount of money that she can save each period is $y - c - \varepsilon$, where ε is the cost that she has to incur for saving the money on her own. But if she joins a ROSCA this cost disappears and the maximum she can save is $(y - c)$.

a. Show that, *ex ante* (that is, before she knows when she will be getting the pot relative to other participants), every saver-borrower is willing to join the ROSCA.

b. In order for a ROSCA to work well, the organizers decide that those members who quit the ROSCA before all of the participants have received the pot will face a punishment P:

i. Show that if $P > B$, then the mechanics of a ROSCA will survive in that no one would want to abscond. Note that, as in Appendix 3A, B is the value of the good to be purchased with the ROSCA pot.

ii. Show that if $P < 1/2\ B$, then the mechanism that holds the ROSCA together collapses.

iii. Again, using the notation from appendix 3A, and considering: $T = 100$, $\theta = \$10$, $y = \$20$, $c = \$12$, $\varepsilon = \$3$, $B = \$80$, $P = \$79$ and $n = 78$, can participants borrow from a ROSCA? What about when $n = 120$?

4. Consider 3 villagers who live for 10 periods and have linear, additive utility functions as follows:

$$\text{Villager 1: } U_1 = \sum_{i=1}^{10} 0.6^i c_i^1$$

$$\text{Villager 2: } U_2 = \sum_{i=1}^{10} 0.8^i c_i^2$$

$$\text{Villager 3: } U_3 = \sum_{i=1}^{10} c_i^3$$

Where c_i^n is the consumption (both of durable and nondurable goods) at time i of villager n. And 0.6, 0.8, and 1 are the discount factors of villagers 1, 2, 3, respectively. Note that villager 1 is the most impatient, and villager 3 the least impatient. Assume that at each period, each villager earns $y = \$140$, and the subsistence level of consumption for all of them is $\underline{c} = \$80$, so the maximum amount that each villager can save at each period is $(y - \underline{c})$. A durable good costs $B = \$360$, and if a villager buys it the utility he receives from it equals that of consuming $\theta = \$2500$ each period, for two periods.

Consider a ROSCA, organized as follows. At the first meeting, which takes place at the end of the second period, the pot will go to the member who makes the highest bid, which must be at least $A_1 = \$1000$. Villagers who do not take the pot each get ½ of the bid. At the second meeting, the villager who got the pot in the first meeting is excluded from bidding. The pot will go to the villager who makes the highest bid again in this round, which must be at least $A_2 = \$200$ and will be given to the other participants. At the third meeting, the remaining villager will get the pot, and the ROSCA ends. Meetings occur every two periods, and every villager contributes $60 every period to the pot.

a. Which villager will get the pot at the first meeting, at the second meeting, and the third meeting?

b. Assume that if the villagers do not turn up to make their contributions after receiving the pot, they will be punished so severely that their utility will be $-\infty$, and that all events occur at the end of the periods. What does this exercise tell us about social sanctions in microfinance operating in close-knit village economies?

5. Relative to Credit Cooperatives, ROSCAs have some disadvantages.
a. Compare the main disadvantages of ROSCAs relative to credit cooperatives.
b. In light of such disadvantages, explain why ROSCAs are so common in nearly all low-income economies these days.

6. ROSCAs often are considered to be predecessors of today's microfinance institutions.
a. In what way have microfinance institutions resolved some of ROSCAs' limitations?
b. Assuming that microfinance institutions resolve the main limitations of ROSCAs, why have ROSCAs survived even in those countries which are thick with microfinance?

7. Consider a village inhabited by 3 risk-neutral individuals: a borrower, an inside lender, and an outside lender. The first two are part of a credit cooperative. The borrower wants to invest in a project that costs $K = \$100$. If she exerts effort, the project will be successful with probability 0.9 and will yield a return of $y = \$240$. Otherwise, the project fails and her return is zero. If she "shirks" (i.e., if she does not put in enough effort), her probability of success is only 0.5. The cost of her effort is $e = \$30$. The inside lender can lend at most $b = \$60$ to be used as investment with a gross interest rate $R = 160\%$. The outside lender will lend the rest of the funds needed to start the project at a gross interest rate of $R = 210\%$. In case of default, the outside lender can seize an amount $\varphi = \$50$ offered as collateral by the inside lender. As she is interested in the result of the project, the inside lender can choose whether to monitor the behavior of the borrower, which would imply a monitoring cost of $P = \$20$. If she monitors, she knows the behavior of the borrower. In the event that misbehavior is discovered, the borrower will then be punished and incur a penalty equivalent to $A = \$9$. Assume that all agents are rational, and that they understand the following time line: lending takes place first; then monitoring decisions are made; choices about effort are made next; and, finally, returns are realized and the borrower decides whether or not to repay.
a. What strategies will the borrower and the inside lender choose and why?
b. Will these strategies change if the inside lender increases the interest rate to $R = 200\%$? Briefly explain your answer.

8. Consider an economy where there is an inside borrower, an inside lender and an outside lender, and assume the three are risk neutral.

The inside borrower has a project that yields a return of y with probability p and a return of zero with probability $(1 - p)$ after one period. The project requires an investment of b, which can be borrowed from the outside lender. Since the inside borrower has no wealth, the inside lender offers her the following contract: the inside borrower provides wealth w to the inside lender to be used as collateral, as well as half of her project returns, net of debt payments. The inside lender lends the necessary funds b to the inside borrower and receives either R_b if the project is successful or simply seizes w if the inside borrower's project fails, where R stand for the gross interest rate (principal plus interest). Finally, the inside borrower can choose her level of effort, which changes the probability of her project's success and incurs an effort cost

$$c_e(p) = \frac{kp^2}{2m}$$

where m is the amount of costly monitoring by the inside lender. This monitoring cost is given by

$$c_m(p) = \frac{tm^2}{2}.$$

Assume that w is sufficiently large to eliminate any ex-post moral hazard problems.

a. Interpret the effort and monitoring cost functions.
b. Solve for the equilibrium effort and optimal monitoring effort in this environment, assuming an exogenously given interest rate. Briefly comment on your results.
c. What happens if the inside borrower adopts a new technology that makes effort less costly for every level of p? Comment on what you expect to happen in this case, and, more generally, on what you expect would happen if the inside lender adopts a new technology that makes monitoring cheaper for any level of m.

9. Consider an economy with *ex ante* symmetric, risk neutral individuals of mass 1, living for 2 periods with an additive, linear utility function on consumption goods (both durable and non durable). At the beginning of the first period, a portion f of the economy will luckily receive high income y_1, while the rest of the economy will get a lower income y_0. An agent's level of income is private information. Assume that every individual in this economy wants to buy a durable good,

which costs B and gives extra consumption θ per period. The subsistence level of consumption in this economy is c (i.e., the total consumption on durable and non durable goods must be greater than or equal to c, assume $\theta - B \geq c$). The unlucky individual doesn't have enough money to buy the durable good in the first period, but the lucky one does. However, in the first period there are enough resources in the economy as a whole for each individual to buy the durable good, and there might be a credit market for consumption of durable goods. In the second period, every one will have the same return y, and $y - B > 0$, so everyone's income is high enough to cover subsistence consumption and purchase the durable good.

a. Suppose that ex ante, individuals in this economy can sign a contract to specify that members can lend l_1 and borrow l_0 at the rate R in the end of period 1, where

$$l_0 = B - y_0$$

$$l_1 = \frac{1-f}{f}(B - y_0) = y_1 - B.$$

b. Define the range for R (to be paid in the second period) in which lucky individuals are willing to lend, unlucky individuals are willing to borrow, and everyone is better off from this transaction. (Assume that θ cannot be used for lending.)

10. Is the result in the preceding exercise still true if we allow the discount rate to be positive? What is the lower bound of the discount rate in this particular case?

11. Follow-up from your answer to the previous exercise: what is the upper bound of the discount rate? Briefly explain your answer.

4 Group Lending

4.1 Introduction

Once every week in villages throughout Bangladesh, groups of forty villagers meet together for half an hour or so, joined by a loan officer from a microfinance organization. The loan officer sits in the front of the group (the "center") and begins his business.[1] The large group of villagers is subdivided into eight five-person groups, each with its own chairperson, and the eight chairs, in turn, hand over their group's passbooks to the chairperson of the center, who then passes the books to the loan officer. The loan officer duly records the individual transactions in his ledger, noting weekly installments on loans outstanding, savings deposits, and fees. Quick arithmetic on a calculator ensures that the totals add up correctly, and, if they do not, the loan officer sorts out discrepancies. Before leaving, he may dispense advice and make arrangements for customers to obtain new loans at the branch office. All of this is done in public, making the process more transparent and letting the villagers know who among them is moving forward and who may be running into difficulties.[2]

This scene is repeated over 400,000 times each week in Bangladesh by members and staff of microfinance institutions inspired by Grameen Bank, and versions have been adapted around the world by Grameen-style replicators.[3] Other institutions instead base their methods on the "solidarity group" approach developed by Bolivia's BancoSol or the "village bank" approach operated by microlenders in seventy countries throughout Africa, Latin America, and Asia (including affiliates of FINCA, Pro Mujer, and Freedom from Hunger).[4] For many, this kind of "group lending" has become synonymous with microfinance.[5]

Group lending generally refers to arrangements by individuals without collateral who get together and form groups to obtain loans from a lender. The special feature of the "classic" Grameen Bank model is that the loans are made individually to group members, but all in the group face consequences if any member runs into serious repayment difficulties. In the original Grameen Bank case, the groups are made up of five people. In the BancoSol case, groups can be as small as three people, and in the village banking system groups can range from ten to about thirty women.[6] The fundamental idea of "group responsibility" (sometimes called "joint liability") coupled with regular group meetings is common across approaches.

In major departures, Grameen Bank has forsworn lending with joint liability, and BancoSol does very little of it now. We describe why in the next chapter, and in this chapter explain the logic of group lending and the rationale for its continuing importance in many institutions. It is still used, for example, by BRAC, Grameen's biggest competitor in Bangladesh, and particularly by institutions working with poorer customers (Cull, Demirgüç-Kunt, and Morduch 2009b).

It is noteworthy that, despite dropping joint liability lending, Grameen Bank retains group meetings. The weekly group meetings have some obvious and simple advantages for the lender and customers. Most immediately, they offer convenience to the villagers; the bank comes to them, and any problems (a missing document, being a few taka short) can be resolved on the spot. The bank thus offers the same convenience as a local ROSCA or moneylender. Meanwhile, transactions costs are greatly reduced for the loan officer since the multiple savings and loan transactions of forty people can take place in a short block of time.

Transacting through groups also has more subtle advantages (and some limitations). In particular, where the joint liability clause is used in contracts, it can mitigate the moral hazard, adverse selection, and enforcement problems that crippled previous attempts at lending to the poor by outside financial institutions. In chapter 2 we described how these problems are caused by information asymmetries, and one implication is that if the bank gets more information, it can always do better. A solution to the resulting inefficiency is thus to create contracts that generate better information.[7]

But the contracts described in this chapter all improve matters *without* the bank necessarily learning anything new. Instead, the contracts take advantage of the fact that group members themselves may have good information about fellow members—and the contract gives the members incentives to use their information to the bank's advantage. This can occur in subtle ways, and we present different scenarios in turn.

While the advantages of group lending will be spelled out, there is another side to the coin. Might groups collude against the microlender by collectively deciding not to repay? If the group of borrowers is not willing to impose social sanctions upon itself, can the group nonetheless provide advantages? Another set of questions relates to peer monitoring. What will happen if the population of potential borrowers is dispersed and local information is thus weak and costly to obtain? If group lending takes place in urban areas, where labor mobility is high and individuals also may not have much information about their potential partners, are there still any advantages for groups? And if borrowers cannot observe each other's effort levels (or are otherwise reluctant to punish shirkers), then group lending can undermine incentives by encouraging "free riding." Borrowers will ask themselves: Why should I work hard if I am liable for a penalty when my partner shirks—even when I cannot control their actions? Sections 4.5 and 4.6 investigate ways that group lending has enabled outside lenders to expand credit access in low-income communities, but we also point to tensions and imperfections in the approach—which suggest turning as well to some of the alternative mechanisms described in chapter 5.

4.2   The Group Lending Methodology

Access to finance via groups is not new. The example of ROSCAs in chapter 3 shows how groups function to give participants access to a pot of communal money, and credit cooperatives similarly function to allow members to obtain loans from their peers. The place of groups in microfinance, however, strengthens and extends earlier uses of groups (although not without some added costs).

To see this, we describe "Grameen-style" group lending. The model has been adapted in different contexts, but replicators have tried to stay true to the main features described in this section. The Grameen Bank itself has undergone changes in the twenty-five years since it started (most recently with a major overhaul dubbed "Grameen Bank II"), and we will describe elements of what is now called the Grameen "classic" system (Yunus 2002). This is the early model that has figured most prominently in economic research.[8] We return to Grameen II in section 4.6.

When the Grameen Bank first got started as an experimental bank in the village of Jobra, near Chittagong University, the first loans were made to individuals without a group responsibility clause (Yunus 1999). Instead, economies of scale motivated the first use of groups. But Yunus and his associates soon realized that requesting potential borrowers to organize themselves into groups had another advantage: the costs of screening and monitoring loans and the costs of enforcing debt repayments could be substantially reduced.[9]

To institute this systematically, the bank developed a system in which two members of each five-person group receive their loans first.[10] If all installments are paid on time, the initial loans are followed four to six weeks later by loans to two other members, and then, after another four to six weeks, by a loan to the group chairperson. (This pattern is known as $2:2:1$ staggering.) At first, the groups were seen just as sources of solidarity, offering mutual assistance in times of need. For example, if a member of a group fails to attend a meeting, the group leader repays on her behalf, and thus the credit record of the absentee borrower remains clean, and so does the group's. The original premise was that perhaps someone might experience a delay in getting a loan if there were a problem within their group, but there would not be further sanctions.[11]

Over time, though, formal sanctions became more common. In principle, if serious repayment problems emerge, all group members will be cut off from future borrowing. The original idea was not that group members would be forced to repay for others, rather it was that they would lose the privilege of borrowing. In practice, of course, a borrower who does not want to lose access to microcredit loans accepts the possibility of having to bail out her fellow group members in times of need. It is not unheard of that a loan officer will stay in a village until group members (or members of the forty-person center) are able to make good on all installments due that week (although the practice is not in keeping with the early vision of top Grameen managers).[12]

In a typical situation, when all goes well with repayments, borrowers are offered a larger loan repayable in the next "loan cycle" (loan cycles—from initial disbursement to repayment of the final installment—were typically a year in the "classic" Grameen system). Thus, if the relationship between Grameen and the borrowers continues, loan sizes grow over the years and credit histories are built up. Eventually loans may be large enough to build or repair a house or to make lumpy investments like purchasing a rickshaw or, in a recent loan innovation, sending a child to university.

4.3 Mitigating Adverse Selection

The adverse selection problem occurs when lenders cannot distinguish inherently risky borrowers from safer borrowers. If lenders could distinguish by risk type, they could charge different interest rates to different types of borrowers. But with poor information, options are limited. As we saw in section 2.3, adverse selection may lead to credit rationing because it induces lenders to charge everyone high interest rates to compensate for the possibility of having very risky borrowers in the customer population. The trouble (and source of inefficiency) arises when safe borrowers are thus deterred from applying for loans. In principle, group lending with joint responsibility can mitigate this inefficiency.[13] The most direct mechanism occurs when customers inform the bank about the reliability of potential joiners, allowing the bank to adjust terms accordingly. We describe a less direct mechanism that may also work, and that does not rely on revealing information to the bank. Because the result is somewhat surprising, we develop it in several steps.

Consider a microfinance institution or a bank committed to covering its costs so that it just breaks even.[14] Assume that the bank introduces the group lending methodology described previously, and that it has no idea about the borrowers' characteristics. Borrowers, on the other hand, know each other's types, and, as in section 2.3, borrowers are either "risky" or "safe." As before, the problem is that the bank wants to charge lower interest rates to safe borrowers and higher rates to risky borrowers, but, since the bank cannot easily tell who is who, everyone has to pay the same rate. In practice, then, the safer borrowers—when they actually decide to apply for a loan at the prevailing interest rates—implicitly subsidize the risky borrowers (who are more costly for the bank to serve). The inefficiency arises when this implicit subsidy is so large that safe borrowers leave the market rather than shouldering the burden— namely, when the presence of risky borrowers raises the interest rate to levels that are simply unaffordable for safer borrowers. The question here is whether group lending can make it possible to *implicitly* charge safe borrowers lower interest rates and thus keep them in the market.

The fact that groups are encouraged to form on their own is the key to the solution; potential borrowers can then use their information to find the best partners. How they sort themselves depends on the nature of the loan contract. Faced with the prospect of joint responsibility for loans, it is clearly better to be grouped with safe types than with risky types. So, given the choice, the safe types stick together. The risky borrowers thus have no alternative but to form groups with other risky types, leading to a segregated outcome often referred to in the labor economics literature as "assortative matching."[15]

How does this help the bank charge lower prices to safe types? Because investment projects undertaken by risky borrowers fail more often than those of safe borrowers, risky borrowers have to repay for their defaulting peers more often under group lending with joint responsibility; otherwise, they will be denied future access to credit. Safe borrowers no longer have to shoulder the burden of default by the risky types. What this boils down to is a transfer of risk from the bank onto the risky borrowers themselves. It also means that, effectively, the safe types pay lower interest rates than the risky types—because they no longer have to cross-subsidize risky borrowers. Strikingly, the result is that the group lending methodology does the trick even though (1) the bank remains as ignorant as ever about who is safe and who is risky, and (2) all customers are offered exactly the same contract. All of the action occurs through the joint responsibility condition combined with the sorting mechanism.

Moreover, because banks are now better insured against defaults, average interest rates for both risky and safe types can be reduced while banks still break even. The lower interest rates in turn bring a secondary positive effect. In the adverse selection problem analyzed in section 2.3, "safe" borrowers were inefficiently pushed out of the market by high interest rates; here, the reduction in interest charges faced by safe types further encourages them to reenter the market, mitigating the market failure.

To see this formally, suppose that the bank requests that borrowers form two-person groups and that each individual in the pair holds herself responsible for her peer.[16] As in section 2.3.2, the analysis is simplified by assuming that individuals try to maximize their expected income without concern for risk. As before, we first present the analysis using algebra and then provide a simple numerical example.

Again, each individual has a one-period project requiring $1 of investment. The fraction of the population that is safe is $q < 1$, and the fraction of the population that is risky is $(1 - q)$. A dollar invested by safe borrowers yields a gross return $\underline{y}$ with certainty.[17] A risky borrower who invests $1, on the other hand, obtains a gross return $\bar{y} > \underline{y}$ if successful, and this occurs with probability $p < 1$. If not successful, they earn 0, which happens with probability $(1 - p)$. Again, to simplify things we assume that both types have identical *expected* returns, so that $p\bar{y} = \underline{y}$. How do the types sort themselves into groups? Since borrowers know each other's types, safe borrowers pair with other safe types, and risky borrowers pair with other risky types (i.e., there will be assortative matching in equilibrium). Now consider more closely situations where both types of borrowers participate in the credit market. Since the fraction of the population that is safe is $q < 1$, this will also be the fraction of groups made up of (safe, safe) types. If, say, a quarter of the population is "safe," then a quarter of the two-person groups will be made up of "safe" couples.

What is the gross interest rate R_b (principal plus interest) that the bank should charge in order to break even? To make the problem interesting, assume that $\bar{y} > 2R_b$ so that, when lucky, a risky borrower can always repay for her peer. Then the expected revenue of the bank if it sets its break-even interest rate at R_b is straightforward to compute: with probability q the bank faces a (safe, safe) pair of borrowers and therefore gets repaid for sure; with probability $(1 - q)$, the bank faces a (risky, risky) pair, in which case it is always repaid unless both borrowers in that pair have a bad draw; we denote the probability that the bank is repaid in this case as g. Since the chance that *both* are simultaneously unlucky is $(1 - p)\cdot(1 - p)$, the chance that one or both are lucky is $g = 1 - (1 - p)^2$. The expected repayment from a given borrower is thus

$$[q+(1-q)g]R_b. \tag{4.1}$$

The equation reflects that a fraction q of groups return R_b always (i.e., the safe groups) and a fraction $(1 - q)$ of groups return R_b just g proportion of the time. This expected payment must be equal to the bank's cost of funds k in order for the bank to break even in expectation. Solving for R_b gives

$$R_b = k/[q+(1-q)g], \tag{4.2}$$

which is smaller than the interest rate in the absence of group lending found in chapter 2 (there, without group lending, we found that $R_b = k/[q + (1 - q)p]$). The fact that the interest rate is smaller here arises because $g > p$; that is, the process of matching means that risky borrowers can pay back their loans more often (thanks to joint liability) than they could if just dealing with the bank as individuals. The risk is thus passed on from the bank to the risky borrowers. The bank can thus reduce the interest rate and lure deserving safe types back into the market.

The beauty of the arrangement is that all borrowers face the *same contract*, but, thanks to assortative matching, the risky types pay more on average. The bank thus effectively price discriminates—without needing to know who is safe and who is risky.

4.3.1 Numerical Example

To see how this works with numbers, return to the numerical example in section 2.3.3. There we showed a situation in which asymmetric information led to inefficiency. Here, we show a group-based contract that solves the problem.

The basic setup is exactly as before. From the lender's viewpoint, half the population is safe (they're always successful) and half is risky (they fail 25 percent of the time). Both safe and risky types are risk neutral and need $100 to undertake a month-long project. Their alternative is to work for a wage of $45. If the bank lends money, it needs to recover costs equal to $40 per month per loan. The gross revenue of safe types is $200, and the gross revenue of risky types is $267. The basic data are shown in table 4.1.

Given this situation, we saw in section 2.3.3 that there was no interest rate at which the bank could cover its costs and still entice everyone to borrow—if it used a standard individual lending contract. Here we show how a contract with joint responsibility can help the bank do better. Consider a contract offered to two-person groups in which the interest rate per borrower is 55 percent, payable only if the borrower's project is successful (i.e., her total payment to the bank is $155, including principal). The contract also specifies that if a borrower succeeds but her partner fails, the borrower is liable for another $45 (which is as much as the bank can extract, given safe types' gross revenues of $200; successful risky types will always claim to be safe types).[18]

Now what happens? Borrowers are asked to choose their partners. Does assortative matching occur? Yes: Groups will never be mixed by type. To see why, consider the expected net returns under the contract. The four possible scenarios are shown in table 4.1. If a safe type matches with a safe type, both borrowers know that they will owe $155 at the end of the month, leaving a $45 net profit. If a risky type matches with a risky type, they know that they will be successful 75 percent of the time. And $0.25 \cdot 0.75$ of the time, they will owe the "joint liability" payment of $45. Their expected payment is thus $0.75 \cdot (\$155 + 0.25 \cdot \$45)$

Table 4.1
Group-lending numerical example: Base data

The economic environment

Lender's cost of capital		$40 per month per $100 loan	
Borrowers' opportunity cost (wage)		$45 per month	
Fraction of safe borrowers in the population		50%	
	Gross revenue if successful	Probability of success	Expected gross revenue
Safe type	$200	100%	$200
Risky type	$267	75%	$200

Group lending contract

Gross interest due if borrower is successful	$155
Payment due if borrower fails	$0
Additional payment due if borrower is successful but partner fails	$45

Borrower's expected net returns under the contract:

		Partner type	
		Safe	Risky
Borrower	Safe	$45	$34
Type	Risky	$84	$75

= $124.69, leaving a $75.31 expected net profit. Can mixed pairs do better? Risky types clearly prefer to group with safe types (expected net profit = $83.75 versus $75.31), but can risky types afford to compensate safe types enough to induce them into partnerships? No, since safe types would demand an extra "side payment" of at least $11.25 (= $45 − $33.75) to compensate for teaming with risky types. But the risky types' expected net gain from teaming with safe types is only $8.44 (= $83.75 − $75.31). So, like matches with like.

The implication is that safe types now earn enough to make borrowing worthwhile. So everybody wants to borrow, and efficiency is restored. Quick calculations will confirm that the bank wants to lend under this contract too, since on average it will just break even.

4.3.2 Group Lending beyond Villages

Not all microfinance programs start with close-knit borrowers with rich information on each other. Karlan (2007), for example, describes village banks in the Andes town of Ayacucho (with a population of

150,000). The FINCA affiliate spreads the word about the village banks, and interested borrowers are invited to come to FINCA's office to put their names on a list; once the list reaches thirty names (typically in less than two weeks), a group is formed. The process is easy and efficient, but a consequence is that few of the group members know each other before joining the village bank.

Section 4.3, in contrast, showed how banks can circumvent credit rationing due to adverse selection through group lending when borrowers are perfectly informed about each other's types. The village banks of Ayacucho represent a different context, one more typical of urban areas such as Mexico City and Bogotá, where populations are highly mobile and often have little information about each other. Can group lending still help to overcome adverse selection? Can group lending carry benefits even if the "getting to know each other" process is slow or imperfect?

Consider the extreme scenario where potential borrowers remain completely anonymous; that is, they do not have any information about the characteristics of their peers. Group lending can no longer lead to assortative matching; instead, it will typically involve mixed pairs of safe and risky borrowers. Is this enough to discourage safe borrowers from applying for a loan? Can an appropriately structured group-lending contract improve on standard "individual-lending" contracts?

As in section 4.3.1, risky borrowers will gain from the possibility of matching with a safe borrower who can always repay for them. But can safe borrowers gain too? Yes, if the contract takes advantage of the possibility that when risky borrowers are lucky, they get higher returns than safe borrowers. The optimal group lending contract will in practice extract more from risky borrowers when they are lucky but paired with an unlucky risky borrower, while the contract will not extract as much from a safe borrower who is paired with an unlucky risky borrower. The reason is "limited liability" as described previously. Group lending here makes risky borrowers indirectly cross-subsidize safe borrowers, allowing the latter to access loans at a lower interest rate than without group lending. Once again, lower interest rates mitigate the credit rationing problem by increasing the participation of safe borrowers in the credit market.

We show the potential for the welfare-improving use of group lending here, using a stylized example based on the analysis of Armendáriz and Gollier (2000). The example follows the spirit of the analysis at the start of section 4.3, and, as previously, our goal is to show the potential for gains, rather than to claim that there will *always* be gains. More formally, again let R_b denote the gross interest rate set by the bank (set so that the bank just breaks even), and again suppose that returns are set such that $\underline{y} < 2R_b < \bar{y}$. In this case, $\underline{y} < 2R_b$ means that the safe borrowers are unable to fully pay for an unlucky partner's failure. Groups are now matched randomly. Since a fraction q of the population is made up of safe types, the chance that a (safe, safe) pair emerges through random matching is q^2.[19] Similarly, the chance that a (risky, risky) pair emerges is $(1 - q)^2$. And the chance that a (safe, risky) pair emerges is accordingly $1 - q^2 - (1 - q)^2$, or, after simplifying, $2q(1 - q)$.

The bank's expected gross revenues are then $2R_b$ from (safe, safe) pairs. This is because both repay the interest rate with certainty. Since the expected fraction of matches that are (safe, safe) is q^2, the bank expects to get $2R_b$ in a fraction q^2 of cases. With probability $(1 - q)^2$ the pair is (risky, risky), and the bank gets $2R_b$ if both are lucky. The chance that both are lucky is p^2 since p is the probability that either independently succeeds (again as in chapter 2). The probability that both risky borrowers fail is correspondingly $(1 - p)^2$; in this case, the bank gets nothing back. And the chance that one is lucky while the other is not is $2p(1 - p)$; in that case, the lucky partner can pay for both, so the bank gets $2R_b$ once more. Finally, with probability $2q(1 - q)$, the bank faces a mixed (safe, risky) pair. We know that the safe partner always does well, so the question is: What happens to the risky partner? If the risky partner is lucky (which happens with probability p), the bank again gets $2R_b$. But $(1 - p)$ of the time the risky partner has bad luck. Note that here the safe partner cannot fully pay for the risky partner (by the assumption that $\underline{y} < 2R_b$). Instead, the bank can only extract the amount $\underline{y}$ from the safe partner by the assumption of limited liability (i.e., the bank cannot extract more than the safe borrower's current revenue).

In equilibrium, the gross interest rate R_b must be set so that the expected repayment per borrower is equal to the bank's full cost of funds k. Since we are analyzing loans to each member in a two-person group, the expected gross repayment must be at least $2k$. Now we can put all of this information together to yield

$$q^2 2R_b + (1-q)^2 (p^2 + 2p(1-p))2R_b + 2q(1-q)\left[p^2 R_b + (1-p)\underline{y}\right] = 2k. \quad (4.3)$$

or, simplifying by dividing by two:

$$q^2 R_b + (1-q)^2 (p^2 + 2p(1-p)) R_b + 2q(1-q)\big[pR_b + (1-p)\underline{y}/2 \big] = k. \qquad (4.4)$$

The next step is to solve for the equilibrium gross interest rate R_b that makes the equation hold. The question is whether the R_b that emerges is lower than $k/[q + (1 - q) p]$, which is the gross interest rate in the absence of group lending (found in chapter 2). After a bit more algebra (which we leave to readers as an exercise), we see that the break-even gross interest rate will indeed be lower than before. The bottom line is quite surprising: in principle, the group-lending contract can help lenders reduce interest rates—even where neither the bank nor the clients have information about who is safe or risky! In the process, adverse selection can be mitigated and a greater number of worthy borrowers can get access to credit.

The intuition is that risky borrowers, if lucky, can always repay their defaulting partners—whether safe or risky. But safe borrowers cannot repay for others due to the fact that their returns are lower and that all borrowers are protected by limited liability. Thus, defaults are de facto shouldered by risky borrowers only. Since risks are thereby passed on to risky borrowers specifically (rather than the average borrower), the bank is able to set interest rates that are low enough to win back the business of the safe borrowers. We end this section where we started, by reminding readers that the analysis only shows the *potential* for gains, and it draws on specific assumptions about the nature of risks and the role of limited liability. All the same, it is a striking example of the potential for group-lending contracts to make improvements— even in situations where it had been thought impossible.

4.4 Overcoming Moral Hazard

Section 4.3 showed how group lending with joint responsibility can mitigate credit rationing due to adverse selection at the group forma-tion stage. But as we pointed out in section 2.4, once loans have been granted, the bank may then face moral hazard problems due to the difficulty of monitoring borrowers' actions. In this section we show how group lending with joint responsibility may circumvent moral hazard problems in lending, thereby further relaxing credit constraints. Here, we draw on the possibility that group members, who often live and work closely together, can impose social or economic sanctions on each other, possibilities that are impossible for an outside bank to impose.

4.4.1 Ex Ante Moral Hazard and the Role of Joint Responsibility

In important early work on the theory of group lending, Stiglitz (1990) and Varian (1990) set out an ex ante moral hazard approach to group lending. Their main argument is that the group-lending contract circumvents ex ante moral hazard by inducing borrowers to monitor each others' choice of projects and to inflict penalties upon borrowers who have chosen excessively risky projects. As Laffont and Rey (2003) argue, the fact that group members are affected by the actions—and inactions!—of other members means that they will take steps to punish anyone who puts in little effort and thus burdens the group with excessive risk.

To see how group lending can address moral hazard, we go back to the ex ante moral hazard model of section 2.4.1, but with two borrowers that are linked by a group-lending contract. As in section 2.4.1, we assume that investment projects require a $1 investment. A nonshirking borrower generates gross revenue y with certainty, whereas a shirking borrower generates gross revenue y with probability p and zero with probability $(1 - p)$. Consider again a borrower's decision whether or not to put effort into her project. If R denotes the gross interest rate (interest plus principal) to be paid to the lender and c is the cost of effort, then a borrower's expected return if she puts in effort equals $(y - R) - c$, as before. Members of the group act to maximize group income, and anyone who deviates is punished with serious social sanctions.

In section 2.4.1, the borrower had the option to put in the requisite effort and get net revenues of $(y - R) - c$. Or, alternatively, the borrower had the option to take a gamble by shirking; in this second case, the borrower only succeeds p percent of the time but does not have to bear the cost of effort. So, effort is only forthcoming if $(y - R) - c > p (y - R)$, which implies that the gross interest rate must be set so that $R < y [c/(1 - p)]$. Interest rates higher than this level will encourage shirking. These inequalities are termed incentive compatibility constraints (or, simply, IC constraints), and they play a key role in understanding the function of contracts.

The group-lending contract allows the lender to do better than this: interest rates can be raised higher without undermining good incentives. To see this, we consider a "group IC constraint." We show that the maximum feasible interest rate that the bank can elicit from the group of borrowers without inducing default is higher because the IC constraint is "more relaxed" (i.e., easier to satisfy) than the individual IC constraint described in the previous paragraph.

We again consider a two-person group. If both put in effort, they both pay back loans and incur the costs of effort. Together, the return is $(2y - 2R) - 2c$. On the other hand, if they both shirk, they expect to be able to pay their full joint obligation $(2y - 2R)$ only p^2 fraction of the time. If the borrowers both shirk and one is lucky but not the other, the lucky one is responsible for the full repayment of both, leaving no surplus left over.

Thus, the group IC constraint under joint responsibility reflects the fact that positive rewards are only received when both projects succeed:

$$(2y - 2R) - 2c > p^2(2y - 2R), \tag{4.5}$$

or equivalently $R < y - c/(1 - p^2)$. Since $p < 1$, it must be that $p^2 < p$, which means that $(1 - p^2) > (1 - p)$. Accordingly, the maximum achievable gross interest rate R under group lending with joint responsibility—namely, $y - [c/(1 - p^2)]$—is strictly larger than the maximum achievable interest rate in the absence of joint responsibility—namely, $y - [c/(1 - p)]$.

The joint liability contract relies on the group's ability to sanction individuals who try to shirk. In the Stiglitz and Varian models, the sanctions are cost-less, but in subsequent work by others, monitoring and enforcement costs are derived as part of the decision framework (e.g., Armendáriz 1999a). Given the contract, in principle both group members will never shirk, so it turns that out the sanctions are never actually used. In principle, all that is needed is the *threat* of their use.

4.4.2 Ex Post Moral Hazard and the Role of Peer Monitoring

Now suppose that everybody works hard, so the kinds of concerns in section 4.4.1 are allayed. But now consider a problem that can occur after production has been completed and profits have been realized. The new concern is that borrowers may now be tempted to pocket the revenues without repaying the lender (i.e., to "take the money and run"). The problem then is that the bank cannot tell which borrowers truthfully cannot repay—versus those borrowers who are seeking to run away with their earnings.[20] To sharpen the tension, assume that, in the absence of peer monitoring, a borrower will default with certainty on her loan (whether or not she in fact has the resources to repay). Everything else equal, we saw in section 2.4.2 that this sort of ex post moral hazard eliminates the scope for lending as no bank will extend credit if it anticipates that the borrower will escape repayment.

Group lending with peer monitoring can, however, induce each group member to incur a monitoring cost k ex post to check the actual revenue realization of her peer. We assume that with this information, the partner can force the peer to repay. As in Armendáriz (1999a), let us assume that by incurring a cost k, a borrower can observe the actual revenue of her peer with probability q, and let d denote a social sanction that can be applied to a borrower who tries to divert due repayments. Then, if R denotes the gross interest rate set by the bank, a borrower will choose to repay if and only if

$$y - R - k > y - k - q^2(d+R) - q(1-q)(d+y) \tag{4.6}$$

That is, the payoff from not defaulting, from the standpoint of an individual borrower, and assuming both borrowers decide to monitor, is: the borrower's gross revenue y minus the gross interest rate (principal plus interest), less the cost of monitoring k. If, on the other hand, the borrower decides to "take the money and run," her payoff is: her gross revenue y, less the monitoring cost k; if both borrowers find out that each has shirked, which happens with probability q^2, $d + R$ is subtracted but if shirking is detected by the borrower's peer only, which occurs with probability $q(1 - q)$, $d + y$ is subtracted.[21] This can be written equivalently as:

$$R < q(d+y)/(1-q). \tag{4.7}$$

This in turn means that borrowers can contract any loans of sizes less than or equal to $q(d + y) / (1 - q^2)$. In the absence of peer monitoring, we had $q = 0$ (zero chance of observing the borrower's actual revenue) and therefore no lending at all in equilibrium. Now, why do we have monitoring (implied by $q > 0$) in equilibrium? The answer is akin to logic developed by Banerjee, Besley, and Guinnane (1994) (see section 3.3.2). In their analysis of credit cooperatives, it was the insider's fear of losing her collateral w which induced her to monitor her peer borrower. Here, it is the borrower's incentive to minimize the probability of suffering from joint responsibility that induces monitoring (provided the monitoring cost k is sufficiently small). Thus, joint responsibility makes lending sustainable by inducing peer monitoring and overcoming enforcement problems associated with ex post moral hazard.

So, the group lending contract again does better than the traditional individual lending contract. But can the microlender do even better than that? Rai and Sjöström (2004) argue in an important theoretical contribution that the answer is yes—and we return to the issue at the end of this chapter.

4.5   Evidence on Groups and Contracts

While the theories of group lending work on paper, how do they work in practice? Is the group lending mechanism in fact the key to the high loan repayment rates boasted by microlenders? Over the past few years empirical researchers have studied these questions, and they have arrived at a series of competing results. Some results support the theories presented here, while others point to tensions and constraints in the group-lending approach.

Cull, Demirgüç-Kunt, and Morduch (2007) provide insight into the impact of group lending from an institutional perspective. The authors use data collected by the Microfinance Information Exchange (the MIX) to analyze the performance of 124 leading group lenders, individual lenders, and village banks. They show that while individual lenders charging higher interest rates face greater levels of default, lenders that use group-based methods do not, suggesting that group contracts mitigate incentive problems as the theory of asymmetric information predicts.

Richard Montgomery (1996) examines the effects of group lending contracts from the opposite perspective—that of individual borrowers at one institution. He turns a critical eye to BRAC in Bangladesh, a Grameen Bank replicator (at least as far as its credit operations go). Montgomery (1996, 289) argues that BRAC's implementation of group lending "can lead to forms of borrower discipline which are unnecessarily exclusionary, and which can contradict the broader (social) aims of solidarity group lending." This is an important reminder: the discussion so far has focused on ways that group lending can improve the bank's performance. We have focused little on how the practice affects borrowers' lives, other than by assuming that improvements are made when group lending improves access to credit for individuals lacking collateral. Montgomery's main concern is that group lending can create peer pressure that works against the poorest and most vulnerable members of the community. In attempting to keep repayment rates up, Montgomery contends, loan officers put sharp pressure on borrowers to repay, even when the borrowers faced difficulties beyond their control. He mentions stories of the "forced" acquisition of household utensils, livestock, and other assets of defaulting members. In one case, a woman's house was pulled down for failure to pay a housing loan (Montgomery 1996, 297). One response raised in chapter 6 involves providing insurance alongside credit, so that borrowers have a way to cope with major risks. Without such insurance, there is a legitimate question as to whether microfinance (whether implemented via group lending or via other methods) can make some borrowers more vulnerable than they had been.[22] As we suggest in chapter 5, there may be other ways to get the benefits of group lending without all of the drawbacks.

Montgomery also suggests that the "reality" of group lending in Bangladesh is that the traditional five-person group ultimately plays a small role in ensuring repayment discipline. Instead it is the larger, village-level group that plays the key role. Montgomery (1996, 296–297) writes the following with regard to this "village organization" (VO):

The VO leaders commonly treat overdue installments as a VO issue. If the individual continues to default on their installments, and the outstanding amount grows or the loan term expires, the VO leader and the group (VO) as a whole comes under pressure from the field staff. Rather than invoking the idea that four other members are jointly liable for the outstanding loan, field staff threaten to withdraw access to loans for VO members in general. The use of this sanction was freely admitted by the program staff in several of the five area offices in which field work was carried out; and it is because of the widespread use of this sanction that it is the VO, not the formal sub-groups within a VO, which becomes the joint-liability group in practice. In reality the 5–6 member joint-liability groups rarely exist, and especially in older VOs ordinary members cannot name the sub-group leaders stipulated in BRAC's formal blueprint of VO structure.

Similar stories have been told about Grameen Bank practices, and it happens often enough that one observer has called it "meeting day joint-liability." The idea is that the loan officer is keenly aware of which borrowers in the larger, village-level group are finishing up their current loans and are about to request a next (often larger) loan. Those individuals are particularly susceptible to pressure to help with problem clients. Loan officers will thus be tempted to tell these soon-to-borrow-again customers that if help in dealing with the problem is not forthcoming, the anticipated loans may be delayed. To make the point sharper, it is not unheard of for the loan officer to refuse to leave the village until the books are completely squared. As Matin (1997) has written, the staggered disbursal of loans helps to ensure that there is often someone in the larger group that is close to qualifying for a next loan—and thus particularly open to suasion.[23]

The practice of "meeting day joint-liability" is not universal, and it is not necessarily a bad thing. Indeed, there is nothing sacred about the number five as the perfect group size. Elsewhere, solidarity groups stretch from three to nine borrowers. And, as described earlier, the village banking model used by FINCA, Freedom from Hunger, Pro Mujer, and others encompasses a single village-level group with up to about thirty members. While the adverse selection story of Ghatak (1999) hinges on the functioning of multiple groups within a village (so that borrowers can freely sort themselves into groups on the basis of risk), the preceding moral hazard stories do not depend critically on whether there is one group or more. Indeed, larger groups may be better able to deal with risks and less vulnerable to collusion (Armendáriz 1999a).

Empirical researchers have tried to shine light on questions around the roles of groups, but getting clean results has not been easy. In the perfect world, empirical researchers would be able to directly compare situations under group-lending contracts with comparable situations under traditional banking contracts. The best test would involve a single lender who employs a range of contracts. But in practice most microlenders use just one main type of contract, leaving little variation with which to identify impacts. Where several different contracts are used, a different problem then emerges: Why do some customers voluntarily choose one contract over another? Or why does a lender offer one version to some borrowers and a different version to others? Making comparisons thus opens up questions of whether "self-selection" or other aspects of the programs (e.g., management style, training policies, and loan officer behavior) are driving results. The best evidence will come from well-designed, deliberate experiments in which loan contracts are varied but everything else is kept the same (e.g., Giné and Karlan 2008).

4.5.1 Lab Experiments
It is easier to study contracts systematically in a lab setting, where the context can be kept exactly the same: the rules of the experiment, the way the participants are treated, and the eventual rewards received by the participants. Experimenters can then change just one aspect (the

way groups are formed) and see what happens holding all else constant. This is the approach Abbink, Irlenbusch, and Renner (2006) use in an experiment on group formation. Participants are invited to the lab to take part in a research experiment. In one case, they must register in groups of four, so that participants presumably sign up with their friends. This case reflects the self-selection into groups at the heart of the Grameen Bank model. In the other cases, individuals register independently and are then placed into groups by the researchers, akin to the practice of the FINCA village bank in Ayacucho, Peru studied by Karlan (2007), in which FINCA forms groups off lists of people who signed up independently.

Abbink, Irlenbusch, and Renner (2006) aim to test the role of social ties by comparing outcomes of the self-selected groups to those of the groups put together by the researchers. To do so, they created a game that attempts to mimic the conditions of joint liability borrowing. Their hypothesis is that stronger social ties should increase repayments. However, they find that to the contrary, there is little difference in outcomes between the two groups; in fact, in some cases the self-selected groups do *worse* in terms of repayment rates.

The finding that groups of strangers do as well as (and, in some cases, better than) groups of friends conflicts with arguments about the role of social capital and social sanctions in microfinance. But the finding has some support in theory,[24] and it is given support in the field by Wydick (1999) whose study of group lending in Guatemala leads him to conclude that social ties per se have little impact on repayment rates: friends do not make more reliable group members than others. In fact, the participants he studies are sometimes softer on their friends, worsening average repayment rates (an interesting contrast to the experimental results in which friends appear to be tougher on each other, at least when dishonesty is perceived). Ahlin and Townsend (2007b) also find that proxies for strong social ties are associated with weaker repayment performance in evidence on group lending in Thailand. Karlan (2007), though, argues that social capital helps in Peru, and Wenner (1995) finds that social cohesion is a positive force in groups in Costa Rica. Wydick too finds that social cohesion helps (as proxied by living close together or knowing each other prior to joining the microfinance group), even if *friendship* specifically creates tensions. Gómez and Santor (2003) find that default is less likely if there is greater trust and social capital, and if members have known each other before joining the groups.

Laboratory experiments like that of Abbink et al. (2006) can help researchers understand the basic logic of contracts, but there is a limit to the amount and kind of information they can provide. The disadvantage of laboratory experiments, of course, is that they proceed in a deliberately artificial setting. For example, in Abbink et al. (2006) no mention was even made of "microfinance" for fear that it would trigger associations with certain kinds of behavior, actual loans are not made, and actual businesses are not operated. Moreover, the participants were students at the University of Erfurt, Germany, not actual microfinance customers. On top of all of that, we have some reservations about how this particular experiment was designed.[25]

4.5.2 Framed Field Experiments

One way to overcome some of the limitations of laboratory experiments is to bring the laboratory to the field. Instead of using university students to shed light on the behavior of microfinance clients, a so-called "framed field experiment" looks directly at how microfinance clients behave. Giné, Jakiela, Karlan et al. (2009) do exactly that. To investigate the mechanisms that underlie microfinance in general and group lending in particular, the researchers created an experimental economics laboratory in a large urban market in Lima, Peru, and invited owners and employees of microenterprises to participate in an experiment. The experiment involves a series of "microfinance games," played in up to ten rounds. At the beginning of each round, participants are given a "loan" and instructed to choose one of two projects to "invest" it in: a project that yields a low return with certainty, or a project that yields either a high return or nothing with equal probability. The former option is conceptually equivalent to a safe investment, the latter to a risky investment. Consequently, the researchers can use participants' project choices to classify their types, as either safe or risky. After participants indicate their choices, a computer calculates the payout for the round by deducting the loan amount from the project returns. Participants who chose the risky project and earned a return of zero cannot repay the loan, so they are forced to default.

In some of the games, participants are grouped in two-person groups featuring joint liability, so if one partner defaults, the other has to repay both of their loans. These games produced several interesting findings. First, as theory predicts, joint liability increases the rate of loan repayment "by forcing borrowers to insure each other" (Giné et al. 2009, 4).

One consequence is that when safer players are matched with riskier players, they choose the risky project more often than they would otherwise, increasing risk taking on the whole.

These findings are broadly consistent with those of another framed field experiment on joint liability. The set up of Fischer's (2008) experiment extends that of Giné et al. (2009): he runs a series of games in which clients of an Indian microfinance institution "borrow" and "invest" according to different types of contracts. Returns are randomized, and players are grouped in pairs and can share risk by making income transfers to their partners. Fischer (2008) finds that joint liability leads to free-riding: risky players made significantly riskier investments when their partners knew only whether or not their projects succeeded. However, under full information—when all of the players' actions and decisions are observable—joint liability didn't encourage greater risk-taking.

Framed field experiments get closer to answering questions about the impact of group contracts in real life. Unlike laboratory experiments, the participants don't stand in for the group the researchers are interested in, they *are* that group. Nevertheless, the experimental conditions are still artificial.

4.5.3   Field Studies

In any study based on survey data (based on actual borrowers and actual loans rather than a lab setting), the job for researchers is to convince readers that the comparisons of situations under different contracts are meaningful—that apples are not being compared to oranges. Gómez and Santor (2003) wrestle with comparability in their study of contracts used by two Canadian microlenders, Calmeadow Metrofund of Toronto and Calmeadow Nova Scotia of Halifax. Both programs make loans using individual-lending and group-lending methods. The individual loans tend to be larger (the median size is $2,700 versus $1,000 for group loans), but interest rates are identical at 12 percent per year plus a 6.5 percent upfront administration fee. As suspected, quite different types of people opt for group lending over individual lending. Group members are more likely to be female, Hispanic, and immigrant. Individual borrowers are more likely to be male, Canadian-born, and of African descent; they are also more likely to have higher income and larger, older businesses, and to rely more on self-employment income. A simple comparison of performance across groups shows that group loans are more likely to be repaid (just over 20 percent of group loan customers have defaulted on their loans versus just over 40 percent of individual loan customers), but the comparison does not take into account other social and economic differences.

The approach taken by Gómez and Santor is to follow the "matching method" approach of Rosenbaum and Rubin (1983).[26] Using a sample of almost 1,400 borrowers, the method involves first pooling all of the data and estimating the likelihood that a borrower will have a group loan (rather than a standard individual loan). Determinants include age, income, neighborhood, education level, and ethnicity. The estimates yield an index of the probability of taking a group loan, with the important feature that borrowers within the same level of the index also have similar observed characteristics. Reliable comparisons are thus achieved by comparing only borrowers within similar levels of the index. In principle, apples are compared to apples, and oranges to oranges. Using this method, Gómez and Santor find that borrowers under group contracts repay more often. The result, they argue, arises both because more reliable borrowers are more likely to choose group contracts and because, once in the group contracts, the borrowers work harder.

The estimation approach is simple and intuitive, but it rests on one vital assumption: that the choice of contract can be explained entirely by the variables in their equation (age, income, neighborhood, etc.). If there are important variables omitted from the equation (say, entrepreneurial ability or inherent riskiness), the method ceases to guarantee consistent estimates: riskier borrowers may more likely end up in individual contracts, for example, and they may also be more likely to default. In this hypothetical case, the correlation between being in an individual-lending contract and having a worse outcome is not a product of behavior induced by the contract. Ideally, we would like to be able to investigate situations in which borrowers are sorted into contracts with some element of randomness—but such situations are rare.

Karlan's (2007) study of the FINCA village bank in Ayacucho, Peru, cleverly takes advantage of a quirk in the way that groups are formed that introduces some randomness into the process. There is only one main kind of contract (FINCA's village banking contract), but there is randomness in which group a borrower is placed. The FINCA contract involves groups of thirty women who meet weekly; each week, they receive new loans, pay installments on existing loans, and/or contribute to savings accounts. Unlike other models, the meeting is not held in the local neighborhood or village; instead meetings are held at the FINCA office in the town center. And, again unlike other models, it is FINCA that forms the groups in Ayacucho. FINCA broadcasts its intention to start village banks and invites prospective borrowers to sign up. A list is posted on a wall, and once thirty names are listed, a group is formed. The next thirty people make up another group, and so forth. The staff find this the quickest way to form groups, and they hope to build social ties between strangers that will deliver independent benefits. In general, clients do not sign up as pre-formed groups, and most people do not know each other before FINCA puts them together. From an econometric standpoint, the fact that FINCA selects the groups in this somewhat arbitrary way minimizes biases due to unobserved characteristics.[27] Specifically, when researchers compare why one group had higher repayments than another, concerns are alleviated that results will be biased due to peer selection based on unobserved strengths. Karlan's tests show that the composition of groups indeed looks similar to the general characteristics of the broader population—groups look like what you would expect from a random draw.

Karlan is most interested in the role of social capital—the links between clients that are foundations of trust and cooperation. Unlike real capital (cash, machines, and equipment), "social" capital cannot be observed and simply counted. To proxy for social capital, Karlan thus considers cultural similarity as indicated by language (Spanish only or Quechua—the most common indigenous language—only?), hair (braided, long, or short?), dress (indigenous *pollera* skirt or Western-style clothes?), and hat (indigenous-style hat or not?), as well as considering geographic proximity (percentage of group members living within a 10-minute walk of each other). These "social capital" measures correlate well with the level of social and business interactions and with who sits next to whom at group meetings.

Do these measures of social capital make a difference to loan repayment rates? There are in fact two types of loan repayment rates. The first pertains to loans made by the central FINCA organization to the local group; these loans were all repaid on time during the period in question (1998–2000). The second pertains to loans made to group members from a pool of savings that was generated by the members themselves; here, repayment rates are much lower: around 20 percent. Karlan finds that larger scores on the measures of geographic proximity and cultural similarity predict lower default rates, a finding in line with the theory we sketched earlier in the chapter in which the threat of social sanctions aids repayment rates (and in line with, e.g., Stiglitz 1990). Interestingly, while Karlan finds that default leads to dropout from the program, the effect is attenuated for clients with more social capital. The finding suggests the possibility of beneficial risk sharing: namely, that clients who are forced to default due to circumstances beyond their control (as opposed to exhibiting moral hazard) are less likely to be forced to leave the program when the clients have strong social ties to the rest of the group.

Karlan's results thus show that the group contract can harness local ties in ways that traditional lending contracts cannot. The limit of the results is that they can not nail down whether the improvements occur because of greater trust (and more effective use of social sanctions) as the stress on "social capital" in the paper's title suggests—or, on the other hand, whether the improvements flow simply from the fact that people who are more similar and who live more closely may have an easier time monitoring each other (or perhaps both) than those who are/do not. The latter interpretation is consistent with Wydick (1999), who finds little support that stronger social ties help in group lending in Guatemala, but finds that repayment rates rise with variables that proxy for group members' ability to monitor and enforce group relationships (e.g., repayments rise with knowledge of the weekly sales of fellow group members). The distinction between the two interpretations may not matter in practice (institutions may just be happy that the contracts help), but the unanswered questions point to future steps for research on contracts.[28]

A different perspective on contracts is provided by the ambitious studies of Ahlin and Townsend (2007a, 2007b). They start with the theoretical models of group lending developed by Besley and Coate (1995), Banerjee, Besley, and Guinnane (1994), Ghatak (1999), and Stiglitz (1990). After putting the models into a comparable theoretical framework, Ahlin and Townsend take them to data, trying to determine which does a better job of explaining patterns in practice. Their data come from 262 joint liability groups of the Bank for Agriculture and Agricultural Cooperatives (BAAC) in Thailand in addition to data on 2,880 households from the same villages. Ahlin and Townsend do not seek to judge group lending versus alternative contracts. Rather, as with some of the other papers described here, their aim is to see what makes group lending work. Their answer is that there is no single universal answer. In the poorer regions of northeast Thailand, expected repayment rates increase when village social sanctions rise. But in the wealthier, central region, the extent of joint liability matters, and the higher joint liability payments are, the higher default rates are. Also, the greater the extent of cooperation among group members (e.g., the more family members are in a group), the higher the default. These latter results suggest that too much social capital can be a bad thing when it fosters collusion against the bank.

4.5.4 A Randomized Trial in the Philippines

To our knowledge, the only field study to date that randomizes group contract design is carried out by Giné and Karlan (2008) in the Philippines. Working with Green Bank, a regulated rural lender, the authors conduct a randomized control trial to test the importance of joint liability.

Green Bank converted the loan terms for a random sample of its group borrowing centers to individual liability, so that all clients selected into joint liability contracts, but some were "surprised" with individual liability. Liability was the only feature of the loan that varied between the study groups—borrowers in the individual liability group still attended regular meetings and made weekly repayments in a group setting. The findings contradict the idea that joint liability is a significant repayment incentive in this setting. After one year and after three years, the repayment rate in centers converted to individual liability was no different than the rate in centers where the Bank maintained group liability. It is an important start, and replications are necessary to determine how widely the result carries.

4.5.5 Group Formation

Empirical evidence also sheds light on the theory of assortative matching, which predicts an efficient outcome when groups self-select based on risk type. Ahlin (2009) looks at whether or not groups actually sort by risk, using BAAC data on 87 groups in 50 different villages. For small loans, BAAC uses joint liability in place of collateral, and for the most part groups are self-selected. Ahlin (2009) creates "sorting percentiles" for each group, with higher percentiles indicating relatively homogeneous risk profiles and lower percentiles indicating heterogeneous risk profiles. He shows that groups are significantly more homogeneous than they would be if they were formed randomly. Though groups are far from perfectly homogenous, the result suggests that when groups self-select, borrowers cluster together by risk type.

With one qualification, this finding is consistent with evidence from the framed field experiment by Giné et al. (2009) discussed above. The authors find that when participants are allowed to select their partner in a joint liability contract, risk averse borrowers are more likely to form groups together, but only under certain conditions. Specifically, risk-averse borrowers pair up only when their access to future loans is conditioned on repayment of the current loan. Conditioning future borrowing on current repayment is a "dynamic incentive," a topic explored in detail in the next chapter.

A final empirical issue involves the role of diversity in groups. The theories that stress the positive roles of social capital and social sanctions suggest that less diverse groups will do better. Where collusion is a possibility, on the other hand, the opposite may hold: greater diversity may aid repayments by diminishing the chance for collusion. Sadoulet (2003) provides another reason that diversity can help: greater diversity means that group members' incomes are less likely to vary together, and thus group members' ability to insure each other increases (i.e., there's a greater chance to provide mutual aid in times of need). Since insurance should help repayment rates, diversity helps.[29] And, if diversity helps, borrowers should try to form groups that are broad, which is exactly what Sadoulet and Carpenter (2001) find in a study of groups in Guatemala. In Thailand, though, Ahlin and Townsend (2007a, 2007b) find that it is positive correlations of income that, holding all else constant, appear to predict entry into group contracts, and Ahlin (2009) finds complementary evidence for risk correlation in self-selected groups.

Results from different parts of the world thus reveal different (sometimes opposing) relationships. Advancing understanding of group lending will thus entail better understanding of the kinds of positive outcomes described in the first part of this chapter—along with understanding of potentially negative scenarios as well.

4.6 Limits to Group Lending: Hidden Costs, Collusion, and Emerging Tensions

We started this chapter by reviewing the standard features of the group-lending methodology introduced by the Grameen Bank in the 1970s. Theorists have been particularly interested in the ways that the model takes advantage of existing local information and social ties. But models that succeed in rural Bangladesh have not succeeded everywhere else. The evidence in section 4.5 shows a mix of results in terms of what works and what does not.

Using social sanctions, in particular, has limitations. Typically, social sanctions involve excluding "problem" borrowers from privileged access to input supplies, from further trade credit, from social and religious events, or from day-to-day courtesies. Commercial banks hoping to move into the "microfinance niche" have particular difficulties invoking these kinds of mechanisms among their clients, but so do NGOs. For example, will the threat of social sanctions be credible in small village communities among very close friends and relatives? Or, at the other extreme, can social sanctions have teeth in urban environments where borrowers come and go and remain fairly anonymous to one another? Practitioners have thus had to tinker with contracts and redesign according to their contexts.

The tinkering and redesigning has had to address the costs inherent in group-lending contracts, as well as the many advantages described previously. The essence of group lending is to transfer responsibilities from bank staff to borrowers. Traditionally, loan officers select clients, monitor performance, and enforce contracts. Under group lending, borrowers share part of these burdens too. The gain for clients is that they obtain loans (and other financial services) at reasonable prices. But, given the choice, most clients would not opt to help start a bank and run it just in order to get loans. Ladman and Afcha (1990), for example, argue that in the case of the Small Farmer Credit Program (PCPA) in Bolivia, it was difficult to find potential borrowers to volunteer to lead their groups, and group leaders had to spend a great deal of time persuading borrowers to accept the group-lending contract. In one village, group leaders had to put in four times as many hours in preparation before initial loan disbursal relative to the time needed under traditional individual lending procedures.[30]

Other concerns hinge on the group meetings that are at the core of group lending models. Attitudes are mixed. One complaint is that attending group meetings and monitoring group members can be costly, especially where houses are not close together. In two of the three Chinese programs studied by Albert Park and Changqing Ren (2001), for example, 8 percent of clients had to walk more than an hour to get to meetings. Overall, attending meetings and travel time took just over one hundred minutes on average. In a survey of dropouts from group lending programs in Uganda and Bangladesh, a Women's World Banking (2003) study found that 28 percent of dropouts in Bangladesh left in part because of the frequency of meetings; this was so for 11 percent of former clients surveyed in Uganda. On the other hand, nearly all current clients of Women's World Banking affiliates in Uganda and Bangladesh report that they enjoy coming to meetings (Women's World Banking 2003, 5). In Uganda, the most-cited reason (65 percent) was that they liked the chance to share ideas and learn from each other; in Bangladesh, the most-cited reason (43 percent) was the social aspect of meetings.

A second issue relates to the fact that group lending works by transferring what are typically the bank's responsibilities to the customers themselves. As we noted, these responsibilities can carry hidden costs. Some borrowers may be tempted to think: I simply want a loan, why am I asked to help run the bank in return? But there is another aspect that goes beyond these kinds of costs. Group lending can bring added risks for borrowers, and if borrowers are risk averse, those risks can weigh heavily, a point stressed by Giné et al. (2009). The risk is embedded in the contract: a borrower is now not just at risk of defaulting on her own, but she also faces the risk that her partners will default also. If monitoring and enforcing contracts is costless—as assumed by Stiglitz (1990) and Varian (1990)—borrowers can address moral hazard effectively and the risks are minimized. This is the great hope of the group lending contract. But, as noted previously, monitoring is not costless, even for individuals living in close proximity. Typically, then, monitoring will be imperfect, opening the way for moral hazard to enter back into the picture. But under the group lending contract, it is now the group that is exposed to the risk, not the bank. The threat of social sanctions can help, as we described earlier, but in practice they are applied only imperfectly too.

This sense of trade-offs carries through in the work of Madajewicz (2004). In an important theoretical analysis, she argues that the benefits of group lending—which have been detailed in the first part of this chapter—are counterbalanced by costs. Those costs emerge when borrowers are risk averse and monitoring is costly. Moreover, the costs grow as the scale of lending grows, since the financial implications of default rise with the size of loans. Madajewicz argues that loan sizes are limited by what the group can jointly guarantee, so clients with growing businesses or those who get well ahead of their peers in scale may find that the group contract bogs everyone down. Below a certain scale, group lending dominates individual lending. But her analysis shows that at a certain size of business, individual lending will be preferred by customers. In an investigation of data from Bangladesh, Madajewicz (2005) estimates that the switch toward the greater net benefits of individual loans already happens for households holding 1.25 acres. Such households would not be considered to be "functionally landless," but they are mainly poor nonetheless.[31]

One implication is that wealthier clients tend to seek individual loans as they move forward, pushing Bolivia's BancoSol and the Grameen Bank, both group-lending pioneers, to introduce new individual-lending contracts for successful clients. A related issue is that some clients simply prefer not having to be obligated to others. As the Women's World Banking (2003, 3) study reports:

This issue was tested further through the question: "Which do you prefer, to have the security that the group will help you out when you are not able to pay back each week, or to assume complete responsibility for your own loan and not having to pay for someone else's loan?" Most customers of both institutions indicated a desire to be independent and to forsake the security of the group. In Bangladesh, 76 percent of the affiliate's current borrowers and 82 percent of dropouts answered that they would want to assume total responsibility for their own loan. In Uganda, 87 percent of the affiliate's current borrowers and 84 percent of dropouts expressed a similar desire for independence.

A third issue is that under some conditions, borrowers in group-lending contracts may collude against the bank and undermine the bank's ability to harness "social collateral."[32] As we saw in section 4.5, stronger social ties within a group can push up repayment rates in some places, while, in others, social ties increase the likelihood of default.

Laffont and Rey (2003) take up these tensions from a theoretical perspective and come to a somewhat optimistic conclusion. In their investigation of moral hazard and group lending, close ties and information sharing among borrowers open the way for contracts that improve on traditional individual-lending contracts. But, on the other hand, the scope for collusion against the lender increases when borrowers share knowledge and social ties. If borrowers do *not* collude, Laffont and Rey show (in a stylized model) that group-lending contracts are superior to individual-lending contracts (because the contracts take advantage of borrowers' knowledge and social ties—as described at the start of the chapter). But even better contracts exist in principle. These include using yardstick competition (judging one member's performance relative to the performances of others) and information revelation mechanisms (such as cross-reporting arrangements).

But what if borrowers collude? In that case, Laffont and Rey show that group lending is superior to these alternative mechanisms. The contract delivers outcomes that are not as good as could be obtained if the lender had full information on borrowers, but it beats any alternatives. Their bottom line is that having more information (either on the part of borrowers or on the part of the lender directly) leads to contracts that improve on standard individual-lending contracts, even when borrowers collude against the lender.

A final issue is whether the group-lending contract is more efficient than alternatives *even when it is successful on its own terms*. At the end of section 4.4.2, we raised this question: Even if the group-lending contract does better than the traditional individual-lending contract, can the microlender do even better than that? Rai and Sjöström (2004) argue that the answer is yes (as do, in somewhat different contexts, Laffont and Rey [2003]). The criticism of the group-lending contract as we see it on paper (and as we have described it above) is that punishments are too harsh. For example, in the widely replicated original Grameen Bank contract with five-person groups, when one borrower defaults, all four others are cut off from future lending, too. It is that threat that drives the "peer monitoring," "peer selection," and "peer enforcement" mechanisms. But what if the defaulter got into trouble because her husband fell ill? Or her cow died? Or prices dropped for the goods she sells? What if the problem occurred despite good monitoring, selection, and enforcement?

Rai and Sjöström's particular criticism does not hinge on the morality of the situation, but rather on its efficiency (in the sense used in chapter 2); in the dispassionate language of economics, the punishment implies a "deadweight" loss. They argue that by using a system of cross-reports (see the end of chapter 5 for more), punishments need not be levied so bluntly. Rai and Sjöström argue that rather than writing a contract and passively following the rules, the bank (and borrowers) can take active steps to gather more information when crises emerge. Their idea of cross-reports is to elicit truthful information about what has happened (e.g., was default due to shirking or to a deeper problem?). This information can be elicited by the microlender by soliciting reports from the problem borrower and her neighbors and showing leniency when all of the independent reports agree with each other. Some overly harsh punishments can thus be avoided. The proposed system of cross-reports is just one way to improve on contracts, and it works well on paper in a specific theoretical context. With modification it might work in practice too, but, even without cross-reports, microlenders are taking steps to address the inefficiencies.

We take the Rai and Sjöström criticism seriously, and microlenders act as if they do as well. Our firsthand observations in Latin America and Asia indicate that group contracts are seldom enforced exactly as they should be on paper. When asked, loan officers respond that they see no reason to automatically punish everyone for the problem of a single person. Instead, loan officers typically spend a great deal of time investigating and managing "problem" cases. In doing so, staff call on defaulters' neighbors for advice and information (in the spirit, loosely, of cross-reporting). And, once the problem has been investigated (and if the defaulter's peers are found to be relatively blameless), microlenders' staff try to get as much of the problem loan repaid as possible and then (if called for) drop just the one defaulter from the group and replace her with an alternative borrower. This is a natural route to improving efficiency (and equity), even as it undermines the strict reading of group-lending contracts.

In a notable break, Grameen Bank's reinvention as "Grameen Bank II" recognizes the tension between what works on paper and what happens in practice by formally introducing mechanisms through which loan officers can address the problems of individual borrowers without invoking punishments for the entire group (Yunus 2002; Dowla and Barua 2006). The heart of Grameen Bank II is comprised of two types of loans. Borrowers first start with a Basic Loan (in Bangla, this is an "Easy Loan"). The new system allows loans of any duration—from three months to three years—and allows for installments to be smaller in some seasons and larger in others. The weekly repayment practice remains, however. Then, if borrowers get into trouble, they will be offered a Flexible Loan (with the penalty of a sharp drop in their loan size limit). The Flexible Loan has easier terms spread over a longer period, and it allows the borrower to get back on track, eventually returning to Basic Loan status. Half of the loan is provisioned for at the time of switching status to the Flexible Loan. Only when the customer fails to repay the Flexible Loans are they expelled, and the loan is fully written off as bad debt. Some see this proposal as a major departure from group lending by the pioneer of the group-lending contract.[33]

4.7 Summary and Conclusions

This chapter took up one of the major innovations of the microfinance movement—group lending. From the lender's perspective, the beauty of the contract is that it's a way to transfer (in whole or part) onto customers the responsibility for jobs usually undertaken by lenders. These jobs include screening potential customers, monitoring their efforts, and enforcing contracts. In return, customers get loans that would otherwise be inaccessible or at least that would not be available at such relatively low interest rates.

From the standpoint of economic theory, the group-lending contract addresses the problems raised in chapter 2, notably information imperfections that cause moral hazard and adverse selection. In principle, the group-lending contract provides a way to achieve efficient outcomes even when the lender remains ignorant or unable to effectively enforce contracts. Moreover, in principle, the group lending methodology can potentially promote social capital, and thus further enhance efficiency.

But if the *borrowers* also lack good information on each other—as may be the case in sparsely populated areas and mobile urban neighborhoods, for example—a bank employing group-lending contracts may end up worse off than it would if other types of contracts are used. In the next chapter we describe alternative lending mechanisms, all of which can be used with or without group lending. Our belief is that the future of microfinance rests in understanding these alternative mechanisms, taking them apart, reconfiguring them, and, possibly, combining them with new, emerging ideas.

Our stress on alternative contracts stems in large part from the mixed results from the empirical work that we surveyed in section 4.5, as well as from anecdotal evidence and theoretical insight in section 4.6. Emerging tensions include borrowers growing frustrated at the cost of attending regular meetings, loan officers refusing to sanction good borrowers who happen to be in "bad" groups, and constraints imposed by the diverging ambitions of group members. In a telling step, the Grameen Bank has undergone a major overhaul to its lending practices, opening the way for greater flexibility. Empirical research on group lending lags behind theory, but the data so far suggest important challenges to the generally optimistic tenor of the theoretical research.

4.8   Exercises

1. Evaluate the merits of the following statement: "Relative to standard contracts where collateral is involved, under group-lending contracts banks elicit more information about the borrowers' trustworthiness."

2. Consider an economy with two types of risk-neutral borrowers. Assume that borrowers are protected by limited liability. There are one-period projects which require a $100 investment each. The bank is operating in a competitive environment, and is only trying to break even. Specifically, the bank wants to cover its gross cost, $K = \$145$ per each $100 loan. If able to borrow, an individual of type 1 is capable of generating a gross return $y_1 = \$230$ with certainty, and if she is denied access to credit, she can work and earn $28 in the labor market. A type 2 borrower, if able to borrow, can invest her loan for a gross return of $y_2 = \$420$ with probability 0.5, or zero with probability 0.5. If denied access to credit, a type 2 potential borrower can work and earn $55 in the labor market. Assume that 40 percent of the population in this economy is of type 1, and the rest is of type 2. Then:

a. If the bank cannot distinguish between the two types, and cannot implement group lending with joint liability, which of the two types of borrowers will be credit rationed? Compute R^*, the gross interest rate for this scenario.

b. Now suppose that the bank is willing to lend to anyone on the condition that all borrowers form pairs, and that each pair accepts a clause making them jointly liable for loan repayment. Specifically, the clause states that if one individual fails to repay, her partner has to pay for her; otherwise, both borrowers will be excluded from access to future loans, which is infinitely costly. Explain how you expect potential borrowers to form groups of 2-borrower pairs.

c. Compute R^{**}, the gross interest rate in this scenario.

d. Suppose the bank charges R^{**}, and that there is one individual of type 1 that has no choice but to form a pair with an individual of type 2. Would the type 1 individual be willing to borrow under a joint liability clause in this particular case? Briefly explain your answer.

3. Consider a similar economy as the one described in the previous exercise. In this case, however, assume 3 types of potential borrowers, all protected by limited liability. If she succeeds, borrower 1 gets a gross return $y_1 = \$300$ with probability 0.9; she gets a return of zero if she fails. Borrower 2 gets a gross return $y_2 = \$333.33$ with probability 0.75

and zero if she fails. Borrower 3 gets a gross return $y_3 = \$500$ with probability 0.5 and zero if she fails. Each type counts for one third of the population in this economy. The opportunity cost (i.e., the labor market wage) for each potential borrower is $40. All three potential borrowers need $150 to carry out their projects, and the lender's cost of capital is $54 for each $150 loan.

a. If group lending is not available as an option, can all potential borrowers gain access to credit to carry out their investment projects? Explain your answer.

b. Now suppose that group lending with joint liability contracts is feasible, that matching is assortative, and that the bank can observe the final returns of all borrowers. The bank will take the entire revenue of the lucky borrower if her partner defaults. Compute the interest R^{**} and briefly explain your result.

c. How relevant is this exercise to the case of solidarity groups in practice?

4. Explain the concept of assortative matching under group lending from the microfinance institutions' standpoint. Focus your explanation on the scope for mitigating adverse selection inefficiencies.

5. A bank is considering extending loans to a population of four potential borrowers with identities A, B, C, and D. Borrowers A and B are of type 1, while borrowers C and D are of type 2. The bank can't observe borrowers' types, but it knows that there are two borrowers of type 1 and two of type 2. With a $100 loan, a type 1 borrower can invest in a project and get a gross return of $y_1 = \$200$ with certainty, while a type 2 borrower can obtain a gross return of $y_2 = \$360$ with probability 0.75. The opportunity cost for a borrower of type 1 is $18, and it is $20 for a borrower of type 2. If denied a loan, type 1 potential borrowers can earn a wage of $18 in the labor market, and type 2 potential borrowers can earn a wage of $20. The gross cost of a $100 loan for the bank is $160. The bank is competitive and aims only to break even. Borrowers are protected by limited liability.

a. If group lending is not possible, will all potential borrowers have access to loans? Derive the interest rate that the bank will charge in this case, and briefly explain your answer.

b. Now suppose that the bank can lend to jointly liable pairs of borrowers, and can observe all borrowers' final returns. Compute the interest rate at which the bank will lend in this case. Briefly explain your answer, comparing it to your answer to part (a).

c. What lessons does this exercise provide with respect to group lending under joint responsibility?

6. This exercise is similar to the previous one, but timing of events is crucial. Consider the following timing: loans are made at date 0, borrowers' types are revealed at date 1, and returns are realized at date 2. Borrowers want to invest in projects that cost $100 at date 0, but they do not have any wealth of their own. Until their types are revealed at date 1, borrowers are identical to the bank; ex ante there is an equal probability (of $\pi = 0.5$) that a borrower will turn out to be type 1 and type 2. The rest of the environment is exactly the same as in the previous exercise.

a. If group lending can't be implemented in this economy, can all agents borrow? What interest rate would the bank charge if they can? Briefly explain your answer.

b. Now suppose that the bank can lend to jointly liable pairs of borrowers and can also observe the final returns of each borrower. Compute the interest rate at which the bank will lend in this case, and briefly explain your answer in light of the results obtained in (a).

c. Explain the kind of credit market inefficiencies this exercise highlights, and the way such inefficiencies are mitigated by group lending under joint liability.

7. Consider again an economy like the one described in exercise 6 in terms of the timing of events, but now suppose that at date 1, the borrower can turn out to be type 1, type 2, or type 3 with equal probability (of $\pi = 1/3$). Type 1 can get a gross return of $300 with certainty, type 2 can get a gross return of $360 with probability $p_2 = 0.75$, and type 3 can get a gross return of $400 with probability $p_3 = 0.5$. Assume that the bank operates under the conditions described in exercise 5, and that the opportunity cost for all borrowers is zero. Compute the interest charged by the bank if group lending is implemented at date 0, and explain clearly whether all potential entrepreneurs will be able to borrow.

8. Consider the following timing: a loan is made first; then monitoring choices are made; next, effort decisions are made and potential borrowers expend effort in their projects; finally, returns accrue to the entrepreneurs. Suppose all entrepreneurs in this economy are identical. These potential borrowers wish to invest in a project that costs $I = \$100$. If successful, it yields a gross return $y = \$300$. If borrowers put in an adequate level of effort, the probability of success will be 1; if they

don't, the probability of success will be $p = 0.75$. Assume that the cost of effort is $c = \$40$ and that the borrowers' opportunity cost is $80. The bank is perfectly competitive, and the gross cost of a loan is $R = \$150$.

a. Can a potential borrower obtain a loan when group lending contracts are not allowed in this economy? Briefly explain your answer.

b. Now suppose that the bank can lend to self-selected groups of 2 borrowers, and that the bank imposes joint liability. A borrower can monitor her partner, which induces return-maximizing effort but costs the monitor $k = \$20$. Assuming that there is simultaneous monitoring and that borrowers are protected by limited liability, compute the interest rate that the bank will charge. Will both entrepreneurs be able to access loans? Briefly explain your answer.

c. Does it make sense to assume symmetry, i.e., that borrowers monitor each other simultaneously?

9. "The only reason why group lending methodologies in microfinance can potentially enhance efficiency is that it lowers transaction costs." Is this statement true? Carefully explain your answer.

10. Assume the following timing: First a loan is made; then returns accrue to the borrowers; next, monitoring takes place, where borrowers assess the nature of their peers' returns (i.e., they verify whether their peers are reporting their returns accurately); finally, borrowers produce a fully verifiable report on their partners' true return realizations. In this setting, the population to which the break-even bank is considering extending loans is identical. The bank knows that any borrower in this economy can invest an amount I and get a gross return of y with certainty, but it is unable to verify borrowers' returns once they've been realized. The gross interest rate on loans is R; thus, when a project yields a return, a borrower can either repay R or lie (e.g., claim that she is unable to repay). If a borrower lies and is found out, she receives a sanction B.

a. Explain what happens when $B < R$ under individual lending contracts without monitoring.

b. Now suppose that the bank lends to pairs of borrowers under a joint liability clause, and suppose that the borrowers can potentially verify each others' return realizations when either borrower states that she cannot repay. Monitoring return realizations costs $k < B < R$. If the group defaults, its members lose future access to credit from the bank. This will incur a loss equivalent to c in present value terms to each member, where $c > k$. Assume for simplicity that $y > 2R$. Can potential

borrowers obtain a loan in this case? Relate your answer to your interpretation of B.

11. Consider the same setting as in exercise 10, and suppose that agents
still have the chance to monitor their peers, but that now monitoring
is imperfect: a borrower can verify her peer's return realizations with
only probability q. If she can prove that her partner is lying, the defaulting partner will have to reimburse the amount R to the bank and will
also be punished with a social sanction W. Create a table summarizing
all possible strategies that the borrowers can follow. What does this
exercise reveal about the efficiency of sanctioning only borrowers who
misrepresent their returns, relative to that of excluding both borrowers
if all individual debts aren't repaid?

12. Several theoretical approaches support group lending as a way to
achieve better outcomes for both microfinance borrowers and banks.
Even though, both empirical and experimental approaches have found
mixed evidence on this issue, and a number of banks have been lately
moving towards individual lending. Which may be the aspects that
explain these different perspectives of group lending benefits?

13. "If borrowers cannot monitor each other any better than the bank
can, joint liability cannot solve the problems of moral hazard." Briefly
explain the merits of this statement.

14. Suppose there are two identical individuals who are risk neutral.
Given start-up capital of size 1, they get a return of y if their project
succeeds. We will assume that y is between 1 and 2. The probability of
success depends on their effort level e. Choosing effort e (which can
vary between 0 and 1) is equivalent to choosing the probability of
success, but it is costly to expend effort. Individuals must pay a cost e^2.
Therefore a self-financing person chooses effort by solving the following maximization problem:

$$\max_e [ey - e^2]$$

a. Explain what the above equation means, and solve for the level of
effort e under self-financing. Is this effort efficient?

b. Let us now assume that the individual cannot self-finance her project
because she is too poor. She must instead take a loan at gross interest
rate R to finance her project. Temporarily assume that the borrower,
though poor, owns a house worth more than R which can we used as
collateral. Explain and solve the new optimization problem:

$$\max_e [ey - R - e^2]$$

Is this effort efficient?

c. Now assume that our borrower has no collateral at all. Explain and solve the optimization problem:

$$\max_e [e(y - R) - e^2]$$

Is this effort efficient? How does the effort level change as R changes?

d. Suppose the lender has already pushed R down as far as it can, and it is still worried about sub-optimal effort. It tries to solve the problem using group lending. The borrowers group themselves in pairs, and the bank makes each borrower liable for the other's debt. We'll call the effort level of the first borrower e_1, and e_2 for the second borrower. Assuming for a moment that monitoring is impossible, explain why the new optimization problem (from agent 1's perspective) is:

$$\max_{e_1} [e_1 e_2 (y - R) - e_1^2]$$

Solve this for e_1. How does this compare with previous effort levels? Without the possibility of monitoring, does joint liability under group lending help or hurt the goal of raising effort to efficient levels?

e. Now let us assume that agents can monitor each other. They choose a monitoring intensity m between 0 and 1. You can think of this as a way for people to bug each other for not working. If agent 2 chooses e_2, she suffers a cost $m_1(1 - e_2)$ when agent 1 chooses m_1. The less she works, the greater is this cost. Monitoring is itself costly, and agents pay a cost αm^2 to monitor, where α is a number less than 1. Explain each of the terms in the following optimization problem:

$$\max_{e_1} [e_1 e_2 (y - R) - e_1^2 - m_2(1 - e_1) - \alpha m_1^2]$$

f. It is possible to solve this problem, but it involves a lot of algebra. The complexity comes from the fact that optimal effort depends not only on the other agent's monitoring, but also on the other agent's effort (and thus on one's own monitoring, which influences the other agent's effort). In order to spare you the algebra, we will modify the problem slightly to avoid this interdependence. The new maximization problem is:

$$\max_{e_1} [e_1 e_2 (y - R) - (1 - e_2)P - e_1^2 - m_2(1 - e_1) - \alpha m_1^2]$$

where P is a penalty that is charged if your partner doesn't pay. This penalty is charged whether your own project was successful or not. In order to solve this problem assume that agents first choose m, then choose e in response. Solve for the optimal monitoring and effort of both agents in this context. How do these effort levels compare to the ones we have seen before?

g. Explain the following: (i) How does effort change as the strength of joint liability (P) increases?, (ii) How does it change as the cost of monitoring (α) decreases?, (iii) In this model, is it possible that effort could ever be higher than would be efficient? (iv) Is this likely to be a problem in the real world?

15. (Based in Laffont and Rey [2003].) Consider an economy where two agents with no wealth have a project that yields an output z when successful and 0 when not. Depending on if the level of effort exerted by the agent is high or low the probability of success will be p_H or p_L respectively with $0 < p_L < p_H < 1$. The cost of exerting a high level of effort is c. There is a profit maximizer bank in this economy, whose funds cost k. The bank has until now used individual lending schemes but is planning to move towards group lending by pairs. The only issue that stops it is the fact that agents may collude, which has no cost for them, and declare that they exerted high effort when they didn't. Show that a contract that states that each borrower will get a fixed payment x^* if both his project and his partners' one are successful (and 0 otherwise) prevent the threat of collusion. Which is the value of x^* in that contract?

5 Beyond Group Lending

5.1 Introduction

The "discovery" of group lending opened up possibilities for microfinance. It is by far the most celebrated microfinance innovation, and with good reason. Group lending showed how unconventional contracts can work where tried-and-true banking practices failed again and again, and the shift in understandings led to other new ideas that borrowed as much from traditional moneylenders as from modern banking practices. Today, group lending is just one element that makes microfinance different from conventional banking.

Many of these other new ideas are also used by institutions practicing group lending. But the mechanisms are not intrinsically linked, and institutions are increasingly finding that they can pick and choose different elements. A case in point is "progressive lending," which is a staple of the "classic" Grameen Bank model but which does not hinge on group lending per se. Progressive lending refers to the practice of promising larger and larger loans for groups and individuals in good standing. Other innovations already present in the classic Grameen model include repayment schedules with weekly or monthly installments, public repayments, and the targeting of women. In addition, microlenders have adopted more flexible attitudes to collateral. The emerging new contracts do not necessarily involve groups, and they have been especially helpful in areas with low population densities or highly diverse populations—and in situations where more established clients seek greater flexibility.

Bangladesh's ASA, with its obsession with maximal efficiency, has weakened joint liability in its lending approach, for example, and even the Grameen Bank has eliminated joint liability in "Grameen Bank II," allowing problem loans to be routinely renegotiated without invoking group pressure.[1] In Bolivia, BancoSol has moved a large share of its portfolio out of "solidarity group" contracts into individual contracts. "Solidarity group" contracts are still used for small loans (from $50 to $2,000) that are offered to less-established clients, but individual contracts (up to $250,000) are the norm for established clients.[2] Bank Rakyat Indonesia, another microfinance leader, eschewed group loans from the start, and it is joined on that path by urban microlenders in Latin America and Eastern Europe.

Table 5.1 provides comparative data for the 890 programs surveyed in the *MicroBanking Bulletin*. Of these "top performers," 277 are individual lenders and the rest either lend through Grameen-type groups of three to nine borrowers, through the larger groups associated with the village banking approach, or use both individual and group lending strategies.[3] Relative to lenders using group-lending methodologies, microlenders focusing on individuals tend to (a) serve better-off clients, as reflected by average loan size; (b) be slightly more self-reliant as proxied by the percentage of their financial costs covered—106 percent relative to 103 for group-lending institutions; (c) serve a smaller population of women clients—on average 51 percent of the clients of individual microlenders are women versus 67 percent for group lenders and 86 percent for village banks; and (d) charge lower interest rates and fees as reflected in the real portfolio yield: 32 percent for village banks, 26 percent for group lenders, and 23 percent for individual lenders. On this latter point, however, it should be noted that village banks and group lenders also have higher expenses relative to loan size. While individual lenders devote 21 cents of each dollar lent to operational costs, group lenders must devote 29 cents, and village banks 35 cents.

The bottom line is that the group lenders and village banks—Grameen or FINCA-style—tend to serve poorer clients and have higher costs relative to loan size. As microlenders have matured and diversified, their push to serve better-off clients and reduce costs has opened the door to individual-lending approaches. But individual-lending approaches also have appeal in sparsely populated regions, areas with heterogenous populations, and areas marked by social divisions, where peer monitoring costs are high and social punishments for noncompliance more difficult to implement. Individual-lending approaches may thus be critical in serving some very poor areas as well.[4]

In section 5.2, we first discuss the recent trend toward bilateral contracting and its emphasis on dynamic incentives via progressive lending techniques. By isolating these lending methods, we aim to shed light

Table 5.1
Performance comparisons by lending methodology

	−1 standard deviation	Average	+1 standard deviation
Average Loan Size (US$)			
Individual	−2409	2720	7848
Solidarity groups	−1216	867	2949
Mixed	−191	242	674
Village Banks	−150	304	758
Fraction Female (%)			
Individual	30	51	71
Solidarity groups	43	67	92
Mixed	62	86	111
Village Banks	70	86	103
Financial self-sufficiency ratio (%)			
Individual	79	106	134
Solidarity groups	74	103	131
Mixed	59	92	124
Village Banks	67	105	142
Portfolio yield (real, %)			
Individual	9	23	38
Solidarity groups	10	26	42
Mixed	5	27	49
Village Banks	10	32	55
Operating expense/loan portfolio (%)			
Individual	−2	21	44
Solidarity groups	0	29	58
Mixed	−1	35	71
Village Banks	7	35	63

Source: Microfinance Information Exchange "2007 database of the *Microbanking Bulletin*" (available at www.mixmbb.org) and calculations by authors. The skewness of the distribution leads to negative values for average loan size and operating expense/loan portfolio.

on alternative variants of the classic group-lending model as described in chapter 4. This in turn can open the door for microfinance to expand to areas where barriers were thought to be too high. We also discuss the use of collateral requirements and the replacement of joint liability clauses with public repayments as a simpler way of maintaining peer pressure, and how these innovations are reshaping the microfinance landscape. At the chapter's end, we revisit the group-lending methodology and the challenges it faces as the microfinance industry moves forward.

5.2 Creating Dynamic Incentives

Even without recourse to peer monitoring, collateral, or social sanctions, microlenders can give incentives to borrowers by threatening to exclude defaulting borrowers from future access to loans. In this way, microlenders have a weapon that was unavailable to failed state-run banks of the past. Those banks were often pressured to extend loans based on political exigencies and could not be counted on to supply a steady flow of financing to small entrepreneurs. One striking finding about India's troubled Integrated Rural Development Program, for example, was that only 11 percent of all IRDP borrowers borrowed more than once (Pulley 1989). If you suspect that you'll only ever take one loan from an institution, the chance that you'll go to great lengths to repay it falls sharply, and it is not surprising that IRDP's repayment rates fell below 50 percent over time.[5] Microlenders ratchet up incentives even further by giving borrowers in good standing access to ever-larger loans, creating the promise of turning startup businesses into steady enterprises.

In this section we present a simple model of debt without collateral to analyze how bilateral contracts work. We then explore the role of "progressive lending" as an additional tool. While a thick, competitive microfinance market ought to be a microfinance dream, we describe cases in which competition has undermined dynamic incentives in microfinance (and led to microfinance crises in Bolivia and Bangladesh). And we describe why credit bureaus are needed to improve matters.

5.2.1 Threatening to Stop Lending
Nearly all moneylenders surveyed by Aleem (1990) rely principally on two devices for eliciting debt repayments from their clients: developing

repeated relationships with the borrowers and making sure that existing borrowers do not contract new loans with other lenders.[6] The two devices make the threat of not refinancing a customer a powerful weapon. We begin by analyzing the theory of these "non-refinancing threats."

Suppose that monitoring costs are very high so that lenders cannot induce repayments via peer groups.[7] As before, we maintain the assumption that borrowers do not have collateral. Moreover, we assume for the moment that social sanctions cannot be used as a way of putting pressure on borrowers to fulfill their contractual obligations. Starting from these basic assumptions, we present a stripped-down version of a model by Bolton and Scharfstein (1990). The model is inspired by the "sovereign debt" problem of the 1980s, which involved lending relationships between "foreign" commercial banks and sovereign nations.[8]

Assume that there are two periods of production and an investment project requires $1. At the end of each period the borrower can generate a gross return $y > \$1$, calculated before repayment of the loan with interest, provided that her current project is financed by the bank. At the repayment stage, however, the borrower may decide to default strategically by simply not repaying the loan. In order to deter the borrower from "taking the money and running," the bank can extend a second-period loan contingent upon full repayment of the first-period obligations. The borrower's penalty for defaulting after the first period is thus that she will not be able to invest in the second period. Is this threat enough to elicit payment from the borrower?

Suppose that the borrower decides to default. Her expected payoff in this case will be $y + \delta vy$, where δ is the borrower's discount factor, and v is the probability of being refinanced by the bank despite having defaulted. The discount factor captures the fact that most people weigh payoffs in the future less than payoffs today. To fix ideas, we assume for simplicity that the borrower needs the bank in order to finance a second-period investment, even in the case where she pockets the entire first-period return realization.[9]

Now suppose that, having done well with her investment, the borrower decides to repay. In this case, her payoff will be $y - R + \delta y$, where R is the gross interest rate payable to the bank (principal plus interest). Here, the bank refinances the borrower's second-period investment for sure, setting $v = 1$. As we argue here, this is an equilibrium strategy.

Clearly, because of the *finite* number of periods (two in this case), the borrower has no incentive to repay at the end of the second period.

So if she repaid in period 1 and is refinanced with certainty, her net expected payoff in period 2—evaluated in period 1—is equal to δy.[10] Similarly, if she defaulted in period 1 and is consequently refinanced with probability $v < 1$, her expected payoff in period 2 (evaluated as of period 1), is equal to $v\delta y$.

Now moving back to period 1, it is easy to see that the borrower will decide to meet her first-period debt obligation if and only if $y + v\delta y \leq y - R + \delta y$. This is an "incentive compatibility" (IC) constraint in the jargon of contract theory, a concept we used in section 4.4.1. As we saw in chapter 4, the constraint determines the largest feasible interest rate that the bank can elicit from the group of borrowers without inducing default. The constraint says that the bank should make sure that the borrower's net present payoff is at least as large when she does not default as when she does. And the obvious way that the bank can do this is by setting an interest rate that is not "too high."

From this, we use the incentive compatibility constraint to derive the maximum gross interest rate R that the bank can elicit from the borrower at the end of the first period is equal to $\delta y(1 - v)$. The expression is maximized by setting $v = 0$ for defaulters, that is, by fully denying access to future refinancing.[11] Thus, the maximum repayment that the bank can request after the first period is simply $R = \delta y$, which is the borrower's opportunity cost of defaulting strategically. It will never pay for the borrower to repay more than δy in this setup.[12] If, say, the borrower's discount factor is 0.90 and the borrower's gross return is 160 percent, the maximum feasible gross interest rate is 144 percent (or a maximum net interest rate of 44 percent). When operating costs are high, the constraint may well bind. And banks will be even more constrained when borrowers have low discount factors or perceive a relatively high chance of getting refinanced despite default. As described in section 5.2.3, competition without coordination—say, without a credit bureau that keeps tabs on defaulters from other banks—may serve in effect to push the effective refinancing probability v above zero.

This simple framework also suggests why maintaining the appearance of stability is important for lenders. If borrowers begin to think that the bank could go under in future periods, they are more likely to default now, since it is not clear whether there will be a future flow of loans. Whether based in fact or not, such speculation can trigger a "borrower run" that becomes a self-fulfilling prophecy. Bond and Rai (2009), for example, describe a ballooning of defaults faced by Childreach, a microlender in Ecuador, in response to rumors that the organization faced a looming financial crisis.

5.2.2 Progressive Lending

Table 5.2 shows that the Grameen Bank not only provides a continuing series of loans but that the loans quickly increase in size. The table shows data for three borrowers randomly chosen from a 1991–1992 sample of thirty Grameen Bank borrowers who each had had six loans to date. The first borrower doubled the value of her loan by the fifth loan; the second borrower had doubled the size by the fourth loan. The final column shows average loan sizes for the entire sample, growing from 2,124 taka for first loans ($57 in 1991) to 4,983 taka ($135) for sixth loans. For the lender, progressive lending cuts average costs since servicing a taka 4,000 loan is not twice as expensive as servicing a 2,000 taka loan. Progressive lending also enables the lender to "test" borrowers with small loans at the start in order to screen out the worst prospects before expanding the loan scale (see Ghosh and Ray 1999).

From the previous analysis, progressive lending has a third, important role with regard to incentives. Microlenders can elicit even larger repayments by offering loans of larger size to borrowers who repay their debts. Specifically, progressive lending schemes increase the opportunity cost of non-repayment and thereby discourage strategic default even further. To see this, suppose that the bank decides to

Table 5.2
Loan size increases (taka), Grameen Bank, Bangladesh

Loan number	Borrower A	Borrower B	Borrower C	Full sample average
1	2000	2000	3500	2124
2	2500	2500	4000	2897
3	3000	3000	3000	3656
4	3500	4000	4000	4182
5	4000	4000	5000	4736
6	4000	5000	4000	4983

Source: Authors' calculations from the World Bank–Bangladesh Institute of Development Studies 1991–1992 Survey. Data are in current taka (in 1991, $1 = Tk. 37; in 1986, $1 = Tk. 30). The final column averages loan sizes over the full sample of Grameen Bank borrowers in the data set (excluding loans used for land/building), and sample sizes diminish with loan number; starting from the first row downward, there are 319, 286, 250, 168, 89, and 30 observations.

increase the size of its short-period loans by a factor $\lambda > 1$ between period 1 and period 2, and that the production technology has constant returns to scale. The opportunity cost of strategic default will then increase by the same factor between the two periods. In particular, by not repaying the gross interest rate R, the borrower now suffers a loss $\lambda \delta y > \delta y$. This in turn relaxes the incentive compatibility constraint, and the bank can now achieve a maximum interest rate equal to $R' = \lambda \delta y > R = \delta y$. Interest rates can be raised while keeping the borrowers happy.[13]

Note though that, as before, the analysis rests on an assumption that may not be fully tenable—that if a borrower defaults in the first period, she nonetheless needs a loan to be able to invest in the second period. In principle, borrowers may be able to keep at least part of the principal from the first period and use that to invest in the second. If so, dynamic incentives are harder to maintain; in this case, borrowers can expect a return of $y - R' + \lambda \delta y$ if they pay their first-period debt. If they do not, their return is $y (1 - \varphi) + \varphi \delta y$, where $\varphi < 1$ is the fraction of the first-period gross return that is invested in the second period. Suppose that, if the borrower defaults, her choice is to hold back a fraction $\varphi = R/y$. That is, from first-period gross returns, she saves for the next period exactly the amount that she would have paid to the bank (had she chosen to repay the loan with interest). In this case, the household will not default if $1 > \varphi$. Since loan sizes are growing ($\lambda > 1$) and since not all of the loan is retained ($\varphi < 1$), this inequality must hold: the borrower will not default. But incentives will erode if loans shrink in size, or if borrowers can scale up their own resources faster than the bank can (for more on this, see Bond and Krishnamurty 2004).

This leads to another observation. A borrower who is disposed to strategically default will wait until loan sizes have grown substantially before ultimately choosing to renege on the loan contract. The lender (if also acting strategically) will in turn carefully determine loan schedules in order to minimize default. More specifically, consider a multi-period debt relationship between the lender and the borrower. If the growth factor λ is large at first (i.e., initial loans increase in size very quickly and then growth slows), the borrower has incentives to default earlier than they would when compared to a steadier path of loan size increases. The incentive problem imposes an upper bound on the desirable growth rate of loan size over time. On the other hand, reputation considerations on the borrower's side (which are absent from the preceding simple model) should mitigate this effect by reducing the borrower's incentive to default (see, e.g., Sobel 2006).

5.2.3   Competition and Incentives

Economists usually view competition as a good thing, and most theoretical models assume that there is perfect competition. So far, we have assumed in fact that microlenders are either perfectly competitive or that they simply wish to break even. But in this section we argue that strong competition can undermine dynamic incentives. If a microlender is a monopolist, its threat to cut access to defaulters has greatest bite since they are the only source of credit. Dynamic incentives can weaken when alternative lenders enter the market (assuming that the defaulter has a chance to borrow from them instead). Not only that, but competition can weaken reputation effects.[14]

Problems with competition have been studied in a variety of contexts. McIntosh and Wydick (2005), for example, report on problems of competition in Uganda, Kenya, Guatemala, El Salvador, and Nicaragua. Focusing on the case of FINCA Uganda, McIntosh, de Janvry, and Sadoulet (2005) show that increased competition led to a decline in both repayment and savings rates. Problems have emerged most notably in two countries where microfinance was first to take hold: Bolivia and Bangladesh. The Bolivian crisis took root when aggressive providers of consumer credit entered the market. In this case, the new entrants were outsiders, notably Acceso FFP, a large Chilean finance company.[15] Acceso came in with streamlined operations and over one thousand highly motivated employees (most of whose pay came in the form of incentives rather than base salary). Within three years, Acceso had ninety thousand loans outstanding, a level that BancoSol had not reached in its twelve-year history. In 1999, the worst year of the crisis, BancoSol lost 11 percent of its clients, and loan overdue rates for regulated microlenders rose from 2.4 percent at the end of 1997 to 8.4 percent by mid-1999. BancoSol saw its return on equity fall from 29 percent in 1998 to 9 percent in 1999.[16]

The immediate problem with competition in Bolivia was borrowers taking multiple loans simultaneously from different lenders. The borrowers then became overindebted, paying one lender's installments by taking a loan from another, leading to a spiral of debt and, too often, financial peril. Carmen Velasco, co-executive director of Pro Mujer, tells of visiting a client in Cochabamba who had loans from two different institutions and was sinking under the weight. The client's husband reported a proposed solution—the next day they planned to seek a loan from BancoSol to help pay off the first two loans![17] While our discussion here concerns problems that occur when borrowers can

turn from one lender to another in sequence (rather than simultaneously), the root of the problem is similar. As long as borrowers believe
that they have multiple options, no single lender will have the power
to clamp down and maintain full discipline.

Pro Mujer declared that clients holding loans from other banks were
henceforth ineligible to borrow, but following up on all financial activities of clients and their families is costly in practice. The general situation in Bolivia improved, though, as regulators tightened rules, the
Chilean financiers retreated, and the early microfinance providers like
BancoSol and Pro Mujer took extra steps to keep their clients satisfied.
Looking forward, the most effective solution would be a credit bureau
that keeps track of the credit histories of all borrowers across the
nation.

The Bolivian crisis occurred around the same time as the crisis in
Bangladesh. The middle and late 1990s saw the explosive growth of
the Grameen Bank, ASA, BRAC, and Proshika. While it is impossible
to accurately count (because borrowers from a given institution also
borrowed from others), around ten million new microfinance clients
signed on over the decade. The main microfinance providers had agreements not to work with the same clients, but that did not prevent a
crisis of simultaneous borrowing along the lines of what occurred in
Bolivia. In Bangladesh the problem has been dubbed "overlapping,"
and Chaudhury and Matin (2002) report that by the end of the decade,
there was more than one microlender operating in 95 percent of eighty
villages surveyed by researchers at the Bangladesh Institute of Development Studies (BIDS). Matin (n.d.) reports on a BIDS study that estimates that 15 percent of all borrowers took loans from more than one
institution. The result, coupled with a broader pattern of lending more
than clients could fully absorb, was a repayment crisis that took
Grameen Bank's reported repayment rates from above 98 percent to
below 90 percent, with greater difficulties in densely served areas like
Tangail district.[18]

The lesson from these experiences is not that monopolies should be
protected. In both Bangladesh and Bolivia, competition has brought a
healthy round of general rethinking that would have not otherwise
happened so soon.[19] The chief lesson is instead that cooperative behavior among microlenders can help to mitigate the problem. Programs
would be aided by the creation of credit bureaus to better share information on credit access and performance history of borrowers. Having

credit bureaus enables lenders to address overindebtedness and to make borrowers face the consequences of strategic defaults (which is not to say that it would be simple to set up credit bureaus in countries like Bangladesh, where there is no system of social security numbers or national ID numbers).

Empirical research on the impacts of credit bureaus suggests that they offer real benefits to lenders. De Janvry, McIntosh, and Sadoulet (2008) take advantage of a natural experiment, paired with a randomized experiment, to analyze the impact of credit bureaus on both supply- and demand-side outcomes. A Guatemalan lender started using a credit bureau, spreading the technology across its branches gradually and without the knowledge of its clients. A year later, the authors ran a training course explaining the credit bureau's existence and function to a random group of clients. They found that the lender's access to information about borrowers led to a significant increase in the number of clients ejected, as well as in the number and size of new individual loans, leading to an improvement in portfolio quality. Efficiency measures also improved, with credit officers approving 55 percent more new borrowers on average. When borrowers learned about the credit bureau, members of large "Communal Banking" groups with good repayment histories and those with little borrowing experience both sought out more loans, but the inexperienced borrowers ran into some trouble repaying. So while the impact of using a credit bureau was substantial and positive for the lender, it was mixed from the borrowers' point of view. The authors take this evidence as support for the role of joint liability as an effective screening mechanism.

No one can force microlenders to join a credit bureau, but the argument in favor of fierce competition cannot be defended without the presence of an adequate regulatory framework.[20] In Bolivia, regulated financial intermediaries like BancoSol are required by law to report both names and national identification card numbers of delinquent borrowers to the Superintendency of Banks and Financial Institutions (González-Vega, Schreiner, Meyer et al. 1997). In return, all regulated financial intermediaries are allowed to view the information provided by the others, and informal arrangements are used to share information with nonregulated microlenders. These measures strengthen dynamic incentives, but lenders must fend for themselves in dealing with "overlapping" clients.

5.3 Frequent Repayment Installments

One important issue that has so far been mainly overlooked by academics is a curious (or at least nonstandard) aspect of microfinance contracts. This is that lenders often expect loans to be paid in small installments, starting soon after the initial disbursement. In the Grameen Bank model, the installments are weekly. Similarly, in Bolivia between 1987 and 1995 the microlender Caja Los Andes demanded weekly repayments from about half of its clients. Another 42 percent made repayments every other week (i.e., biweekly), and the remaining 6 percent made monthly installments. For its competitor, BancoSol, over one-third of clients were asked to repay weekly, about one-quarter paid biweekly, and the rest paid monthly.[21]

While having several installments is not unusual for consumer loans made by commercial banks, it is atypical for loans made (at least on paper) for investing in businesses. In "standard" business loans made by traditional commercial banks, the process is just as you would think: entrepreneurs borrow, invest and grow their businesses, and then— once sufficient profits have been earned—repay the loan with interest. Here, it is quite common to expect repayment to start the next month or week!

Table 5.3 provides more data from Bolivia collected by a research team from the Ohio State University. For both Caja Los Andes and BancoSol, the weekly repayment schedules were demanded on smaller-sized loans, while the larger loans carried biweekly or monthly installments. On average, it is poorer households that are being asked to repay in more frequent installments, since it is poorer households that tend to take smaller loans.

The puzzle is why repayments should be scheduled this way. One explanation is that it creates an early warning system. By meeting weekly, credit officers get to know their clients well by seeing them face-to-face on a regular basis. This information can provide loan officers with early warnings about emerging problems and offer bank staff a protocol by which to get to know borrowers more effectively—and clamp down more quickly when needed. Personalized relationships and regular opportunities for monitoring are thus established, just as with local moneylenders.[22] Drawing on their research in Bolivia, González-Vega et al. (1997, 74) stress the value of the early warning feature, asserting that "the most important tool for the monitoring of borrowers in these lending technologies is requiring frequent

Table 5.3
Loan terms and conditions in Bolivia, BancoSol, and Caja Los Andes, 1995

Repayment frequency	Median amount initially disbursed ($)	Median term to maturity (months)	Effective annual real interest rate (percent per year)
Caja Los Andes			
Monthly	37	1	35
Weekly	62	3	35
Weekly	106	5	34
Biweekly	309	5	33
Monthly	309	6	26
Monthly	309	6	23
BancoSol			
Weekly	62	3	59
Biweekly	72	4	53
Monthly	82	6	48

Source: González-Vega et al. 1997, table 15, 49–50. Amounts are in U.S. dollars at the exchange rate of 4.93 bolivianos per dollar. The effective annual real interest rate is calculated as twelve times the internal monthly rate of return of the contract (in real terms) for loans with median size and median term to maturity. The data reflect loans denominated in bolivianos only; both lenders also provided dollar-denominated loans—in much larger sizes (e.g., the median size for Caja Los Andes was about $2,500) with monthly or biweekly installments, lower real interest rates (30 percent per year or below), and year-long terms to maturity.

repayments followed by immediate reaction in the case of arrears." The observation is reinforced through an example: "After the creation of BancoSol, the proportion of its clients making monthly repayments increased. A couple of years later, BancoSol revised this policy, most likely in response to higher arrears in 1992–93. Thus, the proportion of loans with weekly repayments increased from 27 percent in 1993 to 47 percent in 1995" (González-Vega et al. 1997, 74).

Silwal (2003) also notes the correlation between repayment troubles and the frequency of required installments. He compares repayment performance in nine "village banks" in Nepal and finds that 11 percent of loans were not repaid by the end of the loan period when installments were weekly, while twice that rate (19.8 percent) were delinquent when loans were paid in a single lump-sum payment at the end of the loan's maturity (which was generally 3–4 months). Similarly, when BRAC in Bangladesh experimented with moving from weekly repayments to twice-per-month repayments, delinquencies soon rose, and BRAC—just like BancoSol—quickly retreated to its weekly scheme.[23]

But puzzles remain. After all, the "early warning system" explanation does not answer why it could make sense to demand repayments *before* investments are likely to have borne fruit. Moreover, as González-Vega et al. (1997, 74) argue: "While frequent repayments are critical in keeping the probability of default low, they increase the transaction costs incurred by borrowers and thereby reduce the quality of service to the client." On the face of it, having to pay more frequently does seem to impose an added constraint on borrowers. But we suggest in what follows that this is too simple. For borrowers who have difficulty saving, the frequent repayment schedules can *increase* the quality of service to the client.

Before we get to that, we suggest why it could make sense for the bank to demand initial installments to be repaid so soon after loans are disbursed. One answer is that it helps the bank select less risky clients. The frequent repayment schedule reduces the bank's risk by selecting borrowers who are more likely to be able to repay loans even if their investments fail. This is because households must have some *other* stream of income on which to draw in order to repay the early installments.[24] So, requiring frequent and early installments means that the bank is effectively lending partly against that stream of outside income, not just the proceeds from the project. The bank is therefore taking advantage of the borrower's ability to obtain funds from family members or from household activities apart from the given investment project.

For example, if before borrowing the household has a net income flow of $10 per week after expenses from the husband's wage job, the microfinance institution can fairly safely lend the wife an amount under $520 (52 weeks times $10) to be repaid in a year with the confidence that the household in principle has resources to repay even if the project fails. The example assumes that the husband is happy to help pay off the loan, and to the extent that's not so, the bank would have to reduce its calculations of maximum feasible loan size for the wife. But the example captures the flavor of the way that loan officers assess the repayment ability of their clients. Strikingly, in most of the programs surveyed by Churchill (1999), lenders estimate repayment capacity *without* taking into account expected revenues from the loan in question, and they take into account income flows provided by all household members.[25]

We have to push a bit further, though, to more satisfactorily explain the requirement of frequent installments. One question is: Why not do as before and estimate repayment capacity based on household income (rather than expected investment income) but not require frequent installments? An answer is that the repayment schedule is the easiest way for the microlender to "capture" those other household income flows (which are earned throughout the year) and guarantee that they are put toward paying off the bank loan.

A related part of the story is that frequent installments will be particularly valuable for households that have difficulty holding onto income. This takes us back to issues of savings constraints addressed in the context of ROSCA enforcement in chapter 3—and about which we will say more in chapter 6. If borrowers must wait months before they repay loan installments, part of their earnings may be dissipated as neighbors and relatives come by for handouts, spouses dip into the household kitty, and discretionary purchases command attention. Months later, funds may no longer be there to pay the bank. A repayment schedule with frequent installments instead takes the money out of the house soon after it is earned. The essential insight is that everyone gains by matching repayment schedules as closely as feasible to the cash flowing into borrowers' households. In this way, loan products become like saving products, and the result is the initially puzzling hybrids that we see in practice.[26] It is also why we asserted previously that, for borrowers who have difficulty saving, the frequent repayment schedules can *increase* the quality of service received from microlenders.

The calculation of optimal repayment schedules will then involve the timing and amount of the income that is earned by the household, the difficulty that households have holding onto that income, the bank's desire for early warnings of troubles, and both the bank's and customers' transactions costs associated with collecting repayments. All else the same, if households can save without difficulty and transactions costs are high, the optimal number of installments falls. PRODEM, a rural lender in Bolivia, for example, requires monthly installments because it finds that weekly installments are too costly in the low population density areas in which they work (González-Vega et al. 1997). But where saving is hard and transactions costs are relatively low, weekly repayments are more likely to appeal. The latter scenario will hold with poorer households, where the opportunity cost of time is relatively low, and where the mechanisms to enforce financial discipline are relatively limited. These tendencies are reinforced by the fact that small-scale business like petty trading tends to generate a flow of revenue on a daily or weekly basis, making frequent collections especially desirable in the absence of satisfactory savings facilities. In wealthier households, however, opportunity costs are likely to be higher and revenue costs less frequent, militating toward less frequent loan installments. These arguments are in line with the pattern of weekly versus monthly installment schedules seen in table 5.3, in which bigger loans, which tend to go to wealthier clients, are more likely to be repaid in larger but less frequent installments.

Given the fact that transaction costs increase with repayment frequency, an important question for lenders is whether more installments actually reduce defaults. Field and Pande (2008) explore this question in a field experiment. They use data from an urban microlender in India that uses a group lending methodology with joint liability. The authors find no difference in default rates for groups with weekly repayment schedules and monthly repayment schedules—both groups have nearly perfect performance. Evidence from Uganda corroborates these results. McIntosh (2008) finds no drop in repayment (and a large increase in client retention) when village banks switch from weekly to bi-weekly repayment schedules.

According to Field and Pande (2008), their findings suggest that microlenders could increase their outreach without increasing costs by switching to lower frequency repayment schedules. However, they acknowledge that their findings should be interpreted with caution. First, the financial discipline afforded by frequent repayment might be more important for relatively larger loans. Also, the lender's main repayment incentive is denial of future loans. The lender is the main source of credit in the neighborhoods where the experiment was carried out, but where there are alternatives, more frequent repayments might have an impact on delinquency and default. Finally, the borrowers in the study were pre-selected based on a willingness to borrow at either the weekly or monthly schedule, creating selection bias. Despite the caveats, the result is an important starting point for investigating the relationship between repayment frequency and repayment rates.

One notable problem is that these regular repayment schedules are difficult to impose in areas focused on highly seasonal occupations like agricultural cultivation. Indeed, seasonality poses one of the largest challenges to the spread of microfinance in areas centered on rain-fed agriculture, areas that include some of the poorest regions of South Asia and Africa. (Another major challenge in lending in agriculture is covariant risk, where a bad drought, a pest infestation, or the like can devastate an entire region, debilitating the microlender too.)

The Grameen Bank's new model, "Grameen Bank II," attempts to address this issue in part by maintaining weekly repayment schedules (for all of the reasons discussed earlier) but allowing loan officers to vary the size of weekly installments according to season (Yunus 2002). In low seasons borrowers can ask to pay less in return for paying more during high seasons.

We close this section with a question: Since many lenders appear to judge repayment capacity without taking into account expected revenues from the investment that the loan is intended for, why don't the borrowers simply save up the money needed, rather than taking out a loan with interest? The answer must partly hinge on discount rates (borrowers would rather have assets sooner if possible; see Fischer and Ghatak [2010]) and partly on savings constraints (saving up is not so easy). We suspect that if more households did have better ways to save, the demand for loans would fall considerably. Which takes us to a provocative thought. As Rutherford (2000) notes, the requirement of frequent installments not only builds recognition of saving difficulties into loan products, but also means that some customers with particular problems saving may logically look to the new microfinance loan products as an alternative way to "save"—namely, as a useful mechanism to help convert the small, frequent bits of money that enter the household into a big lump that can be used for a major purchase or investment. For these customers, that the particular financial product is structured and labeled as a "loan product" may be of secondary concern.

5.4   Complementary Incentive Mechanisms

In the rest of the chapter we describe additional means used by microlenders to secure repayments. We describe important mechanisms now in use and one interesting proposal (on "cross-reporting" strategies) that could, in theory, improve on or supplement existing schemes.

5.4.1   Flexible Approaches to Collateral

One premise of microfinance is that most clients are too poor to be able to offer collateral. Loans are thus "secured" through nontraditional means like group lending. But in practice some microfinance lenders do require collateral, the best-known being Indonesia's BRI. In rural Albania, for example, microlenders require tangible assets such as livestock, land, and housing to be put up (in addition to any assets purchased with loans), and the programs have been vigilant in enforcing agreements if clients fail to repay. In urban Albania, a borrower's home or business is typically required as collateral (Benjamin and Ledgerwood 1999).

Microlenders like BRI take a nontraditional view of collateral. While BRI requires collateral in general, the bank is flexible in the assets that it will accept, and in practice collateral is not a major constraint when seeking poor clients. A survey completed in 2000, for example, shows that 88 percent of noncustomers had acceptable collateral of some sort.[27] All the same, the survey shows that non-customers have much less in the way of assets to use as collateral. Table 5.4 shows that the median value of collateralizable assets held by BRI borrowers is roughly 2.5 times the median value of those held by a random sample of noncustomers drawn from the same area. In order to reach poorer customers, BRI has introduced products that require no collateral at all for loans up to Rp. 2 million ($225 in 2003), offered at the discretion of the unit manager.[28]

BRI's view is that the resale value of collateral is far less important than the judgment that the pledged items should be particularly problematic for households to give up. Thus, household items may be considered collateral if they have sufficient personal value for borrowers, even if they are worth relatively little in the hands of BRI. The idea breaks with the traditional banker's view that collateral should be valuable enough so that banks can sell the collateral to cover the costs of

Table 5.4
Collateral value (rupiah x 10,000,000)

	25th percentile	Median	75th percentile
Value x 10,000,000			
BRI borrower	1.1	2.3	4.1
BRI saver only	0.9	1.9	3.8
Noncustomer	0.4	0.91	2.1

Source: BRI survey, 2000. Calculations by Morduch.
Note: Cell size for BRI borrowers, $n = 175$; for BRI saver only, $n = 170$; and for noncustomers, $n = 741$. On June 1, 2000, 10 million rupiah were equivalent to $1,160.

problem loans. In other words, for BRI the value of collateral is determined by the *notional* value of the asset, not the expected sale value.
Land without a certificate of title, for example, may be nearly impossible to sell without the cooperation of the borrower and the local community. It thus has very little value to BRI if the client is hostile. But
BRI still sees such collateral as potentially valuable. In part, it is an
indicator of borrower intent and a guarantee that borrowers have
resources to use if they should get into repayment difficulty.[29]

More formally, we extend this framework to show how collateral
requirements discourage borrowers from defaulting on debt obligations. Let w be the collateral that the bank confiscates at the contracting
stage. Returning to the setup in section 5.2, take $v = 0$ which, again, is
the optimal refinancing strategy from the bank's standpoint. Then, the
borrower's incentive compatibility constraint becomes $y - w \leq y - R +
\delta y$, or, equivalently, $-w \leq -R + \delta y$. This, in turn, implies that the
bank's maximum gross interest rate can be as large as $R = v\delta y + w$.
Thus, with collateral requirements the bank is now able to charge a
higher interest rate while not fearing a greater probability of default.
But note that the bank does not need to take possession of and *sell*
the collateral for this constraint to bind; it only needs to deny the
borrower access to the collateral. The result also says that at a given
interest rate, average default rates will fall, reducing losses for the
bank. In this way, adding a collateral requirement can help the bank
improve profitability without raising interest rates—or even while
reducing charges.

5.4.2 Financial Collateral

The flexible approach to collateral just described is one solution when
borrowers lack assets. Another solution is to address the problem
straight on—to provide ways for borrowers to build up financial assets
and then to base lending on those assets. Many microlenders, for
example, require that borrowers show that they can save regularly for
a period before they become eligible to borrow. Demonstrating the
ability to save demonstrates characteristics like discipline and money
management skills that correlate with being a good borrower. But
saving also leads to deposits in the bank, and that can help directly by
providing security for loans.

At *Safe*Save in the Dhaka slums, the first loan product developed
required that borrowers hold a savings account for three months
before borrowing was allowed. The maximum size of the loan was

determined as (current savings balance) + (10 times the smallest monthly net inflow of savings over the previous three months).[30] While loans are outstanding, savings withdrawals are restricted in some *Safe-Save* loan products.

At Grameen Bank, the policy at the end of 2003 was that borrowers holding loans must deposit between 5 and 50 taka per week into obligatory personal savings accounts (between about 10 cents and one dollar in December 2003), with the amount depending on their loan size.[31] For most loans, an obligatory deposit equal to 2.5 percent of the loan value is also deducted off the top of the loan and placed into the borrowers' personal savings accounts. Another 2.5 percent is put into a "special savings" account. On top of this, borrowers taking loans larger than 8,000 taka (about $145) are required to open a Grameen Pension Scheme (GPS) account with a monthly deposit of at least 50 taka. The GPS requires monthly deposits for a term of from five to ten years. Borrowers in good standing can withdraw from their personal savings accounts at any time, provided they visit the branch with their passbook. The "special savings" accounts, though, have heavier restrictions—for example, withdrawals are not allowed for the first three years. And the GPS is a fixed term account that, if it goes into arrears, is closed and the funds are returned with reduced interest. Loan ceilings are predicated in part on the size of these various loan balances.

How well can these kinds of deposits function as collateral? On the one hand, if borrowers get into repayment trouble, the microlender can, in principle, hold onto the deposits to minimize their exposure to the full extent of the default. Saving up is not easy, so borrowers will surely be careful when their nest egg is at risk. On the other hand, if the outstanding loan is larger than the funds on deposit, the lender remains exposed to the possibility of default on the difference. From this vantage, the use of financial collateral does little more than effectively reduce the capital that borrowers have available to them, since the borrower's savings are tied up with the lender and not available to be invested by the borrower. Since borrowers have to pay higher interest rates on the money that they borrow than on the money they receive as interest on their deposits, the scheme can also add substantial "hidden" costs to borrowing.

This discussion assumes, though, that borrowers see a dollar as a dollar, a peso as a peso, and a taka as a taka. In other words, it assumes that money saved is "counted" the same as money borrowed. But if borrowers attach special worth to money saved over time, the micro-lender might be able to capitalize on financial collateral and its "special" place in the borrower's heart and mind—and in the process to provide larger loans with lower risk. It is often noted, for example, that individuals will prefer to borrow—even at relatively high interest rates—than to draw down the savings that they have diligently built up over years.[32] The bottom line is that using financial collateral can be an effective way to facilitate lending, but it hinges on special assumptions about borrower psychology and constraints that are unlikely to hold for everyone or at all times.

5.4.3 Making Repayments Public

In an important break from its original model, ASA of Bangladesh ultimately weakened its insistence on the group lending mechanism in its credit practices. Customers often still meet as groups, though, making public repayments. Similarly in "Grameen Bank II" the focus shifts from the group to individual relations between borrowers and loan officers. Still, though, customers meet as groups and make public repayments.

A telling story on the importance of public repayments comes from a Grameen Bank replication in Kenya that ran into trouble before instituting monthly public meetings with borrowers. Originally, the lender had instructed borrowers to deposit their installments directly into a bank account, but the incidence of default soared. Repayment rates came under control only after bank officials started meeting in villages with borrowers each month, collecting installments face-to-face.[33]

Public repayment schemes have several advantages for the lender. First, without the ability to secure collateral, microlenders can use the avoidance of social stigma as an inducement for individual borrowers to promptly repay loans (Rahman 1999). Public repayments heighten the ability to generate stigma—or, more powerfully, the *threat* of stigma. Second, by meeting as a cluster of borrowers in scheduled locations, and at scheduled times, some transactions for bank staff might be reduced, even if it adds to clients' costs. Third, the group is often a useful resource through which staff can directly elicit information about errant borrowers and create pressure as needed (i.e., "crossreports" described in section 5.4.4). Fourth, group meetings can facilitate education and training, which may be particularly helpful for clients with little business experience and/or low literacy levels.

The education might aid financial performance or it might be valued intrinsically as a way to improve levels of health and knowledge. Fifth, it is often said that the comfort of clients (many of whom have had no prior experience with commercial banks) is enhanced by encouraging them to approach the bank with their neighbors. And, sixth, by keeping transactions in the open, public repayments can help enhance internal control for the bank and reduce opportunities for fraud.[34]

5.4.4 Targeting Women

The Grameen Bank has bound microfinance to creating opportunities for poor women. Much that is written on Grameen focuses on gender issues, and we devote chapter 7 to this topic. But Grameen did not start with such a strong focus on women. The bank lent originally to large numbers of men, in addition to women, keeping both groups and centers segregated by sex. When the focus shifted in the early 1980s, the move was partly in response to growing repayment problems in male centers, and by the end of that decade well over 90 percent of clients were women. At the end of 2002, 95 percent of clients were women.

As we describe in chapter 7, women seem to be more reliable than men when it comes to repaying their loans (before conditioning on other variables like social status and education). Hossain (1988), for example, argues that women in Bangladesh are more reliable customers, citing evidence that 81 percent of women had no repayment problems versus 74 percent of men. Similarly, Khandker, Khalily, and Kahn (1995) find that 15.3 percent of male borrowers were "struggling" in 1991 (i.e., missing some payments before the final due date), while only 1.3 percent of women were having difficulties. In Malawi, Hulme (1991) finds on-time repayments for women customers to be 92 percent versus 83 percent for men, and Gibbons and Kasim (1991) find that in Malaysia the repayment comparison is 95 percent for women versus 72 percent for men.[35]

The evidence suggests that it may thus be profit-maximizing for banks to lend to women, independent of other concerns about gender equality. Why women often seem to be more reliable customers is up for debate. Todd's (1996, 182) time in two Grameen villages in Tangail leads her to argue that it might be because women are "more cautious" than men, who are more likely to have trouble sustaining membership over the long term. Based on a later village study, Rahman (2001) finds that women instead tend to be much more sensitive to the verbal hostility of fellow members and bank employees when repayment difficulties arise, while men are more likely to be argumentative and noncompliant. In Indonesia, a manager of a Grameen Bank replicator argued that women were better customers because they tended to stay close by the home rather than going out to work. This makes women, on average, easier to find when troubles arise and gives them little way to escape pressures; men, on the other hand, more easily remove themselves (physically) from difficult situations.[36]

In terms of the dynamic incentives analyzed in section 5.2, women will be more likely to repay (than men) if they have fewer alternative sources of credit. Since men may have greater access to formal credit and to informal credit from traders and moneylenders, men may have weaker repayment histories than their wives and sisters.

These observations are surely not universal and are apt to change over time. And not all successful microlenders focus on women. BRI, for example, does not especially target women, but they still boast near-perfect repayment rates. Concerns with gender should thus be seen within the broader context of a lender's approach and objectives, as well as wider social, cultural, and economic constraints—issues taken up further in chapter 7.

5.4.5 Information Gathering by Bank Staff

In the nineteenth-century German credit cooperatives, which we analyzed in chapter 3, borrowers were asked to obtain a loan guarantee from a neighbor. By inducing joint liability, the loan guarantee was a precursor to group lending. More recent experience shows that even without a formal loan guarantee, incorporating neighbors in credit decisions can improve bank performance.

In another step away from traditional bank practices, many microlenders spend considerable time talking with prospective borrowers' neighbors and friends when making lending decisions. One microlender in Russia, for example, relies heavily on staff visits to applicants' businesses and homes, rather than just on business documents (Zeitinger 1996). The idea of relying on outside guarantors has been re-introduced by some microfinance institutions such as VivaCred in Brazil (Janaux and Baptiste 2009). In rural Albania, applicants must often obtain a loan guarantee and character reference from a member of the local "village credit committee." Similarly, Churchill (1999, 55) describes practices at BRI in Indonesia:

At the BRI units, most loan rejections are based on character, not the business assessment. Rejection occurs if the credit officer learns that the applicant is not respected in the community or has misrepresented himself in the application. Almost without exception, the unit staff interviewed for this research identified the neighbor's assessment of the applicant's character as the most important means of predicting a new applicant's future repayment behavior—more important than the business assessment.

At ADEMI in the Dominican Republic, credit officers also check the stability of home life, based on their finding that "troubled homes often become troubled borrowers" (Churchill 1999, 56). At Financiera Cálpia in El Salvador, agricultural extension workers are important informants about some borrowers' character, and accordingly credit officers build ongoing relationships with extension workers.

Thus, even where group lending is not used, novel mechanisms are in place to generate information. Credit officers get out of their branch offices and get to know the neighborhoods in which they work. Microlenders find that the views of shopkeepers, bartenders, schoolteachers, and other central figures in communities can be as helpful in assessing borrowers' creditworthiness as a stack of business plans.[37]

5.4.6 Cross-Reporting

Gathering information from neighbors can be helpful at many stages in the loan process, not just at the application stage. One problem faced by microlenders using the threat not to refinance defaulters is that it's a strong penalty. It's particularly strong when coupled with group lending, since, in principle at least, the entire group should be cut off when any member fails to repay. Rai and Sjöström (2004) argue that these punishments are inefficiently tough, and that "cross-reporting" can improve performance.[38]

Cross-reporting refers to statements made by one borrower about another. If Mrs. Haq is willfully refusing to repay (despite having the necessary resources), the bank can take appropriate action if Mrs. Rahman speaks up about it. If Mrs. Haq's troubles are not self-imposed, Mrs. Rahman can provide helpful input then too (preventing the bank from coming down too hard on Mrs. Haq). Rai and Sjöström describe how cross-reporting can be reliable and improve efficiency. While their focus is on improving group lending schemes, cross-reporting can have wider applications.

In order to work, the bank must credibly commit itself to a system of reward for truthful reports, and the bank must itself check on its borrowers' monitoring activities. One fear is that formalizing such a system may create tensions among individual borrowers or a strong incentive for them to collude. Still, cross-reporting seems promising in a variety of settings, and, as Rai and Sjöström argue, it is already an informal feature of banking relationships, especially coupled with group lending.

5.5 Summary and Conclusions

Group lending with joint responsibility is far from being the only innovation in microfinance. Successfully creating dynamic incentives and creating products that are built around households' cash flows have been as important. Good dynamic incentives are created through attractive long-term relationships. When forward-looking customers know that default means risking losing the relationship, incentives to work hard are strengthened. Helping customers to manage cash flows is also critical, since it helps banks to give banks access to customer resources before they are spent or otherwise dissipated. Weekly or monthly repayment schedules, although a sharp break from traditional banking practices, have been particularly critical in allowing customers to repay loans in manageable bits. Strategic microlenders often attempt to break repayment installments into pieces that are small enough that customers can, if needed, repay loans from household funds other than profits from the given investment project. The bank's risks are considerably reduced as a result.

In order to work effectively in sparsely populated rural areas, in highly transient urban areas, and with more mature clients, it has been necessary to develop additional mechanisms. Even where group lending has been central (e.g., in the densely populated villages of Bangladesh), the additional mechanisms have been put to good use. These additional mechanisms include flexible approaches to collateral (where what matters most is the value that the customer attaches to losing the item, rather than the value that the lender expects to recover from selling the item) and having public repayments, even when joint responsibility is not a part of credit contracts. It is not clear in the end how important group lending is to the continued success of microfinance. We expect that the future will see much more innovation, and the beginning point should be better understandings of existing mechanisms.

But, to date, the innovations described here have been studied far less than group lending, and we know of few systematic attempts to sort out which mechanisms have most power in practice, or how the mechanisms operate together. Progress could be made by experimenting with different mechanisms in a way that would allow researchers to properly infer causality—say, by using different methodologies in different, randomly chosen branches. Microlenders will understandably be reluctant to give over their decision making to a random number generator, but building some elements of randomization into research and development can allow more systematic product testing and piloting—and cleaner answers on what really drives microfinance performance.

5.6   Exercises

1. Refer to table 5.1. What are the main differences between individual lending contracts in microfinance and group lending contracts? What kinds of additional information would you need to have in order to draw sharper comparisons?

2. Give at least two reasons why group lending schemes may be better than individual lending ones, and at least two reasons why they may be worse.

3. Explain three differences between contracts offered by microfinance institutions and standard contracts offered by commercial banks.

4. Comment on the merits of the following statement: "Competition is generally viewed by economists as a good thing, yet microfinance institutions often disagree about this even when they are not pursuing profits."

5. Comment on the merits of the following statement: "Microfinance institutions that extend individual loans often request some kind of collateral, and therefore are biased against the poor." Use table 5.4 as reference.

6. Consider an economy with three types of risk-neutral entrepreneurs. If a type 1 entrepreneur invests $200 she gets a gross return of $400 with certainty. If a type 2 entrepreneur invests $100 she gets $200 with certainty. And finally, if a type 3 entrepreneur invests $100 she gets $300 with probability 0.75 and 0 with probability 0.25. A risk-neutral, competitive lender is considering extending loans to these entrepreneurs. This bank can determine if potential borrowers are of type 1 (henceforth, high-type borrowers), but it can't distinguish between entrepreneurs of type 2 and 3 (henceforth, low-type borrowers), but it does know that half of the low-type borrowers are of type 2, and the other half are of type 3. All borrowers, on the other hand, can recognize each others' types. Under these conditions, the bank decides to extend individual loans to high-type borrowers and group loans with joint liability to low-type borrowers. As a result, a low-type borrower may have to repay for a defaulting peer. The cost of lending to high-types is $20, while the cost of lending to low-types is $30 (because the bank has to put in additional time and effort to ensure that groups are formed and to enforce debt repayments). Assume that the borrowers are protected by limited liability.

a. If the bank only aims to break even, calculate the interest rates charged to high types and to low types. Compare the two rates.

b. Now suppose that the bank holds a pool of loan contracts. It lends to three high-type borrowers and to four low-type pairs with the compositions: (2,2), (3,3), (2,3) and (3,2). Assume that one borrower in group two succeeds, while type 3 agents fail in pairs three and four. Compute the repayment rates that the bank will receive separately for the high and low types loans. Compare the two rates, and explain your answer.

7. Consider an economy with a competitive bank and risk-neutral entrepreneurs whose only source of funds is the bank. The bank and the entrepreneurs interact over two periods, and the timing of events is as follows: At date 0, an entrepreneur wants to borrow an amount I to invest in a project that yields a gross return y with certainty at date 1. The bank cannot verify the return realization on the entrepreneur's project, but it knows that it should be y. If the borrower repays an amount R at date 1, the bank will extend a new loan of size I at date 1. The borrower then invests the entire proceeds from the new loan I, and obtains y at date 2 with certainty. But if the borrower defaults at date 1, the bank does not extend a new loan I at date 1 and therefore the borrower can't invest. The lender's gross cost of lending I is K. Let $\delta < 1$ denote the borrower's discount factor. Assume also that the borrower's consumption starts at date 1.

a. Define the interval for gross repayment R in which the bank would extend a loan and the borrower would repay. Suppose that $y > \delta y > I$.

b. If $I = \$100$, $y = \$200$, $K = \$150$, and $\delta = 0.9$, is there scope for lending and borrowing? Explain your answer.

c. Now suppose that $y = \$360$ and that the rest of the assumptions in this exercise are the same as in (b). Would you expect borrowing and lending to happen in this case? Explain your answer.

8. Consider an economy where a representative entrepreneur is active for three periods, and assume the following timing of events: At date 0, the bank lends an amount I to the entrepreneur (henceforth: the borrower), and she invests the entire loan in a project. At date 1, the borrower obtains a return y. If the borrower repays R_1 to the bank at date 1, she will be able to access a new loan I from the bank with certainty. Otherwise, she will be denied access to a new loan and therefore will not be able to execute the project. At date 2, the borrower faces exactly the same situation: if she invests at date 1, she will obtain a return y with certainty, otherwise she will get nothing. Only if she repays R_2, she is able to receive a loan in the second period, invest I again, and obtain a return y at date 3 with certainty. The borrower's discount factor is δ with $\delta < 1$ and $\delta y > I$, and the borrower's consumption decisions start at date 1. The gross cost of lending I for the bank is K. Assume that the bank sets $R_1 = R_2$, that it has a discount factor equal to 1, and that it just wants to break even. Suppose that the bank cannot verify the borrower's returns at date 1 and 2, but it knows that they should be y.

a. What is the minimum gross repayment R^* for each I loan at which the banks would be willing to lend?

b. What is the maximum gross interest repayment R^{**} for each I loan at which the borrowers would be willing to repay at date 1 and 2?

c. If $I = \$100$, $y = \$300$, $K = \$120$, and $\delta = 0.8$, is the bank willing to lend to the borrower at date 1 and date 2 and the borrower willing to pay back the bank at these two dates?

9. Consider an economy identical to that of the preceding exercise, except that in this economy there is a moral hazard problem: At date 0, provided the borrower puts in an adequate effort level with cost e, she can obtain a gross return y at date 1 with certainty. If the borrower does not put in any effort (so $e = 0$), she can get y with probability $p < 1$ and 0 with probability $1 - p$. The bank cannot verify the return realization of the borrower's project, but it knows that the return should be y. The bank sets a gross repayment R^* at date 1. If the borrower repays at date 1, the bank automatically extends a new loan, the terms of which are identical to those of the previous one. If granted a new loan, the borrower obtains a gross return y with certainty at date 2. Her discount factor is δ and she consumes at date 1 and 2 only. Assume that $\delta y > I$, and that borrowers are protected by limited liability. The gross cost of lending I for the bank is K, $K > I$, and $py < K < y$.

a. What are the conditions on R^* that the bank should set in order to elicit effort from the borrower at date 0, while ensuring that the borrower will be willing to repay at date 1?

b. If $K > \dfrac{\delta y}{2}$, will the bank lend to this potential entrepreneur?

10. Consider the same economy as in exercise 7, but suppose that we now have $y = \$380$, $\delta = 0.75$, and $K = \$150$. Assume that the bank is perfectly competitive, that the borrowers are protected by limited liability, and that the production technology has constant returns to scale (if the loan increases by a factor λ, the borrower's return will increase by a factor λ).

a. Will the bank be willing to extend loans in this case?

b. Now suppose that instead of extending the same loan at date 2, the bank can increase the size of the loan by a factor $\lambda = 1.5$ in period 2. Would you expect the bank to actually offer this contract? Briefly explain your answer.

11. Consider a two-period economy. Suppose that at date 0 a risk-neutral borrower obtains a loan I and invests it in a project which yields a gross return $I \cdot y$ at date 1 with probability p and 0 with probability $1 - p$, where p is exogenous. If the borrower repays her debt obligation R, the bank will offer her a new loan, λ times larger than the previous one, at date 1. If the borrower invests at date 1, her gross return at date 2 is $I \cdot y \cdot \lambda$ with probability p and 0 with probability $1 - p$. Assume that the borrower's production technology exhibits constant returns to scale, and that her discount factor is $\delta < 1$. The borrower's only source of income is the return realization on her project, and she is protected by limited liability.

a. Compute the maximum gross loan repayment R^* that the bank can set without undermining the borrower's incentives to repay at date 1.

b. Consider the case in which $I = \$100$, $\lambda = 1.5$, $y = 3.5$, $\delta = 0.8$, $p = 0.9$, and the gross cost of lending $1 for the bank is $1.2. Assume that the bank just wants to break even. Would you expect both parties to agree on a loan contract? Explain your answer.

12. Consider an economy similar to the one in exercise 9, but with the exception that in this one each borrower has wealth equal to w that can be used as collateral. In other words, if a borrower defaults on her debt obligations the bank can seize w. Define the gross repayment R^* that would enable the bank to elicit effort and debt repayments from the borrower at date 1. In what way does this result differ from the one obtained in exercise 9? Explain your answer.

13. Consider a two-period economy where risk-neutral entrepreneurs with no wealth carry out projects. These projects' return is π with probability p and 0 with probability $1 - p$. There is a bank that will finance the entrepreneurs' projects as long as it can at least break-even. The timing is as follows: At date 0, the bank makes a loan and the borrower makes her investment. At date 1, her project realizes a return, and if she repays her contractual debt obligation R, she is extended a new loan, which she invests in the project for a return at date 2. Define w_p and w_n as positive prizes and negative sanctions imposed by the community at date 1 if the borrower repays or defaults, respectively. Define v as the probability that the borrower will obtain financing for her investment at date 1; if at date 1 the borrower repays the debt obligation for her first loan, $v = 1$. Suppose that the bank's net cost of lending is 0 and that borrowers are protected by limited liability. Additionally, borrowers have a discount factor $\delta < 1$. Assuming that the probability p is exogenous, which means that there are not ex ante moral hazard problems.

a. Refer to the parameters v, w_p and w_n in the context of microfinance institutions in practice. What role does the level of urbanization of the communities where a microfinance institution operates play in this characterization?

b. State the incentive compatibility constraint (ICC) for a borrower. Interpret the role that v, w_p and w_n play in this restriction.

c. Conditional on the assumption that the ICC in (b) holds, state the individual rationality constraint for a borrower.

d. What is the maximum R that the bank can charge without undermining borrowers' incentives to repay? Consider that the bank can manage v.

e. Assume that p is no longer exogenous. Borrowers now can choose their level of effort, which determines the probability that their projects will succeed. The cost of effort to borrowers is given by:

$$c(p) = \frac{kp^2}{2}$$

Under this setup, what value of p will the borrower choose at equilibrium? What value of R will the bank set? As before, consider that the bank can manage v.

f. How could a microfinance institution manipulate v, w_p, w_n and π_{t+1} to provide borrowers with dynamic incentives to repay their loans? Provide concrete examples for each and relate your answer to the equilibrium values you obtained in (e).

14. Consider the case of a borrower with disposable weekly income x. This amount comes from outside sources—i.e., not from an investment the household is seeking microfinance funding to support. This outside income decays by the discount factor d each period, and if it isn't committed to loan repayments, it gets diverted into miscellaneous consumption expenses with probability $(1 - d)$ every week. Assume that these expenses carry no utility.

The bank must set the number of installments ($n = 52/T$) in which the loan will be repaid. T is the amount of time between installments; it is measured in weeks. If the loan is a year in duration, installments may be one time ($n = 1$, $T = 52$), monthly ($n = 12$, $T = 52/12$) or weekly ($n = 52$, $T = 1$), etc. The principal and interest to be repaid sum to the amount L. There is a transaction cost γ associated with each installment payment, borne by the borrower—in other words, each time the borrower pays an installment, she incurs a cost γ. Assuming linear preferences with respect to income, and assuming that the loan is no larger that the outside income that can be put towards loan repayment, the borrower would choose the frequency of installments T that maximize the size of her loan. This is her expected total payment to the bank minus her total transaction cost:

$$f(T) = \max_{T} \left\{ (1 + d + d^2 + \ldots + d^T) \frac{52x}{T} - \frac{52}{T}\gamma \right\}.$$

Assume that $\gamma = 0$, and show that $\forall T \in [1; 52]$, $T \in N$ the function will reach its maximum at $T = 1$. Explain the intuition behind your result.

15. Consider the previous question, and suppose that $\gamma = \$8$, $x = \$20.5$, and $d = 0.6$. Show that the function will still reach its maximum at $T = 1$.

6   Savings and Insurance

6.1 Introduction

Since the early days of microcredit in the 1970s, an influential group of rural financial specialists has argued instead that the priority should go to helping poor households save (e.g., Adams 1978). Microcredit was often dismissed as "microdebt." Wouldn't it be better, the experts asked, if households were helped to build assets rather than to take on more debt? Their argument, though, was no match for the accumulation of stories detailing the social and economic impacts derived from access to credit. Nor was it a match for the assertion that most poor households lack the resources to save in quantity. On top of that, most NGOs were legally able to lend to customers (and could sometimes do so at a profit) but were by law restricted from accepting saving deposits.

The pro-saving argument thus did not go far, and the previous two chapters of this book reflect the emphasis on lending. Three decades later, however, the momentum is moving behind saving, signaled most clearly by the fact that the term *microfinance* has replaced *microcredit* as the most favored catch-all description of efforts to bank the poor.

The change reflects more than mere terminology: the transition from *microcredit* to *microfinance* has brought a change of outlook, a growing realization that low-income households can benefit from access to a broader set of financial services beyond just credit. One result is that new initiatives are under way to create deposit accounts with terms and features that appeal to low-income customers. *Safe*Save, a cooperative working in the slums of Dhaka, for example, sends its sixty-four staff members out on daily rounds, during which customers are visited in their homes or businesses. Each day, customers can choose to make deposits, pay down loans, or to make no transactions at all. There are no limits to how big or small the daily transactions must be. The bank in this case comes to the customers, placing convenience and flexibility for customers above convenience for the staff, and by September 2008 *Safe*Save had established a client base of 13,000 people who live and work in Dhaka's poorest neighborhoods. Each month, they process over 100,000 small transactions.[1]

On a far larger scale, Bank Rakyat Indonesia (BRI), a long-established state-controlled bank, had built a customer base of over 21 million depositors at the end of 2007, achieved by reducing minimum opening amounts and required balances, and by creating a network of nearly 4,100 small suboffices. Most Indonesians can now find a BRI location in the nearest town center.[2] Thailand's large state-owned Bank of Agriculture and Agricultural Cooperatives (BAAC) has followed BRI's lead, and the model has been discussed as a prospect for bank reforms in India and China. In other countries, postal savings services are allowing customers to easily make deposits at their local post office, and the Brussels-based World Savings Bank Institute (WSBI) is promoting over 2,000 regional savings institutions in 92 countries.

The growing focus on saving reorients conversations on microfinance and opens new paths for economics. No area has been as influenced by behavioral economics, the branch of economics at the overlap with psychology (e.g., Thaler 1990; Thaler and Sunstein 2008). Behavioral economists depart from key assumptions that have for decades formed part of the DNA of economics. One casualty is the assumption that people always have perfect foresight and can reliably execute their saving strategies. Behavioral economists instead take seriously that people often have problems with self-discipline. We are only human: we procrastinate, we give in to temptation, and we avoid complexity. As a result, behavioral economists argue, we routinely make choices that are not clearly optimal from the perspective of neo-classical economics, nor even consistent with our own ideals.

"Time-inconsistency" (and the self-control conflict that it often implies) can explain why so many people—rich and poor—save less than they wish to save. But, far more interestingly, behavioral economics shows the hidden logic of successful financial strategies. By taking psychology seriously, we can start to see the value of self-commitment devices of various kinds (the use of ROSCAS as discipline mechanisms is one example we already saw in chapter 3) and we can start to understand seemingly illogical but common behaviors (like taking expensive loans rather than simply drawing down savings accounts). New research based on behavioral insights points to improved designs for saving products that can help poor households save in greater quantities than they would otherwise. The work shows that mechanisms matter: the propensity to save a lot or a little depends in part on the quality of the financial tools available. By definition, the state of being poor means having less money than richer households. In practice, it also means having less reliable and less effective ways to hold onto the money you have (Collins, Morduch, Rutherford et al. 2009).

Recognizing the importance of imperfections in savings devices can help explain some important puzzles—just as credit market imperfections explain other longstanding puzzles. Indeed, we argue in this chapter that the presence of savings imperfections helps to explain one of the most important puzzles of microfinance: the persistence of credit market imperfections. After all, basic economic theory dictates that forward-looking households ought to be able to save their way out of credit constraints if given enough time. The deeper problem may be with overlooked difficulties in saving. This line of thinking shifts the conceptual frame for microfinance.

Some have taken this line even further. Robinson (2001, 21), for example, argues that deposit services are *more* valuable than credit for poorer households. The argument reflects recognition that having assets is a huge benefit for households, rich and poor alike. But it ignores the original insight behind microcredit—i.e., that saving is hard and that credit can deliver needed capital today, not after waiting for savings to accumulate for five or ten or twenty years. The financial diaries reported in Collins et al. (2009) show households at all income levels—from below $1 a day per person to close to $10 a day per person—actively saving *and* borrowing. The two activities often go hand in hand: major investments and crises are typically financed by drawing down savings if you have them and borrowing if you can. For this reason, we reject the priority placed on facilitating saving *instead* of credit. Both are important, even for the poorest.

Much of the borrowing by the poorest households in the financial diaries is for non-business purposes, as is much of the saving. Recognizing the importance of both borrowing and saving for the very poor requires letting go of the notion that borrowing is demanded mainly for business purposes. At the end of the chapter we describe ways that microfinance institutions are creating new emergency loans and other credit products that expand the idea of microcredit and facilitate consumption smoothing.

The fundamental idea that "mechanisms matter" drives recent interest in insurance as well, putting renewed emphasis on product innovation. Insuring farmers against the ups and downs of rainfall, for example, has shown promise relative to traditional crop insurance strategies. Rainfall insurance neatly eliminates concerns with moral hazard and adverse selection, the ubiquitous incentive problems outlined in chapter 2. The ideas are evolving and, as we write this second edition, a "breakthrough" implementation has yet to take place. One problem, highlighted by behavioral perspectives, is overcoming low demand associated with the complexity of products. New ideas in health insurance are emerging too, but they remain relatively small in scale. The promise of a "microinsurance revolution" is exciting but as yet unrealized (Morduch 2006).

We begin by setting the scene in section 6.2. The first part of the chapter examines savings in greater detail, and, in the process, illuminates tensions in modern views of household economies in poor areas. Section 6.3 turns to the varied motivations to save and section 6.4 makes the argument for taking saving constraints seriously. Doing so helps explain the puzzles described in section 6.5: why rotating savings and credit associations (ROSCAs) are so popular as informal financial mechanisms and how savings constraints help explain their workings. Sections 6.5 and 6.6 describe insights from behavioral economics, pointing to new innovations that encourage saving, and section 6.7 describes supply-side challenges. Section 6.8 turns to microinsurance and 6.9 describes credit as a risk management tool.

6.2 Microsaving

From the start, microlenders like Grameen Bank created savings accounts for all clients, but the accounts came with so many strings attached that they hardly looked like savings accounts. Most important, a fixed fraction of loans disbursed had to be deposited into the accounts, and funds in those accounts could only be withdrawn upon leaving the program. For example, in 2000 at the Shakti Foundation for Women—a replicator of the Grameen model in the slums of Dhaka and Chittagong, Bangladesh—compulsory savings included a group tax of 5 percent of the loan principal and weekly compulsory savings of 10 taka (about 20 cents), half of which went into the "Centre Fund" and half of which went into a personal account.[3] The latter account could be accessed at any time, but the other accounts could only be touched when the client left the program—and only if the client had been in for five years or more. A survey of over nine hundred women showed that only 13 percent of its current clients were dissatisfied with this arrangement, but 40 percent were unhappy among those who dropped out.

In principle, the compulsory saving program is meant to help clients build up assets over time and develop the discipline of saving. But to many, these involuntary savings accounts look instead like a way for the bank to acquire relatively cheap capital and to secure a form of collateral from borrowers (since the microlender can seize accumulated savings if the borrower tries to quit the program while in default). It seems like a smart strategy for the microbank, but it is several steps removed from providing the kind of fully voluntary savings possibilities that more affluent customers of traditional commercial banks take for granted (and that are featured, for example, by Bank Rakyat Indonesia). These compulsory savings programs are also several steps away from the kinds of commitment savings devices that customers may voluntarily opt into with a clear end-date when the savings can be withdrawn. With little available in the way of client-driven savings products, it is understandable that many people in the field still speak of microcredit rather than microfinance.

Today, though, the term *microfinance* is used far more frequently (even in the title of this book), and most practitioners accept that low-income households deserve better (i.e., more flexible and convenient) ways to save and insure on top of better ways to borrow. The Grameen Bank itself has radically reversed course, for example, and introduced "Grameen Bank II" in 2001 (Dowla and Barua 2006). In addition to new, flexible loan products, "Grameen Bank II" introduces new, flexible savings products (and a popular way to save over the long-term, the Grameen Pension Scheme). The savings products are marketed to a broader community than just current borrowers, and by February 2009 Grameen was holding deposits equal to 139 percent of its loan portfolio, allowing it to substantially reduce reliance on external financing.[4] The potential benefits of these steps are large.

One example of the power of access to saving accounts was documented in Kenya. In October 2004, a bank opened in Bumala market, a market town along the highway that connects Nairobi, Kenya to Kampala, Uganda. But a year later, fewer than 1 percent of daily income earners had opened an account. The fee to open an account was seen as too high (450 Kenya shillings, about $7 at the time) and the bank was poorly marketed. Overall, just 2 percent of residents had any account in any commercial bank. So in 2006 and 2007, a research team offered to open accounts for a randomly chosen sample of 122 men and women, paying all opening fees. A small group refused (13 percent), and a larger group opened the account but never made a deposit (42 percent). But many others used the account regularly, and the activity of the treatment group was compared to a randomly-selected control group of 81 men and women that did not get accounts. Dupas and Robinson (2008) find that access to the accounts had substantial positive impacts on investment for women, increasing average daily productive investment by about 40 percent ($1.60). But there was substantial heterogeneity: only about half of the women made more than one transaction in the first 6 months after opening the account. For men, there was no impact on investment.

The changes were important for many of the women, however, and the increases in investment for the women paralleled increases in average expenditures. Average daily food expenditures, for example, rose by 13 to 28 percent, an increase consistent with the notion that higher investment levels led to higher income levels. Women with access to savings accounts also appeared better able to cope with health shocks. For these women, access to a safe, convenient bank account made a difference compared to life relying on ROSCAs, saving in livestock, and other informal-sector strategies. The positive findings emerged despite the fact that hefty fees for making withdrawals meant that the bank in Bumala accounts had de facto negative interest rates on savings. The evidence does not say that saving is *more* important than borrowing, but it does say that being able to save can matter substantially.

6.3 Why Save?

The traditional rationale for promoting saving is centered on asset accumulation, but this is too narrow. By the traditional view, savings deposits are valued to the extent that they allow households to build up substantial funds for investment, retirement, and other major outlays. Such long-term accumulation surely matters, but the view obscures a more immediate need for saving by poor households: even if the average household does not accumulate vast sums from year to year, saving can still be an important way to manage resources within a year and across seasons. With savings, not only can households build up assets to use as collateral, but they can also better smooth seasonal consumption needs, finance major expenditures such as school fees, self-insure against major shocks, and self-finance investments.

Table 6.1 reports on a survey of households in Indonesia, for example, that shows that low-income households planned to use their savings for business uses, building up assets, and for future consumption. Nearly as many were saving for working capital (13 percent) as were saving to pay school fees (14 percent) and for general household consumption (13 percent). Savings are mainly used to facilitate large, lumpy expenditures occurring in the short or medium term, but they are also used for long-term needs. Most academic work on the economics of saving begins with these latter needs, building analysis around the "life-cycle" model which describes "low-frequency" saving behavior over the very long term. We turn to this first, and in section 6.3.2 we turn to "high-frequency" saving for the near term.

Table 6.1
Reported uses for savings

	Percentage reporting as primary use
Business uses	16
Working capital	13
Finance new business	0
Buy building, equipment	2
Buy vehicle	1
Nonbusiness consumption	35
School fees	14
Medical expenses	3
Household consumption	13
Purchase jewelry	0
Wedding/funeral/etc.	2
Religious holiday	3
Finance and assets	6
Purchase land	1
Purchase housing	5
Pay loan	0
Other use or not applicable	39

Source: 2000 survey of 201 BRI clients. Calculations by Jonathan Morduch. The sample was drawn from representative regions; results are not weighted to reflect different population levels across sampling units.

6.3.1 "Low-Frequency" Saving

Most households in high-income countries proceed in similar ways: get educated (perhaps borrowing in order to pay for it), get a first job, start saving for later in life, start a family, move up the ladder at work (or move on to other jobs), raise the family, continue saving, retire, then draw down savings, and possibly, leave a bequest. The model in its starkest form implies that households should borrow when very young, save aggressively when in middle age, and dissave when older. Optimal behavior should yield fairly flat consumption over time, rather than ups and downs that track the ups and downs of income and retirement (Ando and Modigliani 1963).

The model does a reasonable job of explaining savings behavior in middle-income and higher-income countries, but it's not perfect. For example, just when the model predicts households should save most for retirement (in the peak-earning years of middle age), households tend to be hit with large demands like college tuitions for their children, the costs of weddings, and so forth. And since much saving takes the form of investing in one's own house, only tracking financial assets will miss much of the story. Also, when young, risk-averse households are typically reluctant to live much beyond their means, even if they might reasonably predict that their incomes will be much higher in the future. Still, all in all, the model provides a reasonable benchmark.[5]

The model's predictive success is much worse in lower-income countries. One of the often-cited reasons is that the model is designed to describe the behavior of nuclear families, not the complex, multigenerational households that often live and eat together in more traditional (low-income) economies. Instead of a standard household with two parents and children, we are as likely to see households that combine grandparents, parents, and grandchildren all living under the same roof or in the same compound. So in multigenerational households, as family members age, as some are born and others die, the average age of the household may hold fairly steady over time. Thus the ups and downs of income (followed by retirement) experienced by a typical household head poorly represents the income flowing into the household as a whole. Another reason that the life-cycle model has less bite in impoverished regions is that retirement periods tend to be shorter than in more affluent countries, with older family members often working close to the end of their lives.

Kochar (1996) takes a close look at cross-sectional data on 4,734 households in Pakistan, in a survey collected as part of the World Bank Living Standards Measurement Survey (LSMS) project. She finds that the plot of the incomes of intergenerational households over time (i.e., as the household head gets older), does not match the pattern of increasing and then decreasing income that emerges when doing the same plot for nuclear households. In fact, the plot for intergenerational households looks as if there was a single, infinitely lived household with steady income over time. That is, it looks as if households continually rebundle themselves as they add and lose members, doing so in a way that minimizes variation in the household's average age and demographic structure. It seems that rather than smoothing consumption by borrowing and saving, the household smoothes its income by rebundling; in this case, if the household simply consumed all of its income in each period, consumption patterns would also be similarly smooth. And if a household can smooth its income, it has little motivation to save for life-cycle purposes; that is, it has little need to borrow and save to make consumption smoother. Simple within-household transfers (e.g., from an adult child to her co-resident elderly parents) should instead be the best means to achieve optimal consumption patterns. If this is the case, life-cycle saving motives are weak in this population.

Remember, though, that the evidence comes from a cross-section of households. The plot has household income on the vertical axis and the household head's age on the horizontal axis; the plot does not actually map changes over time for the same households—since, unfortunately, we lack such data. Instead, the plot shows patterns of different households at a single point in time. The question is whether the cross-sectional plot closely approximates what happens over time to a single family. Kochar (1996) argues that it does not, and this is because, as described previously, relatively few people spend all of their lives in intergenerational households. In particular, Kochar finds that household heads under forty-five are in fact most likely to reside with their nuclear families. This is so for about 80 percent of household heads in their thirties. But after the age of forty-five, the picture shifts sharply so that about 80 percent of household heads who are in their fifties and sixties live instead in intergenerational households (defined as having at least one father co-residing with an adult son or son-in-law). Nuclear households average six members while intergenerational households average nine (three of which are, on average, adult males). In a typical pattern, newly married men live with their parents (and maybe wife and children), but by about age thirty, the young family splits off to form their own nuclear household. Later, as the sons of the nuclear family grow older and marry, an intergenerational household is formed again. The result is that at various points in the life cycle (particularly in one's thirties and forties) there may remain a keen desire to save up over the long term—even in a country like Pakistan where intergenerational households are so common.

The observation helps to explain the popularity of the Grameen Pension Scheme (GPS) in Bangladesh, where intergenerational households are also prevalent. The GPS was introduced in 2001, and although it is called a "pension," the GPS can be used by people of any age. In the GPS, every Grameen borrower with a loan larger than 8,000 taka (about $138) must contribute at least 50 taka (86 cents) per month. Ten years later, the borrower will receive nearly twice the amount (Yunus 2002), earning 12 percent per year in compound interest and ultimately getting back 187 percent of their deposits at the end of the decade (Grameen Bank 2002, note 13.02). Given a low rate of inflation, the return is generous and clients will be able to build up tidy sums through the power of compound interest.

As points of comparison, Grameen's Fixed Deposit savings scheme, for example, which was started in May 2000, pays 8.75 percent to 9.5 percent in annual interest for deposits of one- to three-year durations (Grameen Bank 2002, note 13.01). ASA's deposit rate is 6 percent (Ahmmed 2002, 91), and turning to external sources of funds for comparison, the *Palli Karma Sahayak* Foundation (PKSF) a Bangladesh apex organization, provides microcredit institutions with funding at 7 percent per year. The commercial loan rate is roughly 10–11 percent at minimum (and some businesses pay about 14–15 percent)—and that does not entail the cost of collecting and administering millions of small deposits. The GPS is thus relatively generous, but the high return must be balanced against the restrictions on withdrawals.

While the GPS is compulsory, it also turns out to be popular with customers in its own right.[6] Attractive features are a low minimum monthly installment and a mechanism built around a fixed, structured commitment to saving. In this, the GPS shares features of the ROSCAs described in chapter 3. Unlike the ROSCAs, though, the commitment to the GPS is not short-lived. Ten years is a long time, and the GPS has not yet been operating long enough to know how households will manage to meet their obligations in stressful times. From a financial perspective, the scheme provides a steady inflow of cash for the bank, with early reports that it was bringing in over 100 million taka (U.S. $1.75 million) each month in its early years (Yunus 2002, 14). If Grameen can keep costs down, its clients will benefit considerably from the ability to stow away the money—and Grameen will gain access to a new trove of funds with a bill not due for years.[7]

6.3.2 "High-Frequency" Saving

Low-frequency saving (steady, long-term accumulation) is only part of the savings picture. Another important part is "high-frequency" saving to fund short-term investments and to smooth consumption from month to month or from season to season. Evidence on BURO, a microfinance institution in Bangladesh, for example, shows that even when average balances do not grow much, an open-access savings account may be very popular and very intensively used. At the end of 2000, for example, BURO held just under 27 million taka (about US$290,000) in general savings, a figure that had grown by less than 2 million taka over the year. But the owners of these accounts hadn't been idle—they had deposited more than 62 million taka and withdrawn more than 60 million taka during the year. Similarly, simulations of consumption-smoothing behavior (reducing year-to-year consumption swings by saving and dissaving), described by Deaton (1992), show that effective and active consumption-smoothing may be achieved even with low levels of average assets.

The financial diaries described by Collins et al. (2009) reveal this pattern clearly. In their intensive, year-long studies of poor households in Bangladesh, India, and South Africa, Collins et al. (2009) mainly find low savings balances. The median year-end value in their Bangladesh sample, for example, was $68. In India, it was $115, and $472 in South Africa. The asset levels are relatively small even after adjusting for differences in purchasing power in different countries. When converted using "purchasing power parity" (PPP) exchange rates that approximate equivalences to the cash needed in the United States to buy the same goods and services, the median asset values rise to just $293 for the Bangladesh sample, $637 for India and $1128 for South Africa. But Collins et al. (2009) argue that the year-end balances hide the importance of savings in the economic lives of the "diary" households. The researchers measure "turnover" as the combined flows moving into and out of saving devices, and find that turnover levels are ten times the year-end asset values in rural Bangladesh, 16 times higher in rural South Africa, and 33 times higher in rural India. The ratios in urban areas were lower but still substantial.

This kind of high-frequency saving has generated the most interest by academics investigating saving in lower-income economies, following the lead of Deaton (1992). By and large, they have found that households are both eager to save in the face of recurrent shocks but also that households have problems doing so.

Evidence comes mainly from tests of the permanent-income hypothesis using household survey data. The permanent-income hypothesis was developed by Milton Friedman in the 1950s as a simple characterization of how a rational, forward-looking household would choose to borrow and save when confronted by uncertain future income. Friedman observed that incomes go up and down over time, but some of the changes are permanent (e.g., you get a promotion at work based on your newly acquired skills) while some are transitory (e.g., sales were unusually good this year and your firm gives everyone an especially plump end-of-year bonus). Friedman argues that you should enjoy the permanent changes (assuming they are positive) and increase your expenditures accordingly. But a prudent household should save the transitory increases, expecting downturns later.[8] And when transitory downturns happen, rational households will draw upon savings or borrow in order to maintain fairly steady consumption levels over time. Households facing a lot of income variability—for example, farmers in the semi-arid tropics that stretch across Africa and South Asia—will thus find themselves spending a lot of time trying to smooth consumption.

How well do they do? Before getting to the evidence, we describe the simple idea at the heart of empirical approaches, and then apply it to reality. The basic idea is that if you know that in one year you will earn $4,000 and in the next you will earn $6,000—and if your consumption needs are identical in both years—you would do better to borrow $1,000 and to consume $5,000 each year. The insight in economic terms is that you want to "equalize the marginal utility of consumption in each period." Rather than starting with the idea that you necessarily want to equalize consumption, start with the idea that if spending a dollar now will give you more benefit than holding on to that dollar until later, you should spend it today. And you should keep on spending today until you get to the point at which you are just indifferent between spending the extra dollar now or saving it for later. In our simple example, this is the point at which you consume $5,000 in both years. However, in more complicated models that take changing needs into account, consumption levels need not be equalized—but the "marginal utility" of consumption in all periods should be. Conversely, you should save today if you will benefit more from spending the dollars later—again, up to the point when marginal utility is equal in all periods.

Your choices, of course, must not lead you to exceed your total lifetime resources, which include your current income as well as your assets and any future income that you are able to borrow against. Making the example more realistic involves bringing in (a) the interest rate for borrowing and saving; (b) a discount rate wherein future consumption may be judged to be intrinsically less valuable than consuming right now; and (c) the fact that when you make choices today, you don't know how tomorrow will turn out—you only have your best guess.[9]

Putting this together yields a formal representation of the solution to how much to borrow and how much to save. If you could perfectly smooth consumption, you would want to set the marginal utility of consumption in period t equal to the *expected* marginal value of consumption in a later period $t + 1$ (where the expectation is formed in period t):

$$MU_t = (1+r)/(1+\delta)E_t[MU_{t+1}], \tag{6.1}$$

Where MU_t is the marginal utility of consumption in period t; r is the net interest rate on loans or deposits (assumed to be identical) between the two periods; δ is the discount rate; and $E_t[\cdot]$ indicates that we are interested in the expected value of the item within brackets.

The equation yields a striking conclusion: If you could make choices without constraint (i.e., if you can borrow and save without restriction as long as you don't end up consuming more than you earn or inherit over your lifetime), your consumption choices should be fully independent of when your income arrives. If this year is an unusually bad year, you should borrow—or draw down your savings—to maintain desired consumption levels. And, similarly, you should save when income is unusually good. Equation (6.1) should hold perfectly if markets work perfectly. But imagine that you had difficulty borrowing and saving (for all of the reasons discussed in this book). Then:

$$MU_t = (1+r)/(1+\delta)E_t[MU_{t+1}] + \lambda_{t+1}, \tag{6.2}$$

where $\lambda_{t+1} \neq 0$ reflects the extent of difficulties. When you have difficulty borrowing and saving, your consumption patterns over time
will mirror your income patterns more closely than you would like.
When that is so, λ_{t+1}, the measure of how much your consumption
choices depart from the optimum degree of smoothness, should be
correlated with your transitory income. After making assumptions
about the shape of utility functions, it is possible to learn about λ_{t+1} in
practice.

The trouble is that we do not actually observe λ_{t+1}, thus we have to
make inferences indirectly. There are two relevant cases. In the first,
you face a constraint on the amount that you wish to borrow. Going
back to the example we started with, say that this year your income is
$4,000, and next year it is $6,000—and again ignore interest rates, discount rates, and expectations error. You would like to borrow $1,000,
but are unable to find a willing lender. So, in the extreme case of abso-
lutely no borrowing possibilities at all, you end up consuming $4,000
this year and $6,000 the next. In terms of marginal utility, the marginal
utility of consuming an extra dollar today exceeds that of consuming
that same dollar next year. You would like to set $MU_t = E_t[MU_{t+1}]$, but
instead $MU_t > E_t[MU_{t+1}]$. So it must be, by equation (6.2), that $\lambda_{t+1} < 0$.
Conversely, if you face difficulty saving and this year's income is $6,000
and next year's is $4,000, $MU_t < E_t[MU_{t+1}]$ and by equation (6.2), it must
be that $\lambda_{t+1} > 0$.

With these pieces in place, we can see that when you face a borrowing constraint—that is, in the first example here—the lower your initial
income, the faster consumption levels will grow between periods.
Here, the $4,000 first-year income meant a $2,000 jump between periods
from $4,000 to $6,000. If, instead, income had been distributed $3,000
in year one and $7,000 in year two, there would have been a $4,000
expected jump. Thus, lower initial income is associated with a larger
jump in consumption. To bring matters back to the measure of borrowing constraints, the more negative the correlation is between initial
income and consumption growth, the greater the likelihood is that λ_{t+1}
< 0. If there is no correlation between initial income and consumption
growth, it is fair to assume that $\lambda_{t+1} = 0$, and there are no systematic
borrowing constraints. An important hypothesis is that where borrowing constraints are likely to bind most tightly—for the most impoverished citizens with least collateral—the negative correlation between
initial income and consumption growth should be greatest. For higher-
income households, the correlation should be noticeably smaller.

This is indeed the pattern typically seen. It turns out that for higher-income households, even in lower-income areas like the rain-fed villages of South India, constraints turn out to be small. But for poorer households, the constraints can bind tightly as demonstrated by a large, negative coefficient on the initial income variable in a regression that captures the spirit of the previous discussion. Morduch (1994), for example, reports that landless and near-landless households in rural South India are able to smooth away just a small part of transitory income shocks. This pushes the households to try smoothing income by making more conservative agricultural choices, pushing them to more likely adopt traditional cropping choices, for example, rather than riskier but more profitable high-yielding varieties. Similarly, in rural China, Jalan and Ravallion (1999) find that the bottom 10 percent of households can protect themselves from only 60 percent of adverse income shocks, while the top 10 percent cope well with all but 10 percent. Accumulating evidence from other parts of the world is telling similar stories: The poorest households seek means to address high-frequency fluctuations, but the means are far from perfect.[10]

6.4 Taking Saving Constraints Seriously

While Collins et al. (2009) find that savings devices are used actively by their study households in Bangladesh, India, and South Africa, the devices are nonetheless imperfect in important ways. In particular, the devices are often unreliable (an informal-sector savings club may break up, for example, or money may be stolen), inconvenient, inflexible, and inappropriately structured.

If we go back to the discussion on formal tests for consumption-smoothing, we can see an angle that reveals a place for savings constraints. While most researchers in the consumption-smoothing literature interpret the negative coefficients on initial income as evidence of borrowing constraints, the evidence can also be explained by the presence of savings constraints. In the case of savings constraints, $\lambda_{t+1} > 0$, and households with transitorily high incomes are forced to consume more today than they would like. Consumption growth between today and later periods is thus negative, so again, a negative correlation is generated between income today and subsequent consumption growth. This negative correlation is generally interpreted as a sign that there are borrowing constraints ($\lambda_{t+1} < 0$), but the evidence is consistent with $\lambda_{t+1} > 0$ as well. It remains for future work to better distinguish between the scenarios.[11]

Such savings constraints do not yet have a prominent place in academic explanations of why poor people stay poor, and responsibility rests with two somewhat conflicting attitudes, both of which are due a reassessment. First is the assumption that there is little desire by lower-income households to save: namely, that very poor households are simply too impoverished to save (e.g., Bhaduri 1973). At one level, the logic seems tight: Immediate consumption needs must take priority for households at the brink of subsistence, leaving little (or no) surplus to save for tomorrow. According to this logic, the need to save is far less important than the desire to borrow.

The second assumption, in contrast, is that there are plenty of informal ways to save for those who want to; so, once again, the lack of a formal savings bank is not an immediate cause for concern. Households do indeed use a wide array of informal mechanisms for accumulation, including using money guards (typically a reliable neighbor who holds on to extra cash, and, importantly, gets it out of one's house and away from temptations); rotating savings and credit associations (ROSCAs) described here and in chapter 3; purchasing jewelry and other fairly liquid assets; and, simplest of all, hiding places to stash money at home.[12]

More important may be the less visible ways of saving, such as self-financing a business and purchasing equipment and livestock that—similar to jewelry—can be sold in times of need. In principle, if lower-income households are constrained in their abilities to borrow, they should simply put extra cash directly into their own businesses, typically earning far higher returns than that on money put in the bank. For these reasons—and for the fact that borrowing can yield faster access to a bigger lump of money than waiting to accumulate it by oneself—it was generally perceived that improving the ability to borrow should take precedence over improving the ability to save.

So, why are these positions now up for grabs? First, even very poor households have good reason to save. Basu (1997) points to a logical flaw in Bhaduri's (1973) argument: If they are forward-looking, even the poorest households should see the virtue of saving (even if it is just a bit at a time) so that over the long term they can escape from the constraints imposed by being so close to subsistence. Probably more important in practice is the fact that most households below the poverty line are in truth fairly far from the brink of subsistence. They would have little scope for saving if measures of poverty could be taken literally (where the poverty line is rooted strictly in a notion of minimal needs for subsistence), but poverty measures are only approximate tools. Evidence is mounting that many households well below the poverty line are indeed interested in saving. The slum dwellers of Dhaka who day-by-day contribute their pennies to *Safe*Save accounts testify to the demand for saving services once a well-designed program is in place.

The second statement, that households have sufficient informal means to save, has also been taken apart. Many households are reluctant to tie up all their money in their own risky businesses. Those businesses may not function all year, and investments may be difficult to withdraw in times of need. Other informal means to save may also be risky or may be otherwise burdensome. When a locality as a whole is hit with a crisis, for example, the local market can get flooded with jewelry and assets as households desperately try to generate income. As Dercon (1999) finds in data from Africa, the returns to the assets used by households for "saving" are often positively correlated with incomes. So, when incomes fall, the value of assets fall in turn, and the savings strategy ends up being of only limited help. Saving cash under the mattress or in a secret hiding place would be a better strategy when many in a region are affected by shocks at the same time, but cash is vulnerable to erosion through inflation, and, often more important, through theft or the simple inability to keep temptation at bay. One study (Wright and Mutesasira 2001) in Uganda showed that for 99 percent of households the average loss in savings *per year* was 22 percent.[13]

The figure from Uganda helps to put into perspective the implicit interest rates charged by deposit collectors. Consider the case of Jyothi, a deposit collector in the southeastern Indian town of Vijayawada described by Rutherford (2000). Jyothi works in the slums, and mainly with women. Her job is to take clients' surplus funds, hold them securely, and return the funds (less a fee) at the end of an agreed-upon period. In a typical pattern, Jyothi's clients agree to save a little bit each day for 220 days. The daily amount is fixed, and at the end of the 220 days Jyothi gives her clients the money that they have accumulated— less the fee, which in this case is 9 percent of the total. So if, as in Rutherford's example, a client agreed to save five rupees each day for 220 days, she would end the period with 1,100 rupees. Jyothi then keeps 100 rupees as a fee and hands over the remaining 1,000 rupees to the client. In the meantime, Jyothi holds the savings. The effective cost of her services (taking into account the timing of transactions and putting figures into annualized terms) is equivalent to an annual interest rate on deposits of roughly negative 30 percent per year. The poor women in the slums of Vijayawada are clearly willing to pay well in order to secure safe, convenient savings services.

6.5   Saving and Self Discipline: Lessons from Behavioral Economics

Microcredit proponents insist that credit constraints pose fundamental problems for poor households. So why don't households just save their way out of credit constraints? Economic theory argues that households should, for the same reason that Basu (1997) argues that households should save their way out of subsistence constraints. Theoretical work by Bewley (1976) shows that a credit-constrained household that acts with foresight will always slowly and steadily accumulate until credit constraints are overcome. A similar argument is made by de Meza and Webb (2001) in the context of adverse selection in credit markets. De Meza and Webb argue that when households face credit constraints due to adverse selection (of a sort described in chapter 2), the household always does better if it can wait a bit before investing. Waiting allows the household to accumulate more wealth; and thus to invest more and generate higher income. De Meza and Webb show that it is prudent to prolong waiting until credit constraints disappear altogether.[14] In practice, then, if households can save, we should never see binding credit constraints in equilibrium. These results come from theoretical models and rely on abstractions from reality, but they pose an important challenge: Why does reality seem to look so different? Why are credit constraints so commonly cited in practice?

One immediate response, again from a theoretical perspective, is that households may simply be too impatient to save enough. As Deaton (1992, section 6.2) demonstrates, as long as households are suitably keen to consume today rather than waiting until tomorrow, credit constraints can persist. Specifically, Deaton's notion of impatience flows from the assumption that the rate at which a household discounts future consumption is greater than the interest rate on deposits. In the context of equations (6.1) and (6.2), this means that $\delta > r$.

In this case, households will prefer to consume the marginal dollar rather than save it for later. But why assume that households are so impatient? The assumption stretches plausibility if it is true that households "save" largely by self-financing investments that have large marginal returns to capital (an assumption that is consistent with the typical interest rates on loans charged by microlenders; *Safe*Save, for example, charges 36–48 percent per year). On the other hand, if we take seriously the idea that households have difficulty finding convenient, reliable means to save, and, as in the case of Jyothi the deposit collector, are even prepared to receive *negative* interest on deposits, Deaton's framework becomes perfectly plausible. Discount rates exceed interest rates on deposits because effective interest rates are so low, not because discount rates are necessarily so high.

A different explanation for the inability to save one's way out of credit constraints involves risk. Persistent negative shocks can keep wiping out assets and make accumulation all but impossible. In theory, households should still be able to adequately accumulate in the very long term, but in a risky environment this could require an implausibly long horizon.

A final explanation is put forward by Platteau (2000) based on observations of village institutions in Africa. Platteau argues that difficulties in saving may have origins in social arrangements. Consider, for example, informal risk-sharing arrangements based on reciprocal claims such that you agree to help your neighbors and family when they need assistance, and they agree to help you in return. A problem arises, though, when your neighbors and family assert that they are in need and put claims on your surpluses, preventing you from saving for your own personal gain. Their incentives may in fact be to keep you from accumulating since, once you get wealthy enough, your own incentive could be to bow out of the mutual insurance arrangement and to self-insure. In order to keep the arrangement together, your surpluses thus get "taxed" by the community, making it difficult to save over the long term.[15]

These earlier arguments explain why households may have difficulty accumulating for personal or social reasons. Part of the problem may also be that households lack safe, secure, convenient institutions in which to save. Putting the two issues together takes us to product design. Given the many purposes that individuals save for, and given the varying constraints and objectives they face, a single product design is surely not best for all. Some individuals will do best with a savings account that maximizes flexibility. Others will do better with an account that is more rigid. Insights from behavioral economics suggest that others may do better with both.

6.5.1   Reinterpreting ROSCAs

Insights from behavioral economics can already be seen in the way that informal mechanisms operate. To see that, we continue the discussion of informal rotating savings and credit associations that started in chapter 3. There, we pointed to the use of ROSCAs as methods to save rather than primarily as means to borrow, an observation given support by a survey of ROSCA participants in Bangladesh (Rutherford 1997) and in southeast Asia (Guérin 2010). One can go further, though, and argue that the very existence of ROSCAs—why they do not fall apart—must rest in their value as vehicles for saving (at least for the kinds of ROSCAs that we see most commonly).

In the ROSCAs described in chapter 3, a group of neighbors join together to raise funds, with each person contributing a fixed amount to a pool of money collected weekly or monthly. Each member of the group gets one turn to receive the entire pool until everyone in the group has had an opportunity. One problem with this scheme is that the very last recipient of the pot would appear to have no incentive to participate—because she could instead simply save the money on her own, week after week, and in the end be just as well off as she would have been if she had participated in the ROSCA. The last recipient may even be better off on her own, since she would be free from the rigid structure and schedule of the ROSCA rules. Hence, there is no clear economic gain from ROSCA participation for the last recipient.

The problem is that someone has to be last. And if no one is willing to be last, there can be no ROSCA. The thing falls apart. But ROSCAs are common around the globe, serving as a mainstay of informal economies. Why? One explanation is that the last recipient may not in fact be able to "simply save the money on their own" as previously assumed. As Anderson and Baland (2002) suggest (based on a survey in Nairobi), married female ROSCA members would otherwise have difficulty protecting savings from their husbands' grabbing hands. Or, as Gugerty (2007) argues (also based on data from Kenya), the discipline and communal nature help ROSCA participants accumulate savings in a regular, structured way. Collins et al. (2009) report similarly: in South Africa, even people with savings accounts in local banks often achieve their savings goals by participating in the neighborhood ROSCA (and then might put part of their pot in the bank). In short, ROSCAs may well owe their existence to poor households' desires to save—and their very imperfect alternative options. ROSCAs may thus be a response to the failure of the "market for savings" as much as they are a response to credit market failure (Basu 2008a). [16]

6.5.2 Impatience and Hyperbolic Discounting

The idea that discipline may be attractive only makes sense when self-discipline is a problem. A series of academic studies (outside of the context of microfinance) show how this might be so—e.g., Laibson (1997), Gul and Pesendorfer (2004), Thaler (1990), Thaler and Sunstein (2008). One of the core ideas rests with "hyperbolic discounting." The essential idea is that people may think differently about choices that matter today compared to choices about allocations at some future date. The distinction can be critical when considering saving. To see how this works, consider the study in Karnataka, India described by Bauer, Chytilová, and Morduch (2009). Researchers asked villagers which they would prefer: receiving 250 rupees tomorrow (roughly a week's wage) or 265 rupees in three months. Most opted to take the money sooner rather than later. Then the researchers asked about the choice over 250 rupees tomorrow versus 280 rupees in three months. A few more were now willing to wait. Similar choices continued with steadily rising stakes in three months; the final option was 250 rupees today versus 375 rupees in three months. At that point most people were willing to wait for the much bigger pay-off. The researchers found that the villagers were relatively patient, with women and people in better-off households being more patient than others.

The issue of "hyperbolic" discounting emerged when the researchers asked a second set of questions. They wanted to know about choices over the same amounts of money with the same relative time frame, but now the question entailed getting 250 rupees in *one year* versus 265 rupees in *one year and three months*. The questions were followed up with choices over 250 rupees versus 280 rupees, etc. Everything was kept identical to the earlier questions except the specific dates of the pay-outs.

This time, though, 32 percent of the respondents were more willing to wait the three months for higher pay-outs relative to their choices in the earlier set of questions. Similar results have been found in other regions and in wealthier populations. The shift in choices may seem unsurprising, but it conflicts with the standard assumption of "linear" discounting that is at the heart of basic economic models of saving. With linear discounting, the distance between choices should matter to their relative value (here, one option is available three months after the other) but the nature of the choice should be unaffected by whether the choices occur now or next year. Yet, 32 percent of respondents flipped their choices when asked about consumption at future dates, making decisions consistent with so-called hyperbolic discounting, a phenomenon sometimes called "present-bias."

The "present-bias" exhibited by this 32 percent creates time inconsistency in a specific sense. When members of this group think about choices with consequences well into the future, they recognize the value of patience. But when presented with a similar set of choices but with the possibility of pay-outs now, they are apt to want the pay-out now. So imagine that a person decides to wait for the larger pay-out when asked today about a choice over having 250 rupees in one year or 300 in one year and three months. At least in this abstract way, this person sees the value of saving. But this same person is apt to change their mind if the researchers returned in a year and instead gave the option to take the 250 rupees immediately rather than wait the three extra months for the 300 rupees as previously decided. So much for saving: the switch reveals "time inconsistency." Given this, it's not surprising that Bauer et al. (2009) find that saving is particularly difficult for people exhibiting this kind of "present-bias": the answers to the hypothetical questions predict actual financial behavior. Villagers in their sample who exhibit present bias save less and borrow more— and they are more likely to seek out disciplining devices like self-help groups.

6.6 Commitment Devices, Reminders to Save, and Mental Accounts

There is a solution to the problem above: faced with a conflict between their present and future selves, people can tie their hands to avoid temptations. They can seek structure and commitment. Bauer et al. (2009) argue that such structure is one of the unheralded strengths of the Indian self-help group model. Ashraf, Karlan, and Yin (2006) provide an important study of the way that structure and commitment can be built into a standard commercial savings product. Working together with the Green Bank of Caraga, a small rural bank in Mindanao in the Philippines, they conducted a field experiment to test the efficacy of a commitment savings product. The researchers began by administering a comprehensive household survey of the 1,767 clients of the bank. Then, half of these clients were randomly selected to be offered a new type of account, called a SEED account.

The account restricted access to deposits according to the customer's instructions at the time that the account was opened. No other extra benefits or costs were imposed. The other half of the initial group was either put into a control group and received no contact at all about savings products, or they were put into a group that received promotions about the bank's existing savings products—but received no offer of the SEED account. Of the 710 individuals offered a SEED account, 202 (28 percent) opened one—and they were more likely to do so if they had exhibited "present bias" in a series of hypothetical questions akin to Bauer et al. (2009). After a year, average bank account savings increased by 81 percent for those who opened the account, a figure substantially higher than seen in either of the control groups over the same period. For those who felt they most needed a commitment product, access to it had an economically and statistically significant impact on financial savings.[17] The commitment mechanism clearly mattered.

As Collins et al. (2009, chapter 6) detail with data on Bangladeshi villagers, the Grameen Pension Scheme described above in section 6.3.1 has become very popular since its introduction in 2000—even in an economy in which it was once thought that the poor were not motivated to save. The GPS, as the product is known, serves as a commitment saving device similar to a SEED account. Grameen Bank customers must agree to make fixed monthly contributions (as small as $0.86 in 2006) and can only retrieve the funds (with 10–12 percent interest) after either five or ten years. Collins et al. (2009) describe great interest in the GPS but they also record instances in which customers "break" their GPS and retrieve the funds early, receiving a lower rate of interest but access to needed cash. Both the SEED account and the GPS shift views on saving: they are part of arguments that suggest that poor households save less than they might, not because of impatience but because of a lack of appropriate devices.

Another reason for low saving may be bound up with attention to future needs. In order to save for the future, needs must be "salient"— i.e., they must be recognized and seen as priorities. But with current needs vying to be addressed, future needs often feel less urgent. It is natural to expend less effort on needs that are distant or uncertain. Karlan, McConnell, Mullainathan et al. (2009) develop a model of saving behavior that captures the fact that we sometimes neglect our future needs because present needs are more salient. The model incorporates people's limited attention capacity, and it suggests that making saving more salient—by providing reminders to make a scheduled deposit, for example—could correct the imbalance.

Karlan et al. (2009) test this application in a triad of randomized field experiments, set in Bolivia, Peru, and the Philippines. In each experiment, a bank offering a savings product with scheduled deposits sends saving reminders to some of its clients, selected at random, and sends no reminders to others. The authors predict that reminders will increase individual savings, and they find that this is the case in all three contexts. They examine saving levels and the share of individuals that meet their savings goals, comparing groups that receive reminders against those that don't. Overall, Karlan et al. (2009) find that reminders lead to a 6 percent increase in the total amount of money saved, and a 3 percent increase in the proportion of individuals that meet their saving goals.

Another application of the Karlan et al. (2009) model is to "mental accounting," or the tendency to treat funds differently based on their source and intended use. One saving account (or, say, a ROSCA) may be ear-marked for housing repairs, another for wedding expenses, another for daily consumption needs, and so forth. Such mental accounting is common and can be useful, but it violates the basic assumption of fungibility that underlies standard models of savings behavior (Thaler 1990). In contrast to fungibility, the Karlan et al. (2009) model allows for "mental labels" that associate present income with a specific future need. They argue that mental labels work in part by making future needs salient, thereby preventing the needs from being crowded out by current needs.

The Karlan et al. (2009) experiments on reminders incorporate other randomized treatments that relate to mental accounting. A random subset of the reminders draws individuals' attention to their self-identified savings goals, for instance by including a photograph of what they say they're saving for. While associations with saving goals alone don't have a significant impact on saving levels or goal meeting, the authors find that reminders that mention both particular saving needs and an incentive to save—a higher interest rate as a reward for making every scheduled deposit, for example—increase saving by nearly 16 percent.

6.7 Building Better Savings Banks

Independent of the nature of the savings product, successful banks that provide savings will face institutional design issues as well. From an institutional perspective, collecting deposits appears to be easier than making loans. Most important, the risk lies entirely with the depositor, and the informational asymmetries that undermine bankers when making loans are absent. Here, the table is turned: Now it is the banker who may be subject to moral hazard, and it is the customers who are unsure whether they can trust the financiers. Will the banks adequately safeguard deposits? Will the bank allow withdrawals when needed? Will the bank still exist in a decade? Five years? It has been left to regulators to assuage those concerns and banks must then deal with paperwork, reserve requirements, and other products of regulation. So, one explanation for the lack of deposit services is that regulation makes it too costly to profitably serve small-scale depositors (Christen, Lyman, and Rosenberg 2003).

Another constraint is that—putting aside regulatory costs—collecting small deposits generates higher transaction costs per dollar transacted than collecting large deposits. As a result, banks often exclude poorer depositors through the use of high minimum balance requirements. Richardson (2003), of the World Council of Credit Unions, cites evidence that many banks claim that it is impossible to profit on deposit accounts smaller than $500, leaving many small savers to rely on informal mechanisms.

The track record of credit unions shows that the $500 limit is excessive, though (Richardson 2003). Indonesia's BRI provides one counterexample: The bank successfully (and profitably) collects deposits while insisting that opening balances be only 10,000 rupiah (just over one dollar), with minimum balances equivalent to 57 cents. Most accounts are far larger—although still well below $500. As noted earlier, the average balance at the end of 2002 was $75. By simplifying its mechanisms, BRI is able to serve over 1,200 customers per staff member on average (Hirschland 2003, figure 1) and keep operating costs below 3 percent. Elsewhere, new technology like using mobile telephones for banking and related "branchless banking" innovations show particular promise (Mas and Kumar 2008).

Another challenge is to find adequately high returns for the funds that are deposited. Taking deposits—especially when they are frequent and small—is only profitable if investments are available that offer sufficiently high returns. Finding such returns, while at the same time keeping funds sufficiently liquid, is difficult. The most obvious way to use deposits is to add to the microlender's capital pool for lending to other customers, but this is little help for programs that are running large deficits on the lending side. Improving financial performance in lending may thus be a key to success in taking deposits.

Cost control is an ongoing struggle, and it is made more complicated by the premium that low-income depositors place on convenience and liquidity. One of the lessons from Jyothi, the deposit collector previously described, and from BRI, is that convenience matters. Convenience matters because clients are often trying to convert bits and pieces of income that flow into the household into a useful, large sum to be spent on a major purchase or investment (an observation that Stuart Rutherford built into the design of *Safe*Save). If a bank is not convenient, it is less likely that the little bits of daily savings will make their way into a deposit account. Thus, serving low-income households means finding ways to reduce travel time and hassles for both customers and staff members. In the case of *Safe*Save, for example, staff members are recruited from the slums where they work so that salary costs are relatively low and travel costs are nonexistent.

Another source of costs is the demand for liquidity. Consider the case of BRI. Its important innovation occurred in 1986 after a year of fieldwork, when BRI introduced its "village savings" product, *Simpanan Pedasaan* (SIMPEDES). It quickly became popular, even though BRI paid no interest at all on small deposits. While the largest deposits were paid an interest rate of 12 percent per year, this rate was smaller than the top rate offered on BRI's competing savings product, TABANAS.[18] But TABANAS had the disadvantage of restricting withdrawals to two times per month, while SIMPEDES offered unlimited withdrawals. Patten and Rosengard (1991, 72) argue: "Although very few TABANAS savers actually withdraw funds twice a month, this limitation is an important psychological barrier to the people in rural areas, who seem to fear that they will not have access to their TABANAS savings when they need them." Managing liquidity remains a major concern, but the problem appears to be easily kept within bounds.

As more programs turn toward microsaving, a greater range of lessons and models will be produced, and those will surely spawn new innovations in short order. There is still much that is poorly understood about the saving behavior of low-income households. But the important step of the past decade has been to recognize that the demand for saving services exists, even among the most impoverished households. Providing convenience and flexibility appears critical to creating a solution that works for customers; the interest rate on deposits, it turns out, is most often a secondary concern.

6.8 Microinsurance

The push to provide microcredit started because too few low-income households could get access to loans on "fair" terms. Government banks provided some credit to low-income households but inefficiently and at major losses, while credit from informal-sector moneylenders was in short supply and costly. This reasonably characterizes the insurance sector too: not much access by poor households, inefficient government providers running at large losses, and informal mechanisms that are often very costly. And the problems are similar as well: Providing insurance has all of the incentive problems associated with providing credit—and worse. Most notable, moral hazard and adverse selection are ongoing problems (in ways that parallel our discussion in chapter 2); transactions costs are high; and contract enforcement is difficult. Consider the data on state-supported crop insurance programs collected by Hazell (1992); he finds that for these government programs, costs exceeded revenues by 4.6 times in both Brazil and Japan, by 3.7 times in Mexico, and by 2.4 times in the United States.

Can we do better? So far there has yet to be a breakthrough innovation (of a kind that parallels the innovations described in chapters 4 and 5) that could propel a "microinsurance" movement to become a global phenomenon. Still, a growing movement within microfinance is pushing to provide insurance on top of loans and deposit services. Life insurance has been most successful to date, but health insurance plans are being tried, as well as property and crop insurance.[19]

These innovations hold much promise for improving the lives of customers. In year-long financial diaries collected in *Portfolios of the Poor*, researchers find that half of respondents in Bangladesh and 42 percent of respondents in India suffered at least one major health loss during the year (Collins et al. 2009, table 3.1). The data show that the challenge of poverty entails much more than low average resources, and insurance can, in principle, be a powerful tool.

6.8.1 Life Insurance

Life insurance is often offered as part of a microcredit package. So-called credit-life contracts pay off any outstanding loans and provide the family with a fixed payout in the event of death. Cohen and Sebstad (2003, table 5) describe a program run by FINCA Uganda, for example, that provided about $700 to clients' dependents in the event that the client died an accidental death; their outstanding loan balance was also repaid. If the death wasn't accidental (e.g., from illness), dependents got only $175 and again the loan was paid off. If the client's spouse died by accident, the client received $350. And if any of the client's children died by accident, the payout was $175 per child (up to 4 children). In return for the coverage, clients paid an extra 1 percent on top of interest for each loan that was disbursed. The clients surveyed by Cohen and Sebstad were pleased with the arrangement, particularly because it ensured that their own death didn't impose an undue burden on their families. But it is not particularly cheap and the coverage is restricted—for example, there were no payouts if a spouse or child dies of illness.

For FINCA Uganda the benefits were dual. First, the product generated profit. The actual coverage was provided by the American International Group (AIG), one of the world's largest insurers, and AIG received 45 percent of the premia collected. FINCA kept the rest to defray the administrative burden and to supplement general revenues. The other benefit for FINCA Uganda was that loans were paid off when clients died, sparing them the difficulty of having to chase down relatives during a time of mourning. Cohen and Sebstad (2003) found that insurance premia (for similar coverage) were even higher at other programs. In Tanzania and Kenya, for example, microlenders charged 2.25 percent and 2 percent of loans disbursed, respectively, for credit-life insurance.

The idea of life insurance was greatly welcomed by clients, supplanting informal insurance mechanisms like informal burial societies that pool resources and pay out to participants in the event of a loss. But Cohen and Sebstad (2003) argue that the way microinsurance programs have been implemented has led to ambivalence about their value.

One tension in the FINCA Uganda program was that as loan sizes increased, so did premia. But benefits increased less than in proportion, since a large part of the benefit included fixed-size payouts in the event of death (the value of the other part, repayment of outstanding balances, grows in proportion to loan size). Small-scale borrowers thus got a better deal than large-scale borrowers, and the large-scale borrowers perceived the inequity. Another tension was that coverage only lasted during the duration of a loan; so if you took a break between loans, your coverage lapsed. A third tension was that insurance purchases at FINCA Uganda were mandatory. This was a wise response to adverse selection—since the program avoids facing a self-selected pool that is riskier than average—but it meant that clients who perceived themselves as being fairly safe (e.g., young, healthy borrowers) ended up cross-subsidizing their riskier neighbors. None of these problems are insurmountable, however. At the cost of adding slightly to administrative burdens, premia could be adjusted for age; coverage between loans could be instituted straightforwardly; and cost schedules could be adjusted so that large-scale borrowers get a better deal. Even in the form described above, though, credit-life insurance is generally workable (and very often profitable).

A major part of the success for FINCA Uganda stemmed from the partnership with AIG. The partnership spared FINCA staff from having to deal with the technical side of insurance provision (calculating actuarial tables, calculating appropriate reserves), avoided extra regulation, and ensured that risks were diversified. As a large insurer, AIG had the means to spread risks across its many policies and could reinsure with ease (reinsuring occurs when an insurer sells a fraction of its policies to another insurer in order to reduce exposure). Were FINCA to go at it alone, it would not only be exposed to major administrative burdens, it would also have to find a way to protect itself in the event of larger-than-expected obligations.

Despite the tensions, there is clearly demand for simple life insurance and it can be quite profitable. As Roth (1999) and Collins et al. (2009) show in South Africa, there is also demand for specialized burial insurance products in countries where burials are the occasion for (expensive) community gatherings.

6.8.2 Health Insurance

Relative to life insurance, health insurance programs have been less successful. Part of the problem is that adverse selection is rampant in voluntary programs, a long-known problem. (See the classic articles by Arrow 1963 and Pauly 1968.) When programs are voluntary, less healthy households tend to be overrepresented among those seeking insurance; and insurers, bogged down by imperfect information, are unable to set prices appropriately for different clients. Jowett (2002, 225), for example, shows that in a voluntary health insurance program in Vietnam, individuals self-reporting as being healthy are 41–55 percent less likely to purchase insurance, saddling insurers with a client base that is less healthy than the population average.

Moral hazard can also be a problem, and it tends to take two main forms. First, once insured, customers may be less likely to take due precautions. Second, customers may overuse facilities, seeking medical attention for ailments that are minor and can be treated (if treatment is necessary at all) without a doctor's intervention. In theory, the way to alleviate these problems is to introduce risk sharing mechanisms: a deductible (so that the patient is only reimbursed for expenses over a given minimum), a co-payment (so that the patient also pays a portion of the overall bill), or both. Some microinsurance programs, like Grameen Kalyan, Grameen Bank's health insurance scheme, require co-payments for medical services. Interestingly, Grameen Kalyan views copayments not as a way to curb overuse, but as a way to signal quality of care (Radermacher, Dror, and Noble 2006, 78).[20]

In general, however, insurers have been reluctant to lean heavily on these mechanisms. Part of the reason is that customers want to see quick returns for their premia, which pushes toward covering small losses even though it may not be efficient. High deductibles are also perceived to discourage potential customers considering formal insurance for the first time. Some providers also fear that high deductibles and co-payments are too burdensome for poor customers. On a practical level, they may discourage clients from seeking necessary preventive care and thus could end up being costly to the insurer in the long run. One way around this problem is to organize a parallel lending program to help with co-payments. The cooperative system set up by Union Technique de la Mutualité in Mali, for example, was created for this purpose (Radermacher et al. 2006, 78).

In order to control costs, insurers have thus imposed restrictions on the diseases that they are willing to cover. MicroCare Health Plan of Uganda, for example, covers a range of outpatient and inpatient services—including surgery, X-rays, laboratory analysis, and prescription drugs—but there is no coverage for common (and growing) problems like high blood pressure, diabetes, and ulcers, nor for alcoholism or long-term care associated with chronic illness (Cohen and Sebstad 2003, table 7 and footnote 18). Other programs, like the health insurance program of the Self-Employed Women's Association (SEWA) of Ahmedabad, India, have controlled costs by limiting coverage and relying on public hospital care. Without a new innovation that can cut costs, insurers find themselves with few other options for the time being. Similarly, customers complain that insurance only helps them pay for medical care that, for now, is often of low quality (Cohen and

Sebstad 2003). Quality health services cannot be taken for granted in either the public or private sectors (Das, Hammer, and Leonard 2008), and low quality services have deterred some households from signing up for insurance programs. Paradoxically, though, as more people buy health insurance, the demand for higher-quality medical care—combined with the new ability to pay for it—may be great enough to push providers to make quality improvements such as more widely available medicines, better-trained doctors and nurses, and easier access to facilities. At BASIX in South India, for example, the scale of the insurance program made it possible to certify and contract with high-quality doctors directly. Having the financial clout of the health insurance program was thus a key to helping fix quality deficiencies in healthcare quality. For prominent Bangladeshi institutions, in contrast, quality issues are addressed by providing nearly all health care within the programs' own clinics—which works in practice although at the cost of eliminating competition (Radermacher et al. 2006, 86, 91).

6.8.3 Rainfall Insurance

One of the most promising new insurance lines in recent years is rainfall insurance and other variants of so-called "index insurance" (Carter, Galarza, and Boucher 2007; Skees, Varangis, Larson et al. 2004; Morduch 2006). The idea of rainfall insurance is to avoid the moral hazard and adverse selection problems associated with crop insurance (not to mention the high transactions costs). The strategy is to abandon trying to insure against bad crop yields and instead to insure against bad weather directly. In a typical plan, tamperproof rain gauges are installed in a region; contracts are then written that guarantee payouts in the event of specific events of bad weather (e.g., lack of rainfall by a certain date or, in other cases, too much rainfall).[21] The idea works because farmers are powerless to change the weather, eliminating concern with moral hazard and adverse selection. Costs are also cut since no one needs to verify losses on given plots of land; instead, only the accuracy of the rainfall gauge is needed.

Giné, Townsend, and Vickrey (2007) study how rainfall insurance works in Andhra Pradesh, South India, sold through a partnership between the microfinance institution BASIX and ICICI Lombard, one of India's main commercial insurers. The insurance contract divides the rainy season into three parts, corresponding to different parts of the crop cycle. At sowing time, the main risk is that the monsoon will

arrive too late. At podding and flowering time, the risk is with insufficient rainfall. And at harvest time, the fear is too much rain. The contract thus yields different kinds of payouts in different scenarios. In the
third (harvest) phase, for example, the policy pays out when rainfall
exceeds 70 mm and pays nothing if rainfall is below the threshold.

The idea appeals, but in practice farmers have not rushed to buy
rainfall insurance. The reason is not likely to simply be the price: the
cost for the season is 150–250 rupees (US$3–5), low enough to be acces-
sible to low-income farmers. The culprit is thus more likely to rest with
a low perceived value. One possibility is that farmers expect that if the
season is a true disaster, the government and community will help or
loans will be forgiven (a possibility raised by Giné and Yang 2008 in a
study of low take-up of rainfall insurance in Malawi). A second possibility rests with the low value of rainfall insurance itself. The case for
rainfall insurance relies on there being a high correlation between
incomes and rainfall as measured at the local rain gauge or weather
station. But the rainfall gauge may be relatively far away, or the specific
characteristics of a farmer's plot (elevation, slope, soil quality, irriga-
tion) may mean that rainfall is a less important input for some farmers
than for others. The divergence between the ups and downs of income
for a given plot and the ups and downs of weather is "basis risk," and
Giné et al. (2007) find that basis risk is a force driving low take-up of
the Andhra Pradesh rainfall insurance product. In research underlying
a rainfall insurance pilot in Morocco, to give another example, the correlation between farmers' revenue and rainfall was found to be 60–80
percent. At the low end of that range (i.e., 60 percent), a great many
farmers could suffer losses without getting payouts—or, by the same
token, may have a good year but still get a payout.

One other limit of rainfall insurance, relative to traditional crop
insurance, is that it only covers rainfall-related losses. Index-based agricultural insurance can sometimes do better (Carter et al. 2007 argue the
case with evidence from northern Peru). The idea is to base insurance
pay-outs on the measured average yields in a region, eliminating
concern with moral hazard and adverse selection as long as any given
farmer can do little to affect the regional average. The disadvantage is
that basis risk remains a problem, and, as with traditional crop insurance, yields must still be measured, although a randomized sample
may be adequate.

In sum, rainfall insurance has big advantages and some nontrivial
limits. One of the under-exploited elements of rainfall insurance (and

other kinds of index insurance) is that villagers who are not farmers can purchase contracts. For obvious reasons, crop insurance is marketed only to farmers, but nothing stops the sale of weather insurance to others who want protection from the ups and downs of demand and supply fluctuations. Thus, shopkeepers, craftsmen, traders, and others whose livelihoods are conditioned by the weather will have a chance to gain added protection, even if they do not themselves work the fields.

6.8.4 Other Insurance Lines

The idea of microinsurance encompasses many different kinds of insurance, although most attention has gone to life, health, and weather products. One product which has had success in South America is service warranties, a form of property insurance. Elsewhere, livestock insurance is being developed, as well as general forms of property insurance.

At SEWA in Ahmedabad India, for example, a property insurance product was developed in which clients paid an annual premium of $1.50 for coverage against loss of property due to catastrophic circumstances. Soon after SEWA initiated the plan, it found itself paying out 630 claims against loss due to flash flooding (totaling $5,000), followed the next year by 2,000 claims in the wake of the massive earthquake in Gujarat in January 2001 (totaling $48,000). The insurance delivered $10 to members for each wall that collapsed in their house, and $60 in the event that a member's house was beyond repair. The experiences show that property insurance can work, but they also highlight the importance of having adequate reserves and reinsurance policies in place before big catastrophes hit.[22]

6.9 Microloans and Risk

The turn to microsaving and microinsurance springs from the recognition that vulnerability goes hand in hand with low incomes. As with microcredit, the fundamental problem with exposure to risk is a lack of access to the kinds of financial services that most of us take for granted. The idea of broadening the scope of interventions has had immediate appeal and sets challenges for both practitioners and academics.

Some observers, though, have worried that microloans themselves may actually be sources of risk—so the proposed solution to one problem (low earning power) worsens the other (vulnerability). To sharpen the point, Dale Adams, a longtime critic of subsidizing microcredit, routinely uses the term *microdebt* instead of microcredit. His point is that lenders provide loans, not gifts, and this creates obligations. When misfortunes strike, those obligations cannot always be met, putting the borrower into even greater jeopardy. Emerging evidence of over-indebtedness only increases the concern (e.g., Matin 1997).

From this vantage, the professionalism that microlenders have worked hard to achieve—which translates into uniform treatment of clients and persistent efforts to make sure that borrowers repay their loans—can, in some cases, mean being tough on clients in times of need. Before Grameen Bank instituted its new program (Grameen II), there were many cases in which clients ran into difficulty repaying and loan officers were strict with them, following rules to the letter. This rigidity created ill will and often pushed struggling clients to seek help from others, including the local moneylender.[23] At its worst, debt spirals of the sort described by Matin (1997) occurred, in which Grameen customers turned to moneylenders for help, borrowed more from Grameen to pay the moneylenders, and so forth until the mountain of un-repaid debt became unmanageable. Grameen II was created in part to help customers—and the bank—pick up the pieces and reestablish workable relationships.

The bottom line is that when microfinance providers stick by hard and fast rules in order to reduce costs and enhance transparency, they may impose additional costs on clients. Moneylenders, in contrast, tend to be more flexible. Borrowers therefore may opt to pay more to a moneylender in exchange for the reassurance of knowing that a moneylender typically will extend the loan duration if difficulties make it hard to repay on time, and often without extra interest charges (Collins et al. 2009, chapter 5). In Irfan Aleem's (1990, table 7.3) sample from Pakistan, for example, loans were routinely extended by half a year when needed.

Grameen II incorporates this flexibility into microcredit contracts, offering a "flexi-loan" that can be rescheduled with relative ease. It's designed to create "tension free" microlending by giving staff ways to accommodate clients in temporary crises. As long as rescheduling is used as a last resort, borrower discipline faces little threat of weakening.[24] In addition to uncomplicated rescheduling, flexi-loans feature a top-up facility that mimics the credit lines extended by a formal bank.

Clients can refresh loans to their original amount at any point during the repayment cycle, allowing them access credit as they need it (Collins et al. 2009, chapter 6).

Another South Asian microlender, SKS Microfinance in India, is one of a group of microfinance institutions providing interest-free "emergency loans." At SKS, clients have access to one emergency loan each fiscal year that they can take for any serious crisis, including those related to maternal health, funerals, and hospitalization. In addition to being interest-free, the amount and repayment schedule are determined on a case-by-case basis.

Traditional group lending contracts may provide another type of insurance. They foster mutual insurance relationships wherein group members address problems together before the loan officer is forced to intervene. Drawing on contract theory, Sadoulet (2003) argues that group lending can foster mechanisms in which borrowers down on their luck can get help from fellow group members—in return for helping others later. If this is so, borrowers do better when groups are more diversified, as suggested by Armendáriz and Gollier (2000). Sadoulet and Carpenter (2001) show that in a sample from Guatemala, borrowers do sort themselves into fairly diverse groups (although it cannot be nailed down whether the sorting stems from insurance motives or from other reasons). The other side of this kind of insurance, of course, is the risk of moral hazard explored by Fischer (2008) and Giné, Jakiela, Karlan et al. (2009); the latter study finds evidence of homogenous sorting in a field experiment in Peru.

A different way that microloans may help to reduce risk is by allowing customers as individuals to reduce exposure to income fluctuations by diversifying income streams and facilitating borrowing for consumption purposes. In the language of section 2.3, microlending can thus aid consumption smoothing in part by facilitating income smoothing—though the evidence is not yet established. [25]

6.10 Summary and Conclusions

Microfinance practitioners and policymakers are coming around to the view that facilitating saving should be an important step in building financial systems in poor communities. This is a welcome shift in that many poor households have strong desires to save and often find ingenious ways to do so, but too often lack convenient and secure deposit facilities.

Meanwhile, we see no evidence to support the general premise that having better ways to save is *more* critical than having better ways to borrow. The two are complementary, and in section 6.8 we added into the mix the value of reasonable possibilities to purchase insurance. Being able to save and borrow is, in itself, an important way to self-insure against uninsurable events.

Much can be learned from the experience with microcredit as we turn to microsavings and microinsurance. In particular, the microcredit experience shows the advantage of allowing households to make frequent, small-sized transactions, rather than repaying loans (or depositing funds, withdrawing savings, and paying insurance premia) in large lump sums. The microcredit experience also shows the importance of building strong institutions. Here, the problem is harder as customers' savings must be protected and insurers must be able to deliver payments reliably and quickly when troubles emerge. Regulation and diversification are thus far more imperative when it comes to savings and insurance.

Turning to microsaving initiatives has led us to question assumptions commonly made by economists, even if implicitly—most important, that borrowing constraints are far more serious than savings constraints. We argue in section 6.4 that, as a theoretical matter, the persistence of borrowing constraints is difficult to explain without invoking the possibility of savings constraints as well. In turning to empirical tests for borrowing constraints, we argue that evidence that is taken to be a sign of borrowing constraints can also be explained by the presence of savings constraints. We set out these arguments as a prod to academics, who have yet to see what practitioners are observing in the field: namely, that many low-income households have genuine difficulties saving and, for lack of effective institutions, are forced to take costly measures to build up assets.

The discussion of microsaving has been embedded in the broader literature on saving in low-income communities. In that literature, it is often argued that because households tend to be formed as intergenerational units, the demand for low-frequency saving is small. Important low-frequency events include predictable changes that occur through the life-cycle—such as starting a family, raising children, and retiring. It is argued that for intergenerational households, within-household transfers can do the job that saving has to do in a nuclear household. This is true to some degree, but we need to be careful. Even in places like rural Pakistan where intergenerational households are the norm, individuals still spend substantial parts of their lives in nuclear households. They form into intergenerational households only at later stages. Thus, the demand for low-frequency saving can remain important—and this should inform the design of new savings products. The Grameen Bank's new pension products, which have been very popular since their introduction in 2000, are a case in point.

Much saving is instead "high-frequency": saving and borrowing with the purpose of obtaining insulation from the vagaries of income. When income is highly variable, foresighted households can build up and draw down assets to stabilize consumption levels. Access to consumption loans—rather than loans strongly tied to microenterprise investment—is an important complement to flexible opportunities to save. Making all of this work in practice will require sharply reducing transactions costs for deposit-taking institutions, and innovations like branchless banking may open new doors.

Sections 6.8 and 6.9 turn to issues of risk more directly. Interest in microinsurance is growing, and in many ways the constraints parallel the early constraints facing microcredit. As with microcredit, information problems create inefficiencies due to adverse selection and moral hazard (as described in the credit context in chapter 2), and transaction costs are high. The area has also been plagued by ill-advised and expensive government interventions directed at giving farmers relief from crop failure. New initiatives include providing life insurance tied to loans, health insurance, and insurance against bad weather rather than bad crop outcomes.

Returning to microcredit, section 6.9 describes ways that the design of loan contracts affects customers' exposure to risk. Group lending, for example, can in principle be a way to cement informal, reciprocal self-help agreements among neighbors. But the rigidity of contracts can also penalize customers just at the moment when they are most in need of flexibility.

Taken together, the topics in this chapter suggest the value of focusing on a broad set of financial services, rather than focusing on narrowly defined microenterprise finance. The stories collected by Collins et al. (2009), for example, show that much of the borrowing by low-income households is driven by basic consumption needs and risk management; the loans are taken and repaid, just as business loans are taken and repaid. Still, there remain fears that providing consumption loans can lead to over-indebtedness and to the kinds of exploitative practices on the part of providers exhibited by "predatory lenders" in the United States. There are also fears that consumption loans will do little to change people's lives, unlike the promise of microcredit for microenterprise.

More evidence is clearly needed, and concerns with over-indebtedness need to be taken seriously. At the same time, the sense here is that the reaction against consumer finance springs from a tendency to undervalue the importance of stability that comes with consumption smoothing. The concern also ignores the fact that money is fungible and that loans that are meant for business often get diverted to consumption as it is. Finally, the concern ignores the potential role for microcredit to aid poor households who have jobs but who are looking for ways to better cope with life's ups and downs—and who have no need for business loans. The evidence so far suggests that being able to save and being able to borrow for emergencies and large expenses are often complementary aspirations.

6.11   Exercises

1. If given enough time, why can't households save their way out of credit constraints?

2. Should facilitating microsaving precede microcredit and not the other way around?

3. Crop insurance programs have often failed or have cost governments heavily. Spell out the main advantages and disadvantages of instead directly insuring farmers against bad weather. Describe contexts in which it seems like a better prospect, and places in which it seems less likely to be a winning idea.

4. Women in many poorer regions are less likely than their husbands to hold savings accounts. Suggest three reasons that might explain why women are at present less likely to open savings accounts in commercial banks. How easy would it be to change the status quo?

5. As discussed in chapter 3, ROSCAs are very common across poor and middle income countries. How can precautionary savings be explained under the rationality paradigm? Are precautionary savings always an "optimal" decision in low-income economies? Drawing on lessons from behavioral economics, provide an example of a saving product that can improve upon the status quo when offered as a component of a microfinance program.

6. Arguments for subsidizing small loans have long been made. Can you make similar cases for subsidizing microsaving? On grounds of equity? On grounds of enhancing efficiency? Do the arguments you make seem more or less persuasive than the arguments for subsidizing credit?

7. Explain briefly two reasons as to why it is nearly impossible for individuals living in rural areas to find effective crop insurance.

8. Consider an economy populated by two types of risk-neutral borrowers. And suppose that all potential borrowers live throughout four periods: 0, 1, 2, and 3. At the beginning of each period, every potential borrower needs at least $45 in order to satisfy her basic necessities for the entire period. At date 0, each individual is endowed with $45, which is just enough to survive until date 1. At both dates 1 and 2, investment and job opportunities emerge. Each time, individuals can invest in a project which requires $100 and one period to yield a return. Any individual wishing to take advantage of the investment opportunities presented to them will thus have to obtain a loan. Suppose that the only lender is an NGO that just wants to break even. In particular, the NGO wants to cover its gross cost $K = \$120$ for each $100 loan. If she qualifies for a loan, an individual of type 1 can invest and generate a gross return $y_1 = \$230$ with probability 90 percent, and nothing with 10 percent probability. If she does not borrow, she can work and earn $65. If she obtains a loan, a type 2 individual can invest and succeed with 50 percent probability, in which case her gross return is $y_2 = \$360$. The other half of the time, her investment fails and she earns nothing. Type 2's opportunity cost is $70. The population is made up of 60 percent type 1 individuals; the other 40 percent consists of type 2 individuals. Assume that the NGO cannot observe individuals' types. Moreover, suppose that all individuals are very patient, that is, that their discount factor $\beta = 1$. All borrowers are protected by limited liability. At time 3 there is no investment. All individuals just consume the sum earned in periods 1 and 2. Show that the two types will invest in one project, in period 2 only.

9. Consider the same problem as in exercise 8, except now both types are impatient. The discount factor for type 1 is now $\beta 1 = 0.65$ and the discount factor for type 2 is $\beta 2 = 0.65$. Show that in this case neither type will invest at all.

10. Consider again an economy like the one described in exercise 8, except that in this case all individuals face the risk of a negative shock at the end of period 2. The shock occurs with 50 percent probability. If individuals are hit by a negative shock, all their savings will be totally wiped out. Show that in this case, it is better for both types not to save in period 1. Will there be any investment at date 2? Explain your answer.

11. This exercise shows why microinsurance may work. Empirical evidence suggests that an individual's degree of "absolute risk aversion," A, is decreasing, where A is defined as $(-u''/u')$, with $u(\cdot)$ being the utility of a representative agent, $u' > 0$ (that is, a large amount of consumption is preferred to a small amount), and $u'' < 0$ (that is, the marginal benefit of an additional unit of consumption is decreasing with greater consumption). Suppose that there are two individuals with the same utility function $u = (x^{0.8}/0.8)$. And suppose that both face the same risk to their wealth: a 50 percent probability of losing 10 euros and a 50 percent probability of no loss. The individuals, though, have different incomes: The wealthy one has 70 euros and the impoverished one has 10 euros. Prove that relative to the wealthy individual, the impoverished one is ready to pay a high premium in order to be fully insured. (Full insurance means that both individuals have the same income in all states of the world.)

12. Suppose the following timing for a typical household member in a village economy. There are three periods: 0, 1, and 2. In period 0, effort e must be taken. In period 1 there is a storm with 50 percent probability, and in period 2 the harvest occurs. All working-age individuals in each household are risk neutral. Assume one individual in each household can grow corn that yields a value y at date 2, which is the harvest date. If there is a storm at date 1, all individuals growing corn risk a loss $L < y$ with probability $1 - p$, provided an adequate level of effort is applied at date zero. The cost of this effort is e. In the absence of effort, an individual cannot even recuperate L. Now suppose that there is an insurer. This insurer offers an indemnity I for a premium fee p. Assume that there is no "loading factor" (i.e., no cost of providing insurance, so the insurer sets prices that are actuarially fair) and $\pi < 1/2(1 - p)I$. Show that in order to induce an adequate effort level from the villagers, the insurer should directly contract on bad weather instead of contracting on a bad crop yield.

13. Consider an economy similar to that of the previous exercise. Consider a risk-averse individual who faces the risk of losing L with probability $1 - p$. The probability of not losing L when she puts in adequate effort is $p = \bar{p}$, and when she does not put in any effort, the probability is $p = \underline{p}$ (where $\bar{p} > \underline{p}$). Putting in effort costs e, though. Her expected utility when she puts in effort is $(1 - \bar{p})u(w - L) + \bar{p}u(w) - e$ and her expected utility when she does not put in any effort is $(1 - \underline{p})u(w - L) + \underline{p}u(w) - e$, where the utility function u is an increasing concave function, where w is wealth. An insurer offers an indemnity I in case of loss against a premium fee p (there is no loading factor). Write the participation constraints and the incentive constraint for the individual in this economy to expend effort $p = \bar{p}$. When $I = L$ and $p = I(1 - \bar{p})$, will she put in any effort?

14. Suppose that there are two risk-averse individuals with the same utility function $u = (w^{0.7}/0.7)$, where w is wealth. Their initial wealth endowment is $w = \$70$, but their income is subject to two different kinds of risks. Individual 1 faces the following risk: with 50 percent probability she loses \$10, and with 50 percent probability she does not lose anything. Individual 2 faces the following risk: with probability 1/2 she loses \$20, and with 50 percent probability she loses \$10. Show that relative to individual one, individual 2 is ready to pay a higher premium in order to be fully insured. (Full insurance in this context means that income remains the same in all states of nature.)

15. Consider an economy in which there are two types of risk-averse individuals. Type 1 risks losing \$10 with 40 percent probability and nothing with 60 percent probability. Type 2 is in a riskier situation: with 80 percent probability, she loses \$10, and with 20 percent probability she does not lose anything. Sixty percent of all individuals are of type 1, and 40 percent of type 2. Assume that the two types have the same utility function: $u = (w^{0.6}/0.6)$ where w is wealth. Both types of individuals are endowed with the same initial wealth $w = \$50$. There is a risk-neutral insurer offering full insurance. This insurer is an NGO that just wants to break even, and suppose that there is no "loading factor" (i.e., no cost of providing insurance, so the insurer sets prices that are actuarially fair). The insurer can not distinguish between the two types, and thus has to charge the same premium to both types.
a. Compute the premium fee set by the insurer.
b. With this level of risk premium, which of the two types will purchase insurance? Explain your answer.
c. If the insurer anticipates that only individuals of type 2 will buy insurance, what is the premium charged in this case? Explain whether individuals of type 2 will ultimately buy insurance.

7   Gender

7.1   Introduction

To many, microfinance is all about banking for women. Pioneers such as BancoSol and the Grameen Bank were built around serving women, and microfinance networks such as Women's World Banking and NGOs such as Pro Mujer reinforce the commitment. Not all microfinance institutions focus specifically on women, but the Microcredit Summit Campaign counted that as of the end of 2007, 70 percent of microfinance clients worldwide were women (Daley-Harris 2009). Among those customers classified as the "poorest," the share of women was even higher at 83 percent.[1]

So far we have only touched briefly on gender in microfinance, but in this chapter we address issues directly. We begin by asking why most microfinance borrowers are women, especially the poorest. We then ask whether targeting women is efficient in the strict economic sense. Does it help microfinance enterprises to attain their self-sustainability goals? Does it favor more equality within the household? How might microfinance help to promote social capital and women's empowerment? Is the focus on women limiting?

The Grameen Bank's history is instructive. From the start, Muhammad Yunus recognized the importance of women when confronting poverty. But cultural norms, especially the Muslim practice of *purdah* (which guards a woman's modesty and limits her mobility and social interactions), made it difficult to approach potential female clients. When the bank started, most borrowers were men; just 44 percent of clients were women in October 1983 (Yunus 1983, 11). But figure 7.1 shows that the situation rapidly changed. In 1986, women made up about three-quarters of Grameen's members, rising steadily through

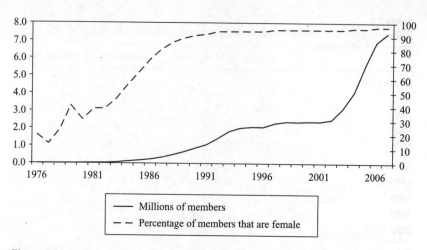

Figure 7.1
Female membership of Grameen Bank, 1985–2007.

the 1990s along with overall membership growth. Now, with barriers fallen, over 95 percent of Grameen's clients are women (Grameen Bank 2008b).[2] The bias in favor of women was reinforced by experience showing that, relative to male borrowers, women had better repayment records. But the belief in the comparative advantage of women as microfinance customers did not stop there; it extended to other dimensions of performance as well. For example, Khandker (2005) asserts that a 100 percent increase in the volume of borrowing by a woman would lead to a 5 percent increase in per capita household nonfood expenditure and a 1 percent increase in per capita household food expenditure, while a 100 percent increase in borrowing by men would lead to just a 2 percent increase in nonfood expenditure and a negligible change in food expenditure. This evidence indicates that serving women can have stronger impacts on households.[3] While recent evidence yields a far more mixed picture—and Khandker's results have been taken apart on methodological grounds—the centrality of gender in microfinance has taken hold. Serving women is seen as according well with the dual objectives of maintaining high repayment rates and meeting social goals.

The importance of women in microfinance in places such as Bolivia and Bangladesh has been helped by other social transformations that started far earlier. Data on fertility rates and illiteracy show how dramatic those changes have been. Table 7.1 shows that fertility rates have

Table 7.1
Falling fertility and female illiteracy rates, selected countries 1970–2000

	Bolivia	Bangladesh	Indonesia	All low-income
Fertility rate				
1970	6.5	7.0	5.5	5.9
1980	5.5	6.1	4.3	5.3
1990	4.8	4.1	3.0	4.4
2000	3.9	3.1	2.5	3.6
Female adult illiteracy rate				
1970	54	88	56	73
1980	42	83	41	65
1990	30	77	27	56
2000	21	70	18	47

Source: World Bank World Indicators 2002b, CD-ROM. Fertility rate is average number of births per woman. Illiteracy is the percentage of women fifteen years and older who cannot read or write.

fallen steadily in both countries—as they have in Indonesia, another country thick with microfinance, and for low-income countries overall. In 1970, women in Bangladesh had seven children on average, leaving limited time for extra work. By 2000, fertility in Bangladesh had fallen to nearly three children per woman, a dramatic decline with clear economic and social implications. The change means that women have more time and resources for self-employment, and it shows that important transformations were already under way within households well before microfinance burst onto the scene. Another important change has been falling illiteracy rates for adult women, from 54 percent to 21 percent in Bolivia between 1970 and 2000, and from 88 percent to 70 percent in Bangladesh. The role of microfinance has been to extend and develop the ongoing transformations, more than to initiate them.

Gender issues in microfinance are only a small part of a global agenda on gender mainstreaming and women's rights, and while progress has been made, much remains to be done within the microfinance sector. Brambilla (2001) points out, for example, that few donors or NGOs have developed systems to monitor and evaluate the gender impact of their programs, projects and policies, or of the gender institutionalizing process within their organizations. It is also important to keep in mind that gender issues are particularly region- and culture-specific, and what holds in one case may not transfer to other contexts.

Results on low returns to female-run micro-enterprise in Sri Lanka (de Mel, McKenzie, and Woodruff 2009a) and the Philippines (Karlan and Zinman 2009a), together with questions about the empirical basis for early claims on the advantages of lending to women (Roodman and Morduch 2009), are pushing researchers to question the automatic assumption that lending to women must lead to gains in income and improved well-being for families. We take a closer look at those studies in chapter 9.

The next section describes trends away from focusing on women as the microfinance movement has become more commercial. Section 7.3 explains the economic rationale for the early focus on women in microfinance, and in section 7.4 we turn to intra-household decision making. We use standard neoclassical models and their extensions to describe channels through which microfinance might alter within-household decisions. In section 7.5 we turn to arguments suggesting that lending to women can have a larger social impact relative to lending to men, and in section 7.6 we turn to the notion of women's empowerment: What does it mean? Are married women better off if their male partners are denied access to microfinance? Section 7.7 takes up debates around the notion of empowerment and section 7.8 concludes with a discussion of frontier questions.

7.2 Commercialization versus Gender Focus?

In table 7.2 we show that the bias in favor of women goes beyond Bangladesh and Bolivia. In all regions of the world, women constitute a majority of the poorest microfinance clients.

When the microfinance landscape is segmented by institutional structure, however, the trends that emerge are more nuanced. The absolute number of female clients has risen for all types of institutions, but the *percentage* of clients that are women has actually fallen for some types of institutions. Specifically, recent studies have shown a correlation between commercialization and a decline in the percentage of female clients as a share of total clients.

In a Women's World Banking Focus Note, Frank (2008) investigates the relationship between commercial transformation and outreach to women.[4] She examines 27 transformed institutions and finds that women make up a smaller fraction of their clients five years after transformation from NGO status, compared to their own client mix before transformation and to that of a control group of nontransformed

Table 7.2
Percent of poorest clients that are women in 2007, as reported to the Microcredit Summit
Campaign 2009

Region	Number of institutions	Percent of poorest clients that are women
Sub-Saharan Africa	935	63%
Asia and the Pacific	1,727	85%
Latin America & Caribbean	613	66%
Middle East & North Africa	85	78%
Developing World Totals	3,360	83%
Industrialized World Totals	192	60%
Global Totals	3,552	83%

Source: Daley-Harris, *State of the Microcredit Summit Campaign Reports 2009.*

institutions. For the transformed set, the percentage of women clients served decreased from an average of 88 percent two years before transformation to 78 percent at transformation and 60 percent five years after transformation. In contrast, the non-transformed institutions increased their fraction of women clients from 72 percent to 77 percent over a parallel five year period. A tension in these findings, however, is that while the transformed institutions served a smaller *fraction* of women, they served twice as many women borrowers in total relative to the non-transformed institutions in 2006, the last year of the dataset. Here, the gains from scale achieved through commercialization offset the dilution of the gender focus (at least in terms of absolute numbers of women reached).

Cull, Demirgüç-Kunt, and Morduch (2009b) present complementary findings. Using a larger dataset from the Microfinance Information Exchange (the MIX), they calculate the percentage of women as a fraction of all borrowers for institutions structured as nongovernmental organizations (NGOs), non-bank financial institutions (NBFIs), and microfinance banks. They find that for more than half of NGOs 85 percent of clients are female, and at least a quarter of the NGOs studied serve women exclusively. NBFIs and microfinance banks, on the other hand, serve only 66 percent and 52 percent women at the median, respectively. A separate analysis of MIX data confirms this relationship. Bauchet and Morduch (2010) find a negative correlation between operational self-sufficiency, a proxy ratio for profitability, and the percentage of women borrowers served. (The authors don't, however, find evidence for this relationship in data from the Microcredit

Summit Campaign, an advocacy organization more focused on social impacts.)

The trends highlighted in this section raise questions about whether and how the way in which women are served will change as microfinance continues to evolve, but for many microfinance programs—particularly those that are structured as NGOs—providing financial access to women remains a primary objective. We turn now to a discussion of the considerations that drive this decision.

7.3   Are Women Better Borrowers?

Formal-sector commercial banks tend to favor men, mainly because men run the larger businesses that commercial banks favor, and men tend to control the assets that banks seek as collateral. Microfinance is a very different business, though. It is aimed at "micro" businesses which most often involve self-employment in the informal sector, and women make up a large and growing segment of informal-sector businesses. The final column of table 7.3 shows that women make up a large fraction of the informal, nonagricultural sector in the countries where data were available; and in just under half, women make up the largest share (particularly in Africa).

Demand for micro loans by women is also shaped by their credit constraints relative to men. Since they tend to have access to fewer alternative sources of credit, women are more likely to select themselves into microcredit contracts with all kinds of strings attached—namely, small loans, training sessions, weekly meetings, and joint responsibility. Women's relative credit-constraints also work to the lender's advantage. The dynamic incentives described in chapter 5 are more powerful when the borrower cannot simply turn elsewhere for future loans; so, where women have few borrowing alternatives the scope of both ex ante and ex post moral hazard is reduced. As Emran, Morshed, and Stiglitz (2007) argue in an important rethinking of missing markets, the logic about the lack of credit alternatives can be extended to other missing markets: where women lack adequate access to labor markets, women will value self-employment opportunities all the more—and will have stronger incentives for diligence in repaying loans.

There are at least three other reasons why lending to women may have advantages from the microfinance institution's standpoint—and may enhance efficiency in a broader economic sense. The first reason has to do with poverty. Women are poorer than men. According to the

Table 7.3
Men and women in the non-agricultural workforce, 1991–1997

	Women's share of the informal sector in the nonagricultural labor force, 1991–1997		Women's share of the informal sector in the nonagricultural labor force, 1991–1997
	Women	Men	
Africa			
Benin	97	83	62
Chad	97	59	53
Guinea	84	61	37
Kenya	83	59	60
Mali	96	91	59
South Africa	30	14	61
Tunisia	39	52	18
Latin America			
Bolivia	74	55	51
Brazil	67	55	47
Chile	44	31	46
Colombia	44	42	50
Costa Rica	48	46	40
El Salvador	69	47	58
Honduras	65	51	56
Mexico	55	44	44
Panama	41	35	44
Venezuela	47	47	38
Asia			
India	91	70	23
Indonesia	88	69	43
Philippines	64	66	46
Thailand	54	49	47

Source: The United Nations 2000, chart 5.13, 122.

UNDP *Human Development Report* (1996), 70 percent of the world's poor, about 900 million people, were women. This accords well with the poverty-reduction mission of a large number of microfinance institutions focusing on women (Armendáriz and Szafarz 2009). Under the standard neoclassical assumptions about the production function, if women have less access to capital than men, returns to capital for women should therefore be higher than for men. Endowing women with more capital can thus be growth-enhancing in principle.[5]

This assumes, though, that capital is not completely fungible within households—that is, the money of all members is not fully pooled and treated as a common resource. Given that the once common assumption of full within-household resource pooling has come under steady attack, the case for a gender focus in microfinance is strengthened. While there is concern that credit directed to women might end up being re-directed to male household heads (who are the ones that are actually carrying out investment projects of their own, with the resources borrowed by women), evidence from Bangladesh sheds light on growing concerns. Goetz and Sen Gupta (1996), for example, report that 40 percent of women in their survey have little or no control over their own investment activities, but optimistic observers respond that this means that 60 percent have full or partial control. Thus, investments do seem to be undertaken by women, despite norms that place restrictions on women. To the extent that—as reported by Goetz and Sen Gupta—women already enjoy a comparative advantage in small-scale microenterprise activities, the efficiency-augmenting argument by neoclassical theorists is further enhanced. Still, section 7.5 shows that the evidence so far is mixed.

The second argument hinges on labor mobility. Women tend to be less mobile than men and are more likely to work in or near the home (a point related to that of Emran, Morshed, and Stiglitz 2007). Bank managers can therefore monitor women at a lower cost. Moreover, less mobility facilitates delegated monitoring under group lending methodologies. Typically, peer borrowers who undertake investment activities at home—and stay at home most of the time—can more easily monitor each other. Similarly, lower mobility reduces the incidence of strategic default under the fear of social sanctions.[6]

This brings us to the third argument in favor of a pro-female bias. Because women are less mobile and more fearful about social sanctions, they tend to be more risk-averse than men and more conservative in their choice of investment projects. This helps women create a reputation for reliability and makes it easier for the bank to secure debt repayments, making women more reliable bets for banks concerned with their financial bottom lines.[7] (On the other hand, where taking greater risk brings greater financial reward for customers, there are opportunity costs for customers who stick with overly conservative strategies—which may explain some of the mixed empirical results in section 7.5.)

As we described in chapter 5, evidence from Grameen Bank—and replications elsewhere in Asia—shows that women are, in fact, better about repaying loans. For example, Khandker, Khalily, and Khan (1995) find that 15.3 percent of male borrowers were struggling in 1991 (i.e., missing some payments before the final due date), while only 1.3 percent of women were having difficulties. That finding is echoed in studies elsewhere in Asia. The field experience of Grameen replications in southern Mexico indicates a similar pattern (Armendáriz and Roome 2008a), and evidence from credit scoring regressions using data from Latin American microlenders confirms this tendency too. (Some of these are studies of repayment rates, in which gender is an explanatory variable.) While the advantage of women in the credit scoring studies falls after considering factors such as age, income, region, and other covariates, it is the simple correlation that is most important in determining the attractiveness of women as customers.[8] In this line, Kevane and Wydick (2001), for example, find that at a group lending institution in Guatemala, female borrowing groups misused funds least often, and, as a result, outperformed male borrowing groups.

In addition to the argument for why women might make better customers, microfinance institutions may have financial reasons for hiring women as loan officers or for other tasks like account keeping, promotion of new products and services, and organizing groups. Data for Albania, for example, offer evidence that default rates are lower for loans handled by female loan officers (Beck, Behr, and Güttler 2009). Furthermore, women's wages are generally lower than those commanded by men in low-income countries. Employing women can thus reduce institutions' operational costs through two separate channels: via enhanced productivity and via low wages relative to male employees. As a result, women don't only make good clients for microfinance institutions, they may also make good employees.

7.4 Neoclassical Approaches to Household Decision Making

Before turning to issues specific to microfinance, we lay out a theoretical framework for how decisions are made within the household.

The traditional neoclassical economic approach to household decision making leaves no room for analyzing conflict between men and women. Households are seen as acting as a single unit, making choices as if household members were in full consensus. Even here, though, a case for targeting on the basis of gender can be made.

The so-called unitary approach goes back to seminal work started by Gary Becker in the 1960s. In particular, in his *Treatise on the Family*, Becker (1981) assumes that male and female preferences can be aggregated into a common household objective function to analyze decisions about expenditures and "noneconomic" investments such as the number, education, and health of children. Households maximize their joint objective utility function subject to constraints on time use, technology, and joint resources. While the time allocation of each household member between the production of market and household output matters (since it may affect total household output), the distribution of income among family members is totally irrelevant. A dollar is a dollar, no matter who in the family earns it. The approach, so focused as it is on efficiency, is sometimes called the "pure investment" model; and it leaves no scope for intrahousehold conflict.

One of Becker's objectives was to understand how households allocate individuals to activities, with household members seeking to gain from their comparative advantages. According to this approach, if the wage in the market sector is higher for males than for females, it would be efficient for men to work more in the market sector and for women to stay in the household (or to work in the informal sector). Becker argues that this is the best way to increase the household's total output, and he claims that this is a good representation of patterns seen in the United States in the 1960s.

In principle, Becker's predictions also apply to developing countries. In most agricultural economies, there are a number of high-wage activities that require certain skills, such as physical strength, for which gender matters. Becker's framework in this case suggests that it is optimal for men to benefit from their comparative advantage by specializing in strength-intensive marketable agricultural activities outside the house. Women, on the other hand, should devote more time to unpaid household work and those marketable activities that require considerably less physical strength, even if the monetary rewards are often low due to market discrimination. It remains unclear whether such unequal specialization within the household truly reflects women's preferences.

Rosenzweig and Schultz (1982) provide early evidence on the pure investment model, finding that survival probabilities for female infants in rural India are higher in areas where opportunities for female employment are greater. Their argument is that asymmetric mortality patterns result because parents are forced to invest in children with the greatest earning potential. It is argued that such strategic decision-making results from the need to sometimes make tragic, brutal choices in the struggle for basic survival.[9]

But microfinance advocates repudiate the helplessness that is implied. First, by helping to raise incomes, advocates argue that microfinance can lift the constraints that force households to make such life-and-death choices. As important, advocates argue that microfinance can also change the nature of basic trade-offs. Rather than taking the structure of wages and employment as given, microfinance advocates aim to improve opportunities and the economic returns to women's work, and thus to change the economic value of females within the home. Raising those returns can, in principle, reduce discrimination of the sort documented by Rosenzweig and Schultz (1982).

The pure investment model is a useful starting point, but microfinance advocates go further. They argue that by raising women's status within families, the nature of decision making can change too. Rather than assuming that households work by consensus, as argued by Becker, economists have recently started deconstructing household choices, finding them to be driven often by inequalities, bargaining, and conflict.[10] Browning and Chiappori (1998), for example, derive implications of a model in which bargaining power is driven by the ability of women to credibly threaten to leave the household. The credibility of those threats will depend on factors like earning power and other factors that affect women's relative power within the household, such as divorce or employment legislation. Access to microfinance can potentially be part of this equation.

To venture further, we first need to turn to a framework in which parents care intrinsically about the education and health of their children (rather than as in the pure investment model, where concern is purely instrumental, restricted to how improving health and education raises earning power). A simple approach is given by Behrman, Pollak, and Taubman (1982), and we follow Strauss's and Beegle's (1996) exposition. We assume that there are two children in a household, a girl and a boy. If the mother is exceedingly averse to inequality in the well-being of her children, she will care most about the child that is worst off. Diagramatically, at the extreme her preferences are L-shaped, or, in the public finance jargon, the mother's preferences are "Rawlsian."[11] This is shown as an "L-shaped indifference curve" in figure 7.2, where the mother has preferences over the health of her son and daughter. In the case depicted, if the daughter's health improves, we will see a horizontal move from A to B in the diagram. This change will not improve the mother's condition, though, because she dislikes inequality. In contrast, take the opposite extreme in which the mother does not care about inequalities between the two children. In this case, the indifference curve will be completely linear, as shown in the downward-sloping line I–I. Here, the mother will invest more in household members whose returns are the greatest (which is the case emphasized by Becker). Preferences between these two extremes are captured by the more plausible indifference curve C, where preferences for equality are traded off against the need to ensure earning capacity.

Such trade-offs shift with income. In particular, at very low income levels, the household may favor males for survival reasons, and mothers may support that decision. Take the example of food, which is often controlled by women. At very low incomes, women's preferences may be biased against females because survival is all that matters, and sons

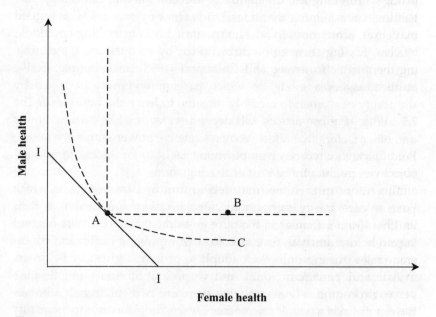

Figure 7.2
The role of preferences in intrahousehold allocation.

may represent higher earning opportunities for the household. Women may therefore allocate more food to males who can potentially bring a higher level of income to the household. Distributions become more equal, though, as the general level of income increases.

Behrman (1988), for example, shows that household nutrient intakes and health outcomes in his sample from India are positively correlated with earning profiles. He also shows that the pro-male bias is more severe during the "lean" seasons, when resources are tight. In particular, households tend to allocate food to members who receive the greatest returns in the labor market, resulting in greater intrahousehold inequality in the lean seasons, but they are more egalitarian in surplus seasons.

Another layer of complexity is added by considering a scenario where men and women may have different preferences, and conflicts are resolved through negotiation. In the context of figure 7.2, women's preferences, say, may tend to be more L-shaped while men's preferences tend toward linearity. The more power a woman has in the household, the more the household's decisions reflect her preferences. Increasing income can thus lead to households changing the pattern of allocations for reasons that get mediated through the bargaining process. Browning and Chiappori (1998), for example, show that in bargaining contexts, preferences tend to shift with income.[12] Microfinance may thus affect household choices through a variety of channels: by changing bargaining power, by raising overall resources, by affecting the returns to investments in human capital, and by influencing attitudes and norms.

7.5   Why May Impacts Be Greater when Lending to Women?

We turn now to reasons why microfinance institutions pursuing social objectives might prefer to work with women. As we noted above, aiming resources to women may deliver stronger development impacts. First, women are overrepresented among the poorest of the poor. In its 1990 *World Development Report*, the World Bank states that women lagged behind in many key indicators of economic development. Literacy rates, for example, were found to be 61 percent of that of men in Africa, 52 percent in South Asia, 57 percent in the Middle East, 82 percent in South East Asia, and 94 percent in Latin America. Moreover, the report finds that, relative to men, women in low-income countries face far greater social, legal, and economic obstacles.[13] Second, when women as policy makers have decision-making power at a macrolevel, their decisions tend to be biased in favor of the provision of public goods helpful for families and communities (e.g., Chattopadhyay and Duflo 2004). Third, relative to men, women's decisions tend to be biased in favor of within-household expenditures, reflecting that women are more likely to be the household members most responsible for children's health and education (e.g., Blumberg 1989).

Region-specific studies on gender bias abound. One stark example is provided by population sex ratios that are so skewed that Sen (1992) has written of a crisis of "missing women."[14] While in developed countries there are approximately 105 females for every 100 males, the ratios are lower in South Asia, the Middle East, and North Africa, due to exceedingly high female mortality rates. The very large female-to-male death ratio in these regions is attributed to parents' neglect for their female infants and, in some cases, to selective abortion of female fetuses. Sen (1992) estimates that the number of missing women (those who died prematurely or who were selectively aborted) in the early 1990s was over 100 million people. Among the reasons that young girls are discriminated against is that they are not viewed as an important source of income and, in some instances, are seen as a burden due to dowry obligations. Less extreme forms of discrimination are manifested in day-to-day living. Poor women, for example, tend to work longer hours for less pay. The World Bank (1990) reports: "Women typically work for longer hours, and when they are paid at all, will be so at lower wages." Studies in numerous developing countries emphasize that when unpaid home-production activities are included, women seem to work even longer hours than men.[15]

Ethical considerations aside, the gender bias has clear implications for policy. Unequal access to health, nutrition, and educational status of women in low-income households has been linked to high fertility rates, low labor force participation, low hygiene standards, and the increased incidence of infectious diseases. And all these variables are clearly related to productivity and household income.

Against this are arguments that male entrepreneurs may more aggressively expand enterprises when given access to credit. There may thus be a trade-off between lending to women in the name of poverty reduction and lending to men in the name of economic growth. De Mel, McKenzie, and Woodruff (2009a) find evidence for this hypothesis among Sri Lankan entrepreneurs. They conduct a randomized experiment on mean returns to capital in Sri Lankan microenterprises, and find that returns to capital are greater for men than for women. Average returns to capital among women-owned microenterprises are not statistically different from zero, whereas their male counterparts earn average returns in excess of 11 percent per month. The authors explore various explanations as to why this might be the case, including risk aversion, different preferences in spending priorities, social conventions which might limit women's ability to travel in search of better places to market their products, and higher bargaining power by men within the household, which in turn gives men greater access to unpaid labor by their children and spouses. The authors rule out these explanations, and suggest instead that relative to men, women have limited access to investment opportunities (investing mostly in equipment for home-stay activities such as ovens and sewing machines), and have a tendency to invest in sectors with lower returns and limited growth possibilities.

Kevane and Wydick (2001), though, find that gender differences in economic responses to credit access are small in the Guatemalan group lending program they investigate. While they find that young male entrepreneurs tend to be more aggressive in generating employment than older male entrepreneurs, older women tend to be more aggressive in generating employment than younger women or older men. Holding all else constant, Kevane and Wydick thus find no statistically significant overall difference in the way that credit affects the ability of female and male entrepreneurs to generate increases in gross sales within an enterprise. Khandker's (2005) evidence, in contrast, suggests that lending to women yields greater social and economic impacts than lending to men. Roodman and Morduch (2009), though, argue that his statistical strategy fails to convincingly demonstrate causal links from credit access to impacts.

While future work remains to clarify the causal links, policymakers tend to strongly presume benefits to targeting women. Their assumption is in line with evidence on the impact of delivering aid for disadvantaged households to women. Food stamps in the United Kingdom and Sri Lanka, for example, and staple food and cash deliveries under the PROGRESA (now called Oportunidades) program in Mexico were directed to women rather than their husbands. The fear is that if such aid was given to men, they might sell the food stamps and misspend the resources—possibly wasting money on gambling, tobacco, and/or alcohol. Skoufias (2001) reports on a randomized experiment showing that PROGRESA/Oportunidades in rural Mexico indeed led to sharp

social improvements: poverty decreased by ten percent, school enroll-
ment increased by four percent, food expenditures increased by eleven
percent, and adults' health (as measured by the number of unproductive days due to illness) improved considerably as well.[16]

Similarly, Thomas (1990) reports that child health in Brazil (as measured by survival probabilities, height-for-age, and weight-for-height)
along with household nutrient intakes, tend to rise more if additional
nonlabor income is in the hands of women rather than men. With
respect to survival probabilities, income in the hands of a mother has,
on average, twenty times the impact of the same income in the hands
of a father. In a subsequent study, also on Brazil, Thomas (1994) reports
that increasing the bargaining power of women is associated with
increases in the share of the household budget spent on health, education and housing as well as improvements in child health. Engle (1993)
similarly studies the relationship between a mother's and father's
income on child nutritional status (height-for-age, weight-for-age
and weight-for-height) for hundreds of households in Guatemala, and
reports that children's welfare improves as women's earning power
increases relative to their husbands'. Schultz (1990) finds that in
Thailand nonlabor income in the hands of women tends to reduce
fertility more than nonlabor income possessed by men. He also finds
that the impact of nonlabor income has different effects on labor
supply, depending on which household member actually controls that
income.[17]

Anderson and Baland's (2002) article on ROSCAs, already discussed
in section 3.2, reports on a survey of hundreds of women in Kenya. An
overwhelming majority of the women responded that the principal
objective for joining a ROSCA was to save, and nearly all of the respondents were married. Anderson and Baland conclude that an important
motive for women joining ROSCAs is to keep money away from their
husbands. Other studies, not necessarily confined to ROSCAs, suggest
that savings considerations (and protection of assets) apply as well
to women's involvement in microfinance institutions (Armendáriz
2010).

Udry (1996) provides related evidence. Using panel data from
Burkina Faso, he finds that, controlling for soil quality and other variables, agricultural productivity is higher in plots that are cultivated
by men. He also finds that relative to plots cultivated by women, the
higher yields of male-cultivated plots are due to a greater intensity
of productive inputs (including fertilizer and child labor). He thus

concludes that productivity differentials are attributed to the intensity of production between plots cultivated by men and women, and not to inherent skill differentials. This outcome is not efficient since there are sharply diminishing returns for fertilizer. Not only are resources not fully shared, they are allocated in ways that diminish total household income. Udry suggests that input reallocation toward plots cultivated by women can thus enhance efficiency. Another solution (i.e., the microfinance solution) is to provide women with credit sufficient to purchase additional inputs. A second way that microfinance can potentially address problems like this is by tackling the social norms that prevent women from having adequate access to inputs and marketing facilities in the first place. This could be done through demonstration effects or from pressure created by the microlender to ensure high returns to borrowers' investments.

7.6 Gender Empowerment

Advocates argue that microfinance can increase women's bargaining power within the household. Women will become "empowered" and enjoy greater control over household decisions and resources. To the extent that group lending in microfinance entails peer monitoring by other borrowers in the same group, microfinance is likely to provide protection to women within their households. In particular, violent acts and abuses by men against women can now be subject to third party scrutiny, as peer borrowers will want to find out why a woman in their group has stopped attending repayment meetings, for example. This, in turn, should act as a deterrent against domestic violence, and, more generally, as an instrument for women to promote their rights and improve their bargaining power vis-à-vis their husbands or other male family members. Rising household incomes in general can also diminish conflicts between husbands and wives by loosening constraints.

Evidence on the effect of microfinance on women's rights delivers an unclear picture, however. Hashemi, Schuler, and Riley (1996) and Kabeer (2001), on the one hand, report that microfinance in Bangladesh has indeed reduced violence against women. This finding is corroborated by recent studies of IMAGE (Intervention with Microfinance for AIDS and Gender Equity) in South Africa which show that microfinance programs that couple loans with gender and HIV education reduce the incidence of intimate partner violence considerably (Pronyk et al. 2007). Kabeer argues that the rationales for targeting women, over and above the desire to empower, include the observations that (1) men are less likely to share their loans with women than women are likely to share loans with men; (2) loans to women are more likely to benefit the whole family than loans to men; and (3) loans to men have little impact on intrahousehold gender inequalities—in fact, they can reinforce them by providing men with a base to prevent wives from engaging in income-generating self-employment.

But the opposite conclusion is reached by Rahman (1999), albeit with evidence from just one village. As many as 70 percent of Grameen borrowers in his survey declared that violence in the household had increased as a result of their involvement with microfinance. Rahman's explanation for the upsurge in violence is that microfinance exacerbates tensions because men feel increasingly threatened in their role as primary income earners in traditional societies.

Armendáriz and Roome (2008a) also raise the concern that women's participation in microfinance may create friction with their husbands, as did Hugh Allen in remarks at the 2006 Microfinance Forum in Beijing. He noted that:

Male exclusion can lead to negative consequences for women who join financial services: they may meet resistance from men who see their exclusive participation as unfair and threatening; their loans may be hijacked. . . . A family whose adult members all have access to financial services is better off than one where half are ineligible.

The perspective that universal access may be better than programs biased toward women has been picked up by some lenders and translated into new approaches. Grameen Trust Chiapas A.C. (GTC)[18] in Mexico, for example, began including men in their formerly women-only solidarity groups in 2003. According to loan officers, the resulting mixed groups have helped the organization to grow rapidly and inspired the country's leading microfinance institution, Banco Compartamos, to consider a similar approach.

Mixed groups can resolve some issues that arise with women-only groups. First, they eliminate ambiguity around how much women are receiving in loans and related conflicts. Husbands tend to overestimate the amount of money that women are handling and react by contributing less to household expenditures. This not only creates friction, but in some cases causes women to redirect loan funds to expenditures on food, health, and education. When husbands join groups, however, they gain an accurate understanding of loan amounts, as well as an appreciation for the terms of lending. In fact, since they are jointly liable for loan repayment, loan officers report that couples in solidarity groups cooperate more: husbands are less likely to complain about time diverted from household chores or steal money from their wives for personal indulgences. The decrease in intra-household conflict attributed to including husbands in solidarity groups has made it easier for women to repay their loans on time. Mixed groups have also been credited with attracting new clients, and new female clients in particular. Normally, women believe they would face a trade-off between being financially independent via credit from GTC or getting married. Since GTC accepts men, the argument goes, women no longer face that trade-off, and are therefore less hesitant to become clients.[19] Experimental research in the Philippines conducted by Nava Ashraf (2009) reinforces the importance of information flows and communication between spouses in determining financial decision making within families.

Another way in which microfinance can affect women's empowerment is with regard to the use of contraceptives. Especially in Bangladesh, microfinance has been promoted as a way to limit the number of children, and positive impacts have been found on contraceptive use (e.g., Rahman and Da Vanzo 1998; Schuler, Hashemi, and Riley 1997). This can be explained by the fact that microfinance increases the opportunity cost of women's time. This substitution effect may be reinforced by peer pressure as women are urged to reduce family size in order to increase education and health expenditure, and to better manage the ability to repay. On the other hand, Pitt, Khandker, McKernan et al. (1999) argue that this substitution effect could be outweighed by a countervailing income effect. In this case, microfinance would be positively associated with *higher* fertility as access to microfinance raises income, and, holding all else constant this should increase the demand for children. Meanwhile, it may raise opportunity costs only slightly since, unlike factory work, women can engage in self-employment activities from home while simultaneously caring for children. They show suggestive evidence from a cross-sectional survey in Bangladesh.[20]

Also working in Bangladesh, Pitt, Khandker, and Cartwright (2006) tackle the empowerment question more directly, estimating the impact of microcredit on an index of empowerment. Their study uses data from a household survey undertaken in 1998–99 that reports on women's responses to questions about female autonomy and gender relations within the household, and builds on an original 1991–92 survey that estimates the difference between household expenditures made by women and men when both had access to microloans. By adding empowerment-oriented questions in the follow-up 1998–99 survey, Pitt, Khandker, and Cartwright (2006) find that microcredit targeted to women produces statistically significant improvements in autonomy with respect to purchasing household assets, access to and control over economic resources, ability to raise emergency funds, role in deciding and implementing household borrowing, power to oversee and conduct major household economic transactions, mobility and networking, awareness and activism, and discussions around family and planning. One concern about their results, however, is that the empowerment questions were not asked in the 1991–92 baseline survey. Without knowing how women perceived their access to credit in connection with empowerment issues back then, it is difficult for researchers to compare the before- and after-intervention responses. Another concern is that the women surveyed in the 1998–99 study are not the same as those in the 1991–92 study. What's more, even if they had been the same women, the vast economic changes taking place in Bangladesh in the 1990s make it difficult to attribute empowerment improvements exclusively to microfinance. Even for the survey respondents themselves, it's difficult to disentangle what can be attributed to microfinance from everything else.

Swain and Wallentin (2007) also use quantitative methods to investigate the relationship between microfinance and women's intrahousehold empowerment. The authors look at a program in India that links informal Self-Help Groups (SHGs) to banks. Using household survey data for 2000 and 2003, they constructed a model for women's empowerment based on responses to survey questions about their economic activities; their reactions to verbal, physical and emotional abuse; and their degree of political participation. In line with the study from Bangladesh discussed above, they found that membership in a SHG increased women's empowerment in India.

The sharpest empirical study on the link between microfinance and women's empowerment is Ashraf, Karlan, and Yin's (2008) follow-up to their 2006 study of commitment saving devices in the Philippines (discussed in chapter 6). The earlier study found that access to commitment savings products led to an increase in saving. In the follow-up, it is shown that access also led to an increase in female decision-making power within the household (as judged by a battery of indicators)— which, in turn leads to greater spending on "female oriented" consumer durable goods. The largest positive impacts are for women who start out with below median decision-making power as measured by the baseline survey. These "female oriented" durables are deemed to include washing machines, sewing machines, electric irons, kitchen appliances, air conditioners, fans, and stoves. No significant impact is found on the consumption of "other durables" like motorcycles or televisions.

While microfinance can potentially empower women within the household, there is less evidence that it has been effective in transforming social norms and traditions. Mayoux (1999), for example, reports on a survey of fifteen different programs in Africa, finding that the degree of women's empowerment is household- and region-specific, and thus, she argues, depends on inflexible social norms and traditions. The findings have to be weighed against the fact that impacts on empowerment will, of course, also depend on how well the particular programs were designed.

7.7 Criticisms

We have argued earlier that microloans have played an important role in the promotion of self-employment in traditional activities where, relative to men, women already enjoy a comparative advantage. By enhancing women's specialization in those activities, microfinance may thus improve efficiency.

The focus on gender empowerment as a broader goal has come under fire from a variety of angles. The ever-provocative Dale Adams (Adams and Mayoux 2001, 4) argues that

the widespread use of the term "empowerment" by the microcredit crowd makes me uneasy. To the unwashed it conveys the impression that smearing a dab of additional debt on a poor woman will transform her into Super Woman. Those who insist on using this bloated term grossly overstate the contribution that indebting crusades play in easing poverty. More debt does not cure malaria or HIV/AIDS. It does not provide clean drinking water or prevent flooding. It does not improve law-and-order or eliminate weeds in a borrower's crops. It does not make crops grow in barren soil or provide secure title to land that squatters occupy. It does not provide schools or teachers for the poor . . .
    A loan provided by the microdebt industry, for say $100, is no more an empowerment tool than is a similar loan from an evil moneylender or a relative, unless the intent of the lender somehow transforms the usefulness of the money borrowed—which it doesn't.

The critique mirrors Adams's broader critique of microfinance as a poverty alleviation tool, discussed earlier in chapter 2. The argument hinges on the (much-disputed) assertion that poor women have adequate access to credit through informal means, so that microfinance might change the terms on which credit is obtained, but it does not open access.[21] The argument also dismisses the role of training or social capital that may be generated through participation in microfinance programs. Mayoux takes Adams to task, but agrees that credit alone is not enough to bring meaningful change to women; empowerment "also depends on how far [programs] are able to build on group organization to enable people to organize on other issues" (Adams and Mayoux 2001, 5).

Mayoux's critique of minimalist, banking-only approaches is taken further by other observers. Rankin (2002), for example, argues that microfinance may entrench—rather than challenge—traditional gender roles. First, she cites the Goetz and Sen Gupta (1996) evidence that it is often men, not the women borrowers, who actually control the microenterprise investments and income. Second, even when women maintain control, Rankin argues that "they are often encouraged to take up enterprises such as sweater knitting that do not disrupt practices of isolation and seclusion within their households (Rankin 2002, 17)." This raises a more complicated question: Is increased specialization within the household a good thing from a gender equity standpoint? Many critics, notably, Gibbons (1995), Goetz and Sen Gupta (1996), and Dawkins-Scully (1997), forcefully argued that it isn't. Within-household specialization, the argument goes, reinforces women's reliance on male family members due to women's limited access to inputs, supplies, and marketing facilities.

One answer to these criticisms is that unskilled women have very few working opportunities outside the household (in the formal sector, at least). So microfinance helps women to make the most out of the traditional activities that they are restricted from in the short run. Meanwhile, the hope is that they acquire new skills and accumulate resources that improve their family's living conditions.[22] Thus, microfinance advocates who stress gender empowerment tend to look to programs that add training and consciousness-raising—such as the training program organized by BRAC, the largest microlender in Bangladesh, or the credit with education strategy of Pro Mujer in Latin America. BRAC not only provides lessons on new productive activities, but they also hold sessions on legal and social rights and basic health practices. Such training is costly, though, and BRAC defrays expenses through funds from the government and international donors.

7.8 Summary and Conclusions

In this chapter we first argued that enhancing opportunities for women can be good for both efficiency and intrahousehold equity. Advocates argue that microfinance can also improve long-term development, as women are the main brokers of children's health and education. In particular, we highlighted the potential for microfinance to play a role in increasing the scale and scope of self-employment opportunities and skill acquisition, protecting women's rights through monitoring by third parties, for facilitating savings, and for enhancing social capital. These are not achievements that will necessarily arrive as a matter of course. Rather, to be achieved, microfinance programs need to be designed with these outcomes in mind. When and whether the goals can be met without sacrificing other goals—such as financial performance—remains an open question. Microfinance practitioners who are most interested in building strong financial systems have viewed discussions of gender empowerment with a wary eye—quite understandably, given the lack of systematic data—but we find a great deal of evidence from other quarters to support the potential for well-designed microfinance products to make a difference here.

In many ways, the discussion in this chapter just scratches the surface, and more research is needed on at least three important dimensions. First, the empirical evidence is scattered and incomplete. In particular we would like to learn more about the relationship of gender and social capital in microfinance; about the impact of microfinance on skill acquisition, education, and women's access to the formal sector; about the limitations that women face in expanding their businesses; and about the effect of microfinance on intrahousehold allocation of resources. The broader interrelationship of gender and class also deserves consideration within the microfinance context.

Second, how does the emphasis on gender affect the design of microfinance institutions? Should financial services be bundled with the provision of complementary inputs and training by NGOs, governments, and/or donor agencies? How should the lending contract or savings devices be modified to increase women's opportunities within the household and the broader community? A third question involves the extent to which microfinance can contribute to changes in social norms, rather than being a vehicle for reinforcing existing norms. These remain "frontier" issues, and will no doubt be revisited regularly.

7.9 Exercises

1. Refer to table 7.1 and comment on the merits of the following statement: "Microfinance might have triggered changes in social norms in both Asia and Latin America."

2. Is there any compelling evidence on gender discrimination in developing economies? Explain your answer.

3. Provide at least three reasons why microfinance can potentially benefit women.

4. Provide at least three reasons why, relative to men, women may be better clients, from the standpoint of a microlender simply interested in maximizing profits. What does this say about empowerment? Is there a contradiction?

5. Consider a household where there are two children, a girl and a boy. Parents in this household derive utility from their children's educational attainment. Suppose that in order to educate their children, parents must spend an amount x per month on the girl's education, and y on the boy's education. Let the household's utility be as follows:

If the income $w < \overline{W}$, then $U = x + 2y$

If the income $w \geq \overline{W}$, then $U = 2 \times \min(x, y)$.

Let $\overline{W} = Tk\ 1500$ and $x + y \leq w$, and do not consider the consumption decision of the household.

a. If the household's income is $w = Tk\ 1100$, what is its optimal strategy for allocating resources to education?

b. Suppose the woman in this household obtains a loan from a microfinance institution and invests it in a project that adds $Tk\ 700$ to the household's income. What is the household's optimal strategy now?

c. Interpret your answers by relating the shape of the household's preferences and its income level.

6. Consider the same situation as in the previous exercise, but now assume that the household has five children, three girls and two boys, and that the household has to spend an amount c on basic consumption goods before it can invest in education. The household's utility is as follows:

If income $w < \overline{W}$, then $U = x_1 + x_2 + x_3 + 3y_1 + 3y_2$, where x_i $(i = 1,2,3)$ is the amount invested in the girl i's education, and y_j $(j = 1,2)$ is the amount invested in boy j's education.

If the income $w \geq \overline{W}$, then $U = 4 \times \min(x_1 + x_2 + x_3; y_1 + y_2)$.

Let $\overline{W} = Tk\ 1800$; $c = Tk\ 1100$.

a. If the household's income is $w = Tk\ 1500$, what is its optimal strategy for allocating resources to education?

b. Suppose the woman in this household obtains a loan from a microfinance institution and invests it in a project that adds $Tk\ 1000$ to the household's income. What is the household's optimal strategy now?

c. Why might the strategy you obtained for part (b) not be strictly Rawlsian? Propose a utility function that will accord the household's allocation strategy with Rawls's distributive argument.

7. Consider a household similar to the one in exercise 4, but in this case its utility is given by:

$$\frac{w_m}{w} U_m + \frac{w_w}{w} U_w = \frac{w_m}{w}(3y+x) + \frac{w_w}{w}[\min(3x; 3y)]$$

where w_m, w_w are the man's income and the woman's income, respectively; $w = w_m + w_w$; and y and x are, respectively, the amount of resources invested in the boy and in the girl.

Let $\dfrac{w_m}{w}$ and $\dfrac{w_w}{w}$ denote the within-household bargaining power with respect to the household's income of the man and the woman, respectively.

a. Interpret the household utility function.

b. Suppose the man is the only source of labor income in this household, and assume that he earns $w_m = Tk\ 1000$ per month. Compute this household's optimal allocation decision.

c. Now assume that the woman can work in a project financed by a microfinance institution, and that as a result she generates an additional amount $w_w = Tk\ 1000$ per month. What would be the optimal strategy for the household in this case? Explain your answer.

8. Consider exercise 6, and compute the threshold rate

$$\frac{w_w}{w_m},$$

below which the woman's preferences have no bearing on the decision
that the household will ultimately take.

9. Consider a man and a woman who request a loan of size I from a
bank. If the loan is obtained by either individual, it can be invested in
either of the following two projects: in project 1, which requires an
investment I and yields $R_1 = \$520$; or in project 2, which also requires
an investment I and yields $R_2 = \$1020$ with probability 0.5 and zero
otherwise. Suppose that the man is risk neutral, while the woman is
risk averse. Her utility function is:

$$u_w = \frac{x^{0.5}}{0.5}$$

Assume that the man and the woman have the same level of initial
wealth, which is zero. Suppose that the gross repayment set by the
bank is $r = \$120$ for the I loan, and that this is fixed. Borrowers are
protected by limited liability. Will the bank decide to lend to the man
or to the woman? Explain your answer.

10. Consider exercise 8, except that in this case the man's utility
function is:

$$u_m = \frac{x^{0.8}}{0.8},$$

and project 2 yields a gross return of \$1120 with probability 0.5 and
zero otherwise. Will the bank decide to lend to the man or to the
woman? Explain your answer.

11. A husband and wife have different preferences over household
spending. The husband's and wife's utility functions are:

$$U_h(b, c) = b(c + 120)$$

$$U_w(b, c) = (b + 120)c$$

where b is spending on alcohol, and c is spending on their children's
education. Imagine these are the only two possible uses of money, so
the household budget constraint is: $b + c = y$. The "household utility
function," which determines household purchases, is a weighted
average of the preferences of the husband and wife:

$$U_H(b, c) = (1 - m)U_h(b, c) + mU_w(b, c)$$

where the weighting factor m is equal to the fraction of the total family income y that belongs to the wife. In other words, if $y = y_h + y_w$, then $m = y_w/y$. Assume that whether income comes from the husband or the wife only matters in determining the balance of power m. Beyond that, the husband and wife have no other "ownership" over their income.

a. Suppose that the husband starts with $100 in monthly income, and the wife has $50. How will the household allocate spending on alcohol and children's education?

b. Now suppose that a microfinance institution can grant a loan to the husband or to the wife, but not to both. Also suppose that the loan to the husband would have a higher return—the husband would get $100 in additional income, while the wife would only get $50. The institution's only objective is to maximize spending on children's education; it doesn't care about spending on alcohol either way. To whom, if anyone, should it make a loan?

12. Evaluate the merits of the following statement: "The only reason why a large majority of microfinance clients are women is because women are the main brokers of health and education."

13. Provide at least three reasons why, relative to men, women may be better clients, from the standpoint of a microfinance enterprise.

14. Some argue that women's preferences are more Rawlsian than men's, so they distribute the resources they control more equally between the boys and girls in their families than men do. If boys hold more earning potential than girls, women's resource allocations do not maximize their families' future earnings. Others claim lending to women has a greater impact than lending to men. At first glance these assertions appear contradictory. Reconcile them.

15. Is there compelling evidence that relative to men, lending to women has more of an impact?

16. Comment on the following statement: "Microfinance empowers women. That is, it reduces the extent of gender bias."

17. Consider a microfinance institution's objectives. What trade-off might it face when deciding between lending to women or to men?

8   Commercialization and Regulation

8.1 Introduction

Some see microfinance as a source of major social transformation. Others see it as the seed of a revolution in banking access. True believers push for both. No matter which path is taken, pursuing the promise of microfinance requires much more than the management acumen required to run strong institutions. It also requires regulators who enable innovation and investors who understand the business proposition.

One of the most unexpected and encouraging turns in the brief history of microfinance is the degree to which leaders who were first driven by social impulses to create NGOs have seized the logic and imperative of engaging with capital markets. The move toward commercialization and regulation offers an opportunity to provide much needed savings facilities to clients. Moreover, it has opened microfinance to serving customers who are not the poorest of the poor—nor even poor by standard measures—but who are nevertheless denied access to loans under traditional bank practices. This has been a tricky transition, given that donors and social investors often gave initial subsidies earmarked for institutions to serve the most disadvantaged. Concerns with "mission drift" from commercialization of microfinance institutions are often voiced and need to be taken seriously.

No single event in the past decade of microfinance has polarized observers as much as the public stock offering of Banco Compartamos, now the largest Latin American microfinance institution, in April 2007. The offering allowed Banco Compartamos's original equity investors to reap impressive returns to their early investments. The $1 million dollar USAID grant that the ACCION microfinance network invested in Banco Compartamos, for instance, increased in value to $300 million.[1]

In total, the $6 million in equity investments that launched the bank in 2000—held by the International Finance Corporation (part of the World Bank Group), ACCION Gateway Fund, Profund, the founding NGO and its leaders, and other Mexican private investors—turned out to be worth $2.2 billion in June 2007 (though the stock price later tumbled).

Outside observers were shocked at the high returns. The event caught the attention of writers at the *Economist*, the *Wall Street Journal*, *Business Week*, and other leading newspapers and magazines. For some, this was a positive event—proof of the fundamental premise that microfinance can be commercially viable and attract private capital without recourse to social motivations. For others, it was an outrage. The high stock prices resulted from Banco Compartamos's high rate of profit and choice to expand rapidly, and those patterns rested on high interest rates charged to borrowers. Interest rates in Mexico are generally high relative to the rest of the world, but Banco Compartamos's customers were paying on average roughly 100 percent per year for loans—while the inflation rate in Mexico was hovering around 4 percent per year.[2]

Muhammad Yunus, founder of Grameen Bank, argued that this was simply moneylending reincarnated. While the announcement of Yunus's Nobel Peace Prize in October 2006 brought microfinance leaders together in celebration of the potential for microfinance to reduce poverty, the Banco Compartamos stock offering revealed important divides around views on the new wave of commercial microfinance.[3] The debate took center stage again at a conference hosted by the World Microfinance Forum in October 2008, pitting Yunus against Michael Chu, the former President of ACCION (Rosenberg 2008). Yunus argued that earning large profits by serving the poor is inherently wrong, and that microfinance can flourish without profit-maximizing investment.[4] Chu, on the other hand, argued that microfinance providers cannot meet the worldwide demand for financial services without private, profit-oriented capital. Competition in the microfinance market, he asserted, would eventually bring down interest rates and profits.[5]

Banco Compartamos's sale was not the first public offering in microfinance. Bank Rakyat Indonesia (BRI) listed on the Jakarta Stock Exchange in 2003, and Kenya's Equity Bank went public in 2006. Moreover, commercial financing through debt has long been a part of the microfinance funding mix. But the Banco Compartamos public offering is set apart by the bank's origins. While BRI was government-owned until its public offering, and Equity Bank initially focused on offering mortgage services, Banco Compartamos, like most microfinance institutions, owes its existence to donor support. Banco Compartamos originated as a donor-funded NGO with a pro-poor mission. However, its management, recognizing the constraints of soft financing, decided to reorganize as a for-profit company. It reasoned that tapping commercial sources of funding would allow the bank to expand its outreach dramatically, and it did: its client base grew from 60,000 in 2000 to over 800,000 in 2007. By May 2009, Banco Compartamos had reached 1.2 million customers.

As a strategic matter, there appear to be middle paths. Banco Compartamos's strategy entailed charging high interest rates to generate retained earnings that could fuel rapid expansion. As a result, the bank's return on equity topped 50 percent in the period leading up to the public offering, and roughly one quarter of interest revenues were pure profit (Rosenberg 2007). In essence, poor and low-income women served by existing branches were paying for the bank's expansion into new branches, raising concerns about monopolistic pricing. Some analysts argued that instead the bank could have lowered interest rates and earned a smaller profit while still expanding, albeit at a slower pace (Rosenberg 2007). Or the bank might have taken on more debt to fund expansion. The controversy around the Banco Compartamos public offering is fueled largely by uncertainty about the nature of these choices: Banco Compartamos decided to keep rates high in the face of plausible alternatives that some see as unambiguously better for the bank's poor client base, but it is easier to criticize after the fact than to consider choices in the context of the constraints and opportunities perceived at the time.

For all of the debate, there are important areas of consensus. All sides agree that the unmet demand for reliable financial services is huge. Recent studies estimate that 40 to 80 percent of the populations in most poor countries lack access to formal sector banking services (Beck, Demirgüç-Kunt, and Martinez Peria 2007). Expanding access to reliable financial services could improve prospects for a substantial portion of the world's poor and unbanked. Funk (2007) estimates that microfinance institutions need $30 billion per year to effectively reach the unbanked across the world, and suggests that capital markets, if allowed to develop, could provide it. With that level of financing, microfinance institutions could broaden their outreach to over 1 billion low-income customers, well beyond the 154.8 million counted in 2007 or the 175 million in the sights for 2015 (Daley-Harris 2009). Moreover, as fully-regulated institutions, banks are generally entitled to collect and intermediate savings, yet another source of funding to increase financial access.

To understand the power and limits of "commercialization," it is important to be precise. The term is used in different ways at different times. Sometimes commercialization is used to indicate that an institution is seeking to operate using commercial sources of funding (i.e., with no direct or indirect subsidy element). However, the term is often used broadly to indicate the application of market-based business principles to the management of microfinance institutions—a concept that could apply as well to subsidized institutions and NGOs. In this chapter, we focus on the move toward purely commercial investment, and, to some degree, we touch upon accompanying changes in governance structure (more broadly developed in chapter 11).

This is the sense in which commercial microfinance institutions are at the heart of the "win-win" proposition of microfinance: that by adopting commercial principles and practices, institutions can do more to reduce poverty. By moving away from subsidy dependence, institutions will be able to grow beyond the limits of donor budgets, expanding their outreach to serve more of the world's poor. If the argument holds, the microfinance path can be broadened by leveraging interest revenues and mobilizing savings deposits.

Here, the most important shift for a commercialized institution is the ability to distribute profits to shareholders. Nothing bars NGOs from earning profits (and below we show that many microfinance NGOs do). However, profit earned by an NGO cannot be distributed to shareholders. Instead, profit is generally re-invested in the institution. With transformation into a fully regulated, commercial business, profit can be earned by investors, providing the opportunity to attract shareholders with only limited (or no) social goals—giving commercial microfinance institutions access to a vast pool of capital.

The debate described above is, of course, a reminder of the many strings that potentially can be attached to that capital—especially as profit-driven shareholders, unlike donors, may have limited social objectives and can use their voice to shape the institution's direction. While seeking profit and serving the poor can in principle be mutually reinforcing, there are often tensions. The greatest tensions result from fears of "mission drift" as commercial MFIs target relatively better-off customers and face trade-offs between the objectives of profitability and outreach to the poor (Morduch 2000; Ghosh and Van Tassel 2008; Armendáriz and Szafarz 2009).

The rest of this chapter introduces key ideas and data. Section 8.2 begins by defining five often-used financial ratios for evaluating and comparing microfinance performance. Section 8.3 puts these ratios to work. We show differences in profitability, costs, and outreach among NGOs, nonbank financial institutions, and commercial banks. Costs are tied to the size of transactions, with NGOs making the smallest loans and facing the highest per unit costs. The chapter then turns to funding. Section 8.4 presents data on interest rates, funding structures and leverage, showing that commercial microfinance banks are achieving far greater leverage than NGOs.

That section also touches upon issues pertaining regulation and consumer protection. The shift from NGO to commercial status typically brings a major change in regulation. Prudential regulation is becoming critical as commercial microfinance institutions look to depositors in the public at large. We describe these issues in section 8.5, which deals with transformation, regulation, and consumer protection. There, we describe evidence on trade-offs between the benefits of strong regulation and the costs it imposes on commercial MFIs (and ultimately on their clients). The chapter concludes with a discussion of efforts to apply consumer protection principles, driven by the realization that good intentions at the top of organizations may be insufficient to guarantee fair treatment for all clients.

8.2   Five Financial Ratios

Five financial ratios are commonly used to compare the financial performance of microfinance institutions. Not all of them are standard in the accounting literature, so it's helpful to start by defining the terms.[6]

The first is the operational self-sufficiency ratio (OSS). This ratio measures the extent to which the operating revenues of a microfinance institution cover its operating costs. Revenues mainly come from interest and fees paid by borrowers, but a typical institution also generates income from investments and from other services (from insurance sales, for example).

$$OSS = \frac{\text{Operating revenue}}{\text{Financial expense} + \text{loan-loss provision expense} + \text{operating expense}}$$

The financial expense in the denominator of the OSS ratio pertains to the cost of raising capital. It includes the interest and fees that the institution pays to commercial banks, shareholders, and other investors. It also includes interest paid to depositors (if savings services are offered). Industry reporting standards published by CGAP (2003) recommended that expenses for loan-loss provisions also be included in the denominator. The loan-loss provision expense is the amount set aside to cover the cost of loans that the microfinance institution does not expect to recover. The third item in the denominator captures basic operating expenses (including rent, staff wages, and transport costs, among others.) Note that operating revenues and operating expenses are calculated net of subsidy.

The ratio is most often presented as a percent. A value of 100 percent for the OSS ratio indicates full operational self-sufficiency, while a value under 100 indicates that the institution must rely on continued outside funding to maintain its current level of operation. An institution with an OSS larger than 100 is often interpreted as being able to continue operating at its present scale without requiring additional subsidies. In this specific sense, a microfinance institution is labeled as "self-sufficient." Subsidies or some other funding strategy would be needed if loan losses mounted or if the institution wanted to expand.

To capture the broader notion of "sustainability," it is necessary to take into account subsidies from "soft" loans and investments. A second important number, the financial self-sufficiency (FSS) ratio, corrects for soft loans by making adjustments that price capital at its market cost. It is also typically presented as a percent.

$$FSS = \frac{\text{Adjusted operating revenue}}{\text{Financial expense} + \text{loan-loss provision expense} + \text{operating expense} + \text{expense adjustments}}$$

FSS takes into account additional adjustments to operating revenues and expenses that model how well the microfinance institution could cover its costs if its operations were unsubsidized and if it were funding its expansion with liabilities at "market" prices. Subsidy adjustments serve two purposes. First, since institutions vary considerably in the amount of subsidy they receive, adjustments that account for subsidies allow for useful comparison across institutions. Second, to the extent that operating on a commercial basis, free from subsidy, is an objective, subsidy adjustments represent how close an institution is to reaching this goal. The question answered by FSS is, roughly, whether an institution can expand without subsidy.

There are two types of subsidy adjustments. The first is a subsidized cost-of-funds adjustment, also called an adjustment for concessionary borrowing. It captures the difference between what an institution pays in borrowing expenses, and what it would pay if all of its borrowing liabilities were priced at market rates. The difference is added to financial expenses. A second type of subsidy adjustment takes into account in-kind donations, or goods and services provided to the institution at no cost or at below-market cost. If FSS is below 100, that is, if adjusted income is below adjusted costs, the institution is considered subsidy dependent.

The FSS ratio is imperfect as a guide to sustainablility. Notably, the adjustment rests on estimates of the market cost of capital, for which there is in practice no standard measure. The *MicroBanking Bulletin*, a widely-used reference, uses the country's deposit rate (as tabulated by the International Monetary Fund) as the "market" price. But this rate is surely too low for the purposes here. The deposit rate is defended as the typical cost that deposit-taking institutions pay savers for capital. But in practice most microfinance institutions do not use deposits as the marginal source of capital and the measure fails to build in the transaction costs of handling deposit accounts.[7] A better measure would be the prime interest rate, the price for capital charged by banks and their most trustworthy customers, plus extra percentage points added to reflect the underlying riskiness of microfinance loan portfolios and the illiquidity of typical investments in microfinance institutions. Cull, Demirgüç-Kunt, and Morduch (2009b) make a modest adjustment (using the prime interest rate plus two percentage points) and find, not surprisingly, that the higher estimate of the price of capital diminishes the appearance of profits and increases the value of implicit subsidies. They find that the median NGO in the *MicroBanking Bulletin* data is no longer profit-making, while microfinance banks are much less affected by the adjustment.

Cull et al. (2009b) also point to a countervailing concern. They note that the FSS analysis is static in a way that undervalues the flexibility of institutions. The FSS ratio is ultimately used as a measure of the ability to operate on commercial terms. That ability, though, is ultimately tied to the ability to shift strategies as required. Let's say that an institution's access to concessional funds and grants dries up; the real question is whether the institution could then shift strategies and reallocate resources as needed. When pushed, could the institution reduce its dependence on subsidy by economizing and becoming more efficient? The FSS ratio is only a rough guide to that strategic question. It usefully reveals current circumstances but gives only a limited sense of possibilities without subsidy.

A third sustainability/profitability ratio is the return on assets (ROA), which measures how well an institution uses its total assets to generate returns.

$$ROA = \frac{\text{Net operating income} - \text{taxes}}{\text{Average assets}}$$

Net operating income is total operating revenue (discussed above) less operating expense, financial expense, and loan-loss provision expense. An institution may either deduct taxes on revenues or profits when calculating net operating income, or it may treat taxes separately. Assets may be averaged for the year, but quarterly or monthly averages are more meaningful because they mitigate distortions resulting from rapidly increasing loan portfolios and seasonal fluctuations.

The fourth measure is the most widely used measure of portfolio quality, the portfolio at risk (PAR) ratio:

$$PAR\,(30\text{ days}) = \frac{\text{Portfolio at risk (after 30 days)}}{\text{Gross loan portfolio}}$$

Portfolio at risk is "the value of all loans outstanding that have one or more installments of principal overdue more than a certain number of days. This system includes the entire unpaid principal balance, including both past-due and future installments, but not accrued interest. It also does not include loans that have been restructured or rescheduled" (CGAP 2003, 6).

For example, consider a customer who borrows $1000, to be repaid in ten monthly installment of $100 each. The first two installments are paid on time, but the customer runs into trouble with the third and can't make the payment. If the third installment remains unpaid a month later, the entire $800 unpaid balance is then classified as part of the institution's "portfolio at risk." In this way, PAR is a sensibly conservative measure. By dividing by the gross loan portfolio, the portfolio at risk measure gives the percentage of loans outstanding that are at substantial risk of default as signaled by difficulties that have already emerged. In addition to considering the 30-day PAR, microbanks also keep an eye on 60-day and 90-day ratios. These ratios are less conservative: the effects of missed installments that are eventually paid two months late will show up in the 30-day PAR, but not the 60-day PAR.

The fifth measure, "portfolio yield" or "yield on gross loan portfolio," is a ratio used to assess revenues. It measures income from the loan portfolio, and is also a measure of the average interest rate charged to borrowers by the institution.

$$\text{Yield on gross loan portfolio} = \frac{\text{Cash financial revenue from loan portfolio}}{\text{Average gross loan portfolio}}$$

This is effectively an average interest rate (including loan-related fees), with weights given by the volume of loans at different prices. The "real yield" is adjusted for inflation as well.

8.3 Financial Performance in a Cross-Section of Microfinance Institutions

Cull et al. (2009b) use the measures presented above to gauge the microfinance landscape. They take advantage of access to the base data used in the *MicroBanking Bulletin* for the years 2002–2004. The data set is relatively large, covering 346 leading institutions with nearly 18 million active microfinance borrowers in total. Using purchasing power parity (PPP) adjusted exchange rates to convert assets into dollars, the institutions hold assets with a combined total of $25.3 billion in effective purchasing power. The numbers are particularly revealing since they are adjusted to show the roles of both explicit and implicit subsidies.[8]

The main analyses focus on NGOs, nonbank financial institutions and microfinance (commercial) banks. Table 8.1 gives the basic data. The first pattern they note is that risk (as measured by the portfolio at risk after 30 days), relative to traditional commercial banks, is low—under 4 percent for the median NGO—and reasonably similar across all the institutional categories. But after that, differences emerge.

Table 8.1
Nongovernmental organizations versus nonbank financial institutions and banks
Return on equity is adjusted net income divided by total equity. Subsidy per borrower numbers are donations from prior years plus donations to subsidize financial services plus an in-kind subsidy adjustment plus an adjustment for subsidies to the cost of funds.

	Nongovernmental organizations				Nonbank financial institutions				Banks			
	25th pctile (1)	Median (2)	75th pctile (3)	Median if profitable (4)	25th pctile (5)	Median (6)	75th pctile (7)	Median if profitable (8)	25th pctile (9)	Median (10)	75th pctile (11)	Median if profitable (12)
1. Portfolio at risk, 30 days (%)	0.74	3.54	7.59	0.81	0.91	2.06	6.91	1.20	0.39*	2.43*	5.23*	4.42*
2. Average loan size/income at 20th percentile (%)	27	48	135	60	71	160	247	164	110	224	510	294
3. Active borrowers (thousands)	3.1	7.4	23.0	11.1	4.1	9.9	23.0	9.4	1.9	20.3	60.7	10.4
4. Women as a share of all borrowers (%)	63	85	100	86	47	66	94	67	23	52	58	49
5. Operating cost/loan value (%)	15	26	38	21	13	17	24	16	7	12	21	11
6. Operating cost/active borrower (PPP$)	84	156	309	157	135	234	491	278	118	299	515	299
7. Real portfolio yield (%)	15	25	37	26	12	20	26	20	9	13	19	14
8. Financial self-sufficiency ratio	0.78	1.03	1.17	1.14	0.86	1.04	1.22	1.16	0.99	1.04	1.15	1.10
9. Return on equity (%)	−10.5	3.4	13.8	11.4	−7.9	3.6	17.8	14.4	1.6	10.0	22.9	15.1
10. Return on assets (%)	−6.0	0.7	4.7	4.1	−2.7	0.9	4.3	3.5	−0.1	1.4	3.2	2.1
11. Subsidy/borrower (PPP$)	72	233	659	199	0	32	747	8	0	0	136	0
12. Noncommercial funding ratio	0.31	0.74	1.00	0.53	0.16	0.46	0.83	0.41	0.00	0.11	0.22	0.03

*Based on fewer than 10 observations.
Source: Cull, Demirgüç-Kunt, and Morduch (2009b), table 3. Data are from the *MicroBanking Bulletin* database (2002–2004, 315 observations).

The second variable is average loan size, a common though imperfect indicator of the poverty level of customers.[9] Smaller average loan sizes indicate greater outreach to the poor. In order to make the data comparable across countries, Cull et al. (2009b) standardize the loan size values via dividing by the average income at the twentieth percentile of the country's income distribution. The ratio is 48 percent for the median NGO, 160 percent for the median nonblank financial institution, and 224 for the median microfinance bank. By this measure, the median bank is considerably further up-market than the median NGO. The result must be treated carefully, though, since the microfinance banks tend to serve more customers than typical NGOs. The median bank is three times larger than the median NGO (there are exceptions, of course—including some very large NGOs in South Asia). With large banks, it's possible to both go up-market and to serve poor and low-income communities in quantity, but the data do not allow that kind of disaggregation.

Data on the percentage of women as clients (row 4) echo the data on average loan sizes. The median bank's customers are roughly half female, while the median NGO's customers are 85 percent female. Whether serving women benefits the microfinance institutions' sustainability objectives is unclear. As chapter 7 describes, the evidence to date shows that women tend to be more risk averse than men, but they also tend to seek smaller loans, increasing the microfinance institutions' transactions costs.

These patterns emerge clearly in rows 5 and 6 of table 8.1, which identify the trade-off. The relatively small average loan sizes typical of NGOs, seen in row 2, translate into relatively high unit costs. For the median NGO, it costs the equivalent of $26 for each $100 lent (before accounting for capital costs). The median microfinance bank is making much larger loans (over 4 times as large) and is thus better able to spread out the fixed costs of lending. As a result, it only costs the median bank $12 for each $100 lent. This result occurs despite the finding in row 6 that microfinance banks spend considerably more per customer over the year; the banks' financial advantage follows largely from the fact that their customers borrow in relatively large quantities. Figure 8.1 shows the data arrayed as a scatter plot.

The consequence of these cost structures is seen in figure 8.2 and in row 7 of table 8.1: the customers at the median NGO pay much higher interest rates than customers of the median microfinance bank. Customers at the median NGO pay, on average, 25 percent per year after accounting for inflation. At a quarter of NGOs, customers pay over 37

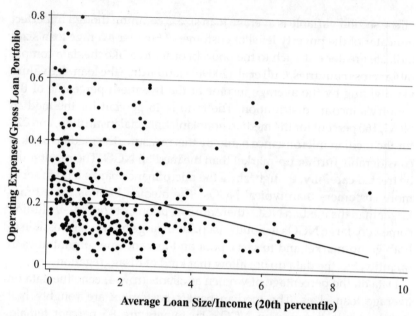

Figure 8.1
Average costs per dollar lent fall as loans get larger. Horizontal axis gives the average loan size as a fraction of the average income of households at the twentieth percentile of the national income distribution. Source: Cull et al. (2009b, figure 3).

percent in real terms. Customers at the median microfinance bank, on the other hand, pay on average just 13 percent per year after accounting for inflation. The highest fees are thus being charged by the institutions most focused on social missions, while the commercial microfinance institutions offer relatively cheap credit.

Row 8 of table 8.1 shows the consequence for profitability: the higher interest rates charged by NGOs offset their greater unit costs. In terms of financial sustainability ratios (FSS), the median numbers look similar across the three categories of institutions at 103–104 percent, and the overall correlation between profitability and loan size is weak.[10] The evidence here thus shows that the higher costs of serving the poor tend to be passed on to customers.

Imagine, though, a scenario in which interest rates and fees could not be adequately raised, perhaps for social reasons, regulatory barriers, public relations issues, or fear of exacerbating the kinds of incentive problems described in chapter 2. In this case, the push for profit necessitates reducing costs. Here, the temptation to move up-market (to a population with the capacity to service larger loans) becomes greatest.

Figure 8.2
Interest rates rise with costs. The "premium" is the excess of the microlender's average interest rate charged to borrowers over the International Monetary Fund's interbank "lending interest rate" that banks in the given countries charge to prime customers (from IMF International Financial Statistics). Source: Cull et al. (2009b, figure 4).

The essential problem is the need to compensate for the high fixed costs of lending in small amounts.

Mission drift is not inevitable. Cull, Demirgüç-Kunt, and Morduch (2007, F110) show that "financially self-sustaining individual-based lenders tend to have smaller average loan size and lend more to women, suggesting that pursuit of profit and outreach to the poor can go hand in hand." Commercialization can even be a great benefit to poor customers. For one thing, when an NGO transforms into a regulated bank, it can start rolling out savings products. For another, commercialization can help fund expansion. But the evidence presented by Cull et al. (2009b) suggests that most NGOs and most commercial banks appear to serve different markets and to operate in fundamentally different ways. The differences run deeper than the institutions' choices of financial structure: the data show that the push for commercialization is apt to have important consequences for who is served and how.

The possibility of cross-subsidization (rather than mission drift) is explored by Armendáriz and Szafarz (2009), drawing on work by

Ghosh and Van Tassel (2008). In the Armendáriz-Szafarz model, cross-subsidization occurs by mixing richer and poorer customers. This helps microfinance institutions to meet their outreach-maximization objectives, particularly when the continued flow of funds from international donors/local governments and socially responsible investors is biased in favor of self-sustainable institutions. Larger average loan sizes do not then mean that the institution is abandoning its poorest customers—in fact, the opposite may be true. In practice, tensions emerge with attempts to cross-subsidize. Focus can be sacrificed, and, with competition, institutions fear that competitors will "cherry pick" richer, more profitable customers.

8.4 Interest Rates, Funding Structures, and Leverage

One of the promises of commercialization is the ability to expand scale by leveraging assets. We turn now to the different sources of revenue and financing microfinance institutions use to fund their operations. Subsidized funding is also an important source of support for microfinance institutions, and we discuss it in detail in chapter 10.

The story of the Banco Compartamos public offering at the beginning of this chapter and the tensions outlined above highlight the interplay between a microfinance institution's pricing policy and its funding mix. On one hand, access to commercial funding fosters financial self-sufficiency by reducing a lender's reliance on subsidies and revenues from interest rates and fees. On the other, only financially viable institutions can access it. Institutions that want to access commercial funding have to pursue sustainability with the tools at their disposal. They are pressed to keep costs low and to generate enough revenue from interest payments on loans to cover those costs.

8.4.1 Interest Rates

In chapter 1 we challenged the assumption that poor borrowers are relatively insensitive to interest rates by unpacking the theory of diminishing returns to capital. Ultimately, the sensitivity of demand for microcredit to changes in interest rates is an empirical issue, and evidence suggests that interest rates can matter. Dehejia, Montgomery, and Morduch (2009) investigate the question directly, using an unanticipated between-branch variation in the interest rate charged by a Bangladeshi credit cooperative to estimate the elasticity of demand for loans with respect to interest rates. They find that a ten percent increase in the interest rate decreases the demand for credit by between 7.3 and 10.4 percent. Furthermore, less wealthy households appear to be *more* sensitive to interest rates than relatively wealthier households. In line with this finding, there is a risk that branches that increased their interest rates would see their customer bases shift away from relatively poorer clients; Dehejia et al. (2009) find suggestive evidence for this shift in their data. Karlan and Zinman (2008) also study consumer sensitivity to interest rates. They find that the demand for high-priced consumer credit is "kinked": it is steep for interest rate increases, but flat otherwise. So while lenders may need to set their interest rates high enough to cover costs, they also should watch how interest rates affect patterns of demand for credit.

The interest rates charged by microfinance institutions are generally considerably lower than those charged by moneylenders, and far below the 100 per year charged by Banco Compartamos at the time of its public offering (inclusive of Mexico's 15 percent value added tax): a global estimate for sustainable institutions put the median rate at about 26 percent (Rosenberg, Gonzalez, and Narain 2009).[11] Yet, 26 percent is still well above the price that wealthier individuals pay for credit. The relatively high cost of making small loans partially accounts for this gap, but operating expenses are not the only use of funds that factor into the price of loans.

In addition to operating expenses, interest rates are comprised by three other main components: cost of funds, loan loss expenses, and profits. Rosenberg et al. (2009) show that operating expenses make up the bulk of interest rates. Whether or not institutions are operating efficiently, that is, keeping operating expenses as low as possible, is a separate but important question. While the loan loss expenses faced by most microlenders are relatively insignificant and thus have little impact on interest rates, microfinance institutions pay more for borrowed money than do traditional banks, and their relatively high cost of funds pushes their interest rates upward (Rosenberg et al. 2009).

The final component of interest rates, profits, is the factor over which managers have the most control and which is the most controversial. In 2006, the average return on assets for sustainable microfinance institutions was 0.7 percent higher than that earned by banks. However, banks had an average return on equity 4.7 percent higher than that of microfinance institutions with large profits (Rosenberg et al. 2009).

The imbalance stems from the fact that banks are typically more lever-aged than microfinance institutions. Most microfinance institutions turn moderate profits that contribute far less to interest rates than do administrative expenses. Rosenberg et al. (2009, 18) show that the median institution could reduce its interest rate by only about one sixth by completely eliminating all profit.

Interest rates turn out to be surprisingly complicated. Collins, Morduch, Rutherford et al. (2009) show that from the customers' per-spective, short-term loans (of, say, a month duration) often carry inter-est rates that are perceived as fixed fees rather than interest per se. Annualizing those rates to calculate APRs (annualized percentage rates) can distort the picture in that customers would likely balk at paying that amount of interest for a longer duration loan (of, say, a year duration). Similar issues come up on the supply side. A 4 month loan—which is typical for Banco Compartamos, for example—seems particularly high when annualized. Yet the *absolute* cost of the loan may in fact be quite reasonable in the context of customers' budgets—and the high *percentage* charged may be necessary for the lender to recover the fixed costs of making small loans with short terms.

8.4.2 Commercial Sources of Funding

Microfinance investment vehicles (MIVs) are funds that invest all or part of their assets in microfinance institutions. Some investors are strictly commercial and expect high returns on their investments, but as of April 2007, these investors accounted for only 12 percent of the microfinance investment funds universe (MicroCapital 2007). More typically, MIVs cater to socially responsible investors and operate with a double bottom line, meaning that they care about social returns as well as financial returns. Yet the majority of investment in microfinance comes from organizations, both public and private, that aren't seeking a financial return at all. As of April 2007, these noncommercial funds made up 63 percent of all investors (MicroCapital 2007). They include microfinance development funds established to promote microfinance, development agencies like the International Finance Corporation, and philanthropic foundations.

Investment in microfinance has been surging in recent years. In December 2008, the Microfinance Information eXchange (the MIX) listed 103 funds investing in microfinance, and the number of private funds grew from 74 in 2006 to 91 at the end of 2007 (CGAP 2008b). Because private investment in microfinance is such a recent phenomenon, data on trends and important indicators like returns is thin, but there are efforts to improve its quality and quantity. Since 2007, CGAP has been working with Symbiotics, a consultancy that specializes in microfinance investment, to track information about private investment in microfinance and produce an annual benchmarks report. In the 2008 publication, the team estimated that the 91 MIVs active at the end of 2007 held $5.4 billion in assets (CGAP 2008b). They also conducted in-depth surveys with 58 MIVs.

To facilitate comparison and analysis, CGAP and Symbiotics segment the private investment universe into 7 peer groups based on their business models, commercial orientation, financial instruments and asset classes. As shown in table 8.2, most of the investment in microfinance is in the form of debt from fixed income investors. While debt accounts for 78 percent of all investment, equity investment is growing rapidly, up 95 percent in 2007 (CGAP 2008b).

Part of the reason for the upsurge in private investment in 2005–7 may be the success of existing funds. Table 8.2 shows that fixed income

Table 8.2
A survey of microfinance funds, 2007

	Fixed Income			Mixed: Blended-value funds	Equity	
	Registered mutual funds	Commercial investment funds	Structured finance vehicles		Private equity funds	Holding companies
Number of funds surveyed	6	5	4	7	4	6
Total assets (US$ millions)	391	437	279	146	62	84
Total microfinance investments (US$ millions)	293	280	268	111	44	70
Equity as % of microfinance portfolio	6%	1%	0%	28%	93%	76%
Debt as % of microfinance portfolio	93%	93%	100%	67%	7%	24%
Return in US$	5.8%	4.8% (euro)	5.3% (AA)	1.5%	NA	NA
Average total expense ratio	2.7%	2.0%	1.3%	6.1%	8.4%	4.1%

Source: CGAP 2008a, "Foreign Capital Investment in Microfinance."

MIVs earned a net return close to money market at 5.8 percent in 2006, and in 2007 they did even better, earning an average 6.3 percent return on their investments (CGAP 2008b). The generally strong financial performance of microfinance institutions gives reason to believe that the average return on equity investment is also good, as does the continued interest of equity investors despite the global economic downturn that started in 2008—two new equity funds were announced in March 2009, with several more on the horizon (CGAP 2009). CGAP and Symbiotics report an internal rate of return of 12.5 percent for private equity funds in 2007 (CGAP 2008b).

Money from private investors is concentrated in a few large, commercial institutions, mostly in Eastern Europe and Central Asia and in Latin America and the Caribbean. Recent trends, however, suggest that the investment landscape is changing. The growth in the number of funds investing in microfinance institutions means that the supply of credit available to leading microfinance institutions has increased, and so too has competition between MIVs. In response to this competition, MIVs have introduced larger and longer-term loans tailored to meet the demand of large microfinance institutions, which has further concentrated investment in the big players. However, investors are also trying to outperform the competition by broadening their client bases, which can mean lending to smaller microfinance institutions that haven't attracted a significant amount of private capital to date, and donors have helped create local funds in places like India and Morocco (CGAP 2008a).

8.4.3 Leverage

The prospect of commercial funding raises the possibility of increasing leverage, the ability to use an institution's existing assets to gain access to a larger amount of capital. Table 8.3 describes the funding picture for the range of institutions covered in Cull et al. (2009b). The table shows that microfinance banks and NGOs have very different financial structures. Turning to the NGOs, 39 percent of funding came from donations and another 16 percent came from noncommercial (soft) loans. But for the banks, donations and soft loans made up just 3 percent of total funding. The greatest quantity, 84 percent, came from commercial borrowing and deposits.

Leverage aids an institution's financial bottom line by allowing the possibility of reaping economies of scale. Here, the NGOs are limited in their ability to gain leverage. Their loan portfolios are not typically

Table 8.3
Shares of total funding by institutional type

Institution type	Shares of total funding					Median noncommercial funding ratio
	Donations	Noncommercial borrowing	Equity	Commercial borrowing	Deposits	
Bank (24 obs)	0.02 [0.09]	0.01 [0.037]	0.13 [0.16]	0.13 [0.19]	0.71 [0.30]	0.11
Credit union (30 obs)	0.11 [0.22]	0.03 [0.11]	0.16 [0.15]	0.06 [0.10]	0.64 [0.29]	0.21
NBFI (88 obs)	0.23 [0.30]	0.11 [0.20]	0.18 [0.24]	0.28 [0.30]	0.21 [0.29]	0.45
NGO (134 obs)	0.39 [0.34]	0.16 [0.25]	0.08 [0.20]	0.26 [0.29]	0.10 [0.18]	0.74
Total (289 obs)	0.26 [0.33]	0.11 [0.21]	0.13 [0.20]	0.23 [0.27]	0.27 [0.34]	0.43

Means [standard deviations in brackets]. Rural banks omitted.
Source: Cull, Demirgüç-Kunt, and Morduch (2009b), table 4.

backed by collateral, making profit-seeking investors wary of taking on the risk. The microfinance banks, in contrast, are more likely to require that their customers pledge collateral, especially given that the banks make larger loans than typical NGOs. The collateral, together with the security afforded by knowledge that the banks are supervised by regulators, in turn increases the microfinance banks' chance to leverage existing assets and to borrow against the loan portfolio. This is the equation that commercially minded microfinance advocates have long pursued. Profitability (which is achieved by many NGOs) is insufficient to maximize leverage.

8.5 Transformation, Regulation, and Consumer Protection

Bolivia's BancoSol is a pioneering commercial microfinance bank in Latin America, but it started first as an NGO, The Foundation for the Promotion and Development of Microfinance Enterprises (PRODEM). It only later became a formal bank, as Rhyne (2001) engagingly describes. Typically, transformation (also called formalization) requires new capital from outside investors, regulatory approval by local banking authorities, and improved governance and internal controls. In return, the shift to becoming regulated generally allows microfinance institutions to mobilize deposits, at least in principle, and offer services beyond loans (Frank 2008, 2). Transformation brings advantages, but it also brings changes. Whereas NGOs and other nonbank financial institutions operate with some flexibility, formalizing means adapting to a more stringent set of rules governing what financial institutions can and cannot do.

Different institutional histories entail different strengths and weaknesses, but all commercial microfinance institutions face the same challenge of complying with regulation. Formal financial institutions are subject to a wide set of rules governing their operations, minimum capital requirements, consumer protection, fraud prevention, establishing credit information services, secured transactions, interest rate limits, foreign ownership limitations, and tax and accounting issues (Christen, Lyman, and Rosenberg 2003). All of these rules represent important concerns, but it's costly for institutions to comply with them, and for regulators to monitor compliance. What's more, because microfinance is a relatively recent phenomenon, financial sector regulation in many countries isn't well adapted to the particularities of providing financial services to the poor.

The challenge, then, is to regulate effectively without unduly burdening either the institutions or the regulators. The fact that many microfinance customers lack ready access to the kinds of identification papers (and property titles, etc.) commonly held by richer customers makes regulating microfinance that much harder.

8.5.1 Prudential Regulation

When discussing the regulation of microfinance, it's useful to distinguish between prudential and nonprudential regulation. According to Christen et al. (2003, 3), prudential regulation "is aimed specifically at protecting the financial system as a whole as well as protecting the safety of small deposits in individual institutions." Most microfinance institutions haven't reached the scale at which their insolvency could undermine the stability of the broader financial systems in which they operate. But deposit-taking institutions guard the savings of their clients, many of whom are relatively poor, and unsound institutions put clients' savings at risk. Governments therefore impose prudential regulations on microfinance institutions mainly to protect the safety of deposits. The flipside of prudential regulation is that in most countries unregulated financial institutions aren't permitted to take deposits from the public. So, if an institution wants to offer savings services, some degree of formalization and prudential regulation is inevitable (Ledgerwood and White 2006).

Prudential regulations set out guidelines for financial intermediation, or using repayable funds (e.g., deposits) to make loans. They are especially important given the challenges of true financial intermediation. As McKee (2005, 27) observes, "[k]eeping assets well matched with liabilities is a complicated balancing act—and losing this balance puts the institution's operating funds and equity at risk. To add to this challenge, liquid deposit products—products that allow withdrawals at any time—heightens the risk of fraud, mismanagement, and illiquidity." These are all serious risks on an institutional level, and as we've seen they also jeopardize the savings of the poor.

But complying with prudential regulations and coping with the associated supervision carries its own nontrivial costs. Prudential regulations typically entail reserve requirements and other measures to ensure the institutions' stability and liquidity. Christen et al. (2003) speculate that the costs for microfinance institutions may be as much as five percent of assets in the first year and 1 percent or more subsequently. Regulatory costs are so high because of limited scale economies. Relative to their assets, smaller banks face higher costs than larger banks in complying with regulations, and microfinance institutions are typically smaller than other types of banks. On top of that, institutions need to hire relatively costly skilled labor to handle the legal and reporting requirements of prudential regulation.

Given the risks and costs associated with intermediation and its regulation, one might wonder why microfinance institutions accept and intermediate savings at all. As discussed in chapter 6, access to reliable saving mechanisms can be important for the poor, so institutions with social missions may want to offer saving services for their value to clients. But integrating deposits into the product mix holds benefits for institutions, too. First, it can help them attract and retain customers. Households often have difficulty saving, and to the extent that this is so, offering reliable, convenient saving devices is a strong selling point. Moreover, it might distinguish a microfinance institution from its competition. Second, intermediating deposits provides microfinance institutions with a funding source that is generally cheaper and more stable than alternatives.

8.5.2 Nonprudential Regulation

In most countries, both commercial and noncommercial microfinance institutions are subject to some form of nonprudential regulation. Nonprudential regulation touches on a broad spectrum of issues, including consumer protection, fraud prevention, establishing credit information services, secured transactions, interest rate limits, foreign ownership limitations, and tax and accounting issues (Christen et al. 2003). Here, we take up three of the major categories of nonprudential regulation.

Consumer protection is an important kind of nonprudential regulation. Calls for consumer protection in microfinance may come as a surprise. By definition, microfinance aims to extend services to the under-served, and the pioneers have combined financial and managerial strategies together with a strong vein of humanity.

But the vision of the leadership is not always fully absorbed by loan officers, and customers may not be well-positioned to make the best choices. Thus, consumer protection efforts have two parts. The first involves truth in lending so that customers can understand contracts and obligations. The second involves protecting customers from abusive practices. In this, we can also include consumer financial education, as well as mediation mechanisms for addressing complaints or disputes.

Nonprudential regulation also encompasses limits on interest rates. As described above, the business of making small loans is expensive. Administrative costs make up a larger portion of total costs for small loans than for larger ones, and lenders need to charge a higher interest rate on small loans in order to cover costs. However, as Christen et al. (2003, 10) explain, "[l]egislatures and the general public seldom understand this dynamic." In some places, governments have capped interest rates below levels at which microlending can be sustainable. While the intention of interest rate limits is to protect the poor from exploitation, in practice they make lenders overly reliant on subsidies or price them out of the market altogether.

A final category of nonprudential regulation is what are sometimes called "know your customer" regulations. These regulations include those related to fraud and financial crime prevention, secured transactions, and credit bureaus. Establishing credit bureaus in the countries where microfinance has a significant presence is both a technical challenge and a question of regulation. Credit bureaus go a long way toward solving the adverse selection problem discussed in chapter 4, and once established they're less costly than the alternatives. But in order for them to be viable and safe, countries need identity-card systems to facilitate the collection and organization of information and legal frameworks that provide incentives for participation while protecting privacy (Christen et al. 2003).

8.5.3 Empirical Evidence

The regulatory environment provides boundaries for microfinance, as well as rules of the game. It has a direct effect on what microfinance institutions do, and it also has an effect on *how* they do. Some studies attempt to answer this latter question by looking at the relationship between regulation and performance. Cull, Demirgüç-Kunt, and Morduch (2009a) investigate the impact of regulation on the profitability of microfinance institutions, paying attention to the channels through which impacts work. They use the same data described in section 8.3 above, focusing on 245 institutions with data on regulation. Their key contribution is to document trade-offs between outreach to poorer customers and prudential regulation and supervision.

Hartarska and Nadolnyak (2007) find that regulation does not directly affect the performance of microfinance institutions either in terms of operational self-sustainability (OSS) or outreach. They find that microfinance institutions that collect savings reach more borrowers, pointing to an indirect benefit from regulation through scale.

Cull et al. (2009a) disaggregate the impact of regulation by constructing two variables: a dummy variable that captures whether an institution faces onsite supervision, and another dummy variable that capture whether the institution is supervised at regular intervals. They find that, even within the same country, some institutions face onsite supervision while others do not, depending on their ownership structure, funding sources, activities, and organizational charter.

In line with Hartarska and Nadolnyak (2007), the Cull et al. (2009a) study shows that microfinance institutions subjected to more rigorous and regular supervision are not less profitable compared to others, despite the higher costs of supervision. But in contrast to Hartarska and Nadolnyak (2007), outreach is clearly affected once the data are disaggregated. Cull et al. (2009a) find that regulatory supervision is associated with larger average loan sizes and less lending to women. They interpret this finding as signaling a likely shift from segments of the population that are more costly to serve. They also find that supervision is associated with having a higher share of staff concentrated in the head office, a natural response to reporting requirements and formalization.[12]

The question left by Cull et al. (2009a) is whether the benefits of supervision in terms of better protection of depositors' funds and improved stability in the microfinance sector outweigh the likely reductions in outreach to the poor and women. Or, to put things more positively, the question is whether it is possible to design regulatory frameworks that avoid undue burdens and that align with social missions.

Policy may also affect microfinance performance indirectly through its effect on the macroeconomy. Ahlin and Lin (2006) review the literature and turn to World Bank data on macroeconomic performance and, like the Cull et al. studies, cross-country, cross-MFI data from the Mix Market. The authors analyze the relationship between macroeconomic performance and four key MFI performance indicators—that is, financial self-sustainability, default rates, costs per borrower, and growth in clientele—and find significant correlations between macroeconomic factors and MFI performance. MFIs in countries with higher rates of macroeconomic growth, for example, have higher levels of financial self-sustainability and lower levels of default. The results suggest that macroeconomic context affects MFIs' performance, but not more so than institutional factors.

8.6 Concluding Remarks

Commercialization raises one of the most contentious issues in microfinance today. To some, it represents the corruption of an idea conceived as a poverty reduction strategy. To others, it is the hope and the future of microfinance. Commercial investment can fund the expansion of microfinance beyond the limits of donor budgets, bringing financial access to more of the world's unbanked. Concerns about how commercialization will change how and to whom services are provided have support in the data we presented in section 8.3. The clientele of banks is, on average, less poor than that of NGOs. However, banks have much wider outreach and operate more efficiently. To us, these differences suggest the need for a balance, where commercial lenders and nonprofit institutions coexist, occupying separate and complementary niches.

Commercial investment, discussed in section 8.4, provides institutions with the opportunity to untether themselves from donor support, but an enabling regulatory framework is as important for institutions to thrive. As we outlined in section 8.5, regulators have no shortage of issues to consider when creating and reforming policies.

One of the most poorly understood possibilities entails the potential for down-scaling large commercial banks. The process of transformation that BancoSol undertook, by starting as an NGO, is one route by which microfinance institutions enter the commercial realm. Other commercial microfinance institutions have been created from scratch, many of them in Eastern Europe. Still others arise through the downscaling of traditional "mainstream" banks and credit unions, moving into lower-income population segments and rural markets. Examples include Bank Rakyat Indonesia's transformation in the 1980s (Robinson 2001) and the transformations of state-run banks like Banco do Nordeste, Banco del Estado, and Thailand's BAAC (Christen and Drake 2002). Downscaling banks, which tend to be well established and already regulated, bring the advantage of reputation and solidity when attracting deposits.

The track record of downscaling banks, however, is mixed so far. While banks are at home in the commercial arena, expanding services down market requires them to change the products they offer and the way they deliver those products. The mere idea of lending to microentrepreneurs without collateral can be hard to embrace. Technical assistance, donor support, and closer dialogue between fully regulated microfinance institutions and downscaling banks are needed. By 2001, however, there were already more than 70 commercial institutions within the field of microfinance (Valenzuela 2001)—a notable increase over the 17 identified only four years earlier (Baydas, Graham, and Valenzuela 1997). The advent of new technologies, such as those that can facilitate branchless banking, holds promise in promoting downscaling further (Mas 2009).

In looking to the future, the issues in this chapter will surely be revisited as policymakers and practitioners address the growth of consumer finance, especially in Latin America and Eastern Europe (Churchill and Frankiewicz 2006). Consumer credit follows a very different model than traditional microfinance (fees are generally very high, defaults are tolerated to a much greater degree, over-indebtedness is more common, technologies like credit scoring are in mainstream use, and the orientation is decidedly for-profit). Yet many of the communities served by consumer credit and microfinance overlap, raising a question of whether and how to draw lines between different kinds of commercial institutions expanding financial access.

The ultimate question is whether the mix of new players can deliver on the promise of wider scale and quality service provision. And, going back to the origins of microfinance, can they deliver the kinds of social and economic impacts for which activists have long fought?

8.7   Exercises

1. Banco Compartamos's success in soliciting public funds through its 2007 public offering was an important event in the commercialization and evolving nature of microfinance. What are some foreseeable advantages of issuing debt or equity? What are some of the trade-offs associated with these changes?

2. In previous chapters we show that in theory, interest rates charged by lenders are limited by borrowers' incentive compatibility constraints, in the sense that excessively high interest rates would undermine borrowers' incentives to repay their debt obligations. Provide a reasonable explanation for the fact that even though Banco Compartamos charges high rates of interest, it achieves high repayment rates. Use a dynamic framework for your analysis.

3. Explain the concept of operational self-sufficiency from the standpoint of any business. Why is this especially important in determining the health of a business?

4. A Ugandan microfinance institution is structured as an NGO. It receives $60,000 in grants each year, gets roughly $10,000 in volunteered services, and earns $50,000 in interest payments and $10,000 in fees from its customers. It currently does not rely on debt financing for its loan portfolio. Its total operating expenses are $40,000 and it has earmarked $10,000 for its loan-loss provision.
a. Is this NGO operationally self-sufficient?
b. Is it likely to be financially self-sufficient?
c. What risks does this NGO face by having its funding structured as it is?
d. Assume that the current market cost of capital in Uganda is 10 percent annually. What is the FSS?
e. Do you think this market interest rate correctly reflects the lending rate for the NGO?
f. How might you be able to obtain a more correct measurement?

5. What are some obstacles in the real world to using FSS as a measure of sustainability? Offer some potential strategic roadblocks to sustainability, especially in the context of a recessionary economy and unstable donor funds.

6. Explain how the Return on Assets ratio is a good measurement of profitability. Calculate the ROA for the NGO in exercise 4 if it reports beginning total assets of $110,000 and ending total assets of $130,000. The NGO also paid $1,000 in taxes in their fiscal year.

7. There is a microfinance institution in Tanzania that is worried about a set of payments that have yet to arrive. Without these payments, it won't be able to disburse as much in the next round of loans as it had hoped to. The gross loan portfolio is valued at $200,000. There are 50 outstanding loans that each have missed two installments of a $200 loan to be paid biweekly over 5 months. Before missing these two consecutive installments, the borrowers each made the first three installments. Calculate the portfolio at risk ratio for 30 days and explain how this affects the security of the loan portfolio.

8. Explain why NGOs charge borrowers higher interest rates, on average, relative to commercial microfinance banks. Under what conditions would it be a bad thing? How might such high interest rates be reduced—and with what costs and benefits?

9. Consider some of the interest rate issues emphasized in this chapter. What are some potential reasons why it is difficult for a microfinance institution to simply increase its interest rates in order to reach financial sustainability? Can you think of any creative solutions to this prevalent challenge?

10. One of the biggest obstacles to taking private companies or organizations public is the cost and time of regulating its activities. When the public has a stake in the well-being of a company, it is invested in its performance, activities and leadership. Compare the advantages and disadvantages of a regulated microfinance institution versus a nonbank financial institution or NGO. What are some particular characteristics of microfinance institutions that present challenges for regulation beyond those posed by traditional banks?

11. The number of microfinance institutions has multiplied in recent years. What are the advantages and drawbacks of increased competition in microfinance?

9 Measuring Impacts

9.1 Introduction

There's much interest in microfinance and many anecdotes about its benefits. But, so far, there are surprisingly few rigorous empirical studies of net impacts. Because of that, there are few hard numbers to inform debates about alternative development strategies and to guide social investments. This chapter describes attempts to measure how much microfinance makes a difference.

The rough notion of "making a difference" can be translated into a precise question that is at the heart of every credible impact study: "How have outcomes changed with the intervention *relative to what would have occurred without the intervention.*" The second part of the question is fundamental. In recent decades, education rates and health conditions have improved almost everywhere. Poverty rates too have fallen steadily in a wide range of countries, even where microfinance has had little or no presence. The impact question centers on how microfinance makes a difference over and above these kinds of underlying trends and conditions.

So far, inspiring stories from around the globe have helped to turn microfinance from a few scattered programs into a global movement. The anecdotes provide the basis for a "theory of change" on which to base investment allocations, but they are not sufficient in themselves. Consider the story of Mrs. Braulia Parra, who lives with a family of seven in a poor neighborhood in Monterrey, Mexico, in a home with cardboard walls and dirt floors.[1] Illiterate and inexperienced in the workplace, Mrs. Parra took her first $150 loan from ADMIC, a local microlender. The loan allowed her to buy yarn and other sewing supplies to make handsewn decorations. Each week she sells about one hundred handmade baskets, dolls, and mirrors, going door-to-door in her neighborhood. After ten loans, Mrs. Parra had earned enough to install a toilet in her modest home, as well as an outdoor shower. Building a second floor was next in her sights.

The story is compelling, but it is not a substitute for careful statistical evidence on impacts from large samples. For every Braulia Parra, was there another customer who fared poorly? Even if Braulia Parra is representative of her community, what would have happened without microfinance?

The number of careful impact studies is small but growing, and their conclusions, so far, are much more measured than the anecdotes would suggest.[2] Microfinance is touted as a way to raise incomes for the very poor, but studies of SEWA Bank in India, Zambuko Trust in Zimbabwe, and Mibanco in Peru sponsored by the United States Agency for International Development (USAID), for example, found that on average borrowers had net income gains only in India and Peru. In Zimbabwe, there were no measurable increases in average incomes relative to those in control groups (Snodgrass and Sebstad 2002).[3] In a recent randomized trial in urban India, business investment was found to increase, but there were no short-term gains to consumption on average (Banerjee, Duflo, Glennerster et al. 2009).

This should not be surprising: the anecdotes are culled to show the potential of microfinance, while the statistical analyses are designed to show typical impacts across the board. Inevitably, some customers will thrive, others will be unchanged, and some may slip backwards. One study of Bolivia's BancoSol, for example, reports that staff estimated that in any given cohort roughly 25 percent showed spectacular gains to borrowing, 60–65 percent stayed about the same, and 10–15 percent went bankrupt (Mosley 1996b). In a 2001 study that ultimately reshaped the strategy of BASIX, one of India's pioneering microfinance institutions, it was found that about half of its best-established microcredit customers reported income increases, about a quarter stayed the same, and a quarter reported a decline.

This chapter provides an introduction to the basic concepts, tools, and value of impact evaluation. We begin by describing the nature of "selection bias" in typical evaluation contexts. Section 9.3 turns to how microfinance affects households. Section 9.4 delivers evaluation basics. Section 9.5 describes studies based on quasi-experiments and instrumental variables methods. Section 9.6 describes the new push to run randomized trials, their advantages, and their limits. It also describes new studies from the Philippines, India, Sri Lanka, and South Africa.

Section 9.7 offers final thoughts on the growing focus on evaluations in the broader context of social performance measurement.

9.2 Selection Bias and the Focus on Causality

No matter what the outcomes of interest are, the most difficult part of evaluating impacts is to separate out the causal role of microfinance (which requires stripping out the various "selection" and "reverse causation" biases common to nearly all statistical evaluations). Even if earnings from microfinance participation are funding new houses, further education for children, new savings accounts, and new businesses, we have to ask whether these changes are more remarkable than what would have happened without microfinance. In Banerjee et al. (2009), for example, 69 percent of their baseline sample from urban India had at least one loan outstanding (from moneylenders, family, or friends) *before* microfinance institutions entered the communities.

Moreover, if we see that richer households have larger loans, we have to ask whether the loans made the households richer—or do richer households simply have easier access to credit (or both) without actually being made much more productive by the loans. This is another way of stating the point of section 9.1: ultimately, the question that every careful evaluation seeks to answer is how would borrowers have done without the programs.

As noted, it is a surprisingly difficult question to answer cleanly in studies that do not involve randomized research designs. One major problem is that many microfinance clients already have initial advantages over their neighbors. In examining village bank programs in Northeast Thailand, for example, Coleman (2006) finds that households that will later become microfinance borrowers tend to already be significantly wealthier than their nonparticipating neighbors before the village bank starts its operations. The household wealth (assets less debts) of village bank members is 574,738 baht, while nonmembers held only 434,154 baht. Moreover, the wealthiest villagers are nearly twice as likely to become borrowers than their poorer neighbors: 81 percent of the uppermost quintile ultimately gained access to the village bank program, compared to only 42 percent of both the first and second quintiles. The wealthiest are also more likely to use their power to obtain much larger loans than others. Alexander (2001) similarly finds that microfinance borrowers in Peru start off considerably wealthier than their nonparticipating neighbors.

In a small sample from Bangladesh, Hashemi (1997) also finds important underlying differences between borrowers and nonborrowers in villages served by Grameen Bank and BRAC. Over half of those who chose not to participate did so because they felt that they could not generate adequate profits to reliably repay loans. Another quarter opted out due to religious and social sanctions that restricted the ability to participate in meetings outside of the home with nonfamily males. If sufficient care is not taken to control for such self-selection into microfinance programs, estimated "impacts" on income and "empowerment" will be misleading. The microfinance interventions will seem more positive than is indeed the case. Unfortunately, this is not an esoteric concern that practitioners and policymakers can safely ignore. It is not just a difference between obtaining "very good" estimates of impacts versus "perfect" estimates—the biases can be large. In evaluating the Grameen Bank, for example, McKernan (2002) finds that not controlling for selection bias can lead to overestimation of the effect of participation on profits by as much as 100 percent. In other cases discussed later, controlling for these biases reverses conclusions about impacts entirely.

9.3   How Microfinance Affects Households

Increasing income and consumption is, of course, not the only metric by which to judge microfinance. Microfinance participation can affect households in many ways. Researchers have analyzed a range of social and economic outcomes beyond household income and consumption—including business profits, nutrition, schooling, fertility, contraception, risk, asset holdings—and a range of measures of empowerment and changes in social consciousness.[4] In the USAID study of Zimbabwe, for example, clients were shown to diversify their income sources more than others, a potentially important means of risk diversification.

So, first researchers have to ask: What are we trying to measure? Microfinance may affect household outcomes through a variety of channels. Most immediately, microfinance may make households wealthier, yielding an "income effect" that should push up total consumption levels and, holding all else the same, increase the demand for children, health, children's education, and leisure. But running microenterprises may also take time (and make that time relatively more valuable than other activities), yielding "substitution effects" that may counterbalance the effects of increased income. With increased female employment, for example, time spent raising children can become costlier in terms of foregone income, pushing fertility rates downward.[5] The need to have children help at home (to compensate for extra work taken on by parents) could decrease schooling levels; and leisure, in this case, may fall if the return to working rises sufficiently. Evaluating impacts on business profits is just a starting point.

The fact that it is often women who are earning the income is not incidental. As described in chapter 7 on gender and microfinance, another way that microfinance can affect household outcomes is by tipping the balance of decision making. With added income, it is argued, women may gain clout within the household, using it to push for greater spending in areas of particular concern to women.

Microlenders may also make direct, nonfinancial interventions that affect client outcomes. Some programs use meetings with clients to advise on family planning, and to stress the importance of schooling and good health practices, taking advantage of group meetings to hold communal discussions and training sessions. Village banks that are run on the "credit with education" model developed by the NGO Freedom From Hunger have made this a mainstay of their approach, for example, and other microlenders like Latin America's Pro Mujer have added training and education components in various ways (Dunford 2001). Taking these kinds of extra benefits into account, McKernan (2002) finds that being a member of the Grameen Bank is associated with a 126 percent increase in self-employment profits *after* accounting for the direct benefit of access to capital.[6] The increase, she presumes, is due to increased social and human capital derived from group meetings.

The multiplicity of channels means that it is typically impossible to assign a given measured impact to the strictly financial elements in microfinance; although there have been attempts to analyze programs that are essentially similar but which differ in specific, limited ways. In order to separate out the role of education programs, for example, ideally one would want to run programs without the "credit with education" training sessions and compare them to similar programs that use the integrated approach. Smith (2002) does this with data on Project HOPE's "health banks" in rural Ecuador and urban Honduras. He finds that the health interventions did indeed improve health care for the participants relative to the health care received by those in credit-only programs, and the health interventions did not diminish the banks' financial performance. There is also hope that health interventions like this might have impacts on household income and spending by reducing the incidence of illness and raising productivity, but results on that score are mixed in Smith's sample. Much is being learned by following Smith's example to gauge the impacts of business training (Karlan and Valdivia 2008), marketing (Bertrand, Karlan, Mullainathan et al. 2008), "consciousness-raising," and other activities often accompanying financial services.

9.4 Evaluation Basics

Disentangling cause and effect is harder than it might seem at first. After all, people can only be in one circumstance at a time. We can't ever know what would have actually happened to specific microfinance customers had they *not* in fact been microfinance customers— just as you can't ever really know what would have happened had you attended a different college, studied different subjects, read different books, or traveled to different places. There are no time machines; we only get one chance to live each moment in life.

This makes an evaluator's life complicated, since ultimately evaluators want to know whether good outcomes for microfinance customers might have been nearly as good (or terrible or much better) without microfinance. To estimate impacts, researchers thus have to find ways to approximate the "counter-factual" (i.e., the prediction of what would have happened without microfinance). Even when it is difficult to form a credible estimate of the counterfactual for a specific individual customer, it can be possible to form a credible estimate for a group of customers taken together.

To be concrete, we focus on attempts to measure the causal impact of microfinance on borrower income.[7] Income can be attributed to many sources. Most immediate, those sources are your job, your business, your pension, and so forth. But here we take one step backward in order to focus on more basic sources such as your age, education, and experience. These attributes are generally measurable. Another category of attributes is far harder to measure, such as your entrepreneurial skills, your persistence in seeking goals, your organizational ability, and your access to valuable social networks. In this latter category, we also include "shocks" such as whether you had a bad flu last winter or an argument with your boss. Another set of attributes has to do with where you live—for example, in a city or village (measurable) or in a place with a thriving local market (measurable, but typically not actually recorded in surveys). A final broad category includes income determinants that tend to be broadly felt, like political upheavals, rampant inflation, or economic booms.

Calculating the impacts of microfinance requires disentangling its role from the simultaneous roles of all of these attributes. The challenge is made harder by the fact that the decision to participate in a microfinance program—and at what intensity—will likely depend on many of those same attributes. Loan officers work hard to screen customers, managers calculate carefully where to locate new branches, products are designed to appeal to the most promising population segments, and people choose to participate in and exit from microfinance programs for strategic reasons often related to their perceived returns. If customers are richer, happier, and more productive than their neighbors, the reason may be because microfinance institutions succeed in targeting richer, happier, and more productive people, not because the institutions have created these conditions. As a result, there is likely to be a high correlation between microfinance participation and, say, your age and entrepreneurial ability. Since researchers can record your age, there are simple ways of controlling for age-related issues. But since entrepreneurial ability is typically unmeasured, researchers need to be careful in making comparisons or else the impact of being a better entrepreneur could misleadingly be interpreted as an impact of microfinance access.

With this in mind, we use figure 9.1 to consider various evaluation approaches. The ultimate goal is to isolate and measure the "microfinance impact" in the bold box. The impact is felt by a "typical" person who gains access to a microfinance program. We term this position T_2, taken to be four years after the program started. Before access to the program, in year 0, this person's income is reflected by position T_1. The difference between T_2 and T_1 is a useful place to start as it nets out the roles of those measured and unmeasured individual attributes that do not change over time, as well as location-related issues. But while the difference captures the microfinance impact, it also reflects broader economic and social changes that occur between year 0 and year 4 and that are independent of microfinance. It would thus be misleading to attribute the entirety of the $T_2 - T_1$ difference to the microfinance impact. The problem is that we cannot parse it without more information.

Identifying a control group is thus critical. Figure 9.1 shows a plausible control group from an area without access to microfinance. It would be very unlikely to find a population that was exactly identical to the "treatment" population. And we see here in this example, base income levels start at a lower level for the control group. Thus,

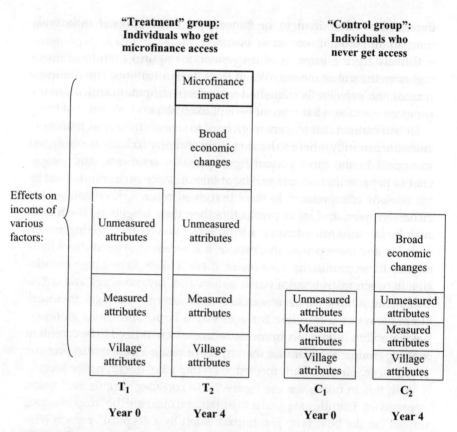

Figure 9.1
Sources of income for treatment and control groups.

comparing the difference between T_2 and C_2 will help address biases due to the broadly felt economic and social changes, but it will not account for the differing base levels. Isolating the true microfinance impact requires comparing the difference $T_2 - T_1$ with the difference $C_2 - C_1$, which is a so-called difference-in-difference approach.

Given the setup in figure 9.1, the difference-in-difference approach is adequate to deliver accurate measures of microfinance impacts. But we have made an implicit assumption that we now need to put on the table. We have taken the impacts of personal attributes like age, education, and entrepreneurial ability to be unchanging over time. Thus, their effects net out when we look at $T_2 - T_1$ and $C_2 - C_1$. But in reality, these characteristics may change over time (perhaps a borrower gets more education or strengthens her social networks, for reasons unrelated to microfinance), or they may directly affect changes over time, so they do not net out as assumed. More capable entrepreneurs will likely have greater earnings *growth*, for example, and not just a higher base level of income. When the relevant variables are not measurable, the problem is mitigated by making sure that control groups are as comparable to treatment groups as possible.

To find comparable treatment groups, we need to consider who joins microfinance programs in the first place. Figure 9.2 gives a plausible scenario, where the focus is just on entrepreneurial ability. Participants tend to have more entrepreneurial ability and nonparticipants tend to have less. Participants thus have higher incomes—and potential for income growth—before the microfinance program even arrives. Comparing microfinance borrowers in a given village to their neighbors who decide not to participate is thus apt to run into problems. As noted earlier, the concern is that unmeasured attributes such as entrepreneurial ability may affect both income growth and initial income levels.

So, imagine that we have access to data from another village that is identical to the one depicted in figure 9.2, except that the second village lacks a microfinance program. It would seem to provide a perfect control group. But how should it be used? Figure 9.2 shows that

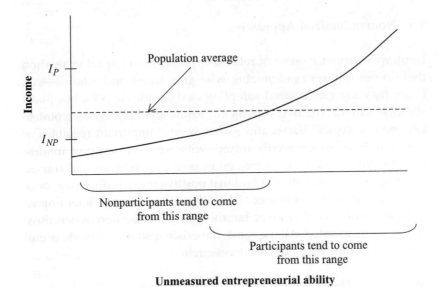

Figure 9.2
The hypothetical relationship between unmeasured entrepreneurial ability and income in a given village.

comparing the income of participants in the treated village to the population average in the control village will also create problems since the former group is self-selected while the latter is not. The problem of course is that by definition there are no participants in the control village since it has no program yet.

Two solutions present themselves. The first solution is to change the question. We have been asking: What is the effect of microfinance participation? We could ask instead: What is the effect of microfinance *access*—whether or not villagers ultimately end up participating? To answer this second question (which may well be more relevant from a policy standpoint), it is only necessary to compare outcomes for the entire population in the treatment village (or, more easily, a random sample drawn from the entire population) against a sample drawn from the control village. A second solution, used by Coleman (1999), is to try to identify future borrowers in the control villages and to compare the actual microfinance participants to the set of future participants. A third approach, that is common but problematic, involves comparing older borrowers in a given village to newer borrowers who are just joining the program. The main difficulty with this approach involves nonrandom attrition, an issue discussed in section 9.5.2.

9.5   Nonrandomized Approaches

Here, we consider a series of related approaches to impact evaluation that do not rely on randomizing who gets access and who doesn't. (They may use randomized sampling designs for surveys, but that's another matter.) The overview is not exhaustive; rather, we point to key methodological issues and gather several important results. The results to date are decidedly mixed, with some evidence of modest positive impacts of microfinance on income, expenditure, and related variables, while other studies find that positive impacts disappear once selection biases are addressed. There have been few serious impact evaluations of microfinance so far, though, so a collection of definitive results is still awaited. All the same, the existing studies provide useful insights and directions for future research.

9.5.1   Using Data on Prospective Clients in Northeast Thailand
A number of recent studies use novel research designs to address selection biases. One approach is to use information on borrowers before

the microfinance program enters. Coleman (1999) and (2006) takes advantage of a particular way a microfinance program was implemented in Northeast Thailand, providing a unique way to address selection bias. He gathered data on 445 households in fourteen villages. Of these, eight had village banks operating at the start of 1995. The remaining six did not, but village banks would be set up one year later. Interestingly (and critically for the evaluation), at the beginning of 1995, field staff from the village bank programs organized households in these six villages into banks, allowing the households to self-select according to the village bank's standard procedures. But then the households were forced to wait one year before getting their first loans.

The unusual procedure on the part of the programs allows Coleman to analyze who joins and who does not *before* the village banks start running. Moreover, it allows him to estimate the following regression equation:

$$Y_{ij} = X_{ij}\alpha + V_j\beta + M_{ij}\gamma + T_{ij}\delta + \eta_{ij}, \tag{9.1}$$

where the variable to be explained Y_{ij} is a household-level outcome—income or profit—for household i in village j. The regression approach allows a refinement of the difference-in-difference approach discussed in section 9.4. Here, "dummy variables" (i.e., variables that only take the values of zero or one) are used to control for location and participation status. Other variables control for factors like age and education.[8] The variables X_{ij} capture household characteristics (and a constant term); and V_j is a vector of village dummy variables that control for all fixed characteristics of the village. The two variables of most interest are M_{ij} and T_{ij}. The first is a "membership dummy variable" that equals one for both actual members of the village banks and those villagers who have opted into the programs (in the control villages) but who have not yet received loans. Coleman argues that M_{ij} controls for selection bias so that δ, the coefficient on T_{ij}, is a consistent estimate of the causal treatment effect. In his application, the variable T_{ij} is the number of months that village bank credit was available to (actual) members, which is exogenous to the household.

Controlling for selection makes an important difference. Coleman (1999) finds that average program impact was not significantly different from zero after controlling for endogenous member selection and program placement. When he extends the estimating framework to differentiate between impacts on "rank-and-file members" and members of the village bank committee (who tend to be wealthier and more powerful), he finds again that most impacts were not statistically significant for rank-and-file members, but there were some noted impacts for committee members, particularly on wealth accumulation.

Coleman cautions, though, that the results need to be put into the context of the larger financial landscape. Thailand is relatively wealthy (at least compared to Bangladesh), and villagers have access to credit from a range of sources—some at low interest rates from government-backed sources. Strikingly, survey households held over 500,000 baht in wealth on average and had over 30,000 baht of "low-interest" debt (excluding village bank debt). Thus, the village banks' loans of 1,500 to 7,500 baht may be too small to make a notable average difference in the welfare of households; in fact, complaints about small loan sizes prompted some women to leave the banks. Coleman argues that one reason that wealthier borrowers may have experienced larger impacts was because they could commandeer larger loans.

9.5.2 Attrition Bias: Problems When Using "New Borrowers" as a Control Group in Peru

A problem in trying to replicate Coleman's approach is that it's not often that a researcher comes upon programs that go through the trouble of organizing villagers but then delay credit disbursement for a period. So, instead, researchers have tried to capture the flavor of the approach by comparing "old borrowers" to "new borrowers" within the same area. Typically this is done with cross-sectional data, yielding an approach that is simple and relatively inexpensive (and which does not require surveying nonborrowers). This procedure has been promoted by USAID through its AIMS project (more on this to come) and by other microfinance organizations (Karlan 2001).

Assuming that the characteristics of people who enter into programs are unchanging over time, the method should account for the fact that borrowers are not a random group of people. But assuming that the relevant characteristics are similar over time requires a leap of faith. Why didn't the new borrowers sign up earlier? Why were the older borrowers first in line? If their timing of entry was due to unobservable attributes such as ability, motivation, and entrepreneurship, the comparisons may do little to address selection biases—and could, in fact, exacerbate bias.

Karlan outlines two additional problems based on his experience evaluating village banks organized by FINCA Peru. Assume that the conditions of selection *are* constant over time so that the same kinds of people become clients today as those who became clients five years ago. All seems well, but there are still two potential biases, both of which are most pronounced when assessing impacts using cross-sectional data. Both are also due to dropouts.

Dropouts are an ongoing microfinance reality. Sometimes borrowers leave because they are doing so well that they no longer need microfinance; but, more often, it is the borrowers in trouble who leave. Wright (2001) gives evidence that dropout rates are 25–60 percent per year in East Africa. In Bangladesh, Khandker (2005) estimates rates for three leading lenders of 3.5 percent per year between 1991 and 1992 and 1998 and 1999 (which is much smaller than the numbers cited by Wright; nonetheless, they can add up over time). González-Vega, Schreiner, Meyer et al. (1997, 34–35) provide parallel data for Bolivia. They investigate the fraction of people who ever borrowed from a given microlender who are still active borrowers at the time of their survey (the end of 1995). The resulting proxy for retention rates shows that just half of BancoSol clients were still active. In rural areas, two-thirds of borrowers from PRODEM were still active, possibly reflecting the fact that there are fewer alternative lending sources in the countryside.

It is likely that these "older borrowers" (i.e., those who remain active) have the positive qualities of survivors, while "new borrowers" have yet to be tested. If the failures are more likely to drop out, comparing old to new borrowers will overestimate impacts. We suspect that this pattern is most often the case, but, as suggested earlier, the prediction is not clear-cut. If it is mainly the successes that move on (leaving weaker clients in the pool), the sign of bias will be reversed, underestimating causal impacts.

The second problem is due to nonrandom attrition independent of actual impacts. If richer households are more likely to leave, the pool of borrowers' becomes poorer on average. Then it could look like microfinance borrowing depletes one's income, when in fact it may have no impact at all. Conversely, when lower-income households leave in greater numbers, impacts will be overstated.

Karlan argues for hunting down the dropouts and including them in the analysis along with the other older borrowers, though it may be costly. A cheaper improvement would be to (1) estimate predictors of dropout based on observable information on older borrowers; then (2) form a prediction of who among the new borrowers is likely to (later on) drop out; and (3) use the prediction to weight the new borrower control group. The method is not perfect, though: in particular, drop-outs who made their decision based in part on the size of impact are not addressed by the reweighting scheme.

9.5.3 Longitudinal Data: USAID AIMS Studies in India, Peru, and Zimbabwe

Some biases can be mitigated by using data collected at several points in time, allowing "before versus after" comparisons as described in section 9.4. Under certain conditions, the approach controls for both nonrandom participation and nonrandom program placement. But when those conditions are not met, the approach is subject to biases due to unobservable variables that change over time—hard-to-observe characteristics such as entrepreneurial spirit and access to markets that are likely to be correlated with borrowing status.[9]

The most ambitious longitudinal studies to date are those sponsored by USAID in the late 1990s, with the hope to demonstrate methods and generate benchmarks.[10] Teams analyzed impacts on members of SEWA (a labor organization and microlender serving women in the informal sector in Ahmedabad, India), Mibanco (an ACCION International affiliate in Peru), and the Zambuko Trust in Zimbabwe. Baseline data was collected and then the same households were resurveyed two years later. Case studies were also conducted alongside the statistical analyses.

The teams selected clients randomly from lists provided by the programs. The trick was then to identify control groups. In India and Peru, the control group was a random sample drawn from nonparticipants in the same regions who met program eligibility criteria. In Zimbabwe, enumerators instead used a "random walk procedure" in which they set off in a given direction to find nonclient households for the control group. As Barnes, Keogh, and Nemarundwe (2001, 19) explain, "for example, when the client's business was in a residential area, from the front of the house the interviewer turned right, went to the first road intersection, turned right and walked to the third intersection and then turned left; from there the interviewer asked a series of questions to identify who met the criteria for inclusion in the study." The criteria used to match treatments and controls were gender, enterprise sector, and geographic location, as well as additional criteria added by Zambuko Trust: "(a) never received credit from a formal organization for their enterprise, (b) be the sole or joint owner of an enterprise at least six months old, and (c) not be employed elsewhere on a full-time basis" (Barnes, Keogh, and Nemarundwe 2001, 19).

The data have potential, and the researchers followed dropouts as best they could to avoid the attrition biases described earlier. With two years of data, the researchers could have analyzed impacts by investigating how changes in microfinance participation affect changes in outcomes. But, surprisingly, the AIMS researchers chose *not* to analyze variables converted to changes over time, which would have eliminated all biases due to omitted variables that do not change over time (i.e., to analyze differences-in-differences as described in section 9.4). The stated rationale is that the "differencing" procedure also eliminates the chance to analyze the roles of variables such as gender and enterprise sector that are also fixed through time, and so alternative methods (analysis of covariance) were used (Dunn 2002). In our view, the costs of that choice far outweigh the benefits.

To see the differencing method (i.e., the method not used), we can modify equation (9.1) to specify that the variables are measured in a given time period t:

$$Y_{ijt} = X_{ijt}\alpha + V_j\beta + M_{ij}\gamma + T_{ijt}\delta + \eta_{ijt}, \tag{9.2}$$

As before, we are interested in estimating the value of δ, but here it is the coefficient on the value of loans received. (The two variables, value of loans and length of membership, are typically very similar since loan sizes and length of time borrowing often move closely together.) The dependent variable, Y_{ijt}, is a household-level outcome (income or profit) for household i in village j at time t. The variables X_{ijt} capture household characteristics at t (and a constant term), and V_j is a vector of village dummy variables that are assumed to be unchanging over time. The dummies will capture village-level features like distance to the closest major city, proximity to major transportation and markets, and the quality of local leadership. Similarly, we assume that the individual-specific variable M_{ij}, the variable that captures nonrandom individual selection into the program, is also unchanging over time. It may reflect, for example, an individual's energy level, management ability, and business savvy. In this case, though, we do not assume that it is observable. Thus, there is a potential bias stemming from its omission when equation (9.2) is estimated.

The problem can be addressed by estimating in differences. Assume that we have the same variables collected in period $t + 1$:

$$Y_{ijt+1} = X_{ijt+1}\alpha + V_j\beta + M_{ij}\gamma + T_{ijt+1}\delta + \eta_{ijt+1}. \qquad (9.3)$$

Then, we can subtract equation (9.2) from (9.3) to obtain

$$\Delta Y_{ij} = \Delta X_{ij}\alpha + \Delta C_{ij}\delta + \Delta\eta_{ij}, \qquad (9.4)$$

where Δ indicates the difference in the variables between periods t and $t + 1$. Here, the village dummies drop out, as do the fixed (and unobservable) individual-specific characteristics (which was the concern that prompted the AIMS researchers not to follow this method). The benefit, though, is considerable: a consistent estimate of the impact δ can be obtained (which is the most important aim).[11]

It turns out that the omitted unobservables in equations like (9.2) do make a large difference, and not addressing them undermines the credibility of the AIMS impact studies. When Alexander (2001) returns to the AIMS Peru data and estimates the equations in differences (akin to equation 9.4), she finds that estimated impacts on enterprise profits fall. In fact when she controls for reverse causality by using an instrumental variables approach (more on this to follow), the estimated impacts shrink and are no longer statistically significant. Selection bias is clearly a problem, but results might have been different if the two surveys had been collected more than two years apart or if other instrument variables had been used. Below we address why finding instrumental variables continues to be a challenge.

9.5.4 Using a Quasi-Experiment to Construct Instrumental Variables: Bangladesh Studies

A different way of approaching the problems above would have been to search for an instrumental variable for microfinance participation. (See Angrist and Pischke 2009, for a broader introduction to instrumental variables.) The instrumental variables method allows researchers to address problems posed by measurement error, reverse causality, and some omitted variable biases. The instrumental variables strategy involves finding an additional variable (or set of variables) that explains levels of credit received, but that has no direct relationship with the outcomes of interest (like profit or income). Then, a proxy variable can be formed based on the instrumental variable, and it can be used to tease out the causal impact of credit access.

The interest rate is a potential instrumental variable—or simply "instrument"—since it can explain how much credit a borrower desires while not being a direct determinant of income in itself (that's testable, at least). The trouble is that interest rates seldom vary within a given program, and the statistical techniques are impossible without some variation. And, while it is true that interest rates vary when comparing clients of different institutions—both formal and informal—it is likely that the variation partly reflects unobserved attributes of the borrowers, undermining the use of interest rates as instruments. Lender characteristics are also candidates for instrumental variables. Similar to all other community-level variables, though, they will be wiped out when including village dummy variables in specifications when there is no variation in program access within a village. In short, the instrumental variables approach can be powerful, but finding convincing instrumental variables for credit has been frustrating.

But when there is within-village variation in program access, rules determining eligibility can be the basis of an evaluation strategy, an approach employed in a series of studies of microfinance in Bangladesh. Over the years 1991 and 1992, the World Bank and Bangladesh Institute of Development Studies surveyed nearly 1,800 households in eighty-seven villages in Bangladesh; most villages were served by microlenders but fifteen were not. In 1998 and 1999, teams were sent back to find the same households, but by then all of the villages were served by microlenders.[12] After losing some households through attrition, 1,638 households were left that were interviewed in both rounds.

In a sign of the rapid spread of microfinance in Bangladesh, about one quarter of the sample included a microfinance customer within the household in 1991–1992, but by 1998–1999 the figure had jumped to about half.[13] The jump makes program evaluation more difficult, but not impossible. To complicate matters, about 11 percent of customers were members of more than one microfinance institution in 1998–1999.

9.5.4.1 Estimates from the 1991–1992 Cross-Section The first round of data has, on its own, generated a series of papers; the most important results have been compiled in Khandker's (1998) *Fighting Poverty with Microcredit*. Completing impact studies with just a single cross-section requires ingenuity and some important assumptions, and the task was made more challenging by the desire to estimate impacts of borrowing by men and by women separately. The studies are intensive in their use of statistical methods to compensate for the fundamental limitations of the data set. One large limitation arises because the researchers were eager to generate results with the first wave of the data rather than waiting for the second. That the studies use heavier statistical artillery than other microfinance studies does not necessarily mean that they deliver results that are more reliable or rigorous than other studies. In fact, as we describe later, the studies are open to serious questions about the validity of the underlying assumptions that prop up the statistical framework, and Roodman and Morduch (2009) have been unable to replicate the original results. We thus put limited stock in the evidence, but the studies are worth examining as examples of this type of approach.

On the face of it, it would seem impossible to get far with just a single cross-sectional data set and without a special setup like that of Coleman (1999). But the way that microlenders in Bangladesh implement their programs opens a door for researchers. To capture the basic insight, figure 9.3 shows two hypothetical villages, one with a program (the treatment village) and one without it (the control village). The villages

"Treatment village"   **"Control village"**
(microlender present)   **(no microlender)**

Figure 9.3
Example of impact evaluation strategies using eligibility rules.

are separated into distinct groups based on their eligibility and participation status; we discuss how eligibility is determined shortly. The
groups within the thick black lines are eligible to borrow (or, in the
case of the control village, *would be* eligible). As a first step, researchers
could compare the incomes and other outcomes of microfinance
participants to nonparticipants just using data from the treatment
village, but it is impossible to rule out selection biases of the sort
described in section 9.3. It is also possible to use the control villages to
compare participants from the treatment villages served by microfinance
to the eligible households from the control villages, but even here there
are potential selection biases since the participants are still a select
group.

A more satisfactory approach is to compare eligible households (all
households within the thick black lines) between the two villages.
Here, the goal is to estimate the impact of microfinance access rather
than actual participation. The benefit is that a clean estimate of the
average impact of access may be more useful than a biased estimate of
the impact of participation. Moreover, if there are no spillovers from
participants to nonparticipants, it is possible to recover a clean estimate
of the impact of participation from the estimate of access (by simply
dividing the latter by the fraction of households in the village that
participate). The assumption that there are no spillovers is strong,
though, and Khandker (2005) finds evidence against it.

The fault with the latter approach is that while selection biases at the
household-level are addressed, it does not address biases stemming
from nonrandom program placement. As mentioned earlier, villagers
served by microlenders may seem to do poorly relative to control
groups just because the microlender chooses to work in isolated, disadvantaged villages. In other cases, villages may be doing better than
average even without the microlender, so the bias would go in the
other direction; estimated impacts would be too high.

A potential solution is at hand, though, provided by the particular
way that the selected microlenders determine eligibility for program
access. Pitt and Khandker (1998) develop a framework for estimating
impacts using the 1991–1992 cross-section. The starting point is the
observation that the three programs being studied—Grameen Bank,
BRAC, and the state-run Rural Development Boards (RD-12)—all share
the same eligibility rule. In order to keep focused on the poorest, the
programs restrict their services to the "functionally landless"; this is
implemented through a rule declaring that households owning over

half an acre of land are not allowed to borrow. The individual programs place some additional restrictions, but the half-acre rule is the
common criterion. So, in terms of figure 9.3, the functionally landless
are encompassed by the thick black lines, and the noneligible lie outside.
The fact that there are ineligible households within villages with programs means that there is another control group that can help alleviate
concerns that the microlenders choose villages that are special in one
way or another.

An improved estimation strategy—but *not* the one adopted by Pitt
and Khandker—is to compare differences-in-differences as described
in section 9.4. It involves comparing the outcomes of households with
microfinance access to the outcomes of households that are ineligible,
but living in treatment villages. The strategy then turns to the control
villages where the ineligible are compared to those who "would be"
eligible. Finally, those two comparisons are pitted against each other.
The result tells us if households with access to microfinance are doing
better than their ineligible neighbors, relative to the difference in outcomes between functionally landless households in control villages
versus *their* ineligible neighbors.

One can do even better by implementing this strategy in a regression
framework that also accounts for a broad range of household characteristics. In the regression framework, the difference-in-difference strategy would be implemented as

$$Y_{ij} = X_{ij}\alpha + V_j\beta + E_{ij}\gamma + (T_{ij}\cdot E_{ij})\delta' + \eta_{ij}, \tag{9.5}$$

The idea is very similar to that of equation (9.1) but two important
changes are made. First, E_{ij} is a dummy variable that reflects whether
or not a household is functionally landless and thus eligible to borrow
from a microlender (whether or not there is in fact a microlender
present in the village). The variable equals one if a household is within
the thick black lines in either village in figure 9.3. The other important
change is the variable $(T_{ij}\cdot E_{ij})$, which is the product of E_{ij} and a dummy
variable that indicates whether or not the household is in a treatment
village; it equals one only if the household is within the thick black
lines in the village with a microlender. The coefficient on the dummy
variable gives the average impact of credit access—after controlling for
being functionally landless, living in a particular village, and having
specific household characteristics.

Morduch (1998) takes the approach in equation (9.5) and finds no
sharp evidence for strong impacts of microfinance on household con-

sumption, but he finds some evidence that microfinance helps households diversify income streams so that consumption is less variable across seasons. The estimates, though, rely on the assumption that the village dummy variables perfectly capture all relevant aspects about the villages that would influence microlenders' location decisions. In this setting, though, the village-level dummies only control for unobservables that affect all households in a village identically (and linearly). Imagine instead that the functionally landless differ from their wealthier neighbors in systematic ways that are not controlled by variables in the regression. In this plausible case, the coefficient on the dummy variable $(T_{ij} \cdot E_{ij})$ could pick up the effects of those inherent differences, biasing estimated impacts, a critique of Morduch (1998) stressed by Roodman and Morduch (2009).

Morduch (1998) also takes a closer look at the eligibility rule on which the strategy rests. As Pitt and Khandker (1998) point out, it is important that landholdings are exogenous to the household—that is, households are not, for example, selling land in order to become eligible to borrow. If that was the case, selection biases would creep back in—even when estimating using equation (9.5)—since unobservably promising borrowers would be taking special steps to switch their eligibility status. Pitt and Khandker cite the fact that in southern India in the 1980s, village land markets tended to be thin, and most land was acquired through inheritance. In that case, landholdings were exogenous to the household and unlikely (or at least much less likely) to be correlated with unobserved potential. But Bangladesh in the 1990s is not southern India in the 1980s, and land markets in the study area turn out to be fairly active—and this is evident upon closer inspection of the landholding module of the data set. On the other hand, Morduch (1998) finds no evidence that households are selling land in order to meet microfinance eligibility criteria. If anything, successful borrowers are buying land, and one explanation for Morduch's inability to find significant impacts on household consumption could be that funds were instead going to land (and other asset) purchases.

The reason that households are not selling land to gain access to microfinance raises another tricky issue. It turns out that the microlenders were not following the eligibility criteria strictly, so many households owning over a half an acre were nonetheless borrowing in 1991–1992. As a result, there was no reason to sell land to become eligible. Khandker (2005) acknowledges the problem and finds that 25 percent of borrowers were over the half-acre line in 1991–1992 and

31 percent were over in 1998–1999.[14] Pitt (1999) follows up on the issue and suggests that households with more land have lower quality land, so they still may be impoverished, even if they are not (strictly speaking) functionally landless. But a problem remains: the eligible households in the control villages were surveyed on the basis of a strict interpretation of the half-acre rule, while the eligible households in the treatment villages include the mistargeted households. Morduch (1998) adjusts the samples in order to maintain comparability, and Pitt (1999) does robustness checks to show that the Pitt and Khandker (1998) results change little when mistargeting is taken into account.[15]

These issues should be borne in mind when turning to the Pitt and Khandker (1998) framework. We start by noting that equation (9.5) (which can be run using ordinary least squares) is closely related to the following instrumental variables approach estimate instead:

$$Y_{ij} = X_{ij}\alpha + V_j\beta + E_{ij}\gamma + C_{ij}\delta'' + \eta_{ij}, \tag{9.6}$$

where Cij is the amount of credit received and $T_{ij} \cdot E_{ij}$ is employed as an instrumental variable.[16] Estimating equation (9.6) using ordinary least squares would bring trouble since households who have received more and larger loans can be expected to be different in unobservable ways from those who have received fewer loans (leading to a variant of selection bias associated with loan size). The instrumental variables method addresses the problem and leads to a clean estimate of δ, the average impact of credit access (subject to the same caveats as village dummy variables noted earlier).

Before moving on to the method used by Pitt and Khandker (1998), note that the instrument $T_{ij} \cdot E_{ij}$ is a dummy variable that only reflects credit access. The estimate of δ thus does not draw on variation in *how much* credit is received, it only depends on whether credit is received. The step taken by Pitt and Khandker is to expand to a larger set of instruments, in effect, by using $X_{ij} \cdot T_{ij} \cdot E_{ij}$ as instruments. The step yields as many instruments as there are X's. (The X's include education and various aspects of household demographics.) The move means that the estimate of δ takes advantage of variation in how much credit households receive.

An important identifying assumption is that the specification in equation (9.6) is correct so that education and demographics affect household outcomes in exactly the same way for the whole sample; otherwise, biases enter back in. In other words, it is assumed that there are no important nonlinear relationships in the ways that age, education, and the other variables influence outcomes of interest.[17] Another critical identifying assumption stems from their use of a Tobit equation to explain credit demand in a first stage in which they are effectively creating the instrumental variables used in the final regressions. The Tobit provides a way to efficiently handle variables with many zero values (like credit); but it requires that, in the second stage estimation, all microfinance impacts are assumed to be identical across borrowers, an assumption that is often made out of necessity but that stretches plausbility here. It also implies (implausibly) that marginal and average impacts of credit are equal. Estimating using a simpler two-stage least squares method would lead to consistent estimates without requiring these assumptions, but the method is less efficient (i.e., coefficients would tend to have larger standard errors). By using the Tobit, the efficiency of the estimators is improved.

Pitt and Khandker take one more step to investigate credit received by men separately from credit received by women (motivated by the concerns raised in chapter 7). To do this, they take advantage of the fact that microlending groups are not mixed by gender in Bangladesh. In the eighty-seven villages surveyed in 1991–1992, ten had no female groups and twenty-two had no male groups (and forty had both, leaving fifteen villages with no groups). Identification in this case comes from comparing how the roles of age, education, and so forth for men with access to male groups compare to the roles for men without access. Similarly, for the characteristics of women with and without access.[18]

Pitt and Khandker's most cited result from the 1991–1992 cross-section is that household consumption increases by eighteen taka for every one hundred taka lent to a woman. For lending to men, the increase is just eleven taka for every one hundred taka lent. Men, according to the estimates, take more leisure when given the chance, explaining in part why household consumption rises less when they borrow. Nonland assets increase substantially when borrowing is by women, but not by men. Schooling of boys increases in general with borrowing, but schooling of girls only increases when women borrow from Grameen—but not when women borrow from the other programs. It cannot be ascertained from the estimates why loans to women have higher marginal impacts than loans to men. Pitt and Khandker interpret it as an indication of a lack of fungibility of capital and income within the household (which is plausible assuming that their basic result is correct). A very different interpretation is supported by the fact that loans to males tend to be larger so that the smaller relative impacts may be explained, at least in part, by the standard theory of declining marginal returns to capital. However, marginal returns would have to be very sharply diminishing, since loan sizes are in the same general ballpark.[19]

The 1991–1992 cross-section has also been used to analyze noncredit program impacts, fertility and contraception choices, and impacts on seasonality and nutrition (for an overview, see Morduch 1999b). Khandker (1998) has used the basic impact numbers described earlier (imperfect as they be) to estimate broad impacts on poverty and to complete cost-benefit analyses (see chapter 10 for a more detailed discussion). The work is ambitious; but, as the previous discussion suggests, the underlying setup is far from perfect. The basic imperfections are not the fault of the researchers, but they have received insufficient attention. A return to the Pitt-Khandker set-up by Roodman and Morduch (2009) re-affirms that the necessary assumptions do not hold up. Roodman and Morduch (2009), like Morduch (1998), do not argue that microcredit makes no difference in the lives of borrowers; instead, they argue that the econometric set-up here is not up to the task. We need to look elsewhere for reliable evidence.

9.5.4.2 Estimates from the Full Panel, 1991–1992 and 1998–1999 A second round of data was collected in Bangladesh in 1998–1999, providing hope that simpler methods might deliver results that are simpler and more robust. With the two rounds of data, Khandker (2005) estimates an equation along the lines of equation (9.4). As with the work on the cross-section, he modifies the equation slightly, to allow for separate impacts when women borrow versus when men borrow. (In other specifications, he explores spillovers to nonborrowers who live in the same villages as borrowers.) As noted earlier, the control villages from 1991 to 1992 all have programs by 1998–1999, so simple before-and-after comparisons in treatment versus control villages are not possible. Complicating matters, the extent of mistargeting became more severe by the end of the 1990s.

The panel data allow us to see trends that help put the microfinance revolution in Bangladesh into perspective. Table 9.1 compiles data from Bangladesh in Khandker (2005). If we just look at the top panel of the table, we see that in program villages, microfinance participants saw important declines in poverty rates (as measured by moderate poverty),

Table 9.1
Falling poverty in Bangladesh: Program participants versus nonparticipants

	Headcount for moderate poverty			Headcount for extreme poverty		
	1991–1992	1998–1999	Difference	1991–1992	1998–1999	Difference
Program area						
All program participants	90.3	70.1	20.2	52.5	32.7	19.8
Target nonparticipants	91.1	72.0	19.1	58.9	44.0	14.9
Nontarget nonparticipants	69.8	50.8	19	23.6	19.3	4.3
Total	83.7	65.5	18.2	45.0	31.4	14.6
No program in 1991–1992						
All program participants	90.8	71.6	19.2	56.6	43.8	13.2
Target nonparticipants	87.4	82.9	4.5	57.0	51.2	6.8
Nontarget nonparticipants	72.7	53.2	19.5	35.5	26.0	9.5
Total	80.3	67.7	12.6	46.6	38.3	8.3

Source: Khandker 2005, table 14, and calculations by the authors.
Note: Program and nonprogram area is based on 1991–1992 program placement. All villages had programs by 1998–1999.

from a rate of about 90 percent in 1991–1992 to about 70 percent in 1998–1999, roughly a 20 percentage point decline. But eligible nonparticipants saw a similar decline (roughly 19 percentage points), as did noneligible nonparticipants (roughly 20 percentage points). Pessimists may thus argue that the poverty declines for micro-finance participants would have happened even without microfinance. Optimists, on the other hand, will argue that the impacts of microfinance have been far-reaching, spilling over to nonparticipants as well. This, they will argue, explains the broad and similar progress in villages with programs.

If the results for program villages are compared to results for those without programs in 1991–1992, we see similar patterns: poverty rates all fell by around 19 to 20 percentage points; except in this case, eligible nonparticipants only saw a poverty decline of about 5 percentage points. Khandker's conclusions, based on his new set of econometric estimates, balances the optimistic and pessimistic vision: he argues that microfinance contributed to roughly one third to one half of these poverty declines. Overall, Khandker finds that (at most) lending 100 taka to a woman leads to an increase in household consumption by as much as eight taka annually. This is considerably less than the 18-taka increase that he found in the earlier cross-section. But it is still large. Khandker's (1998) much-cited finding that microfinance might cause as much as a 5 percent per year drop in poverty thus appears to be far too optimistic, and we have already discussed caveats about the cross-sectional estimation on which that calculation was based.

When Roodman and Morduch (2009) return to the Khandker (2005) results, they find that key identifying assumptions for causal inference do not hold here either. Moreover, Khandker's assertion that the impact of microcredit has been stronger in reducing "extreme" poverty than poverty overall—while plausible—emerges from a simulation exercise requiring an additional set of caveats and assumptions, not from direct estimation. Using estimated baseline poverty levels, Khandker distinguishes between "moderately" and "extremely" poor households, then compares their respective changes in consumption using regression coefficients that make sense only if all households, richer and poorer, experience similar impacts. Given the use of undifferentiated regression coefficients, Khandker's results appear to be an artifact of the way that loans increase with income.

The World Bank and Bangladesh Institute for Development Studies surveys have yielded a broad range of interesting data and have generated much discussion. Given the complicated scene on the ground in Bangladesh (where microlending has spread far and wide, leaving little scope for identifying control groups), as well as econometric problems and difficulties replicating the results, we suspect that the ultimate resolution of how large an impact microfinance can have will be settled by data from elsewhere.

9.6 Randomized Evaluations

Randomized evaluations give hope that we can overcome the important statistical difficulties described above.[20] When done well, randomized control trials (RCTs) can provide clear, transparent, and credible evidence in complicated contexts, and it's not surprising that they dominate clinical research in medicine.

To see the RCT approach at work, let's say that you offered microfinance services to a group chosen randomly from the population (for example, by applying a random algorithm to select people from a census list) and then selected another group randomly who would be denied access to microfinance. Using the same language as in clinical trials of new pills and medical procedures, the first group is the "treatment" group and the second is the "control" group. The result from statistical theory says that the difference between the average outcome of the treated group and the average outcome of the control group is an accurate estimate of the intervention's average impact. We can interpret the result as the *causal* impact—under certain assumptions, it is a clean estimate of the difference made by microfinance.

That's a major result, but note that it's an *average* impact. It could well be that half the treated population gains by 100 percent and half loses by 100 percent, so that the average impact is zero. Zero is a clean estimate of the average impact in this case, but it hides the action. Still, the average impact is an important parameter, and is often just what the social investor wants to know.

To be credible, it must hold that the randomization was completed faithfully and that neither agreement to participate in the study nor the tendency to drop out are systematically related to outcomes of interest. These are not trivial assumptions, even though it turns out that the result still holds if people decide for "random" or exogenous reasons not to participate or decide to drop out.

New work shows that these kinds of concerns can be addressed by posing well-specified research questions and by carefully designing research programs. Much new work takes advantage of pilot phases of projects (or expansion phases), when experimentation and evaluation are particularly valuable for practitioners. Often it is possible to randomize where to place microfinance interventions in a pilot program (i.e., which villages or neighborhoods to choose first) even if it's not sensible to randomize which individuals to serve within those places. Moreover, we often can get clean estimates of *access* to microfinance services (independent of whether people choose to use the services or not) even if we can't as cleanly estimate the average impacts from the *use* of microfinance. From a policy standpoint, this may be the most valuable question anyway. The new work is showing that impact evaluations, when properly done, can be important investments for institutions seeking to improve their services, demonstrate their value, and refine their intuitions.

Still, social science is not medical science, and randomized experiments have limits: they are not always feasible, not always representative, and not always focused on the larger questions of interest. But already we've seen their power in studies described in chapter 2 (Karlan and Zinman 2009b), chapter 5 (de Janvry, McIntosh, and Sadoulet 2008; Giné and Karlan 2008), and chapter 6 (Dupas and Robinson 2008; and Ashraf, Karlan, and Yin 2006). Below, we describe four examples focused on measuring impacts, one from the Philippines, one on the advantages of access to consumer loans in South Africa, one on microfinance in urban India, and the other on returns to capital of small entrepreneurs in Sri Lanka. In section 9.6.6 we return to describe limits of randomization and ways to improve its possibilities.

9.6.1 Analytical Foundations of Randomization

Most evaluations compare outcomes for a treatment group, which receives an intervention, and a control group which does not.[21] The outcome for the former can be written as $(Y_1 \mid T)$. In this notation, Y is the outcome and " $\mid T$" means "given that this person received the treatment." The subscript 1 indicates that the outcome Y is measured after having received the treatment. The notation may seem redundant: the subscript 1 and the notation " $\mid T$" appear to refer to the same condition. But, in a subtle and important way, they do not. To see that, first consider a member of the control group. Their outcomes can be written as $(Y_0 \mid C)$. Here, the subscript 0 indicates outcomes without treatment and the notation " $\mid C$" means conditional on being in the control group. Again, there seems to be a redundancy, this time involving the subscript 0 and the conditioning on C.

As awkward as this notation might seem, it allows us to identify the odd beast which is the prize of our hunt. This is the term $(Y_1 - Y_0 \mid T)$, the causal impact. The term gives the difference between the outcome under treatment and the outcome without treatment, for a person in the treatment group. In the case of microfinance, it could be the net effect of access to credit on the profit of an entrepreneur. Like the unicorn, this is a beast that we don't expect to directly observe in the natural world. We observe $(Y_1 \mid T)$ and $(Y_0 \mid C)$ only, but neither $(Y_0 \mid T)$ nor $(Y_1 \mid C)$. The term $(Y_0 \mid T)$, the expected outcome for an entrepreneur who received a loan, *if she had not received that loan* is not observable. But it is "logically well defined" (Duflo, Glennerster, and Kremer 2007) and the concept helps below.

Randomizing turns out to yield a simple way to get a handle on $(Y_1 - Y_0 \mid T)$. The term can't be measured for an individual person, but its average value can be measured for a group. The result hinges on the properties of averages. To see that, we introduce the expectations operator and write $E(Y_1 \mid T)$ as the average outcome for all members of the treated group (here, microfinance customers) and write $E(Y_0 \mid C)$ as the average outcome for all members of the control group (Angrist 2004). The hunt will turn out to focus on $E(Y_1 - Y_0 \mid T)$.

So how does one capture $E(Y_1 - Y_0 \mid T)$ from $E(Y_1 \mid T)$ and $E(Y_0 \mid C)$? It turns out that $E(Y_1 - Y_0 \mid T) = E(Y_1 \mid T) - E(Y_0 \mid C)$ if the treatment and control groups were formed as random samples of the population at interest. They may include residents of villages selected at random from a list of villages, all of which are identified as plausible sites for microfinance expansion. Or they may include interventions targeted to individuals within communities who are chosen at random to receive access to an intervention before their neighbors. The key element here is that the two groups are expected to be identical before the intervention, because they were formed at random. If that's so, the differences between the groups after the intervention must be due to the intervention itself.

To see where this result comes from, write

$$E(Y_1 \mid T) - E(Y_0 \mid C) = E(Y_1 \mid T) - E(Y_0 \mid T) + \{E(Y_0 \mid T) - E(Y_0 \mid C)\}. \quad (9.7)$$

All we've done is subtract and add $E(Y_0 \mid T)$, which is our unobserved hypothetical outcome. Reorganizing the expression further by using the fact that the expectation operator is a linear operator, so the difference of the expectation is the expectation of the difference, we have: [22]

$$E(Y_1 \mid T) - E(Y_0 \mid C) = E(Y_1 - Y_0 \mid T) + \{E(Y_0 \mid T) - E(Y_0 \mid C)\}. \quad (9.8)$$

Our strategy hinges on the term in braces. If it is equal to 0, then $E(Y_1 \mid T) - E(Y_0 \mid C) = E(Y_1 - Y_0 \mid T)$ and we can measure the impact of the loan by comparing the outcomes of treatment and control groups.

The quantity $E(Y_0 \mid T) - E(Y_0 \mid C)$ represents how both the group with credit access and the control group would have fared if nobody had had access. The unobserved beast, $E(Y_0 \mid T) - E(Y_0 \mid C)$, is "selection bias." It is a devil precisely because it is unobservable. This is where the randomization comes into play: if randomization has been completed successfully, this difference is expected to be 0 and vanishes from the expression, leaving us with our prize:

$$E(Y_1 \mid T) - E(Y_0 \mid C) = E(Y_1 - Y_0 \mid T). \tag{9.9}$$

Randomization promises to banish selection bias, but that pins a lot on the assumption that the randomization has been complete. Without randomizing well, we're back with the troubles that animated the first part of this chapter. That's the fear that microentrepreneurs who apply for and are approved for loans may well be more dynamic, motivated, risk-tolerant, etc. than microentrepreneurs who do not apply for loans. Or that the locations chosen as sites for microfinance institutions may be particularly promising relative to other sites. "Nonrandom" attrition can also cause problems (say, the least promising customers are the first to drop-out). Contamination of the control group (competitors enter during the study period) is also a worry. In our notation, most of these cases will mean that $E(Y_0 \mid T) > E(Y_0 \mid C)$, biasing upward the estimates of impact. Contamination, or other forms of selection bias, might instead lead to downward biases as $E(Y_0 \mid T) < E(Y_0 \mid C)$. Doing randomization well requires that $E(Y_0 \mid T) = E(Y_0 \mid C)$.

One other important note: everything above hinges on the simple properties of expectations of linear operators. That allows us to make claims about average impacts. But the basic set-up does not permit us to say anything about the medians and very little about the distributional features of impacts. And we need to be careful in analyzing data on the impacts for particular subgroups in a population. We return to these issues in section 9.6.6.

9.6.2 Measuring Impacts at the Margin: Consumer Finance in South Africa and Microfinance in the Philippines

Karlan and Zinman (2010) provide an example of a randomized experiment that measures the impact of financial access in South Africa. Here, the institution is not a traditional microlender but a consumer lender that operates commercially and charges high interest rates for short-term (often one month) loans. Unlike most microlenders, the institution tolerates high default rates (loan repayment rates are around 75 percent), and compensates by charging exorbitant interest rates. Still, the study is of interest here since it shows surprisingly positive impacts of consumer lending and demonstrates a creative way to apply randomized methods.

The study design took advantage of the lender's use of credit scoring to allocate loans. In the scoring process, loan applicants are rated on a scale from 100 (most likely to repay) to 0 (least likely to repay). The lender chose a cut-off point below which applicants are excluded from borrowing. The lender, though, feared that the line was too conservative, and the researchers convinced the lender to take a second look at applicants who had narrowly missed being judged creditworthy.

The study focuses on a set of high-risk customers with credit scores in a narrow range just below the cut-off point. From this set, a fraction was chosen (randomly) to be offered a loan. For the lender, the project provided information on the risks and benefits of expanding its approval criteria. For the researchers, the randomization process provided the opportunity to estimate the causal impact of access to the loans. The experiment proceeded by modifying the bank's software. Loan applications were received at the local branch, and loan officers would use proprietary scoring software to evaluate the applicant's creditworthiness. Applicants whose score fell just below the cut-off would normally be denied loans, but the software was modified to reverse the decision for some of them, chosen randomly. Some marginal applicants would literally have a lucky day. With the process in place, the researchers could investigate average outcomes between the lucky borrowers in the treatment group (325 borrowers) versus the unlucky applicants who were rejected (462 applicants) and thus placed in the control group.[23]

The loans were marketed as consumer loans, but some borrowers used the loans to support microenterprises; most did not. Nonetheless, financial access helped people earn income. Notably, the group with access to the loans were more likely to keep their jobs over the study period, which raised their incomes. The median treatment household reported an estimated 16 percent increase in income, and a 19 percent decrease in poverty. Households in the treatment group were

6 percentage points less likely to report that household members had been hungry and 4 percentage points more likely to indicate that food quality had improved in their households since applying for the loan.

The study also showed advantages from the lenders' perspective. First, their credit scoring method proved to have predictive power. The loans approved through the randomization mechanism were indeed less likely to be paid back in full (72 percent for the experimental group versus 76 percent overall). But it also turns out that the additional revenues and costs generated by the experimental loans yielded the lender a net benefit of about US$32 per loan. From the vantage of profit maximization, the credit scoring criteria were too restrictive. In the end, relaxing the lending criteria would be good for client welfare and for the lenders' profits.

Karlan and Zinman (2009a) apply a similar methodology in the Philippines, working again with a commercial lender that made small, uncollateralized loans and charged relatively high interest rates—63 percent when annualized. The institution is First Macro Bank, a for-profit rural bank operating in Metro Manila. This time, however, they targeted low-income microentrepreneurs. Of the 1,601 loan applicants in the sample frame, the credit scoring software randomly approved 1,272 and rejected 329 of them.[24] Researchers conducted follow-up surveys with all of the 1,601 loan applicants. Nearly all of the surveys were completed between one and two years after the individual submitted the loan application.

In this case, the findings were heterogeneous and surprising. Expanding access to credit wasn't associated with an increase in business investment, but access was associated with an increase in profit (mostly for men, particularly people with higher income). How did profits rise? Karlan and Zinman (2009a) show that members of the treatment group let go of unproductive workers, so their businesses actually shrunk. The results suggest that borrowers used credit to shift business strategies toward smaller, lower-cost, and more profitable businesses. It remains unclear why credit was important in prodding the reoptimization.

9.6.3 Urban India
Banerjee et al. (2009) report the first large-scale randomized experiment to measure what happens when microcredit becomes available in a new market. They study 104 similar urban sites in Hyderabad, India.

Their baseline survey revealed that there was virtually no formal borrowing in the area prior to the experiment, from microfinance institutions or from commercial banks. About a third of households operated at least one small business, and average profits were 3,040 rupees (about $61).

Spandana, a large microlender, opened branches in 52 of the 104 sites, selected at random. A follow-up survey, conducted at least 12 months after Spandana entered the local market, revealed that households in the treatment areas borrowed almost 50 percent more from microfinance institutions, and were 32 percent more likely to open a business, compared to those in the control areas. Business owners in treatment areas also reported higher profits, but they did not report employing more workers. For households that were already operating businesses at the start of the experiment, investment in durable goods increased significantly. Households identified as likely to start a business (based on characteristics like literacy and the amount of land owned) *decreased* consumption of nondurable goods such as food and transportation, and of "temptation goods" like alcohol and tobacco in particular. This pattern is consistent with new entrepreneurs' need to make lumpy investments. Households with a low propensity to start a business, on the other hand, increased nondurable consumption. The effects on social outcomes in health, education, and women's empowerment were negligible. The study's relatively short time frame, however, limits the scope of the results and their implications to the short-term. Social outcomes, for example, may take longer to emerge. In the short-run, at least, nothing big and positive leaps out from the evaluation.

9.6.4 Measuring Returns to Capital in Sri Lanka

Suresh de Mel, David McKenzie, and Christopher Woodruff (2008) used another randomized experiment to measure returns to capital for small businesses—a question at the heart of microfinance impacts. As described in chapter 1, economic theory yields a variety of predictions about returns to capital. One often heard claim flows from the notion of diminishing marginal returns to capital: businesses with less capital are able to produce higher profits per unit of capital than firms with more capital. By this logic, small-scale entrepreneurs should be willing to profit handsomely through microfinance and repay high interest rates. But it is not enough to know that entrepreneurs with access to loans earn high profits since both profits and access to capital depend on "attributes of entrepreneurial ability" (de Mel, McKenzie, and Woodruff 2008) and other common causes.

De Mel and his colleagues devised an experiment to introduce randomness in the amount of capital used by businesses. In this way, variation in profits and other outcomes could be pinned on these exogenous increases in capital. The researchers gave some (randomly selected) entrepreneurs larger or smaller grants in cash or equipment/ inventory. Randomization guaranteed that the (positive) increase in capital was not correlated with any characteristic of the entrepreneur or its enterprise.

The experiment was based on a survey of small enterprises in Sri Lanka after the tsunami of 2004. The researchers surveyed about 400 firms nine times over a two-year period (2005–2007). The firms were involved in retail sales, manufacturing, or services activities, such as running small grocery stores, sewing clothing, making bamboo products, or repairing bicycles. All firms had US$1,000 or less in capital, excluding land and buildings, at the time of the first survey wave. The grants given to some entrepreneurs were framed as rewards for participating in the survey, to be allocated by a lottery.

Four separate rewards were used, varying by mode of transfer (cash or equipment/inventory) and size of transfer ($100 or $200). If the transfer was in kind, the entrepreneur would get to select their preferred piece of equipment or inventory and it would be purchased by the research team. These transfers were large in relative terms: $100 represents 3 months of the profits generated by the median enterprise, and $200 represents 110 percent of the median firm's capital at the time of the first wave. Cash grants could be used for any purpose, either business- or family-related, and 58 percent of them were actually invested in businesses.

Researchers studied the impact of the capital increase on three outcomes: capital stock, profits, and number of hours worked by the firm's owner. Profits include earnings from the firm's owner, so particular care was taken to estimate the impact on profits net of the impact on the number of hours worked (see de Mel, McKenzie, and Woodruff 2009b for a sobering follow-up on measuring profits).

The study showed that the enterprises generated returns to capital ranging from 4.6 to 5.3 percent per month, or about 60 percent per year, depending on the estimation technique. These figures are well above the 16–24 percent *nominal* interest rates charged by banks and microfinance institutions in the area.

More striking, results indicated considerable heterogeneity in returns. First, the effect for men was large, but no statistically significant average effect was observed for women. (This is an average: some women did well, others poorly.) The finding runs counter to the idea that women are better positioned to take advantage of credit than men, and it aligns with the mixed results in the other studies above. Second, as expected, returns to capital were larger for microenterprise owners with higher ability, as measured by years of schooling and a test of numeracy and cognitive ability. Third, the variation in impacts was very large: half of women entrepreneurs experienced negative returns, and about 20 percent of men had returns lower than the market interest rates. Finally, differences in levels of risk aversion had no discernible impact on returns to capital.

9.6.5 Where to Randomize

Some studies randomize at the level of the individual, others randomize treatments across neighborhoods, villages, or another grouping. In microfinance, the options for the unit at which to randomize are most often: the individual, the solidarity group, the center, or the village. In many cases, choices are limited by practical constraints. Offering different interest rates to individuals within the same solidarity group, for example, is sure to generate feelings of unfairness within the group. It's probably a bad idea for the group, the microfinance institution, and the study.

The choice of unit of analysis is influenced by two important factors: statistical power and the role of spillovers. (For a more advanced discussion, see Duflo, Glennerster, and Kremer's [2007] excellent toolkit.) When it comes to statistical power, randomizing across groups instead of individuals means that a larger total sample is usually needed to measure the impact of the intervention. Imagine, for example, that villages are assigned to receive a microfinance product or not. To be able to reliably measure effects, the researcher may need to select, say, 100 villages for the treatment group and 100 for the control group. If 20 households are interviewed per village, the total sample would be 4000 households. If, instead, it was possible to randomize by individuals (so that, within the same village, some people are treated and some people not), the researcher might be able to proceed with just 100 households in the treatment group and 100 in the control—for a sample of just 200 in total. The latter is more appealing in terms of simple costs, but it may not be appropriate or feasible.

The existence of spillovers provides one of the challenges when randomizing at the individual level. Spillovers happen when (i) households transfer from the treatment group to the control group or vice-versa, or (ii) members of the control group are inadvertently affected by the treatment. The second kind of spillover effect can happen, for example, when an entrepreneur receiving a new loan shares some of the loan proceeds with a friend who happens to belong to the control group, or when a microfinance client who receives business training shares some of the lessons and tips with another client who was assigned not to receive the training. Or it could be that, say, improved productivity due to the treatment leads to lower prices in the entire community.

The two forms of spillover affect the random assignment at different levels. Because the identification of impacts relies on the randomness of the assignment to either group, and because individuals rarely switch between groups at random, those who switch between groups reintroduce a selection bias in the estimate of impact. The second kind of spillover can reduce (or artificially enlarge) the observed impact of the intervention. For reasons discussed further in the next section, these kinds of spillovers also create a need for a bigger sample. In most cases, some spillovers can be averted by randomizing at the group level rather than the individual or household levels. In a group-lending scheme, for instance, randomly assigning some borrowers inside a group to participate in a program while leaving the others in the control group has a much higher chance of leading to spillovers (and confusion or resentment) than when entire groups are assigned to be either a treatment or control.

9.6.6 Statistical Power

The concept of "power" refers to the ability to reliably detect the impacts of an intervention with statistical methods.[25] Measurement always entails some amount of "noise" due to natural variations in the data and measurement errors. But with a large enough sample, the impact of "noise" can usually be addressed and the effects of interventions emerge clearly. If the sample is too small, the noise may mask the intervention's real effects: measured impacts may be positive and large, but conventional measures of statistical significance would not be able to establish that the measured impacts are nothing other than more noise.

This concern is general, but it is more likely with randomized experiments than other approaches because randomized experiments tend to employ smaller samples. "Power" calculations become critical. The calculations illuminate the likely trade-off between detecting the program's effects and keeping sample size in line with research budgets. Statistical power generally improves with larger sample sizes, but it is not as simple as that. The design of the evaluation matters as well.

In our context, the intervention can be microfinance loans, a savings product, a health program offered to microfinance clients, a new program or new loan product that a microfinance institution is thinking about offering, or any similar intervention. Since asking all clients how the intervention affected them is (generally) too costly, a sample of clients is surveyed and statistical methods are used to determine whether conclusions based on the sample can be generalized to all clients. Intuitively, the larger the sample, the more confident one is that findings based on that sample are valid for all clients. The issue is then to make sure that the sample is large enough, but not so large that budgets are busted.[26]

Power calculations focus on four core elements: (a) the size and variation of the impact, (b) the size of the sample that is used to measure the effect, and (c) two choices about desired levels of statistical significance. The study design matters, so if satisfactory sample and effect sizes cannot be obtained with one design, others should be tried. (We will return to the influence of design elements below.)

Duflo et al. (2007) frame the issue of power in terms of the "minimum detectable effect size" for a given statistical power, significance level, sample size, and study design. The approach is valuable in that it quickly focuses on the trade-off between effect size and sample size. A basic formula for the minimum detectable effect size is

$$MDE = (t_{(1-K)} + t_\alpha) * \sqrt{\frac{1}{P(1-P)}} \sqrt{\frac{\sigma^2}{N}} \qquad (9.10)$$

where $t_{(1-K)}$ captures the level of statistical power, t_α captures the confidence level, P is the proportion of the sample that receives the treatment, σ^2 is the variance of the effect, and N is the total sample size. Without going into all the details,[27] we reproduce the formula here to highlight the relationship between the minimum detectable effect size and the sample size: as N increases, the minimum detectable effect size decreases, and vice versa. For a given study design, power calculations therefore map the relationship between effect size and sample size, with statistical confidence levels typically kept fixed at 5 percent, 10 percent, and 20 percent.

One practical difficulty is, of course, that the effect size is typically unknown, since the project has not happened yet! Several approaches have been developed to address this issue, some very practical and others more conceptual. The first practical approach is to make a prediction based on previous studies. The second is to do a small pilot study. If neither is possible, an estimate is still needed, and it is useful to begin by expressing the effect size in units of the outcome (for example, test scores, dollars of income, number of bed nets used, etc.), or in standard deviations from the mean of the outcome. Cohen (1988) suggests, for example, that an effect of 0.2 standard deviations is small, 0.5 is medium, and 0.8 is large. These numbers, however, need to be placed in the context of the variability of each outcome, and are purely indicative.

The minimum detectable effect size approach and formula also bring to the fore that the relationship between effect size and sample size depends on factors other than the four core elements. First, the proportion of subjects assigned to the treatment and control groups matters. Assigning half of subjects to the treatment group and the other half to the control group makes it possible to detect a smaller effect with a given sample size, or to use a smaller sample to detect a given effect size. We see that since the expression $1/[P*(1 - P)]$ will be maximized when $P = 0.5$. If the study involves several treatments groups and one control group, power calculations can indicate the sample size needed for each group.

Second, as we suggested in section 9.6.5, the level of randomization matters greatly for the sample size. The reason is that group-level randomization creates variation between groups, not individuals. Since individuals in a group share some common characteristics, information obtained from each individual brings less variation in the outcome than when the randomization is done at the individual level. Thus, in the former case, more individuals and groups are needed to detect a similar effect size. What matters here is the proportion of the variance in the outcome that comes from the group effect versus that from the individual effect. The higher the former, the bigger the sample needed or the bigger effect size necessary for detection.

Third, some experimental designs do not directly *assign* subjects to treatment and control groups, but "encourage" them to participate in the treatment—say, through an advertising campaign. People in the treatment group can say yes or no to participation, and members of the control group might take up the intervention despite the lack of encouragement directed to them specifically. This design requires a larger sample to achieve the same level of power or detect the same effect size. In their study of microsavings in the Philippines, for example, Ashraf, Karlan, and Yin (2006) invited a randomly chosen group of individuals to open a new type of savings account. Some did, some did not. The randomness in this project was in the invitation, not in the opening of an account, so the impacts of the new account must be measured by comparing invited and noninvited individuals. Obviously, not all invited people opened an account. The consequence is that the effect measured at the "invitation level" is diluted and a larger sample size is needed.

Finally, well-designed stratified randomized designs can improve the precision of the impact estimate, which makes it possible to use a smaller sample. Stratifying means dividing the sample along one or more observable characteristic, and performing the randomization for each subgroup ("block") separately rather than for the entire sample at once. For instance, a block could be constituted of women over 30 years old, another of women below 30, and two more similar blocks with men. Each block is then assigned to treatment and control. While randomizing individuals into groups create similar groups *in expectation*, stratification is used to ensure that the assignment to treatment or control group is random *in practice* along the dimensions used to stratify. In our example above, we know that there will be an equal proportion of each block in the treatment group and an equal proportion of each block in the control group. In effect, stratifying allows analysts to estimate the effect of the intervention for each block separately, although this is done with statistical methods rather than actually repeating the analysis for each block. Because each block is more homogeneous than the entire sample, a smaller variation in outcomes can be detected with the same sample size, allowing for a smaller total sample to be used.

9.6.7 Criticism of Randomization
Randomized experiments have been embraced as the gold standard for evaluations. In many cases they are. But randomization is not always possible, nor always desirable. Lively debates surround

claims and counterclaims, and recent views include Deaton (2009), Imbens (2009), Banerjee and Duflo (2009), and Ravallion (2009)—and, from a more technical perspective, Heckman and Smith (1995) and Angrist and Imbens (1994). Many of the criticisms are properly lodged against evaluations in general, not at randomized evaluations specifically. (For example: Are the lessons replicable? Is evaluation worth the trouble and expense?) But some apply to randomization more closely.

First, the randomized methodology provides an estimate of the *average* impact of an intervention. It does not teach us anything about the median impact, and offers little about the distribution of impacts. As illustrated in our power example in section 9.6.4 above, the distribution of the outcome value in the treatment and in the control groups are known, but this does not mean that the distribution of the impact is known.

For example, if a project makes one person much better off and all others a little worse off, a randomized experiment might conclude that the average impact was positive if the positive impact for that one person is large enough to offset the sum of negative impacts for everybody else. A policy or intervention that produces such an outcome might not be considered beneficial. Still, it is not impossible to learn about the distribution of impacts. Building in stratification from the start provides one method. Then impacts can be estimated for subgroups, such as men and women, richer and poorer borrowers, and so on. Consideration of impacts on subgroups ought to be built in from the start, or else the researcher risks "data mining" and finding spurious results. In randomized experiments, as in nonrandomized approaches, specifying in advance which subgroups and hypotheses might be relevant, and restricting one's analysis to these, is key to avoiding data mining.

Second, while randomized experiments excel at providing a clean estimate of impact, they are by necessity implemented in a particular setting, and therefore provide limited support to generalizing the findings to other settings. In technical language, they may have high internal validity but not external validity. The idea is that, for instance, a randomized evaluation of flip charts as teachers' aides in schools in Kenya (Glewwe, Kremer, Moulin et al. 2004) only tells us whether the flip charts helped raised test score for these students in these schools in this region of Kenya. One could imagine that students or schools in other parts of Kenya, India, or Latin America have different educational needs, and would benefit differently (or not at all) from their teachers' using flip charts. Nonrandomized approaches, in contrast, are lauded for making use of data coming from large geographical areas, varied contexts, and/or diversified populations, so that their conclusions are applicable to a wider range of situations. On the other hand, these methods are often far less satisfactory in terms of internal validity (the question as to whether estimates are credible on their own terms)— and, without that, they don't amount to much.

The limited external validity of randomized experiments takes several dimensions:

1. As highlighted above, randomized experiments are implemented in a specific context, so their results might only apply to that context. Recognizing this limit, proponents of randomized experiments emphasize the need for replications of the experiment in other settings before drawing general conclusions.

2. Because randomized experiments are typically carefully planned and implemented, expansion to a large scale may yield different results. Regionwide policies can seldom be implemented with the same level of care that goes into pilot studies. Still, testing ideas using pilot studies is a smart policy before applying policies on a wide scale. Randomized experiments are well-suited to addressing that need, and they can provide evidence on whether policy ideas really produce measurable impacts on a small scale and under near-ideal conditions.

3. The third issue with external validity has to do with the fact that randomized experiments impose their logic on the operation of the program being evaluated. Absent an experiment, field partners typically do not deny service to a subset of their beneficiaries, and prefer choosing those beneficiaries who have the highest need for, or potential to succeed in, the program. Because randomized experiments require that these two factors be left aside, not all nongovernment institutions are willing to collaborate with researchers to implement them. If experiments can only be carried out in organizations that accept them, replication will not get rid of the potential selection bias in the choice of field partner. As randomized experiments become more and more common, the hope is that more and more diverse organizations will participate.

Turning back to broader concerns, randomized experiments follow rigorous designs. In particular, they require that participants respect the initial random assignment to receive the intervention or not—and members of the control group do not, say, pose as members of the treatment group in order to receive benefits. The advantages of randomization also cease to exist if there are major spillovers between the two groups, and if a nonrandom subset of participants leaves the study, as highlighted in section 9.6.4. Statistical methods can be employed to correct for spillovers, but at that point the randomness of the assignment has already been undone and experiments have lost some of their edge against nonrandomized approaches.

Fourth, the initial random assignment must be maintained over the course of the study. The problem here is both attrition and contamination. The influence of attrition on the impact estimates is unpredictable, either overestimating or underestimating the impact. Contamination occurs when either the organization being evaluated (or another in the same region) starts working with people in the control areas, or giving added benefits, as a response to the fact that they are not gaining advantages from the treatment.

Fifth, randomized experiments are sometimes criticized on ethical grounds. They indeed require that a portion of the population be denied the intervention that is being evaluated, and the choice of who receives the intervention cannot be made based on fairness considerations ("those who need it most" or "those who deserve it the most"). These concerns are legitimate, and should be taken seriously. In some cases, however, a randomization mechanism may be "fairer" than other selection mechanisms. The selection of beneficiaries of an experimental policy, for instance, or in situations when funding is too limited to serve all eligible individuals, is sometimes fraught with political interventions and favors. Here, publicly randomizing who benefits and who does not can improve the fairness of allocations.

In sum, randomized experiments can be powerful tools to credibly establish that interventions produce impacts. They are not the only method possible, but they have many pluses. Taking their drawbacks seriously as a way to develop improved methods of randomizing and replicating is the next step forward.

9.7 Summary and Conclusions

The microfinance movement was born of the ideal to create new banks with social and economic missions. Completing impact evaluations is an important way to determine if those missions are being achieved. As we have described, there is no study yet that has achieved wide consensus as to its reliability—though, we have described some recent studies that deserve wide attention. The general lack of good studies reflects the inherent difficulty in evaluating programs in which participation is voluntary and different customers use the services with varying degrees of intensity.

Still, a set of solid impact evaluations are emerging. Incorporating experimental designs into the program implementation will be one way to achieve more reliable estimates, and useful lessons can be drawn from the experimental design of Mexico's PROGRESA/Oportunidades education and health program.[28] The discussion in this chapter shows that it matters to get details right, and that, for analytical purposes, having one very reliable evaluation is more valuable than having one hundred flawed evaluations.

The challenges in evaluation arise because no microfinance program lends to random citizens. Instead, lenders carefully select areas in which to work and clients to whom to lend. When the characteristics that make borrowers different from nonborrowers are observable, the relevant conditioning variables (age, education, social status, and so forth) can be accounted for in impact evaluations. Often, though, what makes clients different is not measured—borrowers may, for example, have a more entrepreneurial spirit, enjoy better business connections, or be more focused than nonparticipants. Because these kinds of unobservable attributes are correlated with having credit, what seems like an impact of getting access to credit may in fact largely reflect these unobservable attributes. Estimated impacts of microfinance will be biased if nothing is done about the problem. And the biases can be large.

An important source of selection bias stems from where institutions and their branches are located. Are they set up specifically to serve the underserved in atypically isolated areas? This may lead to apparent negative impacts if control areas are not similarly isolated. Alternatively, the programs may set up where there is good complementary infrastructure (highways, markets, large towns), biasing estimates upward. When evaluating large programs, programs may be placed in different areas for different reasons, so comparisons with control areas need to be made carefully. Some approaches, such as those based on comparisons of outcomes at more than one point in time, can address those characteristics of program location that do not change over time. But they have limitations too—and often unobservable characteristics do change over time.

Still, while some observers have despaired at the impossibility of generating reliable evaluations, their despair is misplaced and too pessimistic. It is true that rigorous statistical evaluations are seldom easy. But an often heard early concern—that since money is fungible within the household, it is impossible to trace the impact of a particular loan to a particular change in enterprise profits—turns out to be a minor limitation; this has been called the "attribution dilemma" by Ledgerwood (2001). Even if a given loan cannot be attached to a given change in profit, it is still possible to evaluate how profits change with capital (i.e., to measure the marginal return to capital) and how borrowing affects household-level variables such as income, consumption, health, and schooling. In many ways, these are more interesting policy questions anyway, relative to narrow issues around sources of microenterprise profit.

Useful evaluations need not be enormous in scale, involving surveys of thousands of households. All else the same, the larger the sample, the better. But some of the smaller studies discussed here turn out to yield more reliable evidence than larger studies that are imperfect in one dimension or another.

Much progress has been made in designing data collection processes that let practitioners quickly gauge their broad impacts by tracking indicators of outcomes for borrowers only. This approach, led by organizations like the Imp-Act project based at the Institute of Development Studies at Sussex, surely provides users with a great deal of helpful data that can lead to program refinements. But they should be distinguished from impact assessments of the kind described in this chapter. Without control groups (or methods that capture the same idea) it is impossible to determine net impacts.[29]

Our argument is not that practitioner-friendly steps should be abandoned. Nor that qualitative evaluations are unhelpful. Far from it: the Imp-Act tools and other "social performance measurement" approaches, such as those adopted by CERISE in France, are helping donors and organizations to better understand their clients' needs, to improve targeting, and to develop appropriate products and marketing. Qualitative evaluations are illuminating institutional processes and the ways that customers use financial tools.[30]

Rather, our argument is that these approaches are not sufficient ways to learn about microfinance. Obtaining more careful, credible impact studies that can garner universal acceptance is vital to push conversations forward. Reliable studies need not be complicated: if well-designed and well-implemented, they can be very simple.

The road does not end with impact evaluations, however. Even with a spotless, perfect impact evaluation, interpreting the results is another matter, and one that has received even less attention. Consideration of the worth of programs typically stops too soon. A clear showing of a positive net impact does not necessarily mean that a program is a good candidate for support. Cost-effectiveness matters too. As described in chapter 10, the microfinance programs that are being evaluated should be judged against the costs and benefits of alternative approaches, including other ways of doing microfinance.

9.8 Exercises

1. List the potential economic, cultural, and psychological impacts of microfinance.

2. Explain the potential effects of microfinance on the economics of the household.

3. Explain at least three different reasons as to why there might be selection biases when trying to measure the impact of microfinance.

4. The most recent trend in program evaluation is the Randomized Control Trial (RCT) methodology, which solves the selection bias problems discussed in question 3. Explain how RCTs overcome selection bias.

5. You've just been hired to evaluate the impact of Vivacred, a microfinance institution operating in Brazil. This institution gives loans to people living in the *favelas* (slums) around Rio de Janeiro.

a. First, imagine that the head of the organization gives you free rein to do the evaluation any way you want. You can direct the organization to give loans however you like, and you can collect whatever data you wish. Write up a plan for what you would do, and why.

b. Now imagine that you don't have total control—you can only observe what the organization has already done. Describe how (if at all) your approach would change, and what you would now do to estimate the impact of the program.

c. Suppose Vivacred is expanding into some new *favelas*, and you collect data on incomes before and after the expansion:

	New Vivacred sites		Still no Vivacred
	Took a loan	No loan	
Before expansion	R$247		R$192
After expansion	R$290	R$255	R$204

Assuming 20 percent of people in the new *favelas* take a loan, construct both the intent to treat (ITT) and treatment on the treated (TOT) estimates of the effect of the program. What assumptions must be true for the estimates to be correct?

6. Contrary to what theory suggests, a number of microfinance institutions have moved to individual lending schemes in recent years. Giné and Karlan (2007) examine how this shift has affected repayment rates in the Philippines. Enumerate the main challenges they may have faced when designing their experiment, and propose solutions.

7. One of the most important criticisms of randomized control trials is the relative weakness of their external validity. Explain this problem and why is it is relevant. What can researchers do to correct or work around it?

8. An economist is interested in studying crop insurance in Kenya. She knows that no formal institutions are providing this kind of service in the area, but she wants to look at the presence of informal community-based arrangements. However, the informality of these mechanisms makes it difficult and costly to measure their presence and intensity. What creative methodology would you propose to her in order to achieve her objective?

9. A researcher wants to estimate the causal effect of access to microfinance on the education of children among poor households in different villages in Bolivia. To this end she proposes to first estimate the following cross-section specification by OLS:

$$Educ_{jv} = X_{iv}\beta_i + M_{iv}\delta_m + \mu^e_v + \varepsilon^e_{iv} \tag{1}$$

Where subscript i stands for the household and v for the village, X_{iv} are observable attributes of the household, M_{iv} is the household's access to microcredit, μ^e_v are village disturbances and ε^e_{iv} are household disturbances.

a. Which problems may affect the estimation of this equation? Will δ_m be the causal effect of interest? Propose solutions for these problems.

b. The researcher suspects that her first specification may have endogeneity problems, and intends to solve it using instrumental variables Z_{iv} in the following first stage specification:

$$M_{iv} = X_{iv}\beta_m + Z_{iv}\rho + \mu^m{}_v + \varepsilon^m{}_{iv} \tag{2}$$

and thus estimate (1) by 2SLS. Which problems may the estimation of this equation have in turn? If these problems are correctly solved, will this methodology lead to an unbiased estimation of the causal effect of interest?

c. Propose an alternative methodology that may help to prevent the sources of biases spelled out in (a).

10. Consider two villages. Village 1 has 10 households, all of which have access to a microfinance program. All we know about these households is the following:

Household	Number of children	Number of children going to school
1	4	3
2	8	5
3	6	4
4	3	3
5	5	2
6	5	4
7	10	5
8	6	4
9	7	3
10	8	3

In addition to having access to a microfinance program, these 10 households enjoy a government grant which targets children's education. The grant enables each household to send one child to school. Now consider village 2. In this village there are 12 households that don't have access to a microfinance program, and do not benefit from a government grant for sending their children to school. The characteristics of these villagers are as follows:

Households	Number of children	Number of children going to school
1	3	2
2	7	2
3	8	3
4	9	5
5	5	4
6	6	4
7	4	3
8	10	5
9	3	1
10	4	2
11	2	2
12	9	1

Compute in percentage terms the level of education in the two villages; then attempt to measure the effect of microfinance on children's education. Can you conclude that microfinance has a positive impact on children's education? If not, propose a way to measure that impact.

11. Consider a bank extending similar loans to people in two identical villages, each of them inhabited by 100 households. All households in both villages are identical, and each loan is worth $100. With a $100 loan, a household can invest in a two-year project. Ex ante, the project succeeds with probability 0.75, in which case the household can get a gross return of $240. If the project fails, which occurs with probability 0.25, the household doesn't get anything. Assume that the cost of extending each individual loan is $20, and that the bank just wants to break even. Individuals are protected by limited liability.

a. What would be the gross interest rate upon signing the loan contract with a borrower?

b. Now suppose that during the course of the two year project, village 1 has been negatively affected by an unexpected aggregate shock that reduced the project's probability of success to 0.50. What will be the financial self-sufficiency ratio for the bank in this case?

c. Instead, suppose that in village 2, the weather conditions were abnormally better than expected, and that this increased the rate of success in this village to 0.85. What is the financial self-sufficiency ratio for the bank in this village? Can we conclude that the bank's program in village 2 is better than that in village 1? Explain your answer.

d. What would you propose in order to correctly estimate the treatment effect of microfinance in this case? Suppose you have data from an unshocked third village that is identical to villages 1 and 2 but where there is no access to credit.

12. Consider a village where all households are eligible for a loan from a microfinance enterprise. Suppose that half of those households borrow from a microfinance enterprise, and that half of them do not borrow at all. The total number of children of participant borrower households is 119 and the number of nonparticipants is 143. Before borrowing from a microfinance enterprise, the number of participant borrowers' children enrolled at school was 51, and of nonparticipants was 71. After joining the microfinance program, the number of children in school of program participants increased to 65, which in turn made the nonparticipants increasingly inclined to send their children to school. Suppose that, on average, for every two additional children that participants in the microfinance program send to school, there is a spillover effect of one additional child from the nonparticipant group who will go to school. Compute the percentage of children that go to school in both the participant and nonparticipant groups once the microfinance program has been set up, assuming that the birth rate in the village throughout the duration of the program is 5 percent. Then evaluate the merits of the following statement: "Microfinance has no effect on education," and explain your answer.

13. Provide and explain at least three reasons why statistical evaluations of microfinance programs might be unsound.

10   Subsidy and Sustainability

10.1   Introduction

The August 20, 2003, *Wall Street Journal* carried a short article on microfinance in Latin America (Kaplan 2003). The article starts with the story of Mrs. Esther Simone Garcia, a shopkeeper in rural Mexico. Mrs. Garcia's $130 loan from Pro Mujer, a leading microlender founded in Bolivia, was enough to improve the range of offerings in Mrs. Garcia's small grocery store. With the debt repaid and business expanding, the *Wall Street Journal* reports that Garcia has started raising her ambitions, and even thinks of sending her daughter to college.

"Now, one of the highly praised tools in the global fight against poverty is also proving it can be a viable business," the article continues, "increasingly drawing investors who seek profits along with the loftier goal of social development." BancoSol's 1996 $5 million bond issue in Bolivia and Banco Compartamos's 2002 $10 million bond issue in Mexico are cited by the *Wall Street Journal* writer to support the case, along with the news of Bank Rakyat Indonesia's plan to sell 30 percent of its equity through an initial public offering in late 2003. These banks are proving part of the promise of microfinance—that microlending can be profitable.

The other part of the promise of microfinance is that it can deliver critical benefits to underserved borrowers such as Esther Garcia in Mexico. Some programs have achieved both promises (profitability *and* deep outreach to the underserved), but most have not—even though many microlenders are now well-established and run impressively efficient (if not actually profitable) operations. BancoSol, Banco Compartamos, and Bank Rakyat Indonesia (BRI) all serve underserved low-income populations, but their outreach to the poorest falls short of the leading programs in Bangladesh and India. Most South Asian programs, however, have not been as commercially successful as BRI or the top Latin American programs. The challenge remains to find ways to deliver small loans and collect small deposits while not sending fees and interest rates through the roof. And if that objective cannot be met, the challenge is then to develop a framework for thinking about microfinance as a social tool that may need to rely, to some degree and in some places, on continuing subsidies.

The reality is that much of the microfinance movement continues to take advantage of subsidies—some from donors, some from governments, and some from charities and socially responsible investors. The *MicroBanking Bulletin* reports that 549 (62 percent) of the 890 institutions in its sample were financially sustainable in 2007 (MicroBanking Bulletin 2008). Cull, Demirgüç-Kunt, and Morduch (2009b) provide a richer picture of subsidy and sustainability in microfinance. They analyze an expanded dataset from the 2005 *MicroBanking Bulletin* and find that 57 percent of the 315 institutions in the sample are financially sustainable, and that these sustainable institutions serve 87 percent of all clients. The remaining 43 percent of institutions receive a total of $2.6 billion in subsidized funds. Of that sum, nongovernmental organizations (NGOs) take 61 percent, which amounts to $233 per borrower at the median and climbs to $659 at the 75th percentile. NGOs' subsidy share is disproportionately large in the sense that they serve only 51 percent of all borrowers, but their clients are considerably poorer on average than those of banks and nonbank financial institutions and the majority of NGOs (54 percent) are actually profitable. So on one hand, the data show that even programs reaching poorer clients can cover their full costs. But, on the other hand, subsidization remains significant. Moreover, Cull et al. (2009b) argue that because the assumed cost of capital is implausibly low in *MicroBanking Bulletin* calculations, the numbers exaggerate profit rates and artificially shrink subsidies.

Even with that caveat, it is important to bear in mind that the microlenders in the *MicroBanking Bulletin* data are a relatively impressive bunch, sustainability-wise. They only include programs that have indicated particularly strong commitments to achieving financial sustainability, and have allowed their financial accounts to be reworked by *Bulletin* staff to improve numbers' conformity with international accounting principles. Bangladesh's Grameen Bank, for example, is not included. In terms of financial management, the programs are thus skimmed from the cream of the global crop. We lack comparable data on the 3,552 programs counted by the Microcredit Summit at the end of 2007, but the bulk presumably show weaker financial performances than the select 890 in the *MicroBanking Bulletin*. Bauchet and Morduch (2009) show that the average operational self-sufficiency ratio of institutions reporting to the Microcredit Summit Campaign is 95 percent, compared to 115 percent for institutions reporting to the Mix Market (the organization that publishes the *MicroBanking Bulletin*; see chapter 8 for definitions).

Given the role of subsidies in microfinance, one might expect to find a mini-industry of consultants with expertise in cost-benefit analysis, plying their trade on data from program after program, quantifying whether the subsidies are used well or not. In a perfect world, microfinance cost-benefit analyses would be routinely pitted against cost-benefit studies from other poverty reduction efforts, following well-established modes in the study of public finance—such as Rosen (2002). These studies could usefully frame policy debates. In chapter 1, for example, we reported the finding of Binswanger and Khandker (1995) that during the 1970s the state banking system in India appeared to have caused increases in nonfarm growth, employment and rural wages. But those programs were inefficient and badly targeted, and there were just modest benefits in terms of agricultural output and none in terms of agricultural employment. Binswanger and Khandker conclude that the costs of the government programs were so high that they nearly swamped the economic benefits.

Microfinance promises to improve on state banks by reducing costs, improving targeting, and maintaining (or expanding) benefits. Even to get a snapshot of microfinance performance, measuring benefits alone is clearly inadequate. To test the full promise, cost-benefit studies pit independent assessments of subsidized program costs against measured benefits. Cost-benefit studies can show that even if a microfinance program delivers less impact than alternative uses of funds (e.g., for schools or health clinics), supporting the microlender could still end up being a more effective use of funds if the microlender delivers more impact for a given budget.

But in fact, we know of just two serious cost-benefit analyses of microfinance programs—and those were completed by researchers rather than by donors. Microfinance is not an outlier with regard to the lack of rigorous evaluations. As Lant Pritchett argues in his paper "It Pays to Be Ignorant," rigorous impact studies of health and education interventions are few as well.[1] Pritchett argues that the general lack of rigorous impact analyses is no accident: most programs have little incentive to be seriously evaluated. After all, why risk a negative assessment? So programs fail to collect the kinds of data required, especially data on appropriate control groups. Collecting data also takes resources away from programs' core missions: *doing* microfinance. In the end, for most programs the costs outweigh the benefits of undertaking cost-benefit studies.

Donors, on the other hand, should be keen on cost-benefit analyses since the studies promise to show donors how to get the most bang for their buck. But donors to date have also shown only limited interest in cost-benefit analyses. One explanation flows from the logic of the promise of financially sustainable microfinance. According to this view, cost-benefit studies pushed in the public finance approach are of limited value since subsidies are only a short-term aid to get microfinance programs up and running. It is of little interest to know the current benefits that subsidies deliver, the argument goes, since subsidies should in the end have no place in microfinance. The *MicroBanking Bulletin* data show that indeed older lenders do look better on average (in terms of financial sustainability) when compared to newer programs—although most older programs remain subsidized.

There are two main reasons why this argument is inadequate. First, it is still useful to assess the costs and benefits of the start-up subsidies relative to alternative uses that they could be put to—building health clinics, buying school textbooks, paving roads, and so forth—even for the programs that eventually achieve financial sustainability. And, second, since reality shows that subsidies remain an ongoing part of doing microfinance for nearly all programs, cost-benefit analyses should nevertheless be a routine part of the evaluation tool kit.[2] An additional concern is that older programs perform worse in terms of depth of outreach, as measured by average loan size in the *MicroBanking Bulletin*. The trend may simply reflect that maturing clients seek larger loans over time or it could reflect "mission drift"; the full story is not clear without more careful studies.

That said, it is far from clear that cost-benefit studies by themselves will resolve key debates. First, doing clean cost-benefit studies can be difficult and costly, and it is often impossible without collecting new data. Inevitably, assumptions must be made in counting costs and benefits, and results will always be open to criticism. Second, even if it can be shown that a dollar used to subsidize an existing microfinance program helps poor households more than the same dollar does in other uses, it might also be that the microfinance program would ultimately help more poor people if it was not subsidized (or if it was subsidized at a much lower level).[3] Thus, demonstrations that benefits of subsidies outweigh costs may not be enough to satisfy critics of subsidies.

More and different kinds of data are required to make a clear policy analysis, and completing a comprehensive quantitative assessment may be daunting. The essential problem is that evaluating microfinance is not like evaluating whether a new bridge should be built or whether a school should expand. In those cases, there are typically clear, fixed projects that are under consideration (or sometimes a limited number of alternative models). Each can be evaluated on its own terms and then be accepted or rejected.

But microfinance programs are not like bridges or schools. They are still evolving, and how they use subsidies affects the nature of products and services that can be offered. As we discussed in chapter 2, interest rates are in part rationing mechanisms (determining who chooses to borrow and who does not), and microlenders' interest rate policies may also affect competitors working in the same markets. Since getting more subsidy generally means that microlenders can keep interest rates lower than otherwise, removing subsidy will, by the same token, put upward pressure on fees charged to clients. Not only that, but the degree of subsidy has implications for how staff are hired and treated, how quickly programs can expand, how large loans can grow, and so forth. (We describe the relationships further in section 10.4.) Thus traditional approaches to evaluation based on the notion of a given, unchanging project (with given, unchanging subsidy levels) fall short.

So, even when faced with a well-done analysis showing that benefits exceed the costs of subsidies, critics will argue that the case for subsidization is still not nailed down. The fundamental problem is that a single cost-benefit study from a given program at a given moment cannot address the value of the existing program versus the continuum of alternative models that would emerge if subsidies were reduced.

In this chapter we lay out a research agenda for getting to the root of these arguments, and we describe how far-existing work can help us sort out questions. In section 10.2 we use the Grameen Bank as a lens to discuss subsidization and the subsidy dependency index. In section 10.3 we analyze subsidies more closely, describing empirical work in Thailand and Bangladesh. In section 10.4 we describe the specific evidence needed to move the debate forward, including measures of supply response and interest rate elasticities. In section 10.5 we introduce the notion of "smart subsidies": carefully designed interventions that seek to minimize distortions, mistargeting, and inefficiencies while maximizing social benefits. Section 10.6 delivers a summary and concluding remarks.

10.2 Counting Subsidies: Evidence from the Grameen Bank

A logical starting point for conversations about subsidies is to figure out how large the subsidies are. This turns out to be harder than it seems. Microlenders take in subsidies in many ways—even those who claim to earn profits. The Grameen Bank, for example, advertises in its annual reports that it has earned profits almost every year since it was started. The sum reported between 1985 and 1996, for example, was $1.5 million (converted into 1996 dollars). These are modest profits, and are in line with Grameen's focus on poverty reduction.[4]

But during this period Grameen also took advantage of subsidies from multiple sources. Sometimes subsidies are direct—for example, grants to help pay for staff training. Other subsidies are indirect, and teasing them out often requires reading the bank's income statements with a calculator at hand. (The amounts cited here are the best approximations feasible given the available published data, but they are nevertheless approximations.)

Grameen's annual reports, for example, indicate that between 1985 and 1996 their direct subsidies totaled $16.4 million. Since these grants are included as income in the bank's income statement, it's clear that when Grameen management writes that they make profits each year, they simply mean that the bank took in more revenue than it spent. By subtracting the $16.4 million in grants from the $1.5 million in reported profits, we can see that in this period Grameen clearly did not earn profits as traditionally calculated.

To get a richer picture, we need to look at other sources of subsidy too. Other forms of subsidy come via "soft loans" from donors. A donor might prefer to support a microlender by making a loan to be repaid in twenty years at an interest rate of 1 percent per year. The subsidy can be calculated as the difference between the 1 percent interest and microlenders' cost of capital from commercial sources. In Grameen's case, between 1985 and 1996 the bank paid an average nominal interest rate of about 3.8 percent per year on the money it borrowed. Once inflation adjustments are made, the average real rate it paid was −1.8 percent per year. Commercial businesses in Bangladesh that have to obtain funds at a rate close to the interbank interest rate, on the other hand, would have paid nominal interest rates greater than 10 percent per year. The implied subsidy in this case is the net gain to the microlender due to their access to cheap capital from the donor. The implicit subsidy amounts to roughly $80.5 million for Grameen between 1985 and 1996. At other times, the subsidy may take the form of tax holidays, loan guarantees, "soft equity," or the assumption of exchange rate risk. The soft equity portion of Grameen's balance sheet, for example, adds another $47.3 million to the bank's effective subsidy in 1985–1996. The total of these direct and implicit subsidies was about $144 million for the period 1985–1996, on average amounting to about 11 cents for every dollar in Grameen's average loan portfolio. We do not take the position that these subsidies are good or bad—we would need reliable data on social and economic benefits to make that judgment. But we recognize that, in principle, well-targeted subsidies can generate much benefit, and Grameen has had an influence that has spilled far beyond Bangladesh's borders.

The subsidy dependence index, created by Jacob Yaron, a finance specialist at the World Bank, is one attempt to systematically account for all of these kinds of subsidies in a clear, concise, policy-relevant way. The measures of "financial self-sufficiency" described in chapter 8 have a similar goal—and are subject to similar caveats. The subsidy dependence index attempts to answer the question: How much higher would the interest rates charged to borrowers need to be in order for the bank to operate without subsidies?

To see how it works, start with a break-even (net) interest rate r^* that solves the equation

$$L(1+r^*)(1-d)+I = L+C+S, \tag{10.1}$$

where L is the volume of loans outstanding before adjustments are made for problem loans, $(1-d)$ is the fraction of the portfolio that is expected to be repaid, I is total income from other investments, C captures total costs (including the cost of capital), and S is the total value of implicit subsidies. The left side gives expected income and the right side gives costs (in the absence of soft loans). To break even the two sides must be (at least) equated. Rearranging shows that the break-even interest rate is thus

$$r^* = [C+S-I+dL]/[L(1-d)], \tag{10.2}$$

and the percentage increase in the current interest rate required for the
bank to break even is

$$(r^* - r)/r = [C + S - I + dL - r(1-d)L]/[rL(1-d)]$$
$$= (S + K - P)/[rL(1-d)], \qquad (10.3)$$

where P is reported net profits and K is direct grants and the value of
discounts on expenses (see section 4 of Morduch 1999c). Reported
profits are gross revenues from lending, grants, and investments (less
repayment of principal and all associated costs). This final formula is
identical to Yaron's subsidy dependence index (SDI), given that appropriate adjustments are made to reported profits and to the volume of
loans outstanding. (In Yaron's formula, the default rate d is assumed
to be folded into L through appropriate provisioning and it is also
assumed implicitly that nonpayment rates of interest are identical to
nonpayment rates of principal (see Yaron 1992; Schreiner and Yaron
2001).

Morduch's (1999c) SDI calculations suggest that Grameen Bank
would have needed to increase its lending rates by about 75 percent in
order to break even without subsidies between 1985 and 1996—holding
all else the same. The calculation is roughly in line with SDIs calculated
by others for the same period. More recently, Grameen has been able
to take advantage of returns to scale and has turned increasingly to
members' savings as a source of capital, so we expect that the SDI
in 2005 should be substantially lower than the SDI a decade
beforehand.

The SDI is a useful tool, but there are important caveats about the
approach described here. The SDI has the merit of systematically
answering a narrowly defined question. That question is: Holding all
else the same, by how much would a lender have to increase its revenue
in order to cover costs if the lender had no access to subsidized
resources? The calculation thus sheds light on how institutions such as
Grameen would fare if they were truly commercial lenders. But the
"holding all else the same" assumption is a strong one—and it applies
also to other widely used measures of financial self-sufficiency. A
tension arises because if Grameen had not had access to such plentiful
and cheap capital, it surely would have organized its business differently. In this sense, the SDI gives an upper bound on how much
revenue would have to rise. Once faced with commercial conditions,
lenders such as Grameen would surely find ways to adapt as best they
could in order to minimize costs.

Second, it is important to note that lenders such as Grameen are driven by their social missions as much as by their economic missions. When subsidized resources are made available to them, it would seem foolish (some might even say unethical) to turn down the resources and not try to pass along the gains to customers. But doing so lowers the SDI. It would be wrong then to infer from their current lack of profitability that lenders such as Grameen would collapse if the subsidized resources dried up. Instead, Grameen could survive in principle, but the nature of services received by clients might have to change in the process. The SDI thus only partially answers the question about how institutions such as Grameen would fare as commercial lenders. By holding constant the lender's current business structure, the answer is unrealistically static. It's more important to know whether the institution has a realistic long-term strategy to remain viable—Grameen's has involved the steady shift from donor finance to obtaining capital from savings deposited by customers within Bangladesh. But gauging the viability of strategies is far harder than measuring whether the short-term financial snapshot involves subsidy or not. As the previous numbers demonstrate, the SDI approach is at the least an important check on accounts presented by lenders who calculate profits in "nonstandard" ways.

10.3   Costs and Benefits of Subsidies

So how do subsidies compare to benefits? We only know of two serious attempts to calculate the costs and benefits of microfinance. Those two studies, reviewed in this section, show that support for microfinance has indeed been a good social investment in Thailand and Bangladesh.[5] As noted earlier, though, this does not nail down the case for continued subsidization. In section 10.5 we discuss additional data we would want in order to make broader policy judgments.

10.3.1   Costs and Benefits in Thailand
The BAAC is a state-run bank that is Thailand's largest microlender, serving about 3.5 million borrowers. Townsend and Yaron (2001) start by accounting for BAAC's subsidies, which means careful analysis of the bank's revenues. In 1995, the bank collected fees and interest from its clients, amounting to 11 percent of the outstanding loan portfolio; this is the "portfolio yield," a rough proxy for the average effective interest rate. Using the SDI method devised by Yaron (e.g., Yaron 1992;

Schreiner and Yaron 2001), Townsend and Yaron argue that BAAC would have had to raise its portfolio yield by 35.4 percent in 1995 in order to be able to survive without subsidies—assuming that all else was unchanged. This means that the resulting financially sustainable portfolio yield would have to be raised from 11 percent to 14.9 percent, still a moderate average interest rate.

Given that the total yield on the 1995 portfolio was 18.5 billion baht, Townsend and Yaron calculate the total subsidy received in 1995 as approximately 4.6 billion baht per year.[6] Much of this subsidy is received directly from the government, but other parts come from the implicit subsidies on soft loans and equity. (The Japanese government was a major source of soft loans in the 1990s.)

The next question is whether or not these subsidies yielded commensurate benefits. Townsend and Yaron do not try to complete a full assessment of BAAC's impacts. Instead, they draw on work by Townsend and Ueda (2006) that considers the benefits that BAAC's 4.5 million customers derive from risk reduction only. (Considering the impacts on average incomes and broader measures of economic and social change would presumably lead to an even larger benefit number than the one reported in this section.)

Townsend and Ueda begin their estimation with a theoretical model that focuses on ways that access to banking helps customers cope with risks such as illness, local weather problems, and other idiosyncratic shocks. The mathematical model is based around a fully dynamic general equilibrium characterization of a hypothetical economy that shares characteristics of rural Thailand, and Townsend and Ueda are interested in its real-world plausibility. Accordingly, they form predictions from the hypothetical world and compare them to the performance of the actual Thai economy between 1976 and 1996. The results are mixed, and in general, households do better in theory than they do in practice. Townsend and Ueda speculate that the problem is barriers of access to banking, and they calculate that the associated loss in welfare is about 7 percent of average household wealth (about 10 percent for middle-income households). Since wealth averaged 876,000 baht in the sample, the 7 percent loss is equal to 61,000 baht. Taking that 61,000 baht loss (which implies a 61,000 baht improvement over the status quo once households get access to BAAC), converting it into annualized terms, and multiplying it times the 4.5 million BAAC borrowers yields a final figure for benefits that BAAC delivers in terms of risk reduction: 13.86 billion baht. Townsend and Yaron conclude that "clearly some nonzero subsidy could be justified."

Assumptions have to be made along the way to deriving the cost (4.6 billion baht) and benefit (13.86 billion baht) figures, and subsequent studies may move the numbers up or down. Monthly data on finances (rather than annual data) might refine the subsidy side, and the benefit figures may look different if estimated directly rather than making inferences from the application of a stylized theoretical model. When Townsend (2000) looks directly at how BAAC access affects risk reduction (during the Thai financial crisis of 1997–1998), he does indeed find evidence that BAAC helps customers cope better, but it is not possible to link that finding to the 13.86 billion baht estimate. Still, the Townsend and Yaron (2001) study puts together the available evidence in an interesting and considered way, and provides evidence that subsidies have been meaningful.

10.3.2 Costs and Benefits in Bangladesh

The Grameen Bank has been in the vanguard of the microfinance movement, reporting repayment rates of 98 percent and modest profits while serving over two million functionally landless borrowers. As noted in section 10.2, these self-reported figures exaggerate Grameen's financial successes, however. Closer examination of the data shows that while the bank reports profits that sum to $1.5 million between 1985 and 1996, the profits rest on $175 million in subsidies, both direct and implicit.[7] These include $16 million of direct grants, $81 million of implicit subsidies via soft loans, $47 million of implicit subsidies through equity holdings, and at least $27 million in delayed loan loss provisions.[8] The real (i.e., inflation-adjusted) costs of borrowed capital paid by Grameen averaged −1.8 percent during 1985–1996, a time when Grameen would have had to pay real interest rates of 5–10 percent to get access to capital had soft loans been unavailable. In 1996, Grameen received a major concessional loan from the Japanese government, but Grameen has received no important external funds since then, and their goal is to shift to self-financing through deposit mobilization within Bangladesh.

Taken together, Grameen's subsidies are relatively modest relative to its scale of operation. The average amount of subsidy as a fraction of the loan portfolio fell from over 20 percent in the mid-1980s to 9 percent by 1996. What have these subsidies allowed Grameen to do?

Like most of the microlenders in Bangladesh, Grameen is committed to serving the poorest households, and their first concern is with fostering economic and social transformation. Studies have linked Grameen's operations to improvements in income, stability, child schooling, and family planning practices.[9]

Khandker (1998) combines estimates of Grameen's subsidies with estimates of impacts to yield a cost-benefit ratio of 0.91. Benefits are measured by the extent of increased household consumption when women borrow from the bank, and Khandker's calculation (which is based on a 1991–1992 survey) implies that it cost society 91 cents for every dollar of benefit received by clients.[10] If instead the resources were directed toward male borrowers, the cost-benefit ratio would be 1.48. As highlighted in chapter 7, the ratio is (arguably) higher since lending to men appears to have a smaller impact on household consumption (based on estimates by Pitt and Khandker [1998]) showing an 18-cent average increase in total consumption when lending a dollar to women, but just an 11-cent average increase when lending a dollar to men).[11] Even the ratio for male borrowers, though, compares favorably to cost-benefit ratios from alternative poverty alleviation programs in Bangladesh. For example, the World Food Programme's Food-for-Work scheme had a cost-benefit ratio of 1.71, and CARE's food-for-work program had a cost-benefit ratio of 2.62.

The microfinance programs of BRAC compare less favorably in Khandker's analysis. Khandker reports cost-benefit ratios of 3.53 when lending to BRAC's female customers and 2.59 when lending to BRAC's male customers. But BRAC staff respond that the costs used here are unduly inflated by including expenses not related to microfinance when accounting for BRAC's subsidies. When accounting is done according to their allocating protocols, BRAC's subsidies shrink—and in the late 1990s BRAC's microfinance operations claimed to be fully financially sustainable. But Khandker may well be right: if the nonmicrofinance activities (like training programs and providing productive inputs to clients) raise BRAC's estimated impacts, then there is a good argument to include the attached subsidies when calculating cost-benefit ratios too.

Khandker (2005) produces new estimates of Grameen's effectiveness. In his new research (which combines the earlier data with data from 1997–1998) he reports that the impact of lending to a woman is found to be an increase in household consumption by 10.5 cents for each dollar lent to a woman (and results for men are small and mixed in significance). This 42 percent decline has striking implications for cost-benefit ratios. If subsidies are unchanged, it is no longer true that it costs society 91 cents for every dollar of benefit to clients. Instead, 91 cents only buys 58 cents of benefit. Still, a cost-benefit ratio of 1.57 (ninety-one divided by fifty-eight) continues to look favorable relative to alternative uses. Moreover, since 2000 Grameen has changed its funding strategies in order to reduce subsidy dependence. New data that account for changing subsidy levels may well show that although the estimated impact is lower, so too are subsidies.[12] Updated data will indicate if shifts in cost-benefit ratios have been advantageous.

10.3.3   Discussion

Townsend and Yaron (2001) and Khandker (1998) provide first cuts at taking costs and benefits seriously. The two studies suggest that investing in microfinance can yield social benefits that beat the costs—although Khandker's estimates are equivocal. Like all simple calculations, though, the studies rest on a series of simplifications. Most immediate, only measurable benefits can be considered: the impact on gender empowerment discussed in chapter 7, for example, is difficult to put into monetary terms, and thus hard to feed into a cost-benefit ratio.[13] Other limits hinge on how the measurable impacts are quantified. For example, Khandker's 0.91 ratio for lending to women by Grameen draws on an estimated 18 cent increase in household consumption for every additional dollar borrowed by women from Grameen (Pitt and Khandker 1998). The estimate is a marginal impact of an additional dollar lent; but the average impact is more appropriate here since the entire program is being evaluated, not just the expansion of scale.[14] Moreover, Morduch and Roodman (2009) raise serious methodological questions about the Pitt-Khandker study, even on its own terms (see chapter 9 for more).

Simple cost-benefit ratios also fail to capture dynamics. Imagine that borrowing allows a client to purchase a sewing machine. Owning the machine (and being able to set up a small-scale tailoring business) creates benefits into the future, and using impacts on current household consumption fails to capture the full value of borrowing since in this case cost is best thought of as a stock variable, while benefit is a flow. In principle, costs should be compared to the present value of the flow of future impacts, not the current impact, and doing so will lower cost-benefit ratios, thereby improving the program's appeal.

What's more, costs and benefits may go beyond localized impacts. Policymakers and donors are often interested in the broader aim of macroeconomic development as well, and factoring long-term, economy-wide effects into the equation further complicates analysis. Isolating the factors behind economic growth is particularly difficult (a fact reinforced by six decades of unsuccessful development strategies); so too is establishing that a program is pro-growth. In the case of microcredit, expanding access to credit might raise GDP in the long-run, but it might instead undermine growth prospects by lowering the use of relatively efficient industrial or entrepreneurial technologies. Ahlin and Jiang (2008) show that the decisive factor is whether self-employed borrowers can graduate to entrepreneurship (i.e., hire employees) by amassing savings, which depends on both average returns and the saving rate. If borrowers can only become entrepreneurs by earning and re-investing substantial returns, the authors predict that microcredit will not lead to economic growth.

Perhaps the most difficult problem—and the one most relevant from the vantage of the current debate in microfinance—is that simple cost-benefit calculations fail to provide insight about all of the relevant counterfactual scenarios. As argued below, cost-benefit ratios will be changed by reducing subsidies slightly, and the simple cost-benefit ratios provide no sense of the optimality of such a move.

10.4 Moving Debates Forward

What kinds of information are needed to move forward on debates about subsidy?[15] First, a clear sense of objectives and social weights. Are impacts on poorer households, for example, weighed in the social calculus more than the same impacts on richer households? The answer must combine both subjective social weights and judgments about the way that marginal increases in income and consumption translate into well-being for different groups.

Second is the impact of subsidy on credit demand and supply. There are two competing effects. One is that demand for loans by current borrowers may fall as interest rates rise, which is the standard result from demand theory. The competing effect emerges in contexts with credit rationing: as programs untether themselves from subsidies, they can increase the supply of loans to the underserved, delivering the opposite result.

The third major impact is on average returns to borrowers. Again there are two competing possibilities. One is that raising interest rates will screen out poor projects and raise average returns, while the competing possibility is that raising rates will exacerbate moral hazard and adverse selection, as pointed out above, and instead worsen net returns.[16]

The fourth major concern is the impact on other (nonsubsidized) lenders, as manifested by changes in their interest rates. One view is that subsidized lenders squeeze out other lenders, so that removing subsidies should both expand overall credit supply and allow those lenders to raise their rates. A contrasting view is that subsidized lenders helpfully segment the credit market; and when subsidies fall, other lenders may be forced to lower their rates given a more diverse pool of potential clients.

The ultimate impact of reducing subsidies is thus the sum of a range of possible mechanisms. There are bits and pieces of data on each, but there is little consensus on the size or sign of the general relationships, and there is clear need for better empirical understandings.

Despite the lack of evidence (or perhaps because of it), experienced practitioners on both sides of the debate strongly hold their views. Discussion about the role of microfinance in development thus remains stalemated early in the game, with assertions checked by counter-assertions and no immediate route to resolution. Those who oppose subsidization tend to assume a relatively flat distribution of social weights, low sensitivity of credit demand to interest rates, positive impacts of interest rates on returns, very low returns to investments by poorer households, and negative externalities of subsidized credit programs on other lenders. Those who are open to strategic subsidization, on the other hand, tend to put greater social weight on consumption by the poor, assume highly sensitive credit demand to interest rates, low impacts (or perhaps negative impacts) of interest rates on returns, moderately high (but not extremely high) returns to investments by poor households, and small or beneficial spillovers onto other lenders.

Fortunately, apart from the social judgments, these are all issues that can be resolved by fairly straightforward empirical studies, and chapter 9 has outlined guidelines and concerns for shaping research agendas. The question is whether donors, who have been eager to spend on new programs and who have had ample funds available for subsidization, are willing to divert funds to assess the value of their interventions.

10.5 Smart Subsidies

Despite the optimistic cost-benefit studies previously discussed, the cheap credit policies of failed state banks have tarred the idea of using subsidies in microfinance (Adams, Graham, and von Pischke 1984). Cheap credit has long been a problem. Lenders charging interest rates that are far below rates available elsewhere in the market are associated with inefficiency, mistargeting, and low repayment rates. The problems stem in part from the low interest rates themselves; and they are reinforced by other aspects of poor program design and management.

When subsidized credit is much cheaper than loans available elsewhere in the market, getting hold of those loans is a great boon. Loans meant just for the poor are thus frequently diverted to better-off, more powerful households. Even when the loans go to the poor, the fact that highly subsidized loans have typically come from state-owned banks (and the fact that the loans are so cheap) make them seem more like grants than loans, and repayment rates fall sharply as a consequence. And because state-owned lending institutions are seldom expected to earn profits, there are few incentives for bank workers and their managers to seek efficiency gains. Political pressures in fact often work against cost-cutting and vigilant loan collection. Poor households may still benefit from loans (especially if there is little pressure to repay loans), but in the long-term the institutions waste precious resources and eventually fall into crises.

That said, the jump from criticizing this kind of cheap credit to criticizing other kinds of subsidies is made far too quickly by leading microfinance advocates (e.g., Adams and von Pischke 1992). These advocates emphasize the need to strengthen financial systems over more immediate efforts to reduce poverty. (The so-called financial systems approach has been associated with the Rural Finance Program at Ohio State University). While there is wide acceptance of subsidies to help institutions get through initial start-up periods wherein costs are high before scale economies can be reaped, there is much less acceptance of the idea of using subsidies in an ongoing way to aid clients. From a theoretical vantage, the argument for using ongoing subsidies is solid, and, in practice, well-designed subsidies may be easy to implement and effective for borrowers. Even skeptics of subsidies recognize that institutions currently use subsidies as integral parts of their programs. With that in mind, we turn to a discussion of "smart subsidies": carefully designed interventions that seek to minimize distortions, mistargeting, and inefficiencies while maximizing social benefits.

10.5.1 "Subsidize the Institution, Not the Customer"

We start with short-term subsidies. Some donors argue for a strategy wherein the aim is to "subsidize the institution, not the borrower." If taken literally, the statement is nonsensical: a program without subsidies must pass along all costs to customers one way or another.[17] Thus, any subsidy to the institution means that fewer costs have to be passed on to customers; directly or indirectly, customers gain through lower prices.

However, if not taken literally, the strategy has some appeal: it simply translates as "subsidize start-up costs, not ongoing operations." In terms of customers, consider a long-term situation in which the institution can be financially self-sufficient when charging an interest rate of, say, 30 percent per year to customers. But, in the first eight years of business, 30 percent would not cover all costs; instead the lender would have to charge, say, 45 percent. Then, the strategy here would be to charge the customers 30 percent from the very first day of operation (and for all time thereafter) and to take a subsidy of fifteen cents per dollar lent for the first eight years.

Figure 10.1 depicts the strategy in a setting where average costs fall over time. The figure shows initial costs start at $r0$ but fall steadily until time t^*, at which time costs have reached the long-term level r^*. A subsidy that covers all costs greater than r^* that are incurred before t^* allows the program to charge borrowers interest rates of r^* from the very start of operations. After time t^*, the program can continue to charge customers r^* and exactly cover the ongoing costs of lending without subsidy. The initial subsidies mean that the customers do not have to help shoulder start-up costs.

As mentioned in chapter 1, the argument echoes the "infant industry" arguments for tariff protection familiar from the theory of international trade. The case is sound in principle, but lessons from trade in practice are less favorable: it has proved hard to wean industries off protection once it starts, and some protected industries are far from their infancy. To be effective, donors need a credible exit strategy based on clear benchmarks (based, for example, on achieving efficiency gains by set dates) that push microlenders to achieve cost reductions in time for the withdrawal of subsidies.

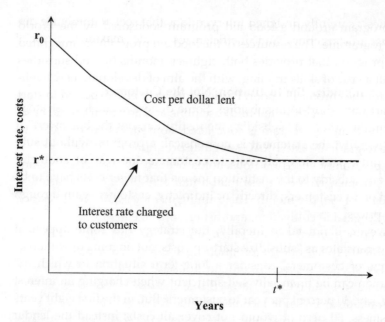

Figure 10.1
Subsidies for startup costs. Customers always face the long-term interest rate r*.

Another form of subsidization that is less controversial than others is to subsidize public goods that the institution might otherwise not provide (notably, data collection and impact evaluations from which others in the field might also benefit). Subsidizing technical assistance (e.g., for setting up a new management information system or designing incentive schemes) also carries little of the negative weight of long-term subsidies since, by its nature, it is short-term and fosters institution-building.

10.5.2 Strategic Short-Term Subsidization of Very Poor Clients

A more interventionist approach would recognize that clients may also benefit from subsidies in a broader way. One approach, which is again limited, is to subsidize those clients that are not yet ready to borrow from microlenders at "market" interest rates. They may, for example, need training first, or they may need time to build businesses that reach a minimum scale.

An example is given by the Income Generation for Vulnerable Group Development (IGVGD) program of BRAC in Bangladesh. BRAC built their program around a food aid program sponsored by the World Food Programme. The resources of the food aid program are integrated into a program that provides both eighteen months of food subsidies and half a year of skills training, with the aim of developing new livelihoods for the chronically poor. Participants were also expected to start saving regularly in order to build discipline and an initial capital base. When the training program is completed, households are expected to be able to graduate into BRAC's regular programs.

The program focused on households headed by women or "abandoned" women who own less than a half acre of land and earn less than 300 taka ($6) per month. The training includes skills like livestock raising, vegetable cultivation, and fishery management.

After an 80 percent success rate in a pilot program with 750 households, BRAC rolled out the program throughout Bangladesh, and by 2000 IGVGD had served 1.2 million households. A follow-up study by Matin and Hulme (2003) showed that the program was associated with dramatic increases in income for households just after completing the program. But within another three years, average income had fallen by nearly 60 percent from its peak. Part of the cause was that when the food subsidy was removed, households sold business assets and used BRAC loans to purchase food rather than invest in businesses, leaving households not much better off than they had been in the beginning. Matin and Hulme thus argue for additional measures to help households from slipping back and to account for the different speeds at which households progress. As Hashemi (2001) points out, two-thirds of IGVGD participants did graduate successfully to regular microfinance programs. But the fact that IGVGD failed to help a significant part of the population it set out to caused BRAC to look for ways it might improve the program.

After reflecting, BRAC initiated a second ultra-poor program in 2002. The Targeting the Ultra Poor (TUP) program builds off lessons from IGVGD, chasing the twin goals of effectively reaching those that are truly the poorest of the poor, and addressing the structural causes of chronic poverty and marginalization. Strict eligibility requirements help it target the most marginalized women in regions where food insecurity is the most severe, and participants receive a range of supports, including asset transfers (e.g., livestock), mentoring, financial literacy training, and health services. The hope is that complementing subsidy for the very poor with training will empower participants and help program impacts endure. TUP is being rolled out in phases to accommodate a randomized impact evaluation by researchers from the London School of Economics and University College London. While the full-scale evaluation won't be complete until 2011, preliminary studies suggest that the program has had better success in sustaining nutritional gains made during its implementation. Haseen and Sulaiman (2007) report that two years after active intervention, the upward trend in food consumption noted during the program period continued.

BRAC has served as an important model for microfinance institutions in other countries hoping to reach the bottom of the pyramid. Programs including SKS and Bandhan in India and Fonkoze in Haiti have launched TUP replications, and while they differ in the details, they share the fundamental approach of targeting and subsidizing the poorest of the poor. The strategy is akin to the infant industry strategy described earlier—only here the point is to subsidize the *client's* start-up costs, and, as long as there are vulnerable and very poor clients that meet the program criteria, subsidies to the institution could continue for a long time.

These subsidies are not large in the scheme of things. Taken together, Hashemi (2001) estimates that IGVGD subsidies per person amounted to about 6,725 taka (about $135 in 2001). The largest component was 6,000 taka for the food subsidy (provided by the World Food Programme), and the remainder was about 500 taka for training costs and 225 taka to support making small initial loans to participants (the first loans were typically about $50).

For $135 per participant, BRAC aimed to forever remove the need for participants to require future handouts. The evolution of the Targeting the Ultrapoor programs signals the challenge in reaching that goal, but the overall vision behind the program remains compelling.

10.5.3 Strategic Subsidization over the Long-Term

Programs like the IGVGD and TUP take us closer to considering strategic subsidization over the long-term. Part of BRAC's costs stem from the fact that initial loans are so small (just 2,500 taka) that BRAC loses money servicing them at the given interest rate (15 percent charged on a flat basis, roughly equivalent to a 30 percent per year effective interest rate). At loan sizes of 4,000 taka and more, BRAC can recover costs with interest earnings, but small loans are too costly per taka lent. The subsidy of 225 taka on a 2,500 taka loan suggests that BRAC would need to raise effective interest rates by about 9 percentage points for small loans; but BRAC fears that effective interest rates of 40 percent would be unaffordable for the poorest borrowers and could undermine social goals.

Figure 10.2 illustrates the general situation. In the figure, servicing small loans costs the microbank more per dollar lent than servicing larger loans, and some of the costs are passed on to customers. But part of the added costs are paid for with subsidy in order to keep interest rates from going too high. Costs start at r_0 but fall until loan size L^*, at which time interest rates have reached the long-term level r^*. At loan size L^*, the program can charge customers r^* and cover all their ongoing costs. In the figure, borrowers seeking small loans pay more than those seeking large loans, but, as with BRAC, it could be that all borrowers are charged the same rate. Or it could be that the smallest loans carry somewhat lower rates than larger loans.

The subsidies depicted in the figure are not associated with "cheap credit" and all of the negative trappings that entails. Instead, they are strategically deployed and targeted to aid the poorest customers. While

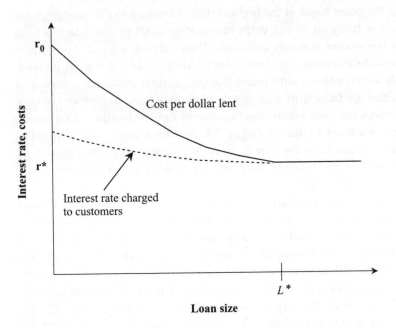

Figure 10.2
Subsidies without "cheap credit." The costs of very small transactions are subsidized, but at rates that mitigate distortions.

it may be possible to use cross-subsidization to cover the extra costs of small loans (using profits from larger loans to offset losses on smaller loans), cross-subsidization runs into trouble when competitors swoop in and steal away top customers with the lure of cheaper interest rates—a problem that happened most dramatically in Bolivia in the late 1990s. Thus it may be that smart subsidies are the most effective way to help programs focused on social transformation ensure outreach and affordability for their poorest clients.

Conning (1999) offers theoretical insight into the problem. He considers programs that have committed to covering their full costs, and argues that if reaching the very poor is impeded simply by high fixed costs associated with making small loans (e.g., having to put in the same paperwork and basic staff time for each loan, no matter the size), then raising interest rates and increasing scale could be a successful way to simultaneously cover costs and have both broad and deep outreach. This, of course, assumes that borrowers can easily generate the returns to pay high interest rates. Subsidies might be used to defray costs for borrowers, justified perhaps in the name of fairness (if not in the name of efficiency).

On the other hand, if the higher costs of lending to the very poor are largely a function of the extra monitoring costs entailed in working with borrowers without collateral, then raising interest rates could exacerbate incentive problems. Recall from chapter 2 that in general, viable loan contracts must provide appropriate rewards for success and penalties for failure. In addition, lenders may need to further enhance incentives for poor borrowers because of limited liability. As a result, poor borrowers require a larger "enforcement rent"—the difference between what they keep in the case of success and what they walk away with in the case of failure—than relatively richer borrowers who can pledge collateral.

Monitoring lowers the enforcement "rent" needed to give incentives to poorer borrowers, so it allows the lender to make larger loans to them. But it also entails real costs, so interest rates must increase with monitoring expenditures for the lender to break even. This means that borrowers with larger, monitored loans take home only slightly more than borrowers with smaller, unmonitored loans, which undermines efficiency gains. Poverty-focused lenders will also have higher staff costs per dollar loaned since they have to provide incentives to the monitors (see the discussion of principal agent theory and incentives in chapter 11). These lenders will be less leveraged: a finding that

Conning tends to confirm with data on seventy-two microlenders. The insight provides a foundation for the downward-sloping cost curve depicted in figure 10.2. In this case, the costs per dollar lent are, in part, a function of the interest rates charged to customers, because interest rates affect borrower behavior and that in turn affects monitoring costs.

Integrated credit models offering clients health services and training with financial services can also benefit from strategically deployed long-term subsidies. To provide these complementary services, otherwise financially self-sufficient microfinance institutions may require continued subsidies. In Nicaragua, Pro Mujer runs a financially self-sufficient credit business with one of the most efficient loan delivery systems in the country. To further Pro Mujer's two-fold mission to provide sustainable and efficient credit services to poor women and promote women's health and empowerment, Pro Mujer offers a wide range of subsidized "credit *plus plus*" services. These include health and empowerment training, as well as direct health service delivery, which require continuous funding. These help Pro Mujer compete and build client loyalty that contributes to Pro Mujer's 79 percent client retention rate. As donors push for sustainability, microfinance institutions with an integrated service model must map out how to secure continued funding for these services, from donors, fees, and revenues from the financial services business. Pro Mujer has gained an understanding of the costs of providing these services, and their benefits, as measured by their value to clients. Clients valued training and health services that address their privacy concerns, yet these received the least subsidy, while highly subsidized direct health care was valued less because it was also available at government clinics. To make the subsidies "smart" the nonfinancial services must follow the same efficiency principles as the credit business, and that involves allocating subsidy resources based on relative gains (Magnoni 2008).

10.6 Summary and Conclusions

Critics of failed state-owned banks have formulated a devastating critique of subsidies. The lessons should be taken to heart, but economic analysis shows that in principle subsidies in modern microfinance can be well-designed. And, if so, they can be part of efforts to achieve meaningful transformations in the lives of clients, without sacrificing the integrity of the institution. Doing it well in practice remains the ongoing challenge, but the growing number of subsidized programs that can boast impressive efficiency benchmarks and high repayment rates gives cause for optimism.

Some microlenders have found ways to achieve full financial self-sufficiency while serving very poor clients. ASA of Bangladesh, the example that led off chapter 1, is frequently cited for its achievements in achieving both financial and social missions. ASA's example is impressive, and we hope that it will be emulated.

At the same time, the fact that financial self-sufficiency can be attained while achieving an impressive depth of outreach does not mean that it can be done always. Some contexts, such as rural Africa and Latin America, are inherently more costly to work in than rural Bangladesh; other contexts offer less scope for internal cross-subsidization. Achievements such as ASA's don't mean that there are no trade-offs involved.

But even if the case for strategic subsidies is stronger than some microfinance advocates have let on, arguments for financially sustainable microfinance continue to have power. One concern is with incentives. While subsidies can help outreach to poor clients, there is always a fear that subsidies make institutions flabby. By subsidizing costs, pressure is removed that would have otherwise pushed management to seek efficiency gains and to experiment with new procedures. Dynamic efficiency may thus be sacrificed in the cause of reducing inequality in the short term. Donors should be prepared to tackle the problem head on and condition receipt of future funds on the achievement of realistic efficiency goals. The objective in principle is to maintain "hard budget constraints" rather than allowing constraints (and incentives) to soften, but this is easier said than done. This is one reason that arguments for limiting subsidies to start-up funds with clear exit strategies, as described in section 10.5.1, have appealed to donors.

As section 10.2 shows, even programs that claim to make profits may in fact use subsidies as a systematic, ongoing part of their operations. Our concern is not with how profits are measured but with how the subsidies are used. In principle, there is nothing inherently wrong with using subsidies, even in an ongoing way. As the discussion of smart subsidies in sections 10.5.2 and 10.5.3 suggests, there is a range of possibilities for using subsidies to maximize the social and economic outcomes enabled by microfinance. But empirical evidence is in short supply, and section 10.3 lays out an empirical agenda that can enrich conversations on how to use subsidies well, as well as how to avoid inadvertently undermining incentives.

Another concern is that relying on subsidies will limit the scale of operations. There are times when this is certainly so, and it is often better to serve more people with less (or no) subsidy per person. But, by the same token, there will be times when advantages flow from serving fewer people, and reaching out to the poorest and most under-served. In practice, the trade-offs may not in fact be so stark. As described in section 10.5.2, BRAC's collaboration with the World Food Programme, for example, shows that using subsidies can actually *expand* the scale of outreach (and not just help with *depth* of outreach).

A third concern is with innovation: the donors' strong push for financial sustainability has forced some microlenders to devise innovations to slash subsidies (a feat thought to be impossible before). Such "induced innovation," to borrow a term from the Danish economist Esther Boserup, suggests that the static framework of cost-benefit analyses may overstate the benefits of subsidies: when push comes to shove, some programs have shown that the subsidies are less vital than once thought.

A final concern emerges from a world in which donors (and the taxpayers who fund them) tend to grow restless and eager to move on to the next project and a new set of concerns. In the rational, analytical world where decisions are made according to cost-benefit analyses, there is no space for "donor fatigue." Instead, if a program is shown to be worthy of support year after year, it should get support year after year. But donors and practitioners are well aware that the actual world looks different, and their warning is that microlenders need to prepare for the day when subsidies disappear as donors choose to move on. In the end, options for using subsidy to maximize the potential of micro-finance may rest in greatest part on how seriously donor fatigue must be taken.

10.7   Exercises

1. Some experts claim that subsidies are sometimes needed for formal banking activities to take off. If businesses expect to eventually earn profits over the long term, how can subsidies be justified?

2. Briefly explain the value of cost-benefit analyses in the context of microfinance. Why may they, at the same time, not be fully persuasive in arguments about the value of subsidies?

3. Consider a risk neutral bank that lends a total amount $L = \$1,000,000$ to poor clients. The total cost of lending is $C = \$200,000$, the total subsidy received from the government is $S = \$50,000$, and the total income from other investments is $I = \$200,000$. The expected fraction to be repaid is 0.80. Compute the interest rate charged by the bank when it is subsidized and when is not. Compute the subsidy dependence index. (Assume that the bank is an NGO and just wants to break even.) Briefly explain your answer.

4. Interpret the expression "subsidize the institution, not the customer" and briefly describe this strategy. To what extent does it make sense as a matter of logic? As a guide for action?

5. What makes a smart subsidy different from subsidies that have long been used to subsidize rural credit in low-income areas?

6. It makes sense for microfinance institutions to be subsidized during their first years of operation. Subsidies lend support for microfinance institutions to reap economies of scale, which in turn enables institutions to operate at lower costs and become self-sufficient. Provide at least one convincing argument against this type of subsidy.

7. Consider an economy where 50 percent of the population is poor and 50 percent is rich. The poor have an income, which is a function of the interest rate r: $y_p = 8,000 \times r^{1/2}$, and the rich have an income with the following functional form: $y_r = 8,000 \times r^{1/2} + 1,500$. Assume that both the rich and the poor have the same utility function: $u(y) = -y^2 + 8,000y + 2,000$. A benevolent government wants to maximize the welfare of the society:

$$\max_r W(r) = 0.5u(y_p) + 0.5u(y_r)$$

It must decide whether to give a subsidy to the bank in order to decrease the interest rate from 22 percent to 20 percent, to keep the interest rate at 22 percent without subsidy, or to raise the rate to 25 percent. What strategy would you suggest to this government to follow? Assume that the maximum income in this economy does not exceed $4,000.

8. Consider an economy inhabited by 100 individuals, where half of the population is poor and the other half is rich. If a poor individual does not get access to credit, then his income is \$90. If he does and is granted a \$100 loan by a microfinance institution, his net income after repayment of the debt becomes $y_p = 125 - 50r - 20r^2$, where r stands for the interest rate charged for the loan. Rich individuals always have access to credit markets, each receiving a \$100 loan, making their income $y_r = 500 - 100r - 45r^2$. The cost of serving clients for the bank implies that the minimum interest rate it can charge in order to break even is 60 percent. Assume there is no risk of default for either type of borrower. Suppose that in this economy an increase in the income of poor individuals has a positive externality on rich individuals (because higher incomes increase their endowments of education and health, thereby improving their productivity, and lead to a decline in the rate of crime, for example). The utility function for both types is $u_p = y_p$ and $u_r = y_r + 0.2\, y_p$.

a. Would a poor individual access credit markets on his own?

b. What is the utility for each type of individual in this case? Calculate the social welfare, i.e., the sum of the utilities of the entire population in this scenario.

9. Suppose the government of the economy in exercise 8 is considering subsidizing credit. Assume that this government works as a social planner, striving to maximize the sum of the utilities of all individuals, net of the cost of subsidies and subject to the bank's break-even constraint. Assuming that the bank charges all borrowers the same interest rate and all loans are therefore equally subsidized, would the government decide to subsidize lending? Calculate the utility of each of the individuals and the social welfare, then compare them with the situation without subsidies in exercise 8. Is subsidization Pareto optimal?

10. Consider a risk-neutral government-subsidized bank. Its average cost of lending each \$100 loan to poor entrepreneurs is a function of the time passed since it first started delivering the subsidy, and it is given by $c = \dfrac{500}{t^2}$, where t stands for the (starting point) year. The maximum net interest rate that the poor can repay is 20 percent.

a. Compute the duration throughout which the government should subsidize the bank, before the bank achieves self-sustainability. Assume that the bank is a profit maximizer, and that repayments from its borrowers are certain.

b. Now assume each year the bank makes 10,000 small loans, and calculate the total amount of subsidies it delivers.

11. Consider a bank in Bolivia. Its average operating cost of lending each peso is a function of the size of the loan L and is given by $c = \dfrac{10}{\sqrt{L}}$. The bank lends 55 loans of 1600 pesos, 55 loans of 1225 pesos, 200 loans of 900 pesos, 185 loans of 3025 pesos, and 200 loans of 3600 pesos. The maximum interest rate feasible for the borrowers is 20 percent per year. Suppose that the bank is a monopoly. Assuming that repayments are certain, can the bank be self-sustainable? What would happen if the bank were operating in a perfectly competitive environment?

12. Consider a bank that conducts businesses in three stages. At stage 0, the bank lends to thirty poor clients, lending $1,000 per person. In stage 1, each individual borrower repays $1,200. The cost of serving each client, however, is $400. In stage 1, if the bank makes losses, it goes bankrupt. If it doesn't, the bank can continue to expand by lending to fifty poor clients. (Assume that the bank can increase its clientele with donor's resources if the bank either breaks even or makes positive profits.) Suppose that all fifty clients access an identical loan size, and that the bank gets an identical return per client in stage 2. Because of economies of scale, the cost of serving each individual borrower now drops to $300 per borrower. Provided that the bank continues to at least cover its costs in stage 2, it can expand its scale of operations by serving an additional one hundred poor clients. Again, the size of the loan per client remains unchanged and is the same for all clients. Now, as a result of economies of scale, the cost of serving each borrower has dropped further, to $100 per borrower. Suppose that each time a poor borrower is served by a formal microfinance institution, the net benefit to society is $5 and the benefit for the borrower is also $5. Finally, assume that all agents in the economy are risk-neutral, and that the economy-wide discount rate is zero. Assess arguments for subsidization of microlenders in this particular case. Would you favor write-offs of all potential losses at each stage?

13. Consider a bank that conducts a microlending program in four stages—at dates zero, one, two, and three. At date zero, the bank lends to thirty-five poor clients an amount 6,000 taka per person. At date one, each individual borrower pays back at most 7,000 taka. The cost of serving each client, however, is 2,000 taka. At date one, if the bank makes losses, it goes bankrupt. If it doesn't, it can continue expanding by lending to sixty-five poor clients. (Assume that the bank can increase its clientele by systematically either breaking even or making positive profits.) Suppose that all sixty-five clients obtain an identical loan size, and that the bank gets an identical return per client in date two. Because of economies of scale, the cost of serving each individual borrower, however, drops to 1,500 taka per borrower. At date two, and provided the bank continues breaking even or making positive profits, it can expand its scale of operations by extending loans to 100 poor clients. Again, assume that the size of the loan per client remains unchanged and that it is the same for all clients. Assume again that, as a result of economies of scale, the cost of serving each borrower drops even further, to 500 taka per borrower. Now suppose that by the virtue of having access to a loan, the borrowers can reduce the risk to their income from 17 percent to 3 percent. Assume that, if the borrower can not obtain a loan from the bank, she has an income of 500 taka. And when she invests with the proceeds of a loan from the bank, she also gets 500 taka after repaying her debt. Finally, assume that all agents in the economy are risk neutral, and that there is no discounting between periods. Would you favor subsidization of formal banking activities in this case? For example, will you favor write-offs of all potential losses at each stage? Explain your answer.

14. Subsidies to microfinance institutions can be helpful, but problematic. Carefully explain a problem that may arise with "smart subsidies." Discuss your answer.

15. Arguments in favor of the use of subsidies for microfinance institutions have often emerged in situations where agency problems play relevant roles. Think of the following two period setting with an ex post moral hazard problem: a start-up risk-neutral microfinance institution is offering loans to poor risk-neutral entrepreneurs in Bolivia, who hold a project that yields a gross return π per every $\$I$ investment after one period. The borrower can at the end of period one either repay her debt obligation, run away from the bank or just lie about the her project return realizations. If the borrower repays, then she is immediately offered a second loan of the same amount which she invests in the same one-year project and which she never repays. The discount factor of the borrower is δ. The short life of the bank implies that she must charge gross repayments as high as $R_N > \delta\pi$ per $\$I$ loan in order to at least break even. Assume that there are no ex ante moral hazard problems, that there are no other lenders in this economy and that the results of the project are not observable.

a. State the incentive compatibility constraint for the borrower. What would be the outcome for this microfinance institution without subsidies?

b. Can the introduction of subsidies solve the problem? Explain your answer.

c. What perverse incentives for the microfinance institution may arise once an "adequate" subsidy has been applied and the borrowers' moral hazard problem has been resolved?

11   Managing Microfinance

11.1   Introduction

In tackling the economics of microfinance, we've focused on how broad arguments and ideas fit together. The successes of microfinance, though, would be nothing without effective management. Economists are right that innovative contract designs help explain microfinance successes. Group lending is especially celebrated, followed by the dynamic incentives described in chapter 5. International donors are also right that financial choices have mattered too, celebrating lenders that judiciously use subsidies and set interest rates at levels that promote saving and wise investment (as described in chapter 9). Still, good contract design and pricing policy are necessary conditions for success, not sufficient conditions. A great deal of what distinguishes failed microfinance from successful microfinance ultimately has to do with management, particularly with how staff members are motivated and equipped to do their jobs.[1] In this, microfinance is no different from businesses that sell soft drinks or haircuts.

If one just read newspaper stories, it would seem that all microlenders can boast repayment rates above 98 percent and are making steady profits; management does not seem to be a big issue.[2] But table 11.1 shows a wide range in levels of productivity indicators from the 2007 microfinance benchmark data of the *MicroBanking Bulletin*. The first column and third columns give the range minus and plus one standard deviation from the mean. (If the indicators are distributed normally, the range should include about two-thirds of the observations, so one-third of programs would be even further away from the average.) The programs vary by age, scale, and location. Were the data made accessible, we could control for these factors, but the raw numbers suggest the basic point: while all of the lenders employ at least some

Table 11.1
Productivity indicators of microlenders by target market (890 institutions)

	−1 standard deviation	Average	+1 standard deviation
Operational self-sufficiency (%)			
Low-end	77	111	145
Broad	85	119	153
High-end	89	124	159
Cost per borrower ($)			
Low-end	−44	88	220
Broad	−29	206	441
High-end	−9	346	701
Portfolio at risk >30 days (%)			
Low-end	−3.0	4.5	12.0
Broad	−2.5	5.0	12.5
High-end	−2.3	5.0	12.3

Source: Microfinance Information Exchange "2007 database of the *MicroBanking Bulletin*" (available at www.mixmbb.org) and calculations by authors. The skewness of the distribution leads to negative values for portfolios at risk. The "low-end" group includes microlenders with average balances under $150 or under 20 percent of GNP per capita. The "broad" group includes microlenders with average balances between 20 percent and 149 percent of GNP per capita. The "high-end" group has average balances between 150 percent and 249 percent of GNP per capita. The "operational self-sufficiency" ratio is operating revenue divided by financial, loan provision, and operating expenses. "Cost per borrower" is operating expense plus in-kind donations divided by the average number of active borrowers. "Portfolio at risk >30 days" is the outstanding balance of loans overdue >30 days divided by the gross loan portfolio.

of the mechanisms described in the previous chapters, much of performance variation is left unexplained by the type of loan contract or financial product.

Consider first the operational self-sufficiency ratio (defined in chapter 8); it indicates whether lenders cover their operating costs (salaries, overhead, and the like). The ratio is a rough measure of efficiency, and the table shows that, on average, all programs are covering these costs. But there is wide variation, with some "low-end" lenders only covering 77 percent of costs, while others in the same category cover over 150 percent.[3] Similarly, the amounts spent per borrower and the management of overdues vary widely; the latter range from near-perfection to delinquencies greater than 10 percent.

The implications are investigated by Woller and Schreiner (2003), who use a regression framework to analyze thirteen village banks in the *MicroBanking Bulletin* data set in the period 1997–1999. By focusing only on village banks, they hold constant the social mission and target group of the institutions. Woller and Schreiner find "interest rates, administrative efficiency, loan officer productivity, and staff salaries to be significant determinants of financial self-sufficiency." The result should not be surprising, and it leads to a next set of harder questions: How can administrative efficiency be improved, loan officer productivity be maximized, and staff salaries be optimally set?

It also leads to the question: How can incentives be provided that enhance financial bottom lines while not undermining social missions? Can institutions design better incentive schemes to meet their varied objectives? Managing microfinance is made particularly challenging by the fact that, unlike the soft drink and haircut businesses, most microlenders pursue both financial and social objectives. The dual goals color hiring practices, compensation policy, and corporate culture in ways that can make being a microlender seem closer to running a school or hospital than a bank.[4] Microlenders also work with populations that have traditionally scared away commercial banks for fear of excessive costs and risks. Thus, traditional banking modes (and management practices) are up for rethinking as microlenders battle to keep costs down. Somewhat surprisingly, however, relatively little has been written on management in microfinance in general, and we know of nothing that brings in recent perspectives from the economics of incentives and contracts. In this chapter we highlight key principles and tensions, drawing in part on advances in the economic theory of incentives and in part on experiences in Latin America and Asia.[5]

We start with a cautionary tale in section 11.2: the story of the rise and fall of Colombia's Corposol, an ACCION International affiliate based in Bogotá (Steege 1998). In section 11.3, we state the multitask-incentive problem formally, and discuss issues that arise in designing incentive schemes (e.g., avoiding myopia, promoting teamwork, and reducing fraud). We draw out the issues, using the example of incentive schemes at PRODEM in Bolivia and BRI—two microlenders operating in very different economic environments. Section 11.4 turns to governance. We review structural issues that affect incentives, including patterns of ownership and how much decision making is delegated to staff. The final section briefly considers lessons from incentive theory for product design.

11.2   The Rise and Fall of Corposol, Bogotá

We start with the story of Corposol, an ACCION affiliate that started with great promise in 1988 (as Actuar Bogotá) but that collapsed in bankruptcy in 1996. The details draw heavily on Steege's (1998) account. At its peak, in 1995, Corposol served nearly 50,000 clients and had a loan portfolio of over \$38 million. Corposol's managers aimed for aggressive growth, partly to reap economies of scale, partly to be able to extend their outreach, and partly as a matter of prestige. They thus rewarded their staff amply for signing up new clients and for renewing loans. The efforts were remarkably effective: at the end of 1990, each loan officer was responsible for 258 clients on average; and by 1992, the average number of clients per officer had risen to 368. The pace continued so that in 1994 and 1995 the dollar value of Corposol's loan portfolio increased by more than 300 percent.

The quality of loans was only a secondary concern, however, and staff members who aggressively expanded volume were given larger bonuses than those who were more conservative.[6] A brewing crisis of borrower overindebtedness emerged in 1994 and 1995 when Corposol diversified the type of loans (or products) it offered, and began giving bonuses to staff based on the number of products (i.e., based on the variety of loans extended to clients), rather than on the number of clients. Then, in 1996, staff members were told to shift gears and expand lending volume rather than the number of products, again with secondary emphasis on the number of clients. The size of loans per client more than doubled in 1995, while the long-term health of the portfolio became ever more precarious. The expansion also brought a shift in orientation. In 1993, 86 percent of lending went to solidarity groups using ACCION-style group lending methods.[7] By 1995, the fraction fell to 30 percent. Instead, loans were increasingly large and made to better-off entrepreneurs.

Corposol's expansion goals were set by top management, and the goals were far greater than what middle management thought was feasible. Still, punishment for noncompliance was tough. In 1995, roughly two employees were fired each month for failure to meet performance objectives. Early on, the president's charisma had motivated workers to do the impossible; but as goals became tougher, motivation more fear-based, and management more arbitrary in its decisions, employees became so disaffected that what had been valued as charisma was soon dismissed as theater.

Delinquency rates followed these trends. (Rates are defined as loans overdue for more than thirty days, as a fraction of the active portfolio outstanding.) Early on, delinquencies were below 2 percent, but they hit 8.6 percent by the end of 1994 and 35.7 percent by the end of 1996 (Steege 1998, 100).[8] In 1996, the superintendency of banks stepped in to halt new lending by Finansol—one of Corposol's main divisions— and bankruptcy ensued.

Corposol originally looked like many other top microlenders in Latin America. Founded by a charismatic leader, Corposol received the backing of ACCION, and built a program around solidarity group lending. But in hindsight we can see that top leadership failed to appropriately decentralize decision making, set realistic and clear goals for staff, create mechanisms for internal control and feedback, balance social objectives while pushing financial ends, and create a culture of openness and professionalism. How to simultaneously motivate staff, balance objectives, and cut costs (especially while trying to rapidly achieve scale) is the ongoing challenge for all institutions.

It is easy to see the failure as only a product of bad choices made by Corposol's staff, but that is too simple. True, senior managers pursued an aggressive growth strategy that focused too heavily on expanding portfolio size and insufficiently on maintaining portfolio quality. But large, regulated institutions like Corposol should have governance mechanisms in place to check and balance the influence of senior management. The board of directors is responsible for overseeing managers and ensuring that the strategies are clear and coherent. In contexts like this, blame might instead be placed on passive boards that fail to effectively question decisions that should raise red flags. Without the benefit of effective board oversight, managers are free to follow unsound strategies to their logical and unfortunate conclusions (Labie 1998). We discuss governance further in section 11.4.

11.3 Microfinance Management through the Lens of Principal-Agent Theory

To put structure on the discussion of how failures like Corposol can happen (and how management successes like ASA of Bangladesh can happen too), we turn again to principal-agent theory (or simply "agency" theory), as used in chapters 2 and 3, to examine relationships between lenders and borrowers. But in applying principal-agent theory to microfinance management, we instead identify the top management as the "principal" and loan officers (and other field staff) as the "agents." The framework then focuses on difficulties that managers have in working with staff members to whom daily decisions have been delegated. The bargaining power of field staff is strengthened here since some of their efforts cannot be fully observed. Managers must then figure out how to adequately reward their unobserved effort in order to most effectively maximize the institution's objectives.

The basic contours of the problem go back to Alfred Marshall's (1890) writings on sharecropping in the late nineteenth century.[9] Much later, Mirrlees (1974, 1976) provided a framework that has been applied to a large variety of contractual relationships, including those between employers and employees, insurance companies and insured individuals, and politicians and bureaucrats (and to the moral hazard problem between lenders and borrowers in chapter 4). The aim is to characterize the best possible contracts that employers can design to elicit maximal (unobservable) effort by workers. The contracts have to take into account that the worker may have other employment options. Thus, a tough contract with harsh penalties for poor performance (a one-million-dollar fine?) may get workers to take the desired action, but in practice it would be hard to get anyone to agree to the terms. This is often called a "participation constraint" or "individual rationality constraint." The employer also has to give workers incentives for appropriate actions, the "incentive constraint."

To simplify, think about an institution with only one manager. She is only concerned with profit, not with risk. Employees, though, care about the ups and downs of their compensation. The manager hires workers who value expected pay and prefer that, all else the same, wages will be fairly predictable. In the first scenario, consider a fixed wage contract that meets the employees' participation constraints. The contract is appealing from the perspective of risk since the employees are guaranteed a given wage regardless of the outcome. But it falls short in terms of incentives: the employees have little incentive to provide additional effort, since additional effort is costly and goes unrewarded. The manager must rely on employees' intrinsic motivation.

Next consider the opposite extreme. Instead of offering a fixed wage, the manager commits to making the employees full owners of the microfinance institution, provided the institution's goals are met within a reasonable period of time (say, poverty is reduced and profitability is attained). Otherwise the employee is fired. This contract gives full incentives for employees to deliver maximum effort, but it obviously burdens them with a lot of risk. We call this a "high-powered" incentive, which is distinguished from "low-powered" incentives. We return to these concepts below.

The trade-off between risk and incentives is well-known, and the optimal contract lies somewhere in between the two extremes: that is, between a fixed wage contract with no incentives and a full ownership contract with lots of risk placed on employees. Sharecroppers around the world, for example, often split output fifty-fifty with landowners. Running a microfinance institution has more dimensions than basic farming, however, and there are not yet well-established rules of thumb for microfinance incentive systems. Instead, below we highlight concerns that should inform contract design.

11.3.1 The Multitask Problem: Poverty Reduction versus Profitability

The first concern rests with the multiple tasks that managers expect their staffs to perform. Let's start with the manager of a microfinance institution whose twin objectives are to reduce poverty and achieve financial self-sufficiency. Mosley (1996b) argues that these two objectives often conflict.[10] The conflict is not a given, but it provides a plausible trade-off to disentangle. His arguments draw on evidence from BancoSol in the early 1990s characterized by figure 11.1. Poverty reduction is on the vertical axis and loan size on the horizontal axis; the downward sloping "poverty reduction" curve indicates that the impact on poverty reduction decreases with loan size. On the other hand, financial performance improves with loan size as economies of scale are reaped. (This is seen in the upward sloping "profitability" curve.) Mosley estimates that in the particular case of BancoSol in the early 1990s, loans larger than $400 improved financial bottom lines but had a negligible effect on poverty.[11] Incentive schemes could push loan officers to make larger loans or, if designed differently, to focus on the low-end; the answer hinges on which objectives managers choose as priorities.

The extent to which the two objectives can be met also depends on employees' constraints. So, how should managers design a contract to maximize the possibility of attaining their goals, subject to employees' participation and incentive constraints? The bonus schemes attempted by Corposol satisfied the participation constraints, but they rewarded the wrong targets. By rewarding loan volume, the Corposol managers gave employees little incentive to train and screen borrowers, and the

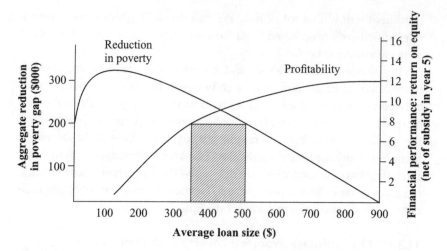

Figure 11.1
The trade-off between poverty reduction and profitability: The case of Bolivia's BancoSol.
Source: Mosley 1996b, 27.

contracts pushed the portfolio upmarket toward better-off customers. If managers had instead only rewarded the number of loans made, the portfolio might have pushed downmarket, but again would not have addressed loan quality. Suppose that instead the Corposol managers had offered large bonuses to employees that were a function of repayment rates only. Employees might then have favored borrowers that were less poor or lived in economically affluent areas (so that they had alternative resources to cover loan losses). But this would have gone against the objective of poverty reduction.

A potential way to resolve the trade-off is by offering bonuses to loan officers based on both high repayment rates and serving a large number of clients.[12] This strategy has been followed by most microfinance institutions, a small sample of which is shown in the 2003 data in table 11.2. In particular, by following such a strategy, lenders like ASA of Bangladesh have attained a high degree of financial sustainability while working with very poor clients, producing financial outcomes that place it among the most effective institutions globally (Rutherford 2009).

This is a start, but in thinking about optimal incentives in microfinance, concerns go beyond risk versus incentives and beyond loan volume versus quality. There is also concern with enhancing teamwork, balancing short-term versus long-term objectives, discouraging

Table 11.2
Governance, incentives, and performance of selected microlenders

Institution	Ownership structure	Sources of funding	High-powered incentive schemes	Operational self-sufficiency ratio	Financial self-sufficiency ratio
ASA (Bangladesh)	Trust	Equity holdings: 38% Donors: 29% Savings: 26%	Bonuses based on repayment rates and number of clients	160%	146%
BSFL (India)	State-owned	Subsidized loans: 81% Equity holdings: 19%	Bonuses based on repayment rates	101%	56%
Fundacion Diaconia FRIF (Bolivia)	NGO	Donors: 99% Commercial loans: 1%	Bonuses based on number of clients, repayment rates, and portfolio volume	Not available	Not available
CAME (Mexico)	NGO	Commercial loans: 45% Donated equity: 33% Subsidized loans: 14% Other: 8%	Bonuses based on number of loans and repayment rates	102%	99%
Cooperative de Ahorro y Credito HARDIN AZUAYO (Ecuador)	Credit Union	Retained earnings: 47% Deposits: 43% Donors: 7% Commercial loans: 3%	Bonuses based on number of clients and number of new loans	108%	97%
PSHM (Albania)	Joint-stock company	Donors: 96% Commercial loans: 4%	Bonuses for number of clients and repayment rates	99%	81%
ESA Foundation (Albania)	Foundation	Donors: 90% Retained earnings: 10%	Bonuses for number of clients and repayment rates	103%	72%
BTTF (Kyrgyzstan)	Foundation	Donors: 100%	Bonuses for repayment rates and other portfolio quality indicators	166%	149%

Source: Godel 2003. Operational self-sufficiency relates to the ability of microfinance institutions to cover their operational costs, and financial self-sufficiency captures the extent to which microfinance institutions can survive without donors' support, subsidized loans included. See chapter 8 for definitions.

fraud, and (holistically) creating an organizational culture of trust. The story of Corposol shows that each of these concerns can be undermined by incentive schemes that are too high-powered and inconsistently administered. The rest of this section takes up these concerns in greater detail.

11.3.2   Unmeasurable Tasks

The multitask problem is made more difficult when performance is ill-defined or is measured by highly visible indicators that are nonetheless noisy (Kerr 1975). In a seminal article, Holmstrom and Milgrom (1991) provide a framework to analyze contracting situations involving a principal (employer) and agents (employees) who are asked to distribute their time among several activities. One key insight is that observability matters. Employers can only directly assess and reward their employees on the subset of tasks they see taking place, whereas performance on other tasks may be important but unobservable. A typical example is that of teachers who have to divide their time between at least two activities, such as teaching and mentoring their students. Of these, only teaching is observed while mentoring is not. The principal of the school, on the other hand, wants teachers to undertake both tasks, but since the principal can only observe teaching (e.g., through teaching evaluations), school principals are limited to offering a compensation scheme based on teaching only. Not surprisingly, teachers end up teaching more than is efficient, at the cost of mentoring—even though school principals perceive both activities to be important.

To better understand the problem, consider the following exposition spelled out by Robert Gibbons (2005) in a review of the literature. Suppose that meeting a desired objective y depends on agents taking two actions, respectively a_1 and a_2. The most simple example is the case in which $y = a_1 + a_2$. Suppose further that the only observable action is a_2, so bonuses can be based on a_2 only. But then the agent will have incentives to concentrate on a_2 only. With maximum performance, his bonus can be huge, but the bonus may make only a limited contribution to meeting the ultimate objective. Optimal outcomes can only be achieved if both a_1 and a_2 are observable.

Next consider a situation with two different objectives, y_1 and y_2 (carrying forward the case at hand, suppose that y_1 = reducing poverty and y_2 = earning profits). Furthermore, consider a trade-off between actions such that

$$y_1 = a_1 - \alpha a_2$$

$$ \tag{11.1}$$

$$y_2 = a_2 - \beta a_1$$

where $0 < a < 1$ and $0 < b < 1$. Here, taking one action (say, working to reduce poverty by seeking out poorer customers and helping them develop business plans) promotes poverty reduction (y_1) but makes it harder to achieve profitability (y_2). Likewise, making larger loans may promote y_2 at the expense of y_1. If only action a_2 is easily observable, incentive schemes will necessarily bias against the objective of poverty reduction. Instituting high-powered bonus schemes with imperfect information will help if the two activities are complements. When the activities are substitutes, strong incentives can worsen outcomes.

So, why just reward staff for their effort? Perhaps in this case making pay contingent on outcomes would be better. If y_1 was indeed observable, it might be possible to reward performance based on outputs rather than inputs, but in practice outputs are not always observable either. In microfinance, social goals such as poverty reduction and female empowerment are notoriously difficult to measure in a simple, regular way. A similar tension runs through education reform in the United States under the "No Child Left Behind" legislation. The strategy provides schools with clear incentives based on how well children do on a battery of standardized tests—because those outcomes are fairly easy to measure. Meanwhile, desired outcomes like creative thinking, which may ultimately be more important, are hard to quantify. Critics argue that test-based incentive schemes can lead teachers "to neglect general education in order to train pupils exclusively for the purpose of doing well at the tests" (Dewatripont, Jewitt, and Tirole 1999). In this same way, rewarding loan officers based on easily collected financial indicators can lead them to neglect other, less tangible social objectives. This takes us to the general issue of high-powered versus low-powered incentives.

11.3.3 High-Powered versus Low-Powered Incentives

Bonus schemes provide high-powered incentives. So-called low-powered incentives, on the other hand, are typically implemented by offering a combination of fixed wages and rewards such as promotions that are granted based on broad achievements. The hope is that employees are induced to balance objectives and not skew efforts too sharply in one direction or another.

The main microlenders in Bangladesh, for example, promise their staff members security of employment, reasonable salaries, and career advancement within the institution—as long as their performance is deemed satisfactory (Morduch and Rutherford 2003). These job characteristics have strong appeal given the severe underemployment in Bangladesh and the country's weak labor laws. Rather than leaning heavily on bonuses (although some are used), the institutions try to set clear, simple targets that help employees understand the behavior that leads to steady promotion. And employees receive nonmonetary awards that are used to publicly recognize the most successful individuals and branches. Organizations have also been successful in making staff members feel that they belong to a special culture, especially committed to serving the poor. Staff training programs encourage this commitment; applicants for jobs at Grameen Bank, for example, are required to interview and write a case history of a poor rural woman.

PRODEM, a microlender operating in sparsely populated rural areas of Bolivia (and described in chapter 8), experimented with various incentive schemes and ended up with a balance of low-powered and high-powered incentives. PRODEM is best known as the organization out of which BancoSol emerged in 1992. But PRODEM has continued as a separate entity (now as a regulated "private financial fund" known as PRODEM FFP) and its Managing Director, Eduardo Bazoberry has paid close attention to how to create constructive incentives in the challenging environment in which PRODEM operates. Bazoberry (2001, 12) describes the importance of low-powered incentives at PRODEM:

To strengthen our hand in a competitive market, PRODEM FFP has developed a complex and creative matrix of incentives to help employees fulfill a variety of personal needs ranging from shelter and security to acceptance and self-fulfillment. The matrix includes financial as well as non-financial incentives, such as staff development, job enrichment and promotional opportunities, extensive health benefits, achievement awards, and the opportunity to take a sabbatical after ten years of service.

As noted above, providing these kinds of low-powered incentives may be superior even with regard to those tasks for which performance is relatively straightforward to measure, for example, financial self-sufficiency. In line with PRODEM, leading microlenders lean on low-powered incentives alongside higher-powered bonus schemes, and the experience of microlenders varies widely. Consider the following data on thirty Latin American microlenders collected by MicroRate.[13] While

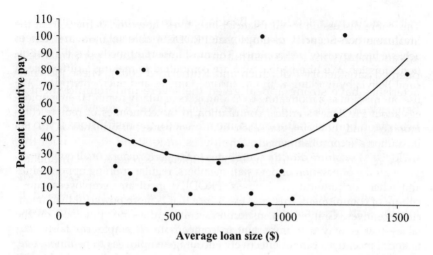

Figure 11.2
Reliance on incentive-based pay versus average loan size.
Source: MicroRate Survey, June 2002 (www.microrate.com).

MicroRate finds that bonus pay as a percentage of base salary varies from zero (not much risk for field staff and low-powered incentives) to 101 percent (high risk for field staff and high-powered incentives), the median percentage is 35 percent, with the twenty-fifth percentile paying bonuses of 13 percent, and the seventy-fifth percentile paying bonuses of 66 percent. These are not necessarily optimal contracts, but they are set at levels that balance risk and incentives.

Figure 11.2 plots the MicroRate data on bonuses against average loan size on the horizontal axis. Average loan size is a rough indicator of how poor clients are at a given institution, and a clear pattern is hard to detect, although the best-fitting curve appears to be gently U-shaped such that institutions serving the poorest households lean on incentive pay more heavily than institutions that serve less poor households, but high-powered incentives again prevail as institutions move to better-off households.

11.3.4 Cultural Implications: Lessons from PRODEM of Bolivia
A different kind of tension with regard to high-powered incentives involves the implications for institutional culture. Bazoberry's experience at PRODEM FFP is instructive, and he places great weight on ways that a positive culture can achieve outcomes that bonus schemes cannot (or may even diminish):

This entire discussion about financial incentives, however, detracts from the invaluable non-financial methods that PRODEM uses to motivate staff to achieve high levels of performance. The most important method is the institution's mission. We hire people who are committed to making a difference in rural Bolivia by working with low-income families and microenterprises. We use our mission as a motivating tool. Managers regularly remind their employees about PRODEM's critical contribution to the economies of remote communities, and how integral each staff member's performance is to the institution's accomplishments.

PRODEM's culture directly contributes to the performance of all employees. Through the orientation of new staff members, regular training opportunities and other communication channels, PRODEM inculcates employees into a culture of commitment, trust and excellence that is more powerful than financial incentives. Granted, an institution's culture does not put food on the table—that is why it is important to compensate all employees fairly. But financial incentives cannot effectively encourage employees to be innovative, to embrace change, to constantly seek ways of doing things better, and to not be afraid to learn from their mistakes. Only the institution's culture can accomplish these objectives, which contribute vitally toward improvements in productivity and efficiency that must occur for an MFI to remain competitive and profitable. (Bazoberry 2001, 12)

Experiences from other sectors are more optimistic than Bazoberry allows, and well-designed bonus schemes have been used to foster innovation and change. But it is not simple. An issue that concerns us here is not just whether bonus schemes are better or worse than nonfinancial incentives (such as creating a strong sense of mission). Our concern also encompasses whether (and when) bonus schemes may actively undermine nonfinancial, mission-based approaches. Indeed, Bazoberry's stress on the role of institutional culture here follows from his negative experience experimenting with bonus schemes (Bazoberry 2001, 11):

During 1993, after looking at the different incentives that MFIs were offering worldwide, we implemented an incentive system that rewarded loan officers for accomplishing goals set in the incentive program. These goals included: the targeted number of clients, the maximum percentage of loans in arrears, and the average portfolio per loan officer. In addition, since PRODEM had different types of branches, we had defined the goals in relation to the potential market and the location of the offices: in rural areas, at the country's borders, in major cities, or in secondary cities.

Rosy Preliminary Results. The incentive program worked as we had hoped. The loan portfolio grew rapidly, the portfolio at risk was under control, the number of clients increased steadily, and profitability improved . . . All of our indicators in 1994–1995 suggested that we made a wise decision in implementing the incentive program.

Things Start to Get Sour. By 1996, we sensed something disruptive occurring. We began to notice a high rate of turnover among our loan officers, including an increase in the number of staff fired because of corruption or for constantly breaking the methodology and rules of the institution. Obviously, we had not managed to gain the loyalty of these loan officers. Instead, we had staff members who were mechanically performing their functions without a real responsibility toward the institution or our clients.

One of Bazoberry's greatest frustrations was that the bonus system was pushing staff members to maximize their own self-interest at the expense of the unified effort of the organization. This was a function both of the direct incentives built into the bonus system and of the indirect, symbolic role that having a high-powered bonus system played in pushing staff members to think of themselves as participants in a competition where the goal was to come out ahead as an individual.

Economists so far have had more to say about the direct role of bonus schemes on incentives than on the indirect symbolic and psychological roles. But an intriguing study shows how important these latter issues can be. Gneezy and Rustichini (2000a, 2000b) make their arguments using two experiments (neither of which involve microfinance but which nonetheless hold lessons). The first study involves wages and bonuses and is most directly applicable.[14]

Gneezy and Rustichini (2000a) created an experiment that involved high school children in Israel. One day each year high school children go from house to house, collecting charity for cancer research, assisting disabled children, and similar social causes. In the experiment, 180 high school children were divided into three groups. The first was a control group; they were given a speech about the importance of the day and of the charitable causes. The second group got the same speech plus the promise of receiving one percent of the day's proceeds as a reward. The third group got the speech plus the promise of a ten percent reward. It was made clear to participants in the second and third groups that the reward money would come from the researchers' pockets, not from the charitable causes. The most money that could be collected was 500 shekels.

It turned out that the group getting a ten percent reward managed to collect more money on average (219 shekels) than the group getting only one percent back (153 shekels)—and the difference was statistically significant. In this sense, monetary rewards seemed to work as expected. On the other hand, neither of the two groups performed as well as the first group (which had no financial incentives, merely a speech on the intrinsic value of the work). The control group averaged collections of 239 shekels, and the difference between this amount and the other amounts was also statistically significant. Gneezy and Rustichini find similar patterns in other cases, and they conclude the lesson by titling their study "Pay Enough or Don't Pay at All."

The results put a different interpretation on statements like that of González-Vega, Schreiner, Meyer et al. (1997, 102), who write, "The low levels of arrears observed [at PRODEM and BancoSol in Bolivia] are outstanding, particularly in the absence of bonus payments to loan officers." Our discussion suggests an alternative possibility: it may not be that the impressive repayment rates occurred despite the absence of bonuses, but rather that they occurred because of their absence. Like PRODEM, BancoSol built a strong culture through nonmonetary incentives like public recognition of successful staff members, development of a shared mission, and trusting loan officers with discretion in making choices about accounts. In addition, "seminars and lectures by expert speakers are frequently offered to the staff [in order to build a commonly held ideology], and a strong esprit de corps is encouraged" (González-Vega et al. 1997, 111).[15] The bottom line is that, given that financial incentives are used, individuals respond positively to stronger incentives. But providing monetary incentives can conflict with attempts to build social cohesion and a sense of shared mission within organizations. Thus, at low levels of monetary bonuses, outcomes are not clearly superior to situations with no financial incentives at all. So, as Gneezy and Rustichini argue, pay enough—so that the benefits of the bonuses outweigh their cultural costs—or don't pay at all.

11.3.5 Incentives in Teams
Bazoberry's frustration that the bonus schemes tried at PRODEM undermined teamwork is echoed by other microlenders, and below we turn to successful solutions adopted by Bank Rakyat Indonesia (BRI). First, though, we continue with the story of PRODEM:

At the same time, some staff members began demanding larger incentives amounts. They were under the false impression that PRODEM's good performance was due solely to their efforts, without realizing that everyone was part of one system of integrated departments, and that other aspects of the organization were also important for PRODEM's performance . . .

As a result, in 1996, PRODEM changed the incentive to an annual bonus awarded for branch performance. All members of a branch received a bonus if their branch met certain performance targets. The largest bonus was worth an additional month's salary . . .

This modification was generally successful in motivating staff and creating teamwork within a branch, but it still had negative side effects. It discouraged staff rotation and cooperation between branches. If employees agreed to transfer to a branch with problems, they reduced their chances of obtaining a bonus. Because some markets were riskier than others, some staff concluded that the bonus involved an element of luck, depending on where one worked. This conclusion generated tension between those who were perceived to have received a bonus because they worked in a good environment and those who failed to earn a bonus even though they worked extremely hard. In such cases, the incentive system discouraged rather than encouraged staff . . .

We decided to eliminate the branch bonus program and instead reward the performance of the whole institution on an annual basis. The collective approach reiterates that we are all in this together. (Bazoberry 2001, 12)

Bazoberry's essay is titled "We Aren't Selling Vacuum Cleaners," presumably because, if they were selling vacuums, teams would not matter so much. In running a microfinance institution, Bazoberry instead found a variety of layers of complication related to team efforts. First, the nature of high-powered incentives promoted an individual orientation among staff members. It was thus natural to shift the scheme so that branch-level performance was rewarded instead. But that created resentments and made employees reluctant to move from "good" branches. So, in the end, rewarding employees based on the performance of the whole institution was chosen as the way to reduce those frictions.

The trade-off, from our viewpoint, is that incentives are then made weaker since the free-riding problem that was evident at the branch-level is even worse at the institution-level. Strong cultural norms are needed to overcome the tendency of employees to not pull their weight, and this, as noted above, seems to be the secret of PRODEM's management success.[16] Thus, in this case the gains from reducing resentments appear to outweigh the losses from dulling the incentive scheme. Other institutions have addressed these tensions in different ways, and we turn next to the example of BRI, a well-run, state-owned commercial bank. BRI's strategy has been to combine incentives at every level: individual, branch, and institution-wide.

11.3.5.1 Combining Incentives: Lessons from Bank Rakyat Indonesia
BRI started as a government-owned rural development bank in 1968,

with the main mission of helping to spur agricultural production.[17] To help both borrowers and depositors, the government mandated that borrowers pay interest rates of 12 percent while depositors received 15 percent under the national savings program. The pro-poor intentions may have been noble, but the negative interest rate spread was untenable, and by the late 1970s the bank was suffering huge operating losses. Indonesia deregulated banks in 1983, and BRI transformed itself with the aim of becoming financially viable without subsidies.

The heart of microfinance at BRI is the "units," small sub-branches set up throughout Indonesia to dispense loans and take deposits from low-income customers. (BRI also does corporate-scale lending through other offices, while microlending is done exclusively through the units.) Before 1983, there was no accounting of profit or loss at the unit level. So while it was clear that the system as a whole was suffering losses, there was no reckoning unit by unit. The 1983 transformation created accounts so that the units became individual profit centers. The key to the policy was to set a "transfer price" to value deposits generated and capital used to make loans at each unit. The transfer price moves closely with the bank's costs of funds and provides a way to calculate profits for each unit.

In addition to yardstick competition as described later, BRI uses three main mechanisms to provide incentives to staff. First, staff get a percentage of the profit of the unit for which they work, capped at 2.6 times monthly wages annually. Most employees get roughly twice their monthly pay through this incentive mechanism. (There is also a component that is, in principle, based on individual performance.) An important aspect of this bonus is that rules are clear, so staff can anticipate it—unlike the often arbitrary and changing bonus rules employed by Corposol (see section 11.2).

Second, bank-wide bonuses are also dispensed, and they are again roughly twice an employee's monthly pay. But since the bank's board of directors decides on bonuses each period and has full discretion, employees cannot count on them as faithfully. Third, staff members are allowed to keep 2 percent of the value of total collections for loans that had been written off by the bank but that are then subsequently collected. This is gives a strong incentive to be vigilant in pursuing defaulters, and it lets customers know that staff are unlikely to let defaults pass without a struggle.

The decision to allow some workers to earn more than others in similar posts was controversial at first, but because incentives were designed so that everyone can in principle gain through hard work (there is no "zero-sum game"), the move has been both popular and effective within the system. The incentive system also works because BRI pursues clear financial objectives. While state-owned, BRI runs on commercial principles and tends to serve low-income customers, who are a few rungs up the economic ladder from the typical customers of the large Bangladeshi microlenders. Social objectives are secondary, freeing BRI from the balancing act faced by microlenders elsewhere. But BRI still wrestles with how to promote unmeasurable tasks (notably, teamwork), and the result is this somewhat elaborate (but clear and understandable) set of bonuses that balances individual and group efforts.

11.3.5.2 Yardstick Competition The specific way that BRI determines bonuses matters as well. The theory of incentives tells us that in situations where the range of individual performance is hard to measure, as is common in microfinance, yardstick competition can help. Contracts are then structured so that employees are rewarded on the basis of their performance relative to other employees.[18] The optimal contract does not create a competition in which there are just a handful of winners. Instead, employees are rewarded when they exceed benchmarks that are set at levels determined on the basis of the past performance of other employees. In principle, if everyone surpassed the benchmarks, everyone would be rewarded. (And in subsequent periods, management may then choose to raise the bar a bit higher in order to induce even more effort.)

BRI uses this basic idea in its microfinance operations. At the end of 2002, BRI operated nearly 4,000 units throughout the country, whose managers enjoy a high degree of autonomy. Yardstick competition among these managers takes the form of unit performance contests. Each semester, the top management creates a list of targets to achieve (e.g., finding new customers, account growth, keeping arrears down, managing savings), and units compete to reach the goals.

The competition is not between units, but relative to the goals so that one unit winning doesn't affect another's chances. The aim is to have ambitious but achievable targets. As at PRODEM, the awards amount to roughly one month's pay or less, and about 30 percent of units win at one of the three award levels. Awards are given out at a large public ceremony, and the prestige of winning may be as rich a reward as the actual financial benefits.

11.3.6 Avoiding Myopia

An additional dimension to incentive schemes involves the time frame. Again we return to Bazoberry's (2001, 11) description of bonuses at PRODEM:

The original scheme awarded a monthly bonus to individuals who met certain performance standards. We learned, however, that this type of incentive had a negative effect on team performance and encouraged a short-term outlook . . .

An annual payment encouraged a long-term perspective. It corrected the "delinquency lag," caused by new loans that go into arrears several months after they were issued. An annual payment also adjusted for the profound seasonal fluctuations that are common in Bolivian microfinance and it allowed PRODEM to complete our audit before issuing bonuses.

The lesson is clear: Bonuses that are based on short-term goals may bias employees away from maintaining the quality of loans over the long-term. Some outcomes, such as poverty reduction, are also achieved over a longer horizon and are best judged at wide intervals. Rewarding employee performance over the span of an entire year addresses the issue of seasonality. Another approach is to base bonuses on year-to-year performance gains even when using monthly or quarterly bonuses (e.g., rewarding improvements between the first quarter of 2010 and that of 2011).

11.3.7 Discouraging Deception

One of the lessons from the experimental evidence of Gneezy and Rustichini (2000a) is "pay enough or don't pay at all." Our discussion earlier focused on what happens when you pay too little—and the advantages of low-powered incentives. Here we describe another problem that arises when you pay too much. The issue is that as incentives to perform to a given level get greater and greater, the incentive to cheat also rises. Not only is it vital to have accurate information on which to assess employees, it is also important to recognize that incentive schemes can themselves lead to biases in the information that gets reported to management. Problems emerge from an accounting standpoint when employees can easily hide default rates or increase the non-repayment period before considering a loan as a defaulted loan. This can in turn make the microfinance institution appear more financially viable than it really is and set up managers for problems down the road.

Bazoberry comments on the scene in Bolivia, describing a consumer credit company that was paying the equivalent of $50 per month as average staff salary. But through bonuses, loan officers were actually earning nearly $900. This is three times what most other loan officers earned in competing companies. Bazoberry argues that this incentive scheme ended up encouraging deception on the part of loan officers. The kinds of unauthorized activities that emerged included the following:

- Frequent rescheduling of loans without much control
- Loan officers forming ROSCAs to pay for clients' arrears, which allows employees to maintain or increase their incentive levels despite worsening portfolio quality
- Creation of "ghost" loans to hide the fact that goals are not met
- Deduction of an arbitrary amount from the clients' loans during disbursement to create a fund to cover bad loans
- Pressure on loan officers to repay clients' arrears from their own salaries
- Utilization of inactive savings accounts to pay for outstanding debts.

(Bazoberry 2001, 12–13)

These kinds of phenomena have been reported widely outside of Bolivia as well, and they provide microfinance skeptics with plenty of fodder. The straightforward solution is to institute greater internal controls. Public repayments, as we noted in chapter 5, can help by making fellow borrowers aware of transgressions of rules. Similarly, pushing for strong management information systems and timely reporting aids oversight and the ability to quickly identify looming problems. Computerization has facilitated the work, and by creating simple data checks, much can be accomplished even in situations where computerization is only partial. But, in the end, the answer may necessitate reducing the reliance on overly high-powered incentives and getting to the root of the problem.

11.3.8 Unbundling Tasks: Lessons from ASA of Bangladesh and PROGRESA of Mexico

One solution to the multitask-incentive problem is to unbundle tasks, so that different staff members are responsible for different jobs and can be rewarded accordingly. To take a term from Dewatripont, Jewitt, and Tirole (1999) the principal can avoid conflicts of interest by seeking "functional specialization" among agents. An example is the state-run PROGRESA program in Mexico, now renamed Oportunidades. Oportunidades's main task is to deliver grants to needy households on the condition that their children go to school and attend health clinics for regular checkups (see Skoufias's 2001 report on PROGRESA for an overview). The government is also interested in microlending, so it launched a second program, FOMIN, to deal primarily with finance. Rather than nesting within Oportunidades, FOMIN is an independent entity that functions in parallel. Thus, staff members at Oportunidades can be rewarded for progress in education and health outcomes, and FOMIN staff can be rewarded for their financial successes. Problems will still arise when the two outcomes are linked (as in section 11.3.2), but one layer of complication is removed.

Another reason for functional specialization (and perhaps a more compelling one) is that it allows managers to hire staff that are best matched to particular tasks, rather than needing to hire employees that can perform well in a wide range of circumstances. For example, by shifting its focus sharply onto providing basic financial services, ASA of Bangladesh, a world innovator in cost-minimization, is able to hire less-educated staff members who are still capable of carrying out the required transactions. Most of ASA's loan officers are thus young and lack college degrees—and therefore cheaper as well. Nevertheless, the job is perceived as a good one, and the staff members are highly motivated (for more on ASA's basic model, see Fernando and Meyer 2002 and Rutherford 2009).

ASA's loan officers had initially been responsible for a half hour of training sessions for customers each week, scheduled as part of weekly group meetings. Topics included health and social problems, and issues under discussion could touch on, for example, oral rehydration therapies, breast feeding practices, and options for divorce. Older, better-educated staff members appear better-equipped to take on these training tasks. So by focusing tasks (and removing training duties from loan officers), ASA can now hire loan officers better suited to their main duties. In addition, by simplifying their loan-making process through publication of a clear manual with a set of rules that govern all choices, ASA has taken away most of the loan officers' discretion (Ahmmed 2002). ASA thus relies on the professionalism of its staff members, but ASA does not need to lean heavily on their decision-making abilities.

11.3.9 Aligning Incentives and Missions

The discussion so far highlights how important it is to align incentives provided to staff members with the organization's broader mission. Grammling and Holtmann (2008) give four examples of how this works, drawing on case studies of PRIZMA, BRAC, BancoSol, and Equity Bank. At BRAC in Bangladesh, the incentive scheme has rewarded the number of outstanding loans and the current outstanding loan portfolio volume, but not explicitly the maintenance of portfolio quality. One consequence of the expansion in scale has been to increase the workers' productivity. But the scheme also risks pushing loan officers to encourage customers to seek larger loans than may be optimal for them, creating a risk of over-indebting customers.

BancoSol uses high-powered incentives to encourage worker efficiency. They also segregate loan officers into five categories, depending on the initial loan sizes of customers. About 60 percent of the loan officers specialize in seeking poorer customers with small loan sizes. This kind of segregation makes sense in light of the discussion of unbundling tasks in section 11.3.8. Loan officers have limited capacity to work with customers outside of their assigned category, narrowing the scope for mission drift and sharpening the provision of incentives.

Equity Bank in Kenya provides an interesting contrast in the way they have taken advantage of the bank's commercial status and recent listing on the stock market. The bank has launched an employee stock ownership plan which allots shares to staff members. In principle, share ownership builds long-term commitment to the bank. To the extent that loan officers are driven to maximize share value, Equity Bank's financial bottom line benefits. But the scheme may make it more difficult to achieve nonfinancial objectives like social goals if workers focus too heavily on propping up stock prices.

11.4 Ownership: Commercialization and Governance

Agency issues arise repeatedly in finance. They define the tensions between customers and loan officers at the heart of traditional credit contracts. In turn, agency issues define the tensions between loan officers and managers described earlier in this chapter. Here, we explore how agency issues help to define relationships between owners, investors, and managers.

The ability to attract capital from outside investors depends in large part on how these agency issues are resolved. The ability to leverage outside funds requires convincing outside investors that incentives and monitoring will remain robust as the institution grows—and that depends on having the right incentive and governance structures in place. The move toward commercialization brings governance to the fore.

As chapter 8 describes, commercialization usually brings a transformation in ownership. The owners of formalized microfinance institutions are its shareholders: those who invest and have an equity stake in the institution. Owners typically fall into four categories: NGOs, private investors, public entities, and specialized equity funds called microfinance investment vehicles (Otero and Chu 2002, 227). The role of NGOs as owners typically arises when NGOs transform their microfinance operations into formal financial institutions, while maintaining the NGO as a separate entity. As part of the transformation process, NGOs often transfer their customer portfolios to the new institution in exchange for a seat on the board and a majority share in the new institution, thereby becoming an owner (Ledgerwood 1999, 112). This is the process by which the Bolivian NGO PRODEM, for example, came to have an ownership stake in BancoSol, a regulated bank.

Different types of investors bring to the table different benefits and types of expertise, as well as different limitations. Investors' interests may be social or purely financial. They may be local or international, and they may have valuable experience in microfinance or in the formal financial sector (Ledgerwood and White 2006, 200). Table 11.3 summarizes the advantages and drawbacks of various investor groups.

Table 11.3 shows that sometimes an institution's employees are also its owners. At PRODEM FFP, for example, employees receive PRODEM shares as part of their annual benefits package (a strategy also used by Equity Bank in Kenya, as described earlier). The hope is that giving employees a degree of direct ownership will strengthen their long-term commitment to the institution's success. Aligning incentives like this can address agency problems, at the risk that employees may focus on securing their financial futures while management also pursues a broader social mission. The problem is that the stock price is unlikely to fully internalize the value of the social mission.

Forming a cooperative (or joint ownership) structure takes the idea of employee ownership further. In cooperatives, the preferences of group members are fully taken into account through voting processes, but as suggested by Ward (1958) and Hart and Moore (1998), in order to maximize their average revenues, incumbent group members may move to restrict entry.[19] In the case of microfinance institutions, this means that older borrowers may restrict the entry of new borrowers—which could defeat the push for broad outreach and reinforce conservatism.

Table 11.3
Pros and Cons of Various Investor Groups

Group	Pros	Cons
Founding NGO	Can help maintain commitment to vision and mission.	With no owners, NGO itself may lack deep pockets in eyes of central bank. Without an owner, NGO may have a weak governance structure and lack accountability.
Founding directors	Personal commitment to success of institution. Example of private risk capital.	Depending on how ownership is structured, may present conflict of interest. May also lack deep pockets.
Multilateral and bilateral donors	Can help maintain commitment to development and poverty mission.	Internal structure and operating procedures often cause delays and may impede effective participation. Environmental and social mandates an create operational challenges.
Socially responsible investors	Allocate experienced staff and resources to monitor performance of MFI; can make quick decisions in case of capital call. Technical know-how can provide confidence for other investors; availability of technical assistance in some cases.	Limited capital; medium-term investment horizon. Potential for conflict of interest when managers of the fund also manage or are linked to the technical assistance provided.
Commercial investors	Profit and efficiency orientation; provide a familiar face to the capital markets.	Danger of short-term, profit-maximizing investors; seeking clear exit strategy.
Employees	Builds employee buy-in to financial future of institution.	Can present risk to staff. Typically staff lack deep pockets to make additional capital calls. Lack of liquidity (market for shares) can also complicate structures.
Local government	May help positive image of MFI; generally have deep pockets; can positively influence regulators.	May scare away other investors; may politically influence decision making with regulators; may be perceived as receiving special treatment.
Clients and community	Community shares in the success of the institution; provides sense of ownership	Difficulties in structuring and in determining who represents the community; typically lack deep pockets expected by regulators; potential for poor governance and conflict of interest.

Source: Ledgerwood and White 2006, table 7.1.

Institutions work to weigh and balance the advantages and drawbacks presented in table 11.3. One general guideline is that shareholders who take an active interest in their investment offer wider benefits than silent investors. These benefits typically play out on the field of governance. Usually, the governance of commercial microfinance institutions "refers to a system of checks and balances whereby a board of directors is established to oversee the management of the MFI" (Ledgerwood 1999, 111). Labie (2001, 2003) argues that governance goes beyond board management and encompasses a wider set of mechanisms which ensure that an organization and its executives make decisions coherent with the organization's mission. For fully commercial microfinance institutions, however, the board of directors is the lynchpin of governance. When an insitution has equity investors, the board is elected by its shareholders to represent their interests. As a result, it "tends to reflect the ownership structure of the institution" (Ledgerwood and White 2006, 221).

Mersland and Strøm (2009) suggest that financial performance also improves when microfinance institutions have local directors. In an analysis of data from microfinance rating agencies, they find that microfinance institutions with international directors have lower operational self-sufficiency ratios and higher operational costs. One possibility is that the international directors in their sample bring to microfinance institutions a "culture of higher costs" (Mersland and Støm 2009, 5).

The most important responsibility of the board of directors is to protect the interests of all stakeholders, including investors, clients, and staff. It does so by overseeing managers, participating in strategic planning, reviewing the business plans prepared by managers, and verifying that they align with the institution's mission and long-term objectives. Also, and perhaps most relevant to management, the board is charged with selecting, supervising, and evaluating the institution's senior managers.

The board also faces challenges. While the board as a whole represents the interests of all stakeholders, specific members may operate with very different priorities. After all, at least some of the members represent particular stakeholders, and different stakeholders have different and sometimes conflicting interests. For example, a representative of the original NGO may be concerned chiefly with ensuring that the MFI continues to meet its social objectives. A representative of a major private investor, on the other hand, may pursue policies that will help the institution turn a healthy profit. Here, unaffiliated directors can play powerful roles as guardians of balance.

Recent evidence suggests the presence of unaffiliated directors is key. Hartarska (2005) studies the impact of governance on the performance of microfinance institutions in Central and Eastern Europe and the Newly Independent States. She examines a range of variables that fall under the umbrella of governance, but her most significant finding is that "MFIs with a higher proportion of unaffiliated directors had better sustainability [as measured by returns on assets] and reached poorer borrowers" (Hartarska 2005, 1635).

Funding structures can also shape incentives. The drive for financial self-sufficiency is typically the main impetus for commercialization, allowing the institution to reduce subsidy dependence. But even institutions with no plans to commercialize may have reason to reduce the use of subsidy. For one thing, doing so limits the scope for politicization that can occur when donors (and possibly the government if they are a major funder) intervene in setting priorities. The problem can be (partly) overcome if the microfinance institution decentralizes, spinning off decision-making authority to a large number of independent "profit centers" (i.e., branches). On the other hand, centralization increases the scope for cross-subsidization among different groups of borrowers and across regions. Cross-subsidization, in turn, may help to achieve overall institutional self-sustainability.

There are times, though, when accepting donor funds can help with incentives, particularly when business imperatives are crowding out social goals. In this case, reputational considerations and the need to look "good" for certain kinds of donors can act as a commitment device that pushes the institution to delegate some authority to professionals who are primarily concerned with social objectives. (Of course, accepting donor funds also has the direct advantage of providing sources of inexpensive finance that can be used to build institutions and push social missions.) In other cases, donors may help strengthen commitments to pursuing cost recovery.

11.5 Summary and Conclusions

We have analyzed how the design of incentive schemes, ownership structures and organizational forms can affect the performance and impact of microfinance institutions. Institutions tend to reward loan officers for making more loans, making bigger loans, and making higher-quality loans (i.e., loans that get repaid). Curiously, relatively few programs explicitly reward cost minimization or measures of poverty reduction.

Tensions in designing optimal incentive schemes hinge on the multitask nature of microfinance, in which institutions seek both profit and social impact. In principle, the task of managers is to give staff members incentives to pursue both ends, although in practice the goals are not always aligned. An important constraint arises when all inputs and outcomes are not observed. Rewarding only easily observed actions (like the number of customers served or on-time collection rates) can skew staff away from other important—but harder to measure—goals, like empowerment or reaching the particularly needy. As a result, low-powered incentives (generated through promises of promotions, training, and interesting assignments in return for steady performance) can dominate high-powered incentives that closely link salaries to observable performance indicators.

Another tension in using (overly) high-powered incentives is that it can undermine institutional culture by creating the sense that loan officers are "out for themselves" as individuals, rather than working for the greater collectivity. The insight holds a lesson for product design, in which tough loan contracts used by microlenders can end up pitting customers against loan officers in what becomes a zero-sum game. Tensions can quickly mount. But when loan officers cannot seize the collateral of borrowers in trouble, cooperation is needed. The Grameen Bank, for example, found that its initial contract system created undue tension between loan officers and customers, and the bank has proposed moving to a more flexible system under Grameen II that aims to be "tension free" (Yunus 2002). While some tension no doubt helps by providing basic motivation to customers, the general insight is useful: maintaining incentives needs to be balanced against the creation of good will, a reserve that may be vital in later periods.

Overly high-powered incentives may also inadvertently increase shortsighted behavior by staff members, encourage fraud, and diminish accurate record-keeping. The theory of contracts and incentives suggests alternative solutions like yardstick competition and the institution of strong internal controls.

These measures can be strengthened by other organizational features beyond staff incentives and ownership structures. The extent to which a microfinance institution is embedded in the community, its degree of centralization or decentralization, and its culture can all influence efficiency. Moreover, while each of these features is important in its own right, their interplay matters even more. Aligning these features is a significant part of management, and misalignment can undermine an organization's efficiency by making it incoherent. Institutions that are highly centralized with most decisions coming down from the top, for example, tend to have difficulty developing organizational cultures that encourage initiative and problem solving.

Part of the relevant structure is determined by institutional type. Self-help groups and village banks, for example, are deeply embedded in the communities in which they work, so they tend to be stable, inclusive and accepted, but they have difficulty accessing capital. Credit unions and cooperatives tend to also be embedded in their communities, and they can benefit from the ability to collect savings. However, these institutions often face governance issues: members who are net savers, for example, often have different priorities from those who are net borrowers. NGOs are typically flexible and innovative, but they can suffer from weak governance because stakeholders are often passive and only weakly influence management. Nonbank financial institutions tend to have more efficient back office processes (e.g., accounting) while retaining the flexibility of less commercial institutions, but they generally are not regulated to raise capital by taking deposits. Commercialized banks can more easily access capital and are regulated, but their front office practices may not be well-designed for efficiently serving the poor.

The discussion is a broad reminder that microfinance entails entwining social and economic relationships. As institutions evolve, so will their needs for governance (Labie and Mersland 2010). While microfinance borrows lessons from successful commercial banks, the task for microlenders is more complicated, and there is still ample room for innovation and new visions.

11.6 Exercises

1. Describe briefly what economists call a multitask agency problem, and relate your answer to the case of microfinance. Describe the main tasks taken on by loan officers and how they might conflict or be complementary.

2. Suggest two potential solutions to the multitasking problem for microlenders. Would the solutions be just as easy to implement in a small organization as in a larger organization?

3. Describe the advantages and disadvantages of microlenders that are privately owned relative to cooperatives.

4. What is yardstick competition? How does it differ from more general uses of competition? Illustrate your answer for the particular case of microlenders.

5. Describe as many situations as you can in which there is a principal and an agent in the context of microlenders. How do the examples relate to one another? Do the proposed solutions to any one of the principal-agent problems you identified help you think about solutions to the other principal-agent problems?

6. In his essay "We Aren't Selling Vacuum Cleaners," Bazoberry suggests that institutions with wider objectives than the pursuit of profit can benefit by instituting team incentive structures. Nevertheless, there is a trade-off associated with the shift from individual incentive schemes to collective ones. Identify this trade-off and suggest some ways that managers can overcome or work around it.

7. It's important to consider intrinsic motivation when designing incentive schemes. Explain this concept and the role it can play in contract structure design. How is this idea related to the experiments in Israel by Gneezy and Rustichini (2000a)?

8. Consider a microfinance institution that has two main objectives: to reduce poverty in the place where it is operating (y_1) and to achieve financial sustainability (y_2). These objectives can be achieved either by providing loans to poorer potential borrowers (a_1), or by offering larger loans to relatively wealthier borrowers (a_2). The problem faced by the institution is that both actions have opposite effects in the outcomes of interest, which can be represented by $y_1 = \sqrt{a_1} - \beta\sqrt{a_2}$ and $y_2 = \sqrt{a_2} - \alpha\sqrt{a_1}$ where $0 < \alpha < \beta < 1$. Assume that there is perfect substitution between actions a_1 and a_2, and that they're compensated equally, so the institution's manager can assign the labor force A freely between them. Additionally, assume that there are no incentive problems among the institution's staff.

a. Explain intuitively the functions for the outcomes of interest for the institutions.

b. How should the microfinance institution distribute its resources between both actions in order to maximize the weighted sum of the outcomes?

c. Suppose that another social institution exogenously implements a program that helps poor borrowers in driving their businesses.

Where would this factor into the microfinance institution's resource allocation?

d. What would be the result in terms of a_1 and a_2?

9. Consider a teacher who has to divide her time between at least two activities: teaching and mentoring her students. The quality of her students depends on the number of hours that she spends with them, both teaching and mentoring. The quality function is: $q = x \cdot y$, where x is the time that the teacher spends teaching, and y is the time that she spends mentoring her students each day. Each day, the teacher can work for only ten hours. Suppose that the principal of the school has a utility function that depends on the quality of her students: $u = q$. The principal can verify teaching activities via teaching evaluations: bad, enough, good, or excellent. (She can observe the time that the teacher is working, but can not fully verify how the teacher allocates her time between teaching preparation and mentoring.) Suppose that in order to attain decent teaching evaluations, the teacher has to spend time (and her salary ultimately depends on this time) as illustrated in the following table:

Evaluations	Teaching time (hours/day)	Salary/day
Bad	1–2	80 Rs the minimum level of salary controlled by the government
Enough	3–5	110 Rs
Good	6–7	160 Rs
Excellent	8 or more	210 Rs

Assume that one hour of teaching per day costs the teacher ten rupees, while one hour of mentoring costs seven rupees, and that the teacher is risk-neutral. (She just wants to maximize her net revenue.) Compute optimal time allocation for both the teacher and the principal. In what way does your answer relate to the problem confronted by managers of MFIs?

10. Suppose the same problem as in the previous exercise, but assume in this case that the teacher must divide her time between three activities: teaching preparation, mentoring, and lecturing. Assume further that the quality function for the students—or the utility function for the principal—is $u = q = x \cdot y \cdot z$ where x, y, and z are,

respectively, the time spent teaching, mentoring, and lecturing. Suppose that the principal can observe teaching activities and lecturing via teaching evaluations: bad, good, or excellent, and pays the teacher accordingly:

Evaluations	Teaching time (hours/day)	Teaching salary/day	Lecturing (hours/day)	Salary for lecturing time/day
Bad	1–2	30 Rs	1–1.5	25 Rs
Good	2–2.6	50 Rs	1.5–2.5	45 Rs
Excellent	3 or more	70 Rs	2.5 or more	65 Rs

The per hour costs for the teacher are as follows: teaching costs ten rupees, mentoring costs four rupees, and lecturing seven rupees. Assume that a working day has ten hours. Compute the optimal time allocation for the teacher and for the principal. Briefly comment on your answer.

11. Suppose that the utility function of a microlender is $u = u_1 + u_2$ where u_1 and u_2 are, respectively, the utility derived from good financial statements and for poverty alleviation. The microlender employs a risk-neutral agent who works eight hours per day. The agent can divide her time between these two activities, namely, between producing good financial statements (i.e., ensuring timely repayments and minimizing costs), and alleviating poverty (i.e., screening the poorer borrowers and instructing them on how to invest wisely). Utility levels u_1 and u_2 are related to the working hours as follows:

u_1	Working hours spent on financial activities	u_2	Working hours spent on alleviating poverty
	1	6.5	1
13	2	13	2
18.5	3	19	3
23	4	21.5	4
26	5	23	5
28	6	25	6
29	7	27	7
30	8	29	8

The manager of the MFI can indirectly verify the effort spent on financially oriented activities (e.g., via the repayment rate), but cannot observe whether the agent is contributing to alleviate poverty. The manager of the MFI thus pays the agent accordingly:

Evaluation	Repayment rate	Salary/day	Working hours spent on financial-oriented activities
Bad	less than 50%	0	Less than 2
Enough	50%–65%	45 Rs	2–3.5
Good	65%–85%	80 Rs	3.5–5.5
Excellent	From 85% on	100 Rs	From 5.5 on

A working hour for financially oriented activities costs the agent 7 Rs, and working for alleviating poverty costs 5 Rs. Compute the optimal time allocation for the manager of the MFI, and for the agent. Explain your answer.

12. Consider two financial institutions. Each institution employs two loan officers (henceforth: agents), and both institutions have the same objectives: financial self-sustainability and poverty alleviation. Assume that the agents are identical and risk-neutral and that they work eight hours per day. Each working hour costs four rupees. Institution A applies a balanced incentive scheme: agents are rewarded for meeting both objectives. Suppose the agents' evaluations take the following form:

Evaluation	Working time division by the manager	Salary/day (rupees)
Bad	If the agent spent less than two hours working for at least one of the two objectives	20 Rs (the minimum level of salary)
Good	If the agent spent 3–3.5 hours working for both objectives	60 Rs
Excellent	If the agent spent four or more hours working for both objectives	100 Rs

Institution B, on the other hand, applies a different incentive scheme: one agent will specialize in obtaining financial self-sustainability, and the other in alleviating poverty:

Evaluation	Working time division by the agent	Salary/day (rupees)
Bad	If the agent spent less than or equal to four hours working for the objective required	20 Rs (the minimum level of salary)
Good	If the agent spent more than or equal to six hours working for the objective required	60 Rs
Excellent	If the agent spent more than or equal to eight hours working for the objective required	100 Rs

The production function (also the utility function for the two institutions) is $q = x^2 + y^2$ where x and y are, respectively, the time spent on financially oriented activities and in poverty alleviation. Show that this production function indicates that specialization will make the agent more effective. Draw the function. Compute the optimal choice for the agent in institutions A and B, and compute the maximum utility for each institution.

13. Consider a model with competitive and risk-neutral principals and a risk-neutral agent. The agent may be of two possible types (abilities) $\theta \in \{1; 0.5\}$ with respective probability $n = -21$ and $1 - n = -21$. There are two periods $t = 1$ and $t = 2$ and no discounting. The agent's output q in each period may take two possible values, zero and ten, with respective probabilities $(1 - \theta\pi)$; $\theta\pi$ where $\pi = 1$ if he exerts effort and $\pi = 0.6$ otherwise (effort is unobservable). The cost of effort for the agent is $e = 1$. Assume that there is perfect competition between alternative principals in order to attract the agent in period 2. Also, neither the agent nor the principals are informed of the ability of the manager. In addition, the principal cannot write contracts conditional on the production level (the production level is observed but not verifiable). The first-period wage is a fixed wage t_1, while the second-period wage may depend on past observation $t_2(q)$. The timing of the model is as follows:

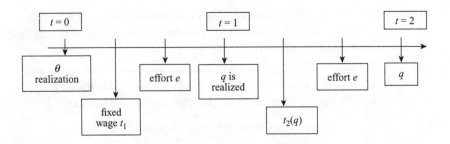

Compute the posterior belief held by the market on the agent's ability after the first period has been observed. Compute the fixed wage t_2 offered to him in the labor market. By comparing the expected payoff when the agent puts forth effort and when he does not put in effort, state whether it pays to put in effort. If the agent lives for one period only, will he put forth any effort?

14. Consider the same scenario as in exercise 13. But in this case, $\bar{\theta} \in \Theta = \{\bar{\theta}; \underline{\theta}\}$ where $\bar{\theta} = 1$; $\underline{\theta} < 1$ and the probabilities of being a high type and low type are respectively v and $(1-v)$. The output can take two possible values, q or 0. And π can be $\bar{\pi}$ or $\underline{\pi}$, and $\bar{\pi} = 1$. The cost of effort is e. Write the incentive constraint of the agent that needs to be satisfied in order to elicit a high level of effort from him.

15. Again, consider a similar problem to the one spelled out in exercise 13, but in this case the agent's effort in each period is observable. His ability remains unknown, however, for both the market and the agent. Compute the explicit incentive constraint that needs to be satisfied in order for the agent to put forth an adequate effort level. Show that implicit incentives can only be imperfect substitutes to the explicit monetary incentives obtained via a wage that is linked to performance.

Notes

1   Rethinking Banking

1. The story of the pledge that marked the start of ASA is re-told from Stuart Rutherford's (2009) engaging recounting of ASA's history and evolution. In the 1970s, the American diplomat Henry Kissinger famously dismissed Bangladesh as an international "basket case." The dynamism of Bangladesh's microfinance sector has been heralded as a refutation of Kissinger's pessimism.

2. Not incidentally, in 2008 ASA counted that 71 percent of its customers were women. We return to the role of gender in chapter 7.

3. ASA's data are taken from www.asa.bd.org. Grameen's are from www.grameen-info .org. BRAC's are from www.brac.net. ASA counted 5.9 million active borrowers in October 2008.

4. There is now a large literature on microfinance oriented to practitioners. Otero, Rhyne, and Houghton 1994 was an important early volume, but it is now dated. Marguerite Robinson 2001 covers some of the same ground as this volume, with particular richness in its descriptions of the Indonesian experience and with a strong tilt toward arguments for creating financially sustainable institutions. Ledgerwood (2001) has written a particularly impressive and comprehensive handbook on practical issues arising in running microfinance institutions.

5. The idea of declining marginal returns in the microfinance context is highlighted in a focus note circulated by the Consultative Group to Assist the Poorest (1996). CGAP is the preeminent microfinance donor consortium, housed in Washington, DC, within the World Bank.

6. The estimates assume standard (Cobb-Douglass) production technologies, where aggregate output Y is a function of an economy's total capital stock K and labor force L such that $Y = f(K, L) = K^\alpha L^\beta$; increasing returns to scale are ruled out when $\alpha + \beta \leq 1$.

7. The role of government interest restrictions in creating financial repression has been highlighted forcefully by McKinnon (1973).

8. Hundreds of academic articles on microfinance have now developed these ideas, and we provide an overview in chapter 2. Microfinance institutions, in turn, have made strides by developing contracts and practices that cheaply overcome information problems, and we describe those in chapters 4 and 5.

9. Not all state development banks have been so problematic. Braverman and Guasch (1986), for example, praise the efficiency and outreach of INVIERNO in Nicaragua in 1975; the rural cooperatives of Korea, Taiwan, and Japan; and Kenya's Cooperative Saving Scheme. Thailand's Bank for Agriculture and Agricultural Cooperatives (BAAC) and the Bank Rakyat Indonesia (BRI) are both state-owned banks that have proved successful at mobilizing savings and efficiently providing loans. The development banks of Germany, France, and Japan have also found praise for their efficacy (Armendáriz 1999b). The Grameen Bank itself was started as a project of Bangladesh's central bank and, although Grameen has taken determined steps to maintain its independence, the government is represented on its board of directors.

10. The IRDP is joined in its troubles by other Indian state banking programs. Meyer (2002) reports that the loan recovery rate for agricultural loans in general was 37–68 percent. Since 2000, the IRDP has been consolidated as the Golden Jubilee Rural Self-Employment Program (*Swaranjayanti Gram Swarojgar Yojna*), and the emphasis has turned to linking "self-help groups" of around fifteen to twenty borrowers (often organized by NGOs) with the formal banking system.

11. See von Pischke, Adams, and Donald 1983 and Adams, Graham, and von Pischke 1984.

12. The econometric findings are also seen in the household surveys of Pulley (1989). Despite the talk of leakage, Pulley's longitudinal survey of the IRDP in Uttar Pradesh found reasonably well-targeted credit, at least from a social viewpoint: 80 percent of IRDP funds went to poor households, and 26 percent went to households that were classified as very poor or destitute; 43 percent went to scheduled tribes and castes, and 17 percent went to women. Moreover, he found that incomes and investment increased for borrowers. This is not what one would guess from the stories about massive distortions and mistargeting.

13. Yunus (1999) tells his story in his own words. See also Counts 2008, Bornstein 1997, and Todd 1996. Dowla and Barua 2006 provide an update on "Grameen II."

14. Microfinance is spreading slowly in Western Europe, and innovative programs are emerging. One is ADIE (Association pour le droit à l'initiative économique), which was inspired by Grameen and uses many incentive mechanisms (www.adie.org). A list of countries and projects that identify as Grameen Bank replications is available at www.grameen-info.org/grameen/gtrust/replication.html. The European Microfinance Network (EMN) provides overviews of European microfinance (www.european -microfinance.org); on France and Belgium, in particular, see Armendáriz (2009). The Microfinance Center (MFC) for Eastern Europe and the New Independent States coordinates efforts in Eastern Europe.

15. The U.S. programs are all inspired to some degree by Grameen but take a variety of forms. Schreiner and Morduch (2002) critically survey the state of microfinance in the United States, where the need to train budding entrepreneurs, cumbersome regulations for new businesses, and usury laws have dramatically slowed the pace and cost-effectiveness of microfinance. Counts (2008) tells the stories of both Grameen Bank in Bangladesh and the translation of Grameen's ideas to the Full Circle Fund in Chicago.

16. This is the most common interpretation of Grameen practices, and it is in this form that the model has been exported from Bangladesh. At home, though, the bank is often more flexible in its approach. We return to issues around group lending in chapters 4 and 5.

17. The literature is surveyed by Ghatak and Guinnane (1999) and by Morduch (1999b).

18. As we describe in chapters 4 and 5, Grameen Bank itself dropped the use of the joint liability contract in 2001 and still reports high loan repayment rates (Dowla and Barua 2006). Throughout the book we cite lenders' repayment rates, but readers should note that different lenders calculate repayment rates in different ways, yielding results that are not always comparable. The measures cited are seldom "on-time collection rates," which give the amount repaid in a given period divided by the amount that was due in that period; the ratio excludes late payments of loans that were initially due in earlier periods. Instead, commonly used ratios often include late payments in the numerator. Late payments are helpful to track since ultimately it makes a big difference whether the loan was never repaid at all or the payment was simply delayed. But it is most useful to track late payments separately from on-time collections for current disbursements. For more on the details of repayment rate calculations, see chapter 8 as well as Rosenberg 1999 and the brief overview in chapter 9 of Ledgerwood 2001.

19. This book focuses mainly on international experiences in developing countries but there are many parallels with issues in richer countries. In the United States, for example, Balkin (1989) and Bates (1997) argue that difficulty in building up assets (rather than just the lack of credit) is at the root of poverty for the self-employed.

20. In this volume we use the term *microfinance* nearly always, while trying to bring out underlying debates.

21. The argument is made in a variety of CGAP documents, but the most nuanced articulation can be found in Robinson 2001, 21, in her discussion of "financial services in the poverty alleviation toolbox." Robinson argues that neither credit nor savings accounts are appropriate for "extremely poor" households (instead, she argues for job creation, skills training, relocation and provision of adequate water, medicine, and nutrition). Providing savings accounts and credit makes sense only for the "economically-active" poor (and richer groups), she continues. But, Robinson argues, *only savings* is right for the poorest among the economically active population. While we strongly agree that access to financial services will not be the answer for everyone, we see neither systematic evidence nor theory that allows us to conclude that saving is *more* appropriate than credit for the poorest who seek financial services.

22. In this sense, the finding that households are often caught in liquidity traps brought on by borrowing constraints (e.g., Deaton 1992) may in fact reflect a deeper problem of "saving constraints."

23. The nutrition-based efficiency wage theory described by Ray (1998) also helps explain why surplus may get consumed rather than saved—since higher consumption generates higher productivity, which in turn generates higher wages. The extent to which the theory holds in practice is up for debate, though. It may hold in some places for the very poorest, but it's less plausible for others (like the ROSCA participants interviewed in Rutherford 1997).

24. The argument that the very poor are bad candidates for credit can be seen in figures 1.3 and 1.4. Think of the figures applied to the "very poor" versus the "less poor" rather than "poorer" versus "richer."

25. More about Banco Compartamos can be found at www.compartamos.com.

26. The effective interest rate cited here is the "portfolio yield," which is calculated as total interest income divided by the average size of the total loan portfolio (see Woller 2000, 8). The Banco Compartamos public offering is described in chapter 8 below and in Rosenberg (2007).

27. While it would shed useful light on debates, there is in fact little sharp evidence of the shape of "returns to capital" functions in different settings. One recent study uses data on Mexican microenterprises collected in 1992, 1994, 1996, and 1998, with about 10,000 enterprises surveyed each year (McKenzie and Woodruff 2006). Each survey covers a range of urban enterprises, from very small to those with up to fifteen employees (which is still small in the big picture, but large for a "microenterprise"). McKenzie and Woodruff find high returns to capital, in keeping with the theory of declining marginal returns to capital described earlier: marginal returns are 15 percent per month for investment levels below $200. Unlike the picture in figure 1.4—and in line with figure 1.1— there is no evidence of scale economies at the low end. McKenzie and Woodruff find weak evidence of scale economies when investments get into the $1,000–$2,000 range, and somewhat stronger evidence of scale economies for the transportation and professional services sectors. Taking all the evidence together, McKenzie and Woodruff argue that there is not strong evidence in their data for patterns of returns to capital of a sort that would lead to poverty traps.

28. In chapter 2 we offer another caveat with regard to raising interest rates: when lenders have imperfect information on their clients (and prospective clients), raising interest rates too high can undermine borrowers' incentives to repay loans and thereby weaken the bank's ability to serve the poor.

29. One reason to be less concerned is that, to the extent that Banco Compartamos works in generally poor areas, it is less important to know that the clients are relatively better or worse off than their neighbors than to know the absolute levels of their living standards. Obtaining impact evaluations and data on absolute conditions would help sharpen conversations.

2 Why Intervene in Credit Markets?

1. Other studies confirm the existence of financing constraints in different contexts. See, for example, the study of business expansion in India by Banerjee and Duflo (2008), where access to subsidized capital turns out to be an important determinant of business expansion for low-income entrepreneurs. Kochar (1997), on the other hand, provides counter-evidence, drawing on the 1981–82 All India Debt and Investment Survey carried out in northern Uttar Pradesh. Kochar finds that in fact demand for credit is fairly low among the farm households that she investigates, and that the extent of credit rationing by formal sector banks is thus typically overstated in the region. Johnston and Morduch (2008) find that in Indonesia many more poor households are judged creditworthy by professional loan officers that are in fact receiving credit from formal-sector banks.

2. The interest rate prescriptions are from Chanakya, who helped to unify India about 2,300 years ago (in the wake of Alexander the Great's invasion). Chanakya further allows for risk by prescribing that traders who must take their wares through the forest can be charged 120 percent, and if by sea 240 percent per year (Reddy 1999).

3. See Ray 1998, chapter 14, which puts the role of moneylenders into perspective and provides an excellent introduction to the theory of rural credit markets. See also Collins et al. 2009, chapter 5, for a view of "the price of money" from the perspective of poor households.

4. Floro and Yotopoulos (1990) document with data from the Philippines that large farmers provide loans to poor neighbors (even on concessional terms) with hope in part that borrowers will default, allowing the larger farmers to seize property.

5. Besley (1994, 39–40) observes that if there are labor market failures, the wages used to value bank workers' time may not accurately reflect true economic valuations. Inefficiencies in the labor market could then spill over to create inefficiencies in the credit market.

6. See Besley (1994) for an excellent, nuanced view of rationales for intervening in credit markets.

7. Borrowers will, of course, only be interested in loans if their returns from investing the borrowed funds are greater than the opportunity cost of their time in alternative activities.

8. Unscrupulous villagers who have no intention of repaying loans may also seek to borrow. Lenders will avoid unscrupulous villagers if they can, but they often lack adequate information. We discuss the resulting agency problem in section 2.3.

9. The theory of monopolistic competition can be traced back to Robinson (1933) and Chamberlain (1933).

10. See, for example, Aghion, Caroli, and Garcia-Peñalosa (1999) and Bourguignon (2001) for surveys on the links between income equality and efficiency.

11. The scenario is described by Besley (1994), drawing on Basu (1989).

12. Evidence on the value of securing land titles as a way to improve credit markets is provided by Migot-Adholla, Hazell, Blarel et al. (1991) for Ghana, Kenya, and Rwanda and Feder, Onchan, and Raparla (1988) for Thailand. Woodruff (2001), however, argues that de Soto's argument lacks strong empirical support.

13. DeMeza and Webb (1987) provide a model that instead allows expected returns to vary for different clients. They show that if safer clients also have higher returns, adverse selection can lead to inefficiently *high* lending to lenders with low returns.

14. Note that the slope of the line relating interest rates to expected profits is flatter in the right section of the figures. This is because only risky types borrow in that range, reducing the rate at which raising fees translates into profits.

15. The gross cost of capital, corresponding to k, is \$1.40.

16. We assume that unlucky borrowers have a support network to help tide them over when their projects fail. Assuming that revenues are zero when luck is bad makes the result easier to see, but it could be relaxed without changing the basic outcome.

17. Why can't the bank lure the safe borrowers back with lower interest rates just for those who departed? The problem is that all borrowers will pretend to be safe and depart in order to obtain the cheaper interest rates.

18. But, as the first scenario showed, it is not always the case that information problems of this sort lead to inefficiencies. The result hinges on the structure of costs and the nature of riskiness in the economy.

19. This type of threat can be quite effective, in particular in the case of sovereign (i.e., country-to-country) lending. See Bolton and Scharfstein 1990 for a dynamic framework where non-refinancing threats may induce sovereign debtors to repay their foreign obligations. We describe these issues (with application to microfinance) in chapter 5.

20. This is a relatively profitable business for *susu* collectors. They return each depositor's accumulated savings each month, holding back one day's worth as a fee. Collectors appear to make a profit of $200 a month, which is six times the average per capita income in Ghana (Steel and Aryeetey 1994).

21. Harper (2002) compares and contrasts the self-help group approach and the Grameen Bank model.

22. Varghese (2004) provides a helpful synthesis of bank-moneylender linkages, on which we have drawn.

23. Alternatively, the bank may be able to use a cross-reporting mechanism to check up on the selection and treatment of clients. Rai (2002) presents an interesting model in this spirit.

24. Bell (1990) reports at least one favorable experience in Malaysia linking to informal-sector lenders. Jain (1998) discusses a different mechanism where banks informally take advantage of the presence of moneylenders, essentially piggy-backing on the local lenders' screening efforts. Varghese (2005) describes a situation where having access to moneylenders aids borrowers' ability to reliably borrow from the formal sector, creating positive feedbacks; his (2004) evidence from rural South India generally supports the proposition.

3 Roots of Microfinance: ROSCAs and Credit Cooperatives

1. The financial diaries take some of the tools of corporate finance (income statements and balance sheets of assets) and apply them to gain a systematic sense of the full financial activities of low-income households. Collins et al. (2009) draw on both quantitative data and stories of individuals and families coping with risk, attempting to save and borrow, and looking for ways to get ahead in life. Samphantharak and Townsend (2008) independently develop and extend a related approach to the study of low-income families, applied to high-frequency data from Thailand.

2. Over time, ROSCA members move in and out of the groups, so that eventually the members may include friends of friends and acquaintances of acquaintances. We discuss how this affects enforcement possibilities. The Indian self-help groups described in chapter 2 are a kind of credit cooperative. In India, chit funds, a kind of commercialized ROSCA, are run as businesses by managers who carefully choose participants who are not necessarily known to each other.

3. ROSCAs are known as *chit* funds in India, *arisans* in Indonesia, and *kye* in Korea. In Africa, they are known as *susu* in Ghana, *esusu* in Nigeria, *upatu* or *mchezo* in Tanzania, and *chilemba* or *chiperegani* in Malawi. In parts of Africa, they are also known as "merry-go-rounds." The term *tontine* is also used to describe burial societies.

4. Interestingly, this finding is not replicated in Siwan Anderson and Jean-Marie Baland's study of ROSCAs in the slums of Nairobi, Kenya. There poorer households used ROSCAs more (Anderson and Baland 2002).

5. Besley, Coate, and Loury (1993) provide a theoretical analysis of ROSCAs, stressing their role for making indivisible purchases. Rutherford (2000), Ardener (1964), and Bouman (1977) provide concise catalogues of ROSCAs and their mechanisms.

6. The example gives the flavor of the model of ROSCAs by Besley, Coate, and Loury (1993). See appendix A1 for a more detailed description.

7. Of course, getting a loan would also solve the problem, but here loans are assumed to be either expensive or unobtainable.

8. An added twist is to randomize the order of the subsequent recipients at each meeting, rather than simply randomizing the order at the first meeting and following that set pattern henceforth. The former plan, which is seen in Brazil, Mexico, and elsewhere, provides better incentives for the last person in line (since no one knows who is last until the penultimate meeting), but it does not improve incentives for the first in line.

9. In line with this, buying jewelry or equipment that can be used as a store of value is a common way to use the pot.

10. Platteau (2000) provides other examples in which individuals have difficulty saving because others (husbands, neighbors, relatives) make claims on surplus resources before the money can be safely stored away.

11. Quotations are from Gugerty 2007, 268. On the following page Gugerty notes that "individuals may have been uncomfortable talking about household circumstances to enumerators, but the overwhelming number of individuals reported difficulties in self-control rather than family or household control issues."

12. One of the most notable features of Crédit Agricole is that it has preserved its cooperative structure in France's traditionally centralized system. Their cooperative programs have been replicated in other contexts where banking was highly centralized, such as Armenia. In 2008 the Grameen Crédit Agricole Microfinance Foundation (GCAMF) was created in partnership with the Grameen Bank, combining Crédit Agricole's focus on farming and the household and the Grameen Bank's emphasis on women. Crédit Agricole also has branchless banking, having collected deposits at hundreds of "points verts." These are local businesses and postal offices that worked with the cooperative as conduits for rural households' savings (Armendáriz 2009).

13. The story continues, anticipating the recent spread of microfinance from Bangladesh to the United States. In the early 1900s, the credit cooperatives of Bengal were so well known that Edward Filene, the Boston merchant whose department stores still bear his name, spent time in India, learning about the cooperatives in order to later set up "friendly societies" in Jewish communities in Boston, New York, and Providence (Tenenbaum 1993).

14. The cooperatives turned out to be a major disappointment in Madras, as funds were captured by the rural elite and arrears skyrocketed. Robert (1979) reports that arrears jumped from 10 percent in 1910 to 63 percent in 1931. The global depression is partly to blame (it cut agricultural prices by half in Madras, crippling farmers), but Robert (1979) places most of the blame on political forces that undermined professionalism and fostered a system notable for its indulgence of bureaucracy and patronage.

15. In having unlimited liability, the Raiffeisen model differs from the competing model advanced by Hermann Schultze-Delizsch (Banerjee, Besley, and Guinnane 1994). The Schultze-Delizsch cooperatives were mainly urban and had larger shares and paid meaningful dividends, while the Raiffeisen cooperatives treated shares nominally, paid no dividends, and were confined to the countryside. The two variants merged in the early twentieth century and spread widely throughout rural Germany.

16. Verifying the result most easily requires calculus. The first-order condition of the maximization problem is $(y - Rb) = (1/m)\, p$, so that $p = m\,(y - Rb)$.

17. In equilibrium, the lender is indifferent between this loan and a loan at the (safe) market rate r. Hence it must be that $pR = m(y - Rb)R = (1 + r)$, which in turn determines R.

18. We take wealth (w) as exogenous here to simplify matters, but w should also be optimized upon as part of the optimal loan contract.

19. To formally derive the relationship among monitoring intensity, collateral, and interest rates, we would need to assume a "cost of monitoring" function (e.g., $1/2\ m^2$). And we would need to formalize the amount of interest that the insider can claim. See Banerjee, Besley, and Guinnane 1994 for a derivation.

20. An additional role that credit unions may potentially play is to mitigate the effects of negative aggregate shocks on individuals' consumption (see Armendáriz 2002).

21. To more closely reflect the model of the Raiffeisen cooperatives described earlier, we would want to assume that the members are risk-averse and that δ is the risk premium attached to the lower variance of local interest rates.

4 Group Lending

1. The loan officer is typically a man and the villagers are typically women, but there are exceptions. Beck, Behr, and Güttler (2009) provide a study of loan officer gender in Albania, finding that default rates there are lower for customers of female loan officers, even after controlling for borrower, loan, and loan officer characteristics.

2. Todd (1996) provides a detailed and unvarnished study of group lending in Bangladesh. Bornstein (1997) offers a journalist's account of group meetings and the Grameen Bank story. See also Fugelsang and Chandler 1993.

3. By December 2007, BRAC counted 260,785 Village Organizations serving 7.37 million members, and the Grameen Bank had 7.41 million members organized into 136,619 centers and 1,169,000 groups. So for Grameen Bank, on average, there were 54.25 individuals per center and 8.56 groups per center. Data are from BRAC 2008 (see www. brac .net) and Grameen Bank 2003 (see www.grameen-info.org).

4. FINCA is the Foundation for International Community Assistance. See www .villagebanking.org.

5. In chapter 5, though, we argue that there is much more afoot in microfinance than group lending, although it has played a historically important role.

6. Both the Grameen Bank and BancoSol now also make many loans on a strictly bilateral basis, without the "group responsibility" contract. The "individual" contract (as opposed to the "group" contract) is viewed as being more appealing to better-off, better-established members.

7. Such "information revelation mechanisms" are described by Rai and Sjöström (2004). They provide an interesting example of a hypothetical mechanism that reveals information by inducing villagers to "cross-report" on each other, and they show conditions under which cross-reporting can dominate the Grameen-style contract described here. We return to their proposal in chapter 5.

8. An excellent overview of the theory of group lending is provided by Ghatak and Guinnane (1999).

9. Grameen restricts membership to people who do not possess more than half an acre of land, although the rule is followed more in spirit than in letter. This definition obviously does not apply to other countries where the Grameen methodology has been replicated.

10. The maturity period varies across borrowers and countries. But most replicators are advised to extend one-year loans that are to be repaid weekly, that is, in 52 installments. As of 2007, Grameen offers four different loan products with variable terms, but its Basic Loan maintains the original weekly repayment plan.

11. Jonathan Morduch interview with Muhammad Yunus, December 15, 2002, Dhaka. One advantage of the 2:2:1 staggering, pointed out to us by Imran Matin, is that it increases the chance that a group member is awaiting a new loan when another group member runs into repayment trouble.

12. González-Vega, Schreiner, Meyer et al. (1997, 88) report that in BancoSol's version of group lending in Bolivia, loan officers refuse to accept partial loan repayments from a group. So if one member cannot come up with the required money in a given week, the loan officer will not accept any group member's individual contribution for that week—and all members are seen to be in arrears. Funds are only accepted when everyone has 100 percent of their contributions ready to submit. Like the Grameen Bank rules, this creates strong incentives (if enforced) to encourage group members to work hard, manage funds wisely, and help their peers.

13. The exposition here follows treatments by Ghatak (1999) and Armendáriz and Gollier (2000); also see Ghatak 2000. Varian (1990) includes an early treatment of group lending and adverse selection, and Laffont and N'Guessan (2000) provide a later treatment.

14. Henceforth we will use the word *bank*, bearing in mind that the institution is special in that it is committed to just breaking even, or that it is in a perfectly competitive market so that it cannot charge more than its costs.

15. The question arises as to why risky types (who earn higher profits than safe types in good periods) cannot simply pay safe types to join with them. Ghatak (1999) provides a proof of why risky types cannot adequately compensate safe types to induce the safe types into mixed safe-risky groups. The numerical example shows this too. In contrast with the assortative matching stand taken by Ghatak (1999), Armendáriz and Gollier (2000), deliver the rationale behind improvements when groups are not homogenous (i.e., they are not matched assortatively). Whether in practice adverse selection is mitigated via assortative or non-assortative matching (or through other mechanisms) remains under-researched.

16. Analyzing five-person groups is straightforward but adds complications with little extra insight. Similarly, considering risk aversion alters the main results only slightly.

17. By working with gross returns and gross interest rates, we define returns as not being net of the cost of borrowing. The safe types' net returns are $(y - R_b)$, for example.

18. This is not the optimal contract that the bank could use, but it is sufficient to show how group lending can restore efficiency in the face of adverse selection. Note that the bank can determine whether a borrower has been successful or not, but it cannot see exactly how successful; thus, there is no way for the bank to tell ex post if the borrower is a risky or safe type. Joint liability/group responsibility contracts cut off all group members if any one of them defaults. Implicitly this means that they must find a way to make good on the defaulter's debts in order to escape sanctions. We assume that the

debts are simply paid by the partners, but an informal loan might be used rather than a grant to the defaulter.

19. The probability that two independent events occur is the product of probabilities. If you randomly chose someone from the population, there would be a q chance that they would be safe and a $(1 - q)$ chance that they would be risky. If you instead randomly chose two people from the population, there would be a $q \cdot q$ chance that they would both be safe and a $(1 - q) \cdot (1 - q)$ chance that they would both be risky. The chance that they would be a mixed pair is equal to the chance that they are not both safe nor both risky. That probability is $1 - q^2 - (1 - q)^2$. After simplifying, this probability is equal to $2q (1 - q)$.

20. Important papers on group lending with ex post moral hazard include those by Besley and Coate (1995) and Armendáriz (1999a). See also Rai and Sjöström (2004) and Laffont and Rey (2003) for theoretical approaches drawing from the economics of mechanism design, in which they derive optimal lending contracts in the case of moral hazard; these approaches show how the standard group-lending contract can be improved upon depending on clients' ability to make independent "side contracts between themselves."

21. The implicit assumption here is that both borrowers decide to simultaneously monitor each other, even if even if both have shirked. While we make this assumption for simplicity, our conjecture is that if monitoring decisions are taken sequentially, the main insight remains the same: the magnitude of a borrower's loss from shirking crucially depends on how lucky each borrower is at detecting willful default. We note, however, as is often the case in these types of models, that willful defaulters will nevertheless monitor each other. That is, we are assuming that while they hide their returns, they do not hide from one another because monitoring involves physical presence. While this assumption might seem unrealistic in this simple set-up, it makes sense in set-ups that allow for collusion between borrowers such as Laffont-Rey (2003). While collusive behavior is assumed away here, section 4.6 elaborates on Laffont and Rey's theoretical work.

22. Dale Adams, Emeritus Professor of the Ohio State Rural Finance Program and a microfinance skeptic, is fond of speaking of "microdebt" rather than "microcredit," signaling that loans carry burdens (as well as opportunities) for those who accept them.

23. In the classic Grameen-style practice, typically two people in a five-person group get their loans first, then after a period the next two get loans, and finally after another wait, the last person gets his or her loan.

24. As Ahlin and Townsend (2007b) note, the group lending models of Besley and Coate (1995) and Banerjee, Besley, and Guinnane (1994) predict that greater cooperation can undermine repayments as borrowers collude against the bank.

25. One questionable design feature is that the participants are told that the experiment will stop after exactly ten rounds (if the group gets that far without defaulting). It is a well-known feature of finitely repeated games that in the tenth round strategic players will (in principle) act in a purely self-interested way, without concern for their fellow group members. If players are foresighted, they see that this will happen in the tenth round, and they will realize that they have nothing to lose by acting in a purely self-interested way in the ninth round too. So too for the eighth round, and so forth. Indeed, the whole thing should unravel and no cooperation should be possible from the first round forward. Given this, it is hard to know how to interpret the results of the Erfurt experiment. Clearly everything did not fall apart, and we discuss the results here because we think that this line of research has potential and the results are intriguing (even if the method is not fully satisfying).

26. For more on the methods, see also Dehejia and Wahba 1999 and Rosenbaum and Rubin 1983. An easy-to-use estimator is available in the popular statistical package, Stata.

27. Bias could creep back in when clients drop out of groups and are replaced by friends and neighbors of existing members; Karlan thus limits analyses to initial members.

28. Additional research by Karlan using experimental "trust games" with the same FINCA clients points to the beneficial role that social capital appears to be playing in Peru.

29. Ghatak (1999) finds the opposite result: prospective borrowers will tend to seek out similar people to match with. If there are enough people to choose from, both Sadoulet and Ghatak could be right: safe borrowers seek to match with other safe borrowers (Ghatak), but, within the pool of safe borrowers, preference is placed on those with incomes that covary less with one's own income (Sadoulet).

30. One colleague who read this passage in a draft version of the chapter suggested that part of the problem might simply have been that the particular product was poorly designed—not that the group-lending concept was necessarily flawed.

31. Conning (2005) also provides an important analysis of implications of costly monitoring by borrowers, describing when and how group lending can dominate individual lending—and vice versa.

32. Collusion is also an important possibility considered in the theoretical studies of Besley and Coate (1995), Armendáriz (1999a), and Laffont and N'Guessan (2000).

33. The new flexibility provided by Grameen Bank II has not been implemented widely in practice, perhaps because loan officers remain wary of the complexity (and potential danger) inherent in deviating from simple rules. As chapter 6 describes, Grameen Bank II also brings new savings methods—which may be as important a break for the bank as are the proposed new lending methods (Collins, Morduch, Rutherford et al. 2009, chapter 6).

5   Beyond Group Lending

This chapter draws on Armendáriz and Morduch 2000.

1. Renegotiation occurs by transferring problem borrowers from standard "basic" loans to "flexi-loans" with longer terms and smaller installments. While "Grameen II" allows this possibility, loan officers are simultaneously given incentives to limit renegotiation.

2. Data are from www.bancosol.com.bo/en/productos_cr.html, as posted in April 2009.

3. Village banks operate by placing everyone in the village into one large group with mutual responsibility. Group meetings are often used for training sessions as well as financial matters. For more on village banking, see www.villagebanking.org and Karlan 2007.

4. The work of *Safe*Save in the slums of Dhaka is one example.

5. A credit agency can help address this problem, such that banks can investigate credit histories of prospective clients, but we know of no such agencies serving microfinance populations.

6. See Aleem 1990, table 7.2, 137.

7. See Armendáriz 1999a for a framework where peer monitoring costs are explicitly taken into account. Specifically, if peer monitoring is exceedingly costly, individual (i.e., bilateral lender-borrower) contracts are shown to dominate over group-lending contracts.

8. In the sovereign debt case, there is no international court where foreign creditors can enforce claims on a country, so there can be no use of collateral either. See Bulow and Rogoff 1989a, 1989b.

9. This turns out to be an important assumption. If the borrower could default and hold onto enough principal to easily finance future business operations, the threat of non-refinancing would be considerably weakened. See Bond and Krishnamurty (2004) for a discussion of assumptions needed for threats of non-refinancing to have teeth when this is the case.

10. The model rests on the assumption that the bank can credibly commit to provide a second-period loan, even though it anticipates this new loan will be defaulted upon, which may seem unrealistic. However, it will all depend on the interest rate that the bank charges, which in this setup will be endogenously determined. Note that the probability of default will be substantially reduced in an infinite horizon model. In particular, we know by the "folk theorem" of game theory, that if the discount factor, δ, is large enough, strategic defaults will never be observed in equilibrium. See, for example, Fudenberg and Maskin 1986.

11. This expression reduces to $\delta y(j - v) < \delta y(1 - v)$ if a nondefaulting borrower is refinanced only with probability $j < 1$.

12. Note that the maximum enforceable repayment $R = \delta y$ satisfies the "individual rationality constraint" of the borrower; namely, $y - R + \delta y \geq 0$. This constraint states that an individual borrower must find it profitable to enter into a contractual obligation with the bank—otherwise, she refuses to borrow in the first place.

13. One more step is actually needed. It has to be checked that the interest rate satisfies the borrower's "individual rationality" constraint—namely, is it worth it for the borrower to borrow at that rate?

14. See Hoff and Stiglitz 1998.

15. The Bolivian experience is described by Rhyne 2001, chapter 7, from which this account is taken.

16. Data on number of clients are from Rhyne 2001, 142. Data on overdues rates are from pp. 148–149, and data on BancoSol's return on equity are from p. 149.

17. The story is related in Rhyne 2001, 145.

18. Grameen Bank, *Annual Report* 1995 and *Annual Report* 2000 (Grameen Bank 1996, 2001). Matin (1997) tells a richly observed story of how "overlapping" led to severe difficulties in villages in Tangail.

19. Grameen Bank's "Grameen Bank II" is the most notable example. For early assessments, see and Dowla and Barua (2006) and Collins, Morduch, Rutherford et al. (2009).

20. The need for credit bureaus is made forcefully by McIntosh and Wydick (2005) who show cases where, in principle, competition can worsen the lot of the poorest households.

Competition can, in particular, make it difficult to cross-subsidize the poorest borrowers.

21. Data on Bolivia are reported by González-Vega et al. (1997), 74.

22. A theoretical formalization of this notion would follow the treatment of repeated lending contracts described in Parikshit Ghosh and Debray Ray (2001).

23. Morduch interview with Fazle Abed, founder and chairperson of BRAC, Dhaka, December 2002.

24. Of course, part of the early installments can be (and often is) paid directly from the not-yet-invested principal of the loan. This makes the effective loan size smaller. The practice does not fully answer the puzzle at hand, since it cannot explain the bank's logic in requiring that the first installments are paid so soon. The bank, of course, might not be acting fully logically, but we suspect that there is more to it than that.

25. Jain and Mansuri (2003) offer a different but related story. They argue that if micro-credit borrowers must resort to borrowing from informal lenders to pay off microcredit loans (rather than relying only on the flow of other income coming into the household), then the microlender can piggyback on the informal lender's informational advantage. In other words, if you can't get a microloan without also getting a short-term loan from the moneylender to pay for the initial microloan installments, then only people judged to be creditworthy by moneylenders will demand microloans. The microlender gains due to this implicit screening mechanism. The mechanism is plausible in theory, but we do not know of any evidence that gives it empirical credence. Instead, other family income is most typically used to pay for initial installments, and it is unlikely that this would provide the same kind of helpful piggybacking described by Jain and Mansuri.

26. Our discussion here is influenced heavily by conversations with staff members at Bank Rakyat Indonesia about how they determine loan terms and by Stuart Rutherford 2000, which considers lending mechanisms in the context of savings problems. We present a more "formal" discussion in Armendáriz and Morduch (2000).

27. The survey of customers and non-customers was completed by Bank Rakyat Indonesia and analyzed by Morduch.

28. Personal communication with Don Johnston, a microfinance expert based in Jakarta, January 29, 2003.

29. BRI's policy is consistent with the view of collateral as a lever to improve credit contracts. In some cases, requiring collateral may be a lender's way of obtaining assets from the poor. Ray (1998), for example, argues that in India moneylenders sometimes require collateral and are pleased when borrowers default since it allows asset transfers from poor borrowers to wealthier moneylenders. This is not the case in microfinance.

30. Product data are from personal communication with Stuart Rutherford, January 2004. Similar data are available at www.safesave.org.

31. Data are from Stuart Rutherford, personal communication, January 2004.

32. Morduch personal communication with Monique Cohen, president of Microfinance Opportunities, an organization based in Washington that is focused on better understanding how microfinance customers use financial services, March 2004.

33. This story is related in Rai and Sjöström 2004, drawing on Espisu, Nasubo, Obuya et al. 1995. An alternative explanation of the story offered by Stuart Rutherford is that "people pay when they are asked to, and tend not to pay if they're not asked (the oldest rule in banking)."

34. Thus, a lender like *Safe*Save, that bases its operations on one-on-one visits by staff to client homes rather than public transactions, has one less lever to use in maintaining internal control.

35. The data from Hossain 1988, Hulme 1991, and Gibbons and Kasim 1991 is taken from Hulme and Mosley 1997 as cited in Wright 2000, 23.

36. Morduch interview with George Oetomo, general manager for operations, Yayasan Dharma Bhakti Parasahabat (www.ydbp.com), March 2003.

37. Churchill (1999) describes similar monitoring and information-collection mechanisms in individual lending programs run by the Alexandria Businessman's Association in Egypt and the Cajas Municipales of Peru, and he is the source for the information on Financiera Cálpia cited previously.

38. Armendáriz (1999a) provides an alternative view.

6 Savings and Insurance

1. Full disclosure: Jonathan Morduch is, at the time of writing this book's second edition, a member of the *Safe*Save cooperative, effectively serving as a board member.

2. BRI's coverage is particularly impressive given that the population of Indonesia is roughly 238 million. One way in which BRI deposits are less convenient is that clients have not been able to deposit or withdraw at any branch other than their local unit, although with ongoing computerization that limit should be overcome.

3. Program details and the survey results below are from Women's World Banking 2003.

4. In collecting deposits from the broader community, Grameen is taking full advantage of their official status as a bank, not an NGO. Thus, Grameen can do what ASA, BRAC, and other rivals cannot do as of this writing: Grameen can collect savings from clients who do not borrow.

5. Deaton 1992 remains an essential reference.

6. Personal communication with Stuart Rutherford, December 2003. Client perspectives on Grameen II are the subject of Chapter 6 of Collins et al. (2009).

7. Field experience in Chiapas, Mexico reveals that poorer clients typically have time horizons that are rather short, suggesting limited prospects for long-term savings products in that context.

8. Blanchard and Fischer (1989) provide a guide to newer work in this spirit, building up from dynamic optimization problems under uncertainty.

9. For a more thorough and general treatment of the problem, see Deaton's excellent exposition (1992) and the lecture notes collected in Blanchard and Fischer (1989).

10. See Morduch 1999a for further evidence on addressing risk through informal mechanisms. Jalan and Ravallion's evidence is derived from a similar framework that focuses

on risk-sharing within communities rather than intertemporal consumption smoothing per se. The frameworks, though, tend to capture similar difficulties—that consumption and income track each other more closely than households would like. The literature on consumption-smoothing and risk-sharing is large and growing. For further evidence on addressing risk through informal mechanisms, see Fafchamps 2004; Dercon 2004; Dercon and Hoddinott 2004; and Morduch 2004.

11. One approach would be to distinguish between the role of initial income when shocks are negative (creating a case in which borrowing constraints are expected to bind), versus situations in which shocks are positive (creating a case in which savings constraints are more apt to bind).

12. See Rutherford 2000 for a rich description of some common (and some not so common) mechanisms. Collins et al. (2009) also describe a range of informal risk-sharing and saving mechanisms.

13. See Morduch 1999a for more on the hidden costs of informal mechanisms and related inefficiencies.

14. Specifically, de Meza and Webb (2001) argue that when adverse selection leads to credit rationing in the model of Stiglitz and Weiss (1981), borrowers face an infinite marginal cost of funds. As a result, they're better off delaying the project to accumulate more wealth. Continued delay means more wealth, reducing the need for credit.

15. In a similar way, it may be difficult to keep funds away from your spouse. As noted earlier, Anderson and Baland (2002) find that women in Nairobi save in ROSCAS in order to keep money out of the house and away from husbands. When it is harder to keep money from your spouse, it will be harder to accumulate savings.

16. Collins et al. (2009) find many households in South Africa that have savings accounts but who, nonetheless, choose to accumulate funds through participating in local ROSCAs and savings clubs. Having a bank account does not, in itself, make saving possible.

17. The nature of commitment is not totally nailed down by the study. Another aspect of the SEED account entailed customers committing to save for a given purpose. Thus part of the impact of the SEED product could come from its accommodation to people's "mental accounts"—i.e., creating a product that aligns with the desire to have independent accounts for separate purposes.

18. BRI also provides depositors with coupons for a semiannual lottery. The chance of winning is proportional to the size of the account, and lotteries are much-anticipated local events. Awards range from a car or motorcycle to clocks, radios, and washing machines; overall, the value of awards in 1995 was about 0.7 percent of balances. (BRI Unit Products, p. 17, Jakarta: BRI.) In January 2003, the maximum interest rate on SIMPEDES deposits was 9.5 percent per year.

19. The literature on microinsurance (most of it oriented toward practitioners) is growing. Institutions such as the Grameen Bank and SEWA have long offered insurance products, and today organizations including the International Labor Organization and Micro-Save Africa are taking up the cause. The CGAP microfinance gateway (available at www.microfinance.org/gateway) has links to a range of resources. Early introductions to the literature include Brown and Churchill 1999, 2000 and, from a broader vantage, Morduch 2006 and Karlan and Morduch 2009.

20. Radermacher et al. (2006, 78) contend that "over-use does not appear to be a major problem in developing countries, where there is a lack of adequate healthcare and therefore access is usually restricted indirectly by related opportunity costs." Grameen Kalyan's copayments are seen as signaling quality of care because clients equate price with quality.

21. For more on the ideas behind rainfall insurance, see Miranda 1991, Skees et al. 2004, and Morduch 2006.

22. Data are from the CGAP Microfinance Gateway, "Earthquake in Gujarat: SEWA delivers on insurance claims," an article from 2001. Available at www .microfinancegateway.org/microinsurance/highlight_sewa.htm.

23. Todd (1996) and Rahman (2001) describe situations where difficulties emerged; bear in mind, though, that they are not necessarily representative.

24. In the first two years of Grameen Bank II's implementation, field reports indicated that loan officers were reluctant to adopt the new, flexible lending mechanism. One reason is that the flexibility also brings more variation, and that makes it more costly to keep track of clients. Another reason for the reluctance to embrace the new flexibility is fears that giving too much latitutde may inadvertently undermine repayment discipline.

25. Morduch (1998) puts forward empirical evidence from Bangladesh consistent with the notion that microcredit borrowing enhanced income smoothing, showing that across seasons, households with access to microloans have smoother income streams (and thus smoother consumption patterns) relative to control groups. Roodman and Morduch (2009) describe the limits of the data and question the pattern of results, suggesting that the earlier result is not dispositive.

7 Gender

1. The Microcredit Summit Campaign defines the "poorest" as "those who are in the bottom half of those living below their nation's poverty line, or any of the nearly 1 billion people who live on less than US$1 a day adjusted for purchasing power parity (PPP), when they started with a program" (Daley-Harris 2009).

2. See chapter 5, Yunus (1999). An important step in serving women was to reconceive rural finance as nonfarm enterprise finance, rather than as lending for crops. Women tend to have greater autonomy in the former, while farming tends to be a man's domain in Bangladesh.

3. Roodman and Morduch 2009 question the causal link on which this evidence is based. Similar claims are made by Pitt and Khandker (1998), using just the first year of the data used by Khandker (2005).

4. Transformation refers to the process through which a nongovernmental organization becomes a regulated, commercial financial institution. See chapter 8 for further discussion.

5. Neoclassical production functions (and their limits) are discussed in chapter 1.

6. See Armendáriz 1999a for a theoretical treatment of microfinance with a focus on monitoring.

7. At the same time, we note that inducing women to be too conservative, that is, to invest in traditional activities that are not skill-intensive, may increase the gender gap and not be efficient.

8. Information is based on Morduch's conversation with Mark Schreiner, a consultant on credit scoring in microfinance, November 2003.

9. Poor households are often biased against elderly women too. In a recent article on Tanzania, for example, Miguel (2005) shows an extreme example. At exceedingly low subsistence levels, male household members have been known to murder elderly women in order to preserve the nutritional status of the household. The incidence of such violence is intensified when villages are hit by a negative aggregate shock.

10. It should be noted that Becker's results are also consistent with household choices made unilaterally by a dictatorial head (which is another way of creating consensus).

11. Rawlsian preferences relate to an approach to the issue of a just society and, in particular, distributive justice—which has been proposed by philosopher John Rawls in his *Theory of Justice* (1971). According to Rawls, justice requires maximum concern for those in the worst position.

12. See Bergstrom 1996 for a comprehensive review of bargaining models and theories of the family.

13. Strauss and Beegle (1996) provide a comprehensive survey.

14. See also Klasen and Wink 2001.

15. See Evenson, Popkin, and King-Quizon 1980, Folbre 1984, and King and Hill 1993.

16. Promoting women to powerful positions in villages and regions may, by the same token, bring social benefits. In a recent paper on India, Chattopadhyay and Duflo (2004) show that by empowering women and, in particular, by allowing them to be elected to local councils, spending on public goods most closely linked to women's concerns increased.

17. Evidence from India also shows that there is a positive correlation between the relative size of a mother's assets (notably jewelry) and children's school attendance and medical attention (Duraisamy 1992).

18. Grameen Trust Chiapas, A.C., is one of the first Grameen replications in Latin America, alongside AlSol. Both NGOs were launched by Beatriz Armendáriz with technical assistance from Grameen Trust Bangladesh, and with the financial support of the Deutsche Gesellschaft für Technische Zusammenarbeit.

19. Based on anecdotal evidence from GTC loan officers, Armendáriz is collaborating with researchers from Innovations for Poverty Action (IPA) to design and implement a randomized impact assessment of allowing husbands to join otherwise women-only solidarity groups (see Allen, Armendáriz, Karlan et al. 2010).

20. Morduch (2001) confirms this result in the cross-section, using the same survey but fails to find a similar result when investigating fertility trends before and after introduction of the programs.

21. Disputes over the extent of credit constraints and the strength of informal markets are discussed in chapter 2.

22. It may still be the case that a fraction of women, typically with high skills, have access to formal employment activities. The enhancement of self-employment opportunities via microcredit is unlikely to have a direct effect on these women. However, suppose that as a result of gender discrimination, wages of women in the formal sector are maintained at their reservation utility level. Microfinance might then have a positive externality on these women also, as it increases their reservation utility, and, therefore, their bargaining power in the formal sector.

8 Commercialization

1. For details, see Rosenberg 2007, Malkin 2008, and ACCION International 2007. Chuck Waterfield has usefully assembled primary data and discussion on the Banco Comparta-mos offering, available at www.microfinan.com/compartamos.htm. The discussion here draws largely on those primary source materials, as well as on data and analysis in Cull et al. 2009b.

2. The debates on "allowable" profit and the setting of fees are part of much wider arguments around the nature of "social investment." As Kinsley (2008) demonstrates through a series of conversations with leading business and academic leaders, the fundamental arguments touch on the basic possibilities and limits of what Bill Gates calls "creative capitalism" and Yunus (2008) calls "social business." Microfinance serves as the best-developed laboratory for examining issues of prices and profits in social business.

3. Carlos Danel, one of the founders of Banco Compartamos, reflects that the outsize profitability was essential to attract the attention of a market unfamiliar with—and perhaps wary of—microfinance (personal communication with Jonathan Morduch, April 23, 2008).

4. Hudon (2007) explores the idea of ethical interest rates, distinguishing four different approaches to "fair" rates. While they vary in their ethical foundations, the deontological, consequentialist, demand for credit, and procedural approaches share in identifying an underlying tension between the interests of an institution's clients and its other stake-holders. Hudon (2007) acknowledges that interest rates can be important for sustain-ability, but he argues that over-emphasizing sustainability objectives can be dangerous, because donors, local governments, and socially responsible investors might withdraw essential support for nascent institutions and further innovation if they perceive current interest rates as being unfair. He argues that financial and social objectives should be viewed as mutually reinforcing and uses the term "social sustainability."

5. The assertion that competition will reduce interest rates is often heard but not obvi-ously true (though there is evidence that this has been the case in Bolivian microfinance). In practice, competition between banks is often resolved through nonprice competition (e.g., over the diversity and convenience of services). Moreover, the entry of a handful of competitors can result in oligopoly, yielding only limited competitive pressure.

6. The discussion and definitions draw on a variety of sources. Among the most useful are the Mix Market Web site (www.mixmbb.org) and the various issues of the *MicroBank-ing Bulletin*.

7. The *MicroBanking Bulletin* adjustments are also too limited with regard to the oppor-tunity costs for equity holders. The only adjustment is an adjustment for inflation, not

for returns on alternative investments. Manos and Yaron (2008) make similar points in arguing for the superiority of Yaron's "subsidy dependence index." We see the criticism of the FSS adjustments as separate from arguments about competing (but very similar) measures.

8. Bauchet and Morduch (2010) analyze differences between the Mix Market data set (of which the *MicroBanking Bulletin* data are a subset) and the Microcredit Summit Campaign database. They find that the latter data are more heavily tilted toward South Asia and the former toward Latin America.

9. Gonzalez and Rosenberg (2006) provide support for using loan size as a proxy for the income of customers. Cull et al. (2009b) note: "In their data, a 10-percentage point increase in the fraction of small loans is associated on average with a 9-percentage point increase in the self-reported fraction of poor borrowers served. Self-reporting bias could explain some of the correlation, but the link between smaller loans and greater outreach to the poor appears to be fairly tight when comparing across institutions." The finding addresses the worry of Armendáriz and Szafarz (2009) that increases in average loan size are ambiguous in terms of "mission drift."

10. As discussed in section 8.2, though, the FSS figures for NGOs are aided by the relatively low choice of a "market" price of capital. All FSS ratios will fall if the choice of "market" price for capital rises, but Cull et al. (2009b) find that the FSS ratios for NGOs will fall furthest given their greater use of subsidy and noncommercial funding.

11. By excluding unsustainable institutions, this figure tells us how much institutions covering their costs were charging.

12. The analysis is made complicated by the fact that being regulated is a choice made by institutions. It is not a choice made lightly or randomly, and the correlations described above could stem from omitted variables rather than underlying causal relationships. Cull et al. (2009a) attempt to allay the concern by using an instrumental variables methodology. The instruments should influence whether an institution is regulated, but they should not directly affect the institution's performance (this is the critical "exclusion restriction"). The instruments capture (1) the general propensity to supervise formal financial institutions in a country; (2) whether an institution was originally chartered as an NGO or as a nonbank financial institution; and (3) whether the institution takes deposits. The analysis hinges on the validity of the exclusion restrictions, and a split sample test (used to compare institutions with similar types of commercial funding) is used as an added robustness check. This is likely the best that can be done methodologically without a true source of exogenous variation in the propensity to be regulated.

9   Measuring Impacts

1. This story was taken from accion.org/insight/meet_meet_our_borrowers.asp in mid-2003. The site also contains stories of other ACCION customers.

2. Ledgerwood (2001, 49–50), for example, concludes that "Few [microlenders] invest much in impact analysis, and the literature on microfinance and microenterprise development has been remarkably short on discussions of the subject."

3. Even in Peru, a second look at the data shows that the results are not 100 percent robust. As we describe later, Alexander (2001) shows strong, positive results on income even after controlling for household-level unobservables, but the results are not robust

when econometrically treating the problem of reverse causality from income to credit using instrumental variables methods.

4. See Sebstad and Chen 1996 for an overview of the range of outcomes that have been evaluated.

5. Pitt, Khandker, McKernan et al. (1999) show evidence that these substitution effects may be weak in the case of fertility in Bangladesh, since most microenterprises are based in the borrowers' home, making it possible to simultaneously raise children and run new businesses without the added burdens that jobs outside the home would entail.

6. Grameen does not use the "credit with education" model, but they do incorporate some social components into their activities, and the very act of meeting in village groups may have some intrinsic benefits for participants. McKernan's estimates also imply that a 10 percent increase in capital will, on average, yield a 20 percent increase in profit—a result that is so large that it leads us to wonder about the robustness of the specification. Malgosia Madajewicz, in her Harvard Ph.D. dissertation, suggests that McKernan's results weaken when capital is disaggregated into a fixed capital component and a working capital component.

7. The brief introduction to evaluation here is extended by others, including Angrist and Pischke (2009).

8. For more on regression approaches, see, for example, Kennedy's (2004) *Guide to Econometrics*.

9. The reliability of methods based on differences is reduced as the time periods get closer together, reducing temporal variation. Differencing noisy data can also exacerbate measurement error; in the "classical" case this leads to attenuation bias. Noisy recall may thus bias downward coefficients that show program impacts. See Heckman and Smith 1995 and Deaton 1997 for more detailed discussions of methods.

10. An earlier set of longitudinal studies includes Mosley (1996a and 1996b). Quality control problems have diminished their relative value as more careful studies have been completed (see Morduch 1999c).

11. All fixed household-specific variables drop out as well (such as education level, for example) so their effects cannot be independently estimated in equation (8.4), which was a concern of the AIMS researchers (although one that was weighted too heavily in our view). There are two important caveats here. The first is estimating that equation (8.4) can exacerbate attenuation bias due to measurement error (it can make positive coefficients shrink toward zero). Second, time-varying unobservables are not addressed. Both concerns suggest that instrumental variables methods are required for consistent estimation.

12. The survey focused on customers of Grameen Bank, BRAC, and RD-12, a government program. But by 1998–1999, a variety of other lenders were operating within the survey area, including ASA and Proshika.

13. Data on the surveys and household characterisitics are taken from Khandker (2005).

14. In a demonstration of how loosely the targeting rules were taken, Khandker (2005) shows that in 1998–1999, 22 percent of households with over two and a half acres in fact included microfinance borrowers, as was true for 42 percent of households holding between one acre and two and a half acres.

15. Had the eligibility rules been followed to the letter, it would have been possible to apply a regression discontinuity design approach, comparing outcomes of households just below the line to those just above.

16. The equation will then be exactly identified: there is one endogenous variable and just one instrument.

17. Pitt and Khandker (1998) demonstrate that their results are robust to allowing flexibility in the specification for the landholdings variable but do not show results with flexible treatments of other variables.

18. The fact that a man is in a village with no male groups may say something about the unobserved qualities of the men and the strength of their peer networks in that village; so identification relies on the assumption that group structures are exogenous to individuals.

19. In 1991–1992, men borrowed slightly more on average than women from Grameen (15,797 taka for men versus 14,128 taka for women). For BRAC, males cumulatively borrowed 5,842 taka versus 4,711 taka for women; and for BRDB, males borrowed 6,020 taka versus 4,118 taka for women (Morduch 1998).

20. This section draws heavily on Bauchet and Morduch (2009).

21. The treatment here draws on Angrist (2004), Duflo et al. (2007), and Deaton (2009).

22. The fact that "the difference of the expectation is the expectation of the difference" is simply that if, say, you asked a group what their income was last year and you asked them what their income was the year before that, the average change in income for the group could be calculated as either the group's average income change or, equivalently, the group's average income last year minus the group's average income from the year before.

23. The researchers measured the impact of the loans on financial access, household welfare, and profitability for the lender. They used administrative data from the lender, credit bureau data about the randomized applicants, and a household survey conducted 6 to 12 months after the start of the experiment (the experiment lasted 2 months, and the loans were standard 4-month loans).

24. The approval rate came from the study's two randomization windows—approve with 60 percent or 85 percent probability. Ultimately, "due to loan officer noncompliance and/or clerical errors," 332 of the approved applicants did not receive a loan and 5 of the rejected applicants did (Karlan and Zinman 2009a).

25. Duflo et al. (2007) is valuable, and once again we draw from it in this section.

26. This section focuses on how power calculations are used to determine a sample size, pre-study. Power calculations are also used post-study to estimate the level of power obtained with a given sample size.

27. A full treatment is available in Duflo et al. (2007) and Bloom (1995, 2005).

28. See the references on PROGRESA and further discussion (in a different context) in chapter 10.

29. Similar practitioner-friendly tools have been created by USAID's AIMS project and by CGAP.

30. See, for example, Servet (2010) for qualitative discussions and current debates on social indicators and Corporate Social Responsibility (CSR). See de Lutzel (2009) for a discussion of socially oriented investments during the 2008–9 financial crisis, Heal (2008) delivers a comprehensive analysis of social indicators and CSR relevant to microfinance.

10   Subsidy and Sustainability

1. See Martens 2002 for a complementary view.

2. The economic approach to microfinance suggests that ongoing subsidies may be justified in principle, depending on the nature of costs and benefits. Detractors argue (without data) that in practice the costs will surely outweigh the benefits.

3. For example, Consultative Group to Assist the Poorest 1996.

4. Data on Grameen's finances are taken from Morduch 1999c, which draws on data published in Grameen Bank annual reports. The focus is on Grameen Bank here in large part because the bank has been very open in providing easy access to its detailed yearly income statements.

5. Schreiner's doctoral dissertation from Ohio State University develops an alternative framework to consider the cost-effectiveness of microfinance; see Schreiner 2003.

6. The figure equals 18.5 billion baht multiplied by (14.9%–11%).

7. While Grameen is audited by leading accountants in Bangladesh, the audits focus on detecting fraud rather than on placing Grameen's figures into internationally accepted formats. Grameen is chartered as a bank (meaning that it can take deposits) by a special act of the government, and it is not expected to conform to all of the regulations and accounting standards faced by other banks in Bangladesh.

8. Data are from Morduch 1999c. The remaining $4 million of subsidy is from miscellaneous sources.

9. Chapter 9 describes methodological debates over details of some studies, but the overall weight of the evidence suggests that microfinance has helped bring substantial positive change to rural Bangladesh.

10. See also Mark Schreiner (1997, 2003), who presents a framework for considering cost-effectiveness applied to Bolivia's BancoSol and the Grameen Bank. Schreiner argues (based on his own cost analyses and a synthesis of the impact literature) that Grameen's lending has been cost-effective.

11. See chapter 9 for a discussion of debate around these estimates and chapter 7 for a discussion focused on gender.

12. Preliminary results calculated by Morduch show that subsidy rates have fallen by about half between 1991 and 1998, which, if substantiated through additional research, would lead to improved cost-benefit ratios—even though benefits have fallen too.

13. Collecting data on gender empowerment is feasible (see, e.g., Hashemi, Schuler, and Riley 1996). The more difficult step is boiling numbers down to monetary terms.

14. If average benefits were used instead, and if marginal returns diminish with amounts borrowed, the cost-benefit ratio will be overstated (making supporting Grameen more

attractive). But if there are large fixed costs in production technologies, marginal returns may well be higher than average returns, weakening support for Grameen. The econometric structure required for identification in fact rests on the assumption that marginal and average impacts are the same, but this is just an assumption (and not very plausible); Pitt and Khandker interpret the impacts as marginal. As discussed in chapter 9, average impacts estimated with more limited econometric structure are weaker.

15. This section draws heavily on Morduch 1999b, where a mathematical formalization of the arguments is provided.

16. The effect depends on the fundamental economic structure. The view here follows the much-cited model of adverse selection by Stiglitz and Weiss (1981) in which the riskiest borrowers earn the highest expected returns, but de Meza and Webb (1990) derive alternative results by assuming that the riskiest borrowers earn lower expected returns than others.

17. This statement assumes that the institution operates in a perfectly competitive environment. If instead, the microbank made profit, but reduced the profit in start-up stages to cover initial costs, receiving subsidies to cover those costs could be used to increase profit without affecting what the customer is charged. In a sense, one kind of subsidy (from the owners, taken in the form of reduced profit) is substituted for another (external subsidies).

11 Managing Microfinance

1. Jain and Moore (2003) argue the point as well, although some of what they consider good management practices (like regular repayment schemes), we consider to be contract design issues (e.g., see chapter 5).

2. Articles questioning the Grameen Bank's record, notably the *Wall Street Journal* article by Pearl and Phillips (2001), are an exception to generally very positive coverage in the media.

3. The numbers are suggestive only: operational self-sufficiency is a product of costs and revenues, so that poorly managed programs with high fees may still have favorable ratios. Furthmore, Bauchet and Morduch (2010) show that Microfinance Information eXchange data tend to be biased toward sustainability, particularly in comparison with those reported by the Microcredit Summit Campaign.

4. Some microlenders purely pursue profits and happen to operate in the microfinance market niche. Issues around dual objectives are not central for them. The bulk of microlenders, however, are driven to a great extent by social objectives.

5. Robinson's (2001) *The Microfinance Revolution*, a wide-ranging overview published by the World Bank, offers detailed discussions of the problems of excessive subsidies, but just three pages on management issues. This is not meant as a criticism of her book, but as a comment on priorities in the literature on which she draws. Books and articles that focus on management in microfinance include Churchill (1999), Holcombe (1995), Ahmmed (2002), Jain and Moore (2003), and Christen (1997). See also the separate literature on governance issues.

6. In 1989, monthly bonuses were as much as 20–30 percent of base salaries, although the financial incentives were dropped later, to be reintroduced in 1995 (Steege 1998, 43–44).

7. ACCION-style solidarity groups are composed of three to seven members and feature group responsibility for loan repayments.

8. These figures do not reveal problem loans hidden by refinancing.

9. Sharecropping is a contractual arrangement between a landlord and a tenant whereby the landlord provides land and the tenant labor. Output is then divided according to a prespecified formula. When comparing sharecropping with rental contracts, Marshall argued that sharecropping was inefficient because it did not provide the tenant with the appropriate incentives to expend enough effort—as he knew that part of the fruits of any additional labor would accrue to the landlord. Detailed studies on sharecropping abound; see, for example, Cheung 1969, Stiglitz 1974, and the discussion in Ray 1998.

10. By helping microlenders expand scale (by untethering themselves from limited donor funds), pursuing profits can help institutions reach more low-income people. Thus, it has been argued that pursuing profits and reducing poverty are, in general, mutually self-reinforcing. But practitioners have come to see tensions between the depth of outreach to the poor and financial self-sufficiency. This observation is in line with Cull, Demirgüç-Kunt, and Morduch's (2009b) analysis showing that on average, nongovernmental organizations serve poorer clients than nonbank financial institutions and banks, but they face significantly higher operating costs as a percent of loan value. NGOs compensate for these higher relative costs by charging higher interest rates. See Morduch's (2000) discussion of the "microfinance schism" for a critical discussion of the "win-win" vision of profitability and poverty reduction.

11. On the other hand, increasing the number of customers borrowing beyond the $400 loan size could in principle help poorer households indirectly if the microlender chose to cross-subsidize.

12. Holtmann (2001) reports that, more broadly, the main indicators used are: number of loans to first-time borrowers, number and volume of outstanding loans, number and volume of loans disbursed, and portfolio quality. More recently, institutions have also rewarded staff for promoting saving and insurance.

13. The data are from June 2002 and available at www.microrate.com.

14. We are grateful to Oriana Bandiera of the London School of Economics for pointing us to this literature. Gneezy and Rustichini (2000b) consider the case in which fines are levied on activities that had previously only been enforced by social sanctions (e.g., inducing guilt). The specific context they investigate involves parents picking up their children from daycare programs on time. When small fines were imposed for lateness, parents' behavior actually worsened. Gneezy and Rustichini argue that the reason is that "a fine is a price" so that, under the scenario with the fine, parents could pick up their children, pay the fine, and leave with a guiltless conscience. Without the fine, guilt weighed more heavily on parents—and daycare workers were more likely to be able to get home on time.

15. The quote is from González-Vega et al. (1997), 111. Gonzalez-Vega et al. also note that by late 1995, BancoSol was considering introducing a bonus system. The lesson here is that to be successful such systems should provide meaningful rewards and managers should be aware of consequences for the organization's culture.

16. Mark Schreiner, a microfinance consultant and scholar at Washington University in St. Louis, related the following story to us about PRODEM's strong corporate culture: "I remember one Friday night, after a hard day of consulting [at PRODEM], finishing up

work while waiting for some other people to go on home so that I would not be the first to leave. Six o'clock. Seven o'clock. Eight o'clock. Nine. Finally I left at ten."

17. This account draws heavily on personal communication with Don Johnston, a resident advisor to BRI in Jakarta, January 29, 2003. For more on BRI's transformation, see Patten and Rosengard 1991 and Robinson 2001.

18. The theory of yardstick competition is developed by Shleifer (1985) in the context of the cost-minimization problem in monopolies. He draws a parallel to the practice of insurers reimbursing doctors according to the average costs of various procedures, rather than to the doctors' actual costs; the practice gives doctors incentives to reduce their own costs (since they get to keep any savings).

19. Our focus is on cooperatives in which members have full votes in management decisions. The Grameen Bank is formally a cooperative: all borrowers are also members, and a handful of borrowers have seats on the board of directors, but their sway in decision making is effectively limited by their minority status on the board.

References

Abbink, Klaus, Bernd Irlenbusch, and Elke Renner. 2006. "Group size and social ties in microfinance institutions."*Economic Inquiry* 44(4): 614–628.

ACCION International. 2007. "Following up: Replies to remaining Compartamos IPO webcast questions." Accessed December 13, 2008. Available at http://www.accion.org/Page.aspx?pid=713.

Adams, Dale W. 1978. "Mobilizing household savings through rural financial markets." In J. D. von Pischke, Dale W Adams, and Gordon Donald, eds., *Rural Financial Markets in Developing Countries: Their Use and Abuse*. Baltimore: Johns Hopkins University Press.

Adams, Dale W. 1984. "Are the arguments for cheap agricultural credit sound?" In Dale W Adams, Douglas H. Graham, and J. D. von Pischke, eds., *Undermining Rural Development with Cheap Credit*. Boulder, CO: Westview Press.

Adams, Dale W. 1995. "Using credit unions as conduits for micro-enterprise lending: Latin-American insights." Poverty-Oriented Banking working paper no. 12, Enterprise and Cooperative Development Department, International Labor Office, Geneva.

Adams, Dale W, Douglas H. Graham, and J. D. von Pischke, eds. 1984. *Undermining Rural Development with Cheap Credit*. Boulder, CO: Westview Press.

Adams, Dale W, and Linda Mayoux. 2001. "Crossfire." *Small Enterprise Development* 12(1): 4–6.

Adams, Dale W, and J. D. von Pischke. 1992. "Microenterprise credit programs: Déjà vu." *World Development* 20(10): 1463–1470.

Aghion, Philippe, and Patrick Bolton. 1997. "A theory of trickle-down growth and development." *Review of Economic Studies* 64: 151–162.

Aghion, Philippe, Eve Caroli, and Cecilia Garcia-Peñalosa. 1999. "Inequality and economic growth: The perspective of the new growth theories." *Journal of Economic Literature* 37(4): 1615–1660.

Ahlin, Christian. 2009. "Matching for credit: Risk diversification in Thai microcredit groups." Michigan State University Working Paper.

Ahlin, Christian, and Neville Jiang. 2008. "Can micro-credit bring development?" *Journal of Development Economics* 86(1): 1–21.

Ahlin, Christian, and Jocelyn Lin. 2006. "Luck or skill? MFI performance in macroeconomic context." BREAD working paper No. 132.

Ahlin, Christian, and Robert Townsend. 2007a. "Selection into and across credit contracts: Theory and field research." *Journal of Econometrics* 136(2): 665–698.

Ahlin, Christian, and Robert Townsend. 2007b. "Using repayment data to test across models of joint liability lending." *Economic Journal* 117(517) (February): F11–F51.

Ahmmed, Mostaq. 2002. *Key to Achieving Sustainability: Simple and Standard Microfinance Services of ASA.* Dhaka: ASA.

Akerlof, George. 1970. "The market for lemons: Quality uncertainty and the market mechanism." *Quarterly Journal of Economics* 84 (August): 488–500.

Aleem, Irfan. 1990. "Imperfect information, screening, and the costs of informal lending: A study of a rural credit market in Pakistan." *World Bank Economic Review* 4(3): 329–349.

Alexander, Gwen. 2001. "An empirical analysis of microfinance: Who are the clients?" Paper presented at 2001 Northeastern Universities Development Consortium Conference.

Allen, Treb, Beatriz Armendáriz, Dean Karlan, and Sendhil Mullainathan. 2010. "Inviting husbands into women-only solidarity groups: Evidence from southern Mexico. Typescript. IPA–Harvard–University College London research paper (forthcoming).

Anderson, Siwan, and Jean-Marie Baland. 2002. "The economics of ROSCAs and intrahousehold allocation." *Quarterly Journal of Economics,* 117(3): 983–995.

Anderson, Siwan, Jean-Marie Baland, and Karl Ove Moene. 2009. "Enforcement in informal savings groups." *Journal of Development Economics* 90(1): 14–23.

Ando, Albert, and Franco Modigliani. 1963. "The life-cycle hypothesis of saving: Aggregate implications and tests." *American Economic Review* 53: 55–84.

Angrist, Joshua D. 2004. "American education research changes tack." *Oxford Review of Economic Policy* 20(2): 198–212.

Angrist, Joshua D., and Guido Imbens. 1994. "Identification and estimation of local average treatment effects." *Econometrica* 62(2): 467–476.

Angrist, Joshua D., and Jörn-Steffen Pischke. 2009. *Mostly Harmless Econometrics: An Empiricist's Companion.* Princeton, NJ: Princeton University Press.

Aportela, Fernando. 1999. "Effects of financial access on savings by low-income people." MIT Department of Economics Dissertation Chapter 1.

Ardener, Shirley. 1964. "The comparative study of rotating credit associations." *Journal of the Royal Anthropological Institute* 94(2): 201–229.

Armendáriz, Beatriz. 1999a. "On the design of a credit agreement with peer monitoring." *Journal of Development Economics* 60: 79–104.

Armendáriz, Beatriz. 1999b. "Development banking." *Journal of Development Economics* 58 (February): 83–100.

Armendáriz, Beatriz. 2002. "A theory of credit unions." Harvard University Department of Economics Working Paper.

Armendáriz, Beatriz. 2009. "Microfinance in industrialized countries: Contrasting Crédal in Belgium with Adie in France." Typescript. Solvay Brussels School of Economics and Management, Université Libre de Bruxelles, Belgium.

Armendáriz, Beatriz. 2010. "Women and microsavings." In Beatriz Armendáriz and Marc Labie, eds., *The Handbook of Microfinance*. London: World Scientific Publishing, forthcoming.

Armendáriz, Beatriz, and Christian Gollier. 2000. "Peer group formation in an adverse selection model." *The Economic Journal* 110(465) (July): 632–643.

Armendáriz, Beatriz, and Marc Labie, eds. *The Handbook of Microfinance*. London: World Scientific Publishing, forthcoming.

Armendáriz, Beatriz, and Jonathan Morduch. 2000. "Microfinance beyond group lending." *The Economics of Transition* 8(2): 401–420.

Armendáriz, Beatriz, and Jonathan Morduch. 2004. "Microfinance: Where do we stand?" In Charles Goodhart, ed., *Financial Development and Economic Growth: Explaining the Links*. London: Macmillan/Palgrave.

Armendáriz, Beatriz, and Nigel Roome. 2008a. "Gender empowerment in microfinance." In Suresh Sundaresan, ed., *Microfinance: Emerging Trends and Challenges*. New York: Edward Elgar Publishing, Ltd.

Armendáriz, Beatriz, and Nigel Roome. 2008b. "Empowering women via microfinance in fragile states." Working Paper, WP—CEB No 08–001.RS. Centre Emile Bernheim, Brussels Solvay Business School of Economics, Business and Management, Université Libre de Bruxelles, Belgium.

Armendáriz, Beatriz, and Ariane Szafarz. 2009. "On mission drift in microfinance institutions." Working Paper, WP–CEB No. 09-05. Centre Emile Bernheim, Brussels Solvay Business School of Economics, Business and Management, Université Libre de Bruxelles, Belgium.

Armendáriz, Beatriz, and Annabel Vanroose. 2009. "Uncovering three microfinance myths: Does age matter?" *Reflets et perspectives de la vie économique*, Tome XLVIII(3): 7–17.

Arrow, Kenneth. 1963. "Uncertainty and the welfare economics of medical care." *American Economic Review* 53(5): 941–967.

Aryeetey, Ernest, and William Steel. 1995. "Savings collectors and financial intermediation in Ghana." *Savings and Development* 19(2): 189–199.

Ashraf, Nava. 2009. "Spousal control and intra-household decision making: An experimental study in the Philippines." *American Economic Review* 99(4): 1245–1277.

Ashraf, Nava, Dean Karlan, and Wesley Yin. 2006. "Tying Odysseus to the mast: Evidence from a commitment savings product in the Philippines."*Quarterly Journal of Economics* 121(2): 673–697.

Ashraf, Nava, Dean Karlan, and Wesley Yin. 2008. "Female empowerment: Impact of a commitment savings product in the Philippines." Yale University Working Paper.

Balkin, Steven. 1989. *Self-Employment and Low-Income People*. New York: Praeger.

Banerjee, Abhijit. 2004. "The two poverties." In Stefan Dercon, ed., *Insurance Against Poverty*. Oxford: Oxford University Press.

Banerjee, Abhijit, Timothy Besley, and Timothy Guinnane. 1994. "Thy neighbor's keeper: The design of a credit cooperative with theory and a test." *Quarterly Journal of Economics* 109(2) (May): 491–515.

Banerjee, Abhijit, and Esther Duflo. 2005. "Growth theory through the lens of development economics." In Philippe Aghion and Steven N. Durlauf, eds., *Handbook of Economic Growth*. Amsterdam: Elsevier.

Banerjee, Abhijit, and Esther Duflo. 2007. "The economic lives of the poor." *Journal of Economic Perspectives* 21: 141–167.

Banerjee, Abhijit, and Esther Duflo. 2008. "Do firms want to borrow more? Testing credit constraints using a direct lending program." Working paper, Department of Economics, MIT.

Banerjee, Abhijit, and Esther Duflo. 2009. "The experimental approach to development economics." *Annual Review of Economics* 1: 151–178.

Banerjee, Abhijit, Esther Duflo, Rachel Glennerster, and Cynthia Kinnan. 2009. "The micracle of microfinance? Evidence from a randomized evaluation." MIT Department of Economics and Abdul Latif Jameel Poverty Action Lab (J-Pal) Working Paper.

Banerjee, Abhijit, and Andrew Newman. 1993. "Occupational choice and the process of development." *Journal of Political Economy* 101: 274–298.

Banerjee, Abhijit, and Andrew Newman. 1994. "Poverty, incentives, and development." *American Economic Review Papers and Proceedings* 84(2) (May): 211–215.

Bangladesh Bureau of Statistics. 1992. *Statistical Pocket Book of Bangladesh 1992*. Dhaka: Government of Bangladesh, Ministry of Planning.

Barnes, Carolyn, Erica Keogh, and Nontokozo Nemarundwe. 2001. "Microfinance program clients and impact: An assessment of Zambuko Trust, Zimbabwe." USAID AIMS Report, October.

Basu, Karna. 2008a. "Hyperbolic discounting and the sustainability of rotational savings arrangements." University of Chicago Working Paper.

Basu, Karna. 2008b. "A behavioral model of simultaneous borrowing and saving." University of Chicago Working Paper.

Basu, Kaushik. 1989. "Rural credit markets: The structure of interest rates, exploitation, and efficiency." In Pranab Bardhan, ed., *The Economic Theory of Agrarian Institutions*. Oxford: Oxford University Press.

Basu, Kaushik. 1997. *Analytical Development Economics: The Less Developed Economy Revisited*. Cambridge, MA: MIT Press.

Bates, Timothy. 1997. *Race, Self-Employment, and Upward Mobility: An Elusive American Dream*. Baltimore: Johns Hopkins University Press.

Bates, Timothy. 2005. "Financing disadvantaged firms." In Patrick Bolton and Howard Rosenthal, eds., *Credit Markets for the Poor*, New York: Russell.

Bauchet, Jonathan, and Jonathan Morduch. 2009. "An introduction to impact evaluations with randomized designs." Financial Access Initiative Framing Note.

Bauchet, Jonathan, and Jonathan Morduch. 2010. "Selective knowledge: Reporting bias in microfinance data." *Perspectives on Global Development and Technology*, forthcoming.

Bauer, Michal, Julie Chytilová, and Jonathan Morduch. 2009. "Behavioral foundations of microcredit: Experimental and survey evidence from rural India." New York University Working Paper.

Baydas, Mayada M., Douglas H. Graham, and Lisa Valenzuela. 1997. "Commercial banks in microfinance: New actors in the microfinance world." USAID Microenterprise Best Practices Report.

Bazoberry, Eduardo. 2001. "We aren't selling vacuum cleaners: PRODEM's experiences with staff incentives." *MicroBanking Bulletin* 6 (April): 11–13.

Beck, Thorsten, Patrick Behr, and André Güttler. 2009. "Are women better loan officers?" Tilburg University, Goethe University Frankfurt, and European Business School Working Paper.

Beck, Thorsten, Asli Demirgüç-Kunt, and Ross Levine. 2007. "Finance, inequality and the poor." *Journal of Economic Growth* 12: 27–49.

Beck, Thorsten, Asli Demirgüç-Kunt, and Maria Soledad Martinez Peria. 2006. "Banking services for everyone? Barriers to bank access and use around the world." World Bank Policy Research Working Paper Series 4079.

Beck, Thorsten, Asli Demirgüç-Kunt, and Maria Soledad Martinez Peria. 2007. "Reaching out: Access to and use of banking services across countries." *Journal of Financial Economics* 85(1): 234–266.

Becker, Gary. 1981. *A Treatise on the Family*. Cambridge, MA: Harvard University Press.

Beegle, Kathleen, Rajeev H. Dehejia, and Roberta Gatti. 2003. "Child labor, crop shocks, and credit constraints." National Bureau of Economic Research Working Paper 10088.

Behrman, Jere R., Robert Pollak, and Paul Taubman. 1982. "Parental preferences and provision for progeny." *Journal of Political Economy* 90(1): 52–73.

Behrman, Jere R. 1988. "Nutrition, health, birth order and seasonality: Intrahousehold allocation in rural India." *Journal of Development Economics* 28(1): 43–63.

Bell, Clive. 1990. "Interactions between institutional and informal credit agencies in rural India." *World Bank Economic Review* 4(3): 297–327.

Bell, Robin, Annie Harper, and Dyson Mandivenga. 2002. "Can commercial banks do microfinance? Lessons from the Commercial Bank of Zimbabwe and the Cooperative Bank of Kenya." *Small Enterprise Development* 13(4) (December).

Benjamin, McDonald, and Joanna Ledgerwood. 1999. "Case studies in microfinance: Albania—Albanian Development Fund." World Bank, Washington, DC, May.

Bennett, Lynn, Mike Goldberg, and Pamela Hunte. 1996. "Ownership and sustainability: Lessons on group-based financial services from South Asia." *Journal of International Development* 8(2): 271–288.

Bergstrom, Theodore C. 1996. "A survey of theories of the family." In Mark Rosenzwerg and Oded Stark, eds., *Handbook of Population and Family Economics*. Amsterdam: North-Holland.

Bertrand, Marianne, Dean Karlan, Sendhil Mullainathan, Eldar Shafir, and Jonathan Zinman. 2008. "What's advertising content worth? Evidence from a consumer credit marketing field experiment." Yale University Economic Growth Center Working Paper.

Besley, Timothy. 1994. "How do market failures justify interventions in rural credit markets?" *World Bank Research Observer* 9(1) (January): 22–47.

Besley, Timothy, and Stephen Coate. 1995. "Group lending, repayment incentives, and social collateral." *Journal of Development Economics* 46(1): 1–18.

Besley, Timothy, Stephen Coate, and Glenn Loury. 1993. "The economics of rotating savings and credit associations." *American Economic Review* 83: 792–810.

Besley, Timothy, and Alec Levenson. 1996. "The role of informal finance in household capital accumulation: Evidence from Taiwan." *Economic Journal* 106 (January): 39–59.

Bewley, Truman. 1976. "The permanent income hypothesis: A theoretical formulation." *Journal of Economic Theory* 16: 252–292.

Bhaduri, Amit. 1973. "A study in agricultural backwardness under semi-feudalism." *Economic Journal* 83: 120–137.

Bhaduri, Amit. 1977. "On the formation of usurious interest rates in backward agriculture." *Cambridge Journal of Economics* 1: 341–352.

Bhagwati, Jagdish. 1988. *Protectionism.* Cambridge, MA: MIT Press.

Binswanger, Hans, and Shahidur Khandker. 1995. "The impact of formal finance on the rural economy in India." *Journal of Development Studies* 32(2) (December): 234–262.

Blanchard, Olivier, and Stanley Fischer. 1989. *Lectures on Macroeconomics.* Cambridge, MA: MIT Press.

Bloom, Howard S. 1995. "Minimum detectable effects: A simple way to report the statistical power of experimental designs." *Evaluation Review* 19: 547–577.

Bloom, Howard S. 2005. "Randomizing groups to evaluate place-based programs." In Howard S. Bloom, ed., *Learning more from social experiments.* New York: Russell Sage.

Blumberg, Rae. 1989. "Entrepreneurship, credit, and gender in the informal sector of the Dominican Republic." In *Women in Development: A.I.D.'s Experience, 1973–1985,* vol. 2. Washington, DC: USAID. Center for Development Information and Evaluation.

Bolton, Patrick, and David Scharfstein. 1990. "A theory of predation based on agency problems in financial contracting." *American Economic Review* 80: 93–106.

Bond, Philip, and Arvind Krishnamurty. 2004. "Regulating exclusion from financial markets." *Review of Economic Studies* 71(3): 581–913.

Bond, Philip, and Ashok Rai. 2009. "Borrower runs." *Journal of Development Economics* 88(2): 185–191.

Boone, Peter. 1996. "Politics and the effectiveness of foreign aid." *European Economic Review* 40(2) (February): 289–329.

Bornstein, David. 1997. *The Price of a Dream: The Story of the Grameen Bank.* Chicago: University of Chicago Press.

Bose, Pinaki. 1998. "Formal-informal sector interaction in rural credit markets." *Journal of Development Economics* 56: 256–280.

Bottomley, Anthony. 1975. "Interest rate determination in underdeveloped areas." *American Journal of Agricultural Economics* 57(2) (May): 279–291.

Boucher, Stephen R., Michael R. Carter, and Catherine Guirkinger. 2008. "Risk rationing and wealth effects in credit markets: Theory and implications for agricultural development." *American Journal of Agricultural Economics* 90(2): 409–423.

Bouman, Fritz. 1977. "Indigenous savings and credit societies in the developing world." *Savings and Development* 1(4): 181–214.

Bouman, Fritz. 1995. "Rotating and accumulating savings and credit associations: A development perspective." *World Development* 23(3): 371–384.

Bourguignon, François. 2001. "Can redistribution accelerate growth and development?" Paper presented at 2000 DELTA—EHESS, ABCDE Conference, Paris.

BRAC. 2008. *Annual Report 2007*. Dhaka: BRAC.

Brambilla, Paola. 2001. "Gender and monitoring: A review of practical experiences." Paper prepared for the Swiss Agency for Development and Co-operation, BRIDGR (Development-gender).

Braverman, Avishay, and Luis Guasch. 1986. "Rural credit markets and institutions in developing countries: Lessons for policy analysis from practice and modern theory." *World Development* 14(10/11) (October/November): 1253–1267.

Braverman, Avishay, and Luis Guasch. 1989. "Institutional analysis of credit cooperatives." In Pranab Bardhan, ed., *The Economic Theory of Agrarian Institutions*. Oxford: Oxford University Press.

Brett, John. 2006. " 'We sacrifice and eat less': The structural complexities of microfinance participation." *Human Organization* 65(1): 8–19.

Brown, Warren, and Craig Churchill. 1999. "Providing insurance to low-income households, part 1: A primer on insurance principles and products." Microenterprise Best Practices Project. Bethesda, MD: DAI/USAID. Available at www.usaidmicro.org/pubs/mbp-res.asp#npm.

Brown, Warren, and Craig Churchill. 2000. "Providing insurance to low-income households, part 2: Initial lessons from micro-insurance experiments for the poor." Microenterprise Best Practices Project. Bethesda, MD: DAI/USAID. Available at www.usaidmicro.org/pubs/mbp-res.asp#npm.

Browning, Martin, and Pierre-André Chiappori. 1998. "Efficient intrahousehold allocation: A general characterization and empirical test." *Econometrica* 66(6): 1241–1278.

Browning, Martin, and Annamaria Lusardi. 1996. "Household saving: Micro theories and micro facts." *Journal of Economic Literature* 34(4): 1797–1855.

Bulow, Jeremy, and Kenneth Rogoff. 1989a. "A constant recontracting model of sovereign debt." *Journal of Political Economy* 97(1) (February): 155–178.

Bulow, Jeremy, and Kenneth Rogoff. 1989b. "Sovereign debt: Is to forgive to forget?" *American Economic Review* 79(1) (March): 43–50.

Burgess, Robin, and Rohini Pande. 2005. "Do rural banks matter? Evidence from the Indian social banking experiment."*American Economic Review* 95(3) (June): 780–795.

Calomiris, Charles, and Indira Rajaraman. 1998. "The role of ROSCAs: Lumpy durables or event insurance?" *Journal of Development Economics* 56: 207–216.

Carter, Michael, Francisco Galarza, and Stephen Boucher. 2007. "Underwriting area-based yield insurance to crowd-in credit supply and demand." UC Davis Working paper 07-003. Giannini Foundation of Agricultural Economics.

Centre for the Study of Financial Innovation (CSFI). 2008. "Microfinance banana skins 2008: Risk in a booming industry." New York: CSFI.

Chamberlain, E. H. 1933. *The Theory of Monopolistic Competition*. Cambridge, MA: Harvard University Press.

Charness, Gary, and Garance Genicot. 2007. "Informal risk sharing in an infinite-horizon experiment." University of California, Santa Barbara and Georgetown University Working Paper.

Chattopadhyay, Raghabenda, and Esther Duflo. 2004. "Women as policy makers: Evidence from a randomized policy experiment in India." *Econometrica* 72(5): 1409–1443.

Chaudhury, Iftekhar A., and Imran Matin. 2002. "Dimensions and dynamics of microfinance membership overlap: A micro study from Bangladesh." *Small Enterprise Development* 13(2): 46–55.

Cheston, Susy, and Larry Reed. 1999. "Measuring transformation: Assessing and improving the impact of microcredit." *Journal of Microfinance* 1(1) (Fall): 20–43.

Cheung, S. N. S. 1969. *The Theory of Share Tenancy*. Chicago: University of Chicago Press.

Christen, Robert Peck. 1997. *Banking Services for the Poor: Managing for Financial Success*. Washington, DC: ACCION.

Christen, Robert Peck, and Deborah Drake. 2002. "Commercialization: The new reality of microfinance." In Deborah Drake and Elizabeth Rhyne, eds., *The Commercialization of Microfinance*. Bloomfield, CT: Kumarian Press.

Christen, Robert Peck, Timothy R. Lyman, and Richard Rosenberg. 2003. "Microfinance consensus guidelines: Guiding principles on regulation and supervision of microfinance." Washington, DC: CGAP/World Bank.

Churchill, Craig. 1999. *Client-Focused Lending: The Art of Individual Lending*. Toronto: Calmeadow.

Churchill, Craig, and Cheryl Frankewicz. 2006. *Making Microfinance Work*. Geneva: International Labor Office.

Clarke, George R. G., Lixin Colin Xu, and Heng-fu Zou. 2006. "Finance and income inequality: What do the data tell us?" *Southern Economic Journal* 72(3): 578–596.

Cohen, Jacob. 1988. *Statistical Power Analysis for the Behavioral Sciences*, Second Edition. Hillsdale, NJ: Erlbaum.

Cohen, Monique, and Jennefer Sebstad. 2003. "Reducing vulnerability: The demand for microinsurance." MicroSave-Africa Report, March.

Cole, Shawn A., and Gauri Kartini Shastry. 2008. "If you are so smart, why aren't you rich? The effects of education, financial literacy, and cognitive ability on financial market participation." Harvard Business School Working Paper 09-071.

Coleman, Brett. 1999. "The impact of group lending in northeast Thailand." *Journal of Development Economics* 60: 105–142.

Coleman, Brett. 2006. "Microfinance in northeast Thailand: Who benefits and how much?" *World Development* 34(9): 1612–1638.

Collins, Daryl, Jonathan Morduch, Stuart Rutherford, and Orlanda Ruthven. 2009. *Portfolios of the Poor: How the World's Poor Live on $2 a Day*. Princeton: Princeton University Press.

Conning, Jonathan. 1999. "Outreach, sustainability and leverage in monitored and peer-monitored lending." *Journal of Development Economics* 60: 51–77.

Conning, Jonathan. 2005. "Monitoring by delegates or by peers: Joint liability loans under moral hazard." Hunter College Department of Economics Working Paper.

Conning, Jonathan. 2008. " 'Ventas piratas': Product market competition and the depth of lending relationships: rural credit in Chile following trade liberalization." Hunter College Department of Economics Working Paper.

Conning, Jonathan, and Jonathan Morduch. 2007. "Social finance." New York University Working Paper.

Conning, Jonathan, and Christopher Udry. 2007. "Rural financial markets." In Robert Evenson, Prabhu Pingali, and T. Paul Schultz, eds., *Handbook of Agricultural Economics*, Vol. 3. Amsterdam: North-Holland.

Consultative Group to Assist the Poorest (CGAP). 1996. "Microcredit interest rates." *Occasional Paper*, Number 1, August.

Consultative Group to Assist the Poorest (CGAP). 2000. "Exploring client preferences in microfinance: Some observations from *Safe*Save." Focus Note 18, Washington DC.

Consultative Group to Assist the Poorest (CGAP). 2002. "Microcredit interest rates." Occasional Paper 1, revised. Washington, DC: CGAP.

Consultative Group to Assist the Poor (CGAP). 2003. "Microfinance consensus guidelines: Definitions of selected financial terms, ratios, and adjustments for microfinance." Washington, DC: CGAP/World Bank.

Consultative Group to Assist the Poor (CGAP). 2008a. "Foreign capital investment in microfinance." Washington, DC: CGAP.

Consultative Group to Assist the Poor (CGAP). 2008b. "MIV survey benchmarks 2008." Washington, DC: CGAP.

Consultative Group to Assist the Poor (CGAP). 2009. "Microfinance funds continue to grow despite the crisis." CGAP Brief, April. Washington, DC: CGAP

Counts, Alex. 2008. *Small Loans, Big Dreams: How Nobel Prize Winner Muhammad Yunus and Microfinance are Changing the World*. Hoboken, NJ: John Wiley & Sons.

Cull, Robert, Asli Demirgüç-Kunt, and Jonathan Morduch. 2007. "Financial performance and outreach: A global analysis of leading microbanks." *Economic Journal* 117(517): F107–F133.

Cull, Robert, Asli Demirgüç-Kunt, and Jonathan Morduch. 2008. "Banks and microbanks." World Bank and Financial Access Initiative Working Paper, November. Washington, DC: World Bank.

Cull, Robert, Asli Demirgüç-Kunt, and Jonathan Morduch. 2009a. "Does regulatory supervison curtail microfinance profitability and outreach?" World Bank Policy Research Working Paper. Washington, DC: World Bank.

Cull, Robert, Asli Demirgüç-Kunt, and Jonathan Morduch. 2009b. "Microfinance meets the market." *Journal of Economic Perspectives* 23(1) (Winter): 167–192.

Daley-Harris, Sam. 2007. *State of the Microcredit Summit Campaign Report 2007.* Washington, DC: Microcredit Summit.

Daley-Harris, Sam. 2009. *State of the Microcredit Summit Campaign Report 2009.* Washington: Microcredit Summit.

Das, Jishnu, Jeffrey Hammer, and Kenneth Leonard. 2008. "The quality of medical advice in low-income countries." *Journal of Economic Perspectives* 22(2) (Spring): 93–114.

David, Cristina. 1984. "Credit and price policies in Philippine agriculture." In Dale W Adams, Douglas H. Graham, and J. D. von Pischke, eds., *Undermining Rural Development with Cheap Credit.* Boulder, CO: Westview Press.

Dawkins-Scully, Nan. 1997. "Micro-credit no panacea for poor women." Available at www.developmentgap.org/micro.html.

Deaton, Angus. 1992. *Understanding Consumption.* Oxford: Clarendon Press.

Deaton, Angus. 1997. *The Analysis of Household Surveys: A Microeconometric Approach to Development Policy.* Baltimore: Johns Hopkins University Press.

Deaton, Angus. 2009. "Instruments of development: Randomization in the tropics, and the search for the elusive keys to economic development." National Bureau of Economic Research Working Paper 14690.

Dehejia, Rajeev, and Sadek Wahba. 1999. "Causal effects in non-experimental studies: Re-evaluating the evaluation of training programs." *Journal of the American Statistical Association* 94(448): 1053–1062.

Dehejia, Rajeev, Heather Montgomery, and Jonathan Morduch. 2009. "Do interest rates matter? Credit demand in the Dhaka slums." NYU Wagner Graduate School and Financial Access Initiative Working Paper.

de Janvry, Alain, Craig McIntosh, and Elisabeth Sadoulet. 2008. "The supply- and demand-side impacts of credit market information." University of California-Berkeley and University of California-San Diego Working Paper.

de Lutzel, Emmanuel. 2009. "Paradox et defies de la microfinance; une industrie qui résiste à la crise, une nouvelle classe d'actifs." In *Rapport sur l'argent dans le monde.* Paris: Association d'Economie Financière.

de Mel, Suresh, David McKenzie, and Christopher M. Woodruff. 2008. "Returns to capital in microenterprises: Evidence from a field experiment." *Quarterly Journal of Economics* 123(4): 1329–1372.

de Mel, Suresh, David McKenzie, and Christopher M. Woodruff. 2009a. "Are women more credit constrained? Experimental evidence on gender and microenterprise returns." *American Economic Journal: Applied Economics* 1(3): 1–32.

de Mel, Suresh, David McKenzie, and Christopher M. Woodruff. 2009b. "Measuring microenterprise profits: Must we ask how the sausage is made?" *Journal of Development Economics* 88(1): 19–31.

De Meza, David, and David Webb. 1987. "Too much investment: A problem of asymmetric information." *Quarterly Journal of Economics* 102 (May): 281–292.

De Meza, David, and David Webb. 1990. "Risk, adverse selection, and capital market failure." *Economic Journal* 100(399): 206–214.

De Meza, David, and David Webb. 2001. "Saving eliminates credit rationing." LSE Financial Markets Group Discussion Paper 391.

Demirgüç-Kunt, Asli, Thurston Beck, and Patrick Honohan. 2007. "Finance for all?: Policies and pitfalls in expanding access." World Bank Policy Research Report. Washington, DC: World Bank.

Dercon, Stefan. 1999. "Income risk, coping strategies, and safety nets." Background paper for World Bank, *World Development Report 2000/2001: Attacking Poverty*. Washington, DC: World Bank.

Dercon, Stefan. 2004. "Risk, insurance, and poverty: A review." In Stefan Dercon, ed., *Insurance Against Poverty*. Oxford: Oxford University Press.

Dercon, Stefan, and John Hoddinott. 2004. "Health, shocks, and poverty persistence." In Stefan Dercon, ed., *Insurance Against Poverty*. Oxford: Oxford University Press.

De Soto, Hernando. 2000. *The Mystery of Capital: Why Capitalism Triumphs in the West and Fails Everywhere Else*. New York: Basic Books.

Dewatripont, Mathias, Ian Jewitt, and Jean Tirole. 1999. "The economics of career concerns, part II: Application to missions and accountability of government agencies." *Review of Economic Studies* 66(1), Special Issue (Contracts): 199–217.

Dewatripont, Mathias, and Jean Tirole. 1994. *The Prudential Regulation of Banks*. Cambridge, MA: MIT Press.

Diagne, Aliou. 1997. "Default incentives, peer pressure, and equilibrium outcomes in group-based lending programs." International Food Policy Research Institute Working Paper, Washington, DC.

Dowla, Asif, and Dipal Barua. 2006. *The Poor Always Pay Back: The Grameen II Story*. Bloomfield, CT: Kumarian Press.

Drake, Deborah, and Elisabeth Rhyne, eds. 2002. *The Commercialization of Microfinance: Balancing Business and Development*. Bloomfield, CT: Kumarian Press.

Duflo, Esther, Rachel Glennerster, and Michael Kremer. 2007. "Using randomization in development economics research: A toolkit." In T. Paul Schultz and John Strauss, eds., *Handbook of Development Economics*, Vol. 4. Amsterdam: North-Holland.

Duflo, Esther, Michael Kremer, and Jonathan Robinson. 2006. "Understanding technology adoption: Fertilizer in Western Kenya. Evidence from field experiments." J-Pal Massachusetts Institute of Technology Working Paper.

Dunford, Christopher. 2001. "Building better lives: Sustainable integration of microfinance and education in health, family planning and HIV/AIDS prevention for the poorest entrepreneurs." *Journal of Microfinance* 3(2): 1–25.

Dunn, Elizabeth. 2002. "Research strategy for the AIMS core assessments." AIMS working paper. Available at www.mip.org/componen/aims/publications.htm.

Dupas, Pascaline, and Jonathan Robinson. 2008. "Savings constraints and microenterprise development: Evidence from a field experiment in Kenya." University of California, Los Angeles and University of California, Santa Cruz Working Paper.

Duraisamy, Paul. 1992. "Gender, intrafamily allocation of resources and child schooling in South India." Working Paper 667, Economic Growth Center, Yale University.

Easterly, William. 2006. *The White Man's Burden: Why the West's Efforts to Aid the Rest Have Done So Much Ill and So Little Good.* New York: Penguin.

Emran, M. Shahe, A. K. M. Mahbub Morshed, and Joseph E. Stiglitz. 2007. "Microfinance and missing markets." George Washington University, Working Paper.

Engle, Patrice. 1993. "Influences of mothers' and fathers' income on children's nutritional status in Guatemala." *Social Science and Medicine* 37: 1303–1312.

Espisu, E., G. Nasubo, M. Obuya, and K. Kioka. 1995. *Lending through Chikola Groups: Four Years of Experience.* Kenya Rural Enterprise Evaluation Report No. 28, Nairobi, Kenya.

Evenson, Robert, Barry Popkin, and Elizabeth King-Quizon. 1980. "Nutrition, work and demographic behaviour in rural Philippine households: A synopsis of several Laguna household studies." In H. Binswanger, R. Evenson, C. Florencio, and B. White, eds., *Rural Household Studies in Asia.* Singapore: Singapore University Press.

Fafchamps, Marcel. 2004. *Rural Poverty, Risk and Development.* Cheltenham: Edward Elgar.

Feder, Gershon, Tongroj Onchan, and Tejaswi Raparla. 1988. "Collateral guarantees and rural credit in developing countries: Evidence from Asia." *Agricultural Economics* 2: 231–245.

Fernando, Nimal, and Richard Meyer. 2002. "ASA—The Ford Motor model of microfinance." *ADB Finance for the Poor* 3(2): 1–3. Manila: Asian Development Bank.

Field, Erica, and Rohini Pande. 2008. "Repayment frequency and default in microfinance: Evidence from India." *Journal of the European Economic Association* 6(2–3): 501–509.

Field, Erica, and Maximo Torero. 2006. "Do property titles increase credit access among the urban poor? Evidence from a nationwide titling program." Harvard University Department of Economics Working Paper.

Fischer, Greg. 2008. "Contract structure, risk sharing and investment choice." Institute for Financial Management and Research Centre for Micro Finance Working Paper 24.

Fischer, Greg, and Maitreesh Ghatak. 2010. "Spanning the chasm: Uniting theory and empirics in microfinance research." In Beatriz Armendáriz and Marc Labie, eds., *The Handbook of Microfinance.* London: Scientific World Publishing, forthcoming.

Floro, María, and Debraj Ray. 1997. "Vertical links between formal and informal financial institutions." *Review of Development Economics* 1(1): 34–56.

Floro, María, and Pan Yotopoulos. 1990. *Informal Credit Markets and the New Institutional Economics: The Case of Philippine Agriculture.* Boulder, CO: Westview Press.

Folbre, Nancy. 1984. "Household production in the Philippines: A non-neoclassical approach." *Economic Development and Cultural Change* 32(2): 303–330.

Forster, Sarah, and Xavier Reillie. 2008. "Foreign capital investment in microfinance: Balancing social and financial returns." CGAP Focus Note 44. Washington, DC: World Bank.

Frank, Christina. 2008. "Stemming the tide of mission drift: Microfinance transformation and the double bottom line." Women's World Banking Focus Note.

Freixas, Xavier, and Jean-Charles Rochet. 2008. *Microeconomics of Banking*, Second Edition. Cambridge, MA: MIT Press.

Fudenberg, Drew, and Eric Maskin. 1986. "The folk theorem in repeated games with discounting or with incomplete information." *Econometrica* 54: 533–556.

Fuentes, Gabriel. 1996. "The use of village agents in rural credit delivery." *Journal of Development Studies* 33(2): 188–209.

Fugelsang, Andreas, and Dale Chandler. 1993. *Participation as a Process—What We Can Learn from Grameen Bank, Bangladesh*, rev. ed. Dhaka: Grameen Trust.

Funk, Steven. 2007. "Remarks by Steven Funk, founder and member of the Dignity Fund Board." *Microcredit Summit E-News* 5(1) (July).

Galor, Oded, and Joseph Zeira. 1993. "Income distribution and macroeconomics." *Review of Economic Studies* 60: 35–52.

Genicot, Garance, and Debraj Ray. 2003. "Group formation in risk-sharing arrangements." *Review of Economic Studies* 70: 87–113.

Gertler, Paul, and Jonathan Gruber. 2002. "Insuring consumption against illness." *American Economic Review* 92(1): 51–70.

Ghatak, Maitreesh. 1999. "Group lending, local information and peer selection." *Journal of Development Economics* 60(1) (October): 27–50.

Ghatak, Maitreesh. 2000. "Screening by the company you keep: Joint liability lending and the peer selection effect." *Economic Journal* 110(465) (July): 601–631.

Ghatak, Maitreesh, and Timothy Guinnane. 1999. "The economics of lending with joint liability: Theory and practice." *Journal of Development Economics* 60(1) (October): 195–228.

Ghosh, Parikshit, and Debraj Ray. 1999. "Information and repeated interaction: Application to informal credit markets." Boston University mimeo.

Ghosh, Suman, and Eric Van Tassel. 2008. "A model of mission drift in microfinance institutions." Florida Atlantic University Working Paper.

Gibbons, David, ed. 1994. *The Grameen Reader*, 2nd ed. Dhaka: Grameen Bank.

Gibbons, David, and S. Kasim. 1991. *Banking on the Rural Poor*. Center for Policy Research, University Sains, Malaysia.

Gibbons, Peter, ed. 1995. *Structural Adjustment and the Working Poor in Zimbabwe*. Uppsala, Sweden: Nordiska Afrikainstitutet.

Gibbons, Robert. 2005. "Incentives between firms (and within)." *Management Science* 51: 2–17.

Giné, Xavier, Pamela Jakiela, Dean Karlan, and Jonathan Morduch. 2009. "Microfinance games." World Bank Working Paper.

Giné, Xavier, and Dean Karlan. 2008. "Peer monitoring and enforcement: Long term evidence from microcredit lending groups with and without group liability." Yale University Economic Growth Center Working Paper.

Giné, Xavier, Robert Townsend, and James Vickrey. 2007. "Patterns of rainfall insurance participation in rural India." World Bank Policy Research Working Paper 4408.

Giné, Xavier, and Dean Yang. 2008. "Insurance, credit, and technology adoption: Field experimental evidence from Malawi." World Bank Policy Research Working Paper 4425.

Glewwe, Paul, Michael Kremer, Sylvie Moulin, and Eric Zitzewitz. 2004. "Retrospective vs. prospective analyses of school inputs: The case of flip charts in Kenya." *Journal of Development Economics* 74(1): 251–268.

Gneezy, Uri, and Aldo Rustichini. 2000a. "Pay enough or don't pay at all." *Quarterly Journal of Economics* 115(3) (August): 791–810.

Gneezy, Uri, and Aldo Rustichini. 2000b. "A fine is a price." *Journal of Legal Studies* 29: 1–18.

Godel, Moritz Emmanuel. 2003. "Goals, tasks and incentives in microfinance institutions." M.Phil. diss., University College London.

Goetz, Anne Marie, and Rina Sen Gupta. 1996. "Who takes the credit? Gender, power, and control over loan use in rural credit programs in Bangladesh." *World Development* 24(1): 45–63.

Goldsmith, Raymond W. 1969. *Financial Structure and Development*. New Haven: Yale University Press.

Gómez, Rafael, and Eric Santor. 2003. "Do peer group members outperform individual borrowers? A test of peer group lending using Canadian micro-credit data." Bank of Canada Working Paper 2003–33, October.

Gonzalez, Adrian, and Richard Rosenberg. 2006. "The state of microfinance—Outreach, profitability, and poverty (findings from a database of 2600 microfinance institutions)." Presentation at World Bank Conference on Access to Finance, May 30, 2006.

González-Vega, Claudio. 1984. "Credit rationing behavior of agricultural lenders: The iron law of interest rate restrictions." In Dale W Adams, Douglas H. Graham, and J. D. von Pischke, eds., *Undermining Rural Development with Cheap Credit*. Boulder, CO: Westview Press.

González-Vega, Claudio, Mark Schreiner, Richard L. Meyer, Jorge Rodriguez-Meza, and Sergio Navajas. 1997. "An Ohio State primer on microfinance in Bolivia." Manuscript, Rural Finance Program, Department of Agricultural Economics, The Ohio State University.

González-Vega, Claudio, and Marcelo Villafani-Ibarnegaray. 2007. "Las microfinanzas en la profundización del sistema financiero: El caso de Bolivia." *El Trimestre Económico* LXXIV(293) (January–March): 5–65.

Grameen Bank. n.d. *Grameen Bank By-Laws (updated version)*. Reprinted as Annexure 1 of David Gibbons, ed., *The Grameen Reader*, 2nd ed., 1994. Dhaka: Grameen Bank.

Grameen Bank. 1996. *Annual Report 1995*. Dhaka: Grameen Bank.

Grameen Bank. 2001. *Annual Report 2000*. Dhaka: Grameen Bank.

Grameen Bank. 2002. *Annual Report 2001*. Dhaka: Grameen Bank.

Grameen Bank. 2003. "Grameen Bank Monthly Update." December 2002, Issue Number 276, January 25, 2003, Dhaka.

Grameen Bank. 2008a. "Grameen Bank Monthly Update." December 2007, Issue Number 336, January 13, 2008, Dhaka.

Grameen Bank. 2008b. "Grameen Bank Monthly Update." September 2008, Issue Number 345, October 11, 2008, Dhaka.

Grammling, Mattias, and Martin Holtmann. 2008. "The role of staff incentive schemes in balancing social and financial goals—Evidence from four MFIs." Washington, DC: MFN and CGAP.

Guérin, Isabelle. 2010. "The gender of finance and lessons for microfinance," in Beatriz Armendáriz and Marc Labie, eds., *The Handbook of Microfinance*. London: World Scientific Publishing, forthcoming.

Gugerty, Mary Kay. 2007. "You can't save alone: Commitment in rotating savings and credit associations in Kenya." *Economic Development and Cultural Change* 55: 251–282.

Guinnane, Timothy. 2002. "Delegated monitors, large and small: Germany's banking system, 1800–1914." *Journal of Economic Literature* 40(1): 73–124.

Gul, Faruk, and Wolfgang Pesendorfer. 2004. "Self-control and the theory of consumption." *Econometrica* 72(1): 119–158.

Gurley, John G., and E. S. Shaw. 1955. "Financial aspects of economic development." *American Economic Review* 45(4): 515–538.

Hadi, Abdullahel. 1997. "The NGO intervention and women's empowerment—The Bangladesh experience." Manuscript, International Seminar on Women's Empowerment, Department of Demography, Stockholm University.

Hansmann, Henry. 1996. *The Ownership of Enterprise*. Cambridge, MA: Harvard University Press.

Harper, Malcolm. 2002. "Grameen Bank groups and self-help groups: What are the differences?" Draft report.

Hart, Oliver. 1995. *Firms, Contracts, and Financial Structure* (Clarendon Lectures in Economics). Oxford: Oxford University Press.

Hart, Oliver, and John Moore. 1998. "Cooperatives vs. outside ownership." Working Paper No. 1816, Harvard Institute of Economic Research.

Hartarska, Valentina. 2005. "Governance and performance of microfinance institutions in Central and Eastern Europe and the Newly Independent States." *World Development* 33(10): 1627–1643.

Hartarska, Valentina, and Denis Nadolnyak. 2007. "Do regulated microfinance institutions achieve better sustainability and outreach?" *Applied Economics* 39: 1207–1222.

Hartarska, Valentina, and Denis Nadolnyak. 2008. "Does rating help microfinance institutions raise funds? Cross-country evidence." *International Review of Economics and Finance* 17: 558–571.

Haseen, Farhana, and Munshi Sulaiman. 2007. "How sustainable is the gain in food consumption of the CFPR/TUP beneficiaries?" CFPR/TUP Working Paper 18.

Hashemi, Syed M. 1997. "Those left behind: A note on targeting the hardcore poor." In Geoffrey Wood and Iffath Sharif, eds., *Who Needs Credit? Poverty and Finance in Bangladesh*. Dhaka: University Press Ltd.

Hashemi, Syed M. 2001. "Linking microfinance and safety net programs to include the poorest: The case of IGVGD in Bangladesh." *CGAP Focus Note* No. 21, May.

Hashemi, Syed M., Sidney Ruth Schuler, and Ann P. Riley. 1996. "Rural credit programs and women's empowerment in Bangladesh." *World Development* 24(4): 635–653.

Hazell, Peter. 1992. "The appropriate role of agricultural insurance in developing countries." *Journal of International Development* 4: 567–581.

Heal, Geoffrey. 2008. *When Principles Pay: Corporate Social Responsibility and the Bottom Line*. New York, NY: Columbia University Press.

Heckman, James J., and Jeffrey A. Smith. 1995. "Assessing the case for social experiments." *Journal of Economic Perspectives* 9(2) (Spring): 85–110.

Hirschland, Madeline. 2003. "Serving small depositors: Overcoming the obstacles, recognizing the trade-offs." *MicroBanking Bulletin* 9 (July): 3–8.

Hoff, Karla, and Joseph Stiglitz. 1998. "Moneylenders and bankers: Price increasing subsidies in a monopolistically competitive market." *Journal of Development Economics* 55(2): 485–518.

Holcombe, Susan. 1995. *Managing to Empower: The Grameen Bank's Experience with Poverty Alleviation*. Dhaka: University Press Ltd., and London: Zed Books.

Holmstrom, Bengt, and Paul Milgrom. 1991. "Multi-task principal-agent analysis: Incentive contracts, asset ownership, and job design." *Journal of Law, Economics and Organization* 7: 24–52.

Holtmann, Martin. 2001. "Designing financial incentives to increase loan officer productivity: Handle with care!" *MicroBanking Bulletin* (April): 5–10.

Hossain, Mahabub. 1988. *Credit for Alleviation of Rural Poverty: The Grameen Bank of Bangladesh*. Institute Research Report 65, February. Washington, DC: International Food Policy Research.

Hudon, Marek. 2007. "Fair interest rates when lending to the poor." *Ethics and Economics* 5(1): 1–8.

Hulme, David. 1991. "The Malawi Mudzi Fund: Daughter of Grameen." *Journal of International Development* 3(4): 427–432.

Hulme, David, and Paul Mosely. 1997. "Finance for the poor or the poorest? Financial innovation, poverty and vulnerability." In Geoffrey Wood and Iffath Sharif, eds., *Who Needs Credit? Poverty and Finance in Bangladesh*. London: Zed Books, and Dhaka: University Press Ltd.

Imbens, Guido W., and Joshua D. Angrist. 1994. "Identification and estimation of local average treatment effects." *Econometrica* 62(2): 467–475.

Ivatury, Gautam, and Ignacio Mas. 2008. "The early experience with branchless banking." CGAP Focus Note 46.

Jain, Pankaj, and Mick Moore. 2003. "What makes microcredit effective? Fashionable fallacies and workable realities." IDS Working Paper No. 177, University of Sussex, January.

Jain, Sanjay. 1998. "The interaction of formal and informal credit markets in developing countries: Symbiosis versus crowding out." *Journal of Development Economics* 59: 419–444.

Jain, Sanjay, and Ghazala Mansuri. 2003. "A little at a time: The use of regularly scheduled repayments in microfinance programs." *Journal of Development Economics* 72(1) (October): 253–279.

Jalan, Jyotsna, and Martin Ravallion. 1999. "Are the poor less well insured? Evidence on vulnerability to income risk in rural China." *Journal of Development Economics* 58(1): 61–81.

Janaux, Laure, and Venet Baptiste. 2009. "Individual microcredit and social pressure." Typescript, Université Paris-Dauphine, France.

Johnston, Don Jr., and Jonathan Morduch. 2008. "The unbanked: Evidence from Indonesia." *World Bank Economic Review* 22(3): 517–537.

Jowett, Matthew. 2002. Voluntary health insurance in Vietnam: A theoretical and empirical exploration. Ph.D. thesis, Department of Social Policy and Social Work and the Centre for Health Economics, University of York.

Kabeer, Naila. 2001. "Conflicts over credit: Re-evaluating the empowerment potential of loans to women in rural Bangladesh." *World Development* 29(1): 63–84.

Kaboski, Joseph P., and Robert M. Townsend. 2005. "Policies and impact: An analysis of village-level microfinance institutions." *Journal of the European Economic Association* 3(1): 1–50.

Kaplan, Eduardo. 2003. "Microfinancing affords success for some in developing world." *Wall Street Journal*, August 20.

Kapoor, Mudit, Jonathan Morduch, and Shamika Ravi. 2007. "From microfinance to m-finance." *Innovations: Technology, Governance, Globalization* 2(1,2) (Winter/Spring): 82–90.

Karlan, Dean. 2001. "Microfinance impact assessments: The perils of using new members as a control group." *Journal of Microfinance* 3(2): 76–85.

Karlan, Dean. 2007. "Social connections and group banking." *Economic Journal* 117 (February): F52–F84.

Karlan, Dean, Margaret McConnell, Sendhil Mullainathan, and Jonathan Zinman. 2009. "The salience of savings." Yale, Cal Tech, Harvard, and Dartmouth Working Paper.

Karlan, Dean, and Jonathan Morduch. 2009. "Access to finance." In Dani Rodrik and Mark Rosenzweig, eds., *Handbook of Development Economics*. Amsterdam: Elsevier.

Karlan, Dean, and Martin Valdivia. 2008. "Teaching entrepreneurship: Impact of business training on microfinance institutions and clients." Yale University Economic Growth Center Working Paper.

Karlan, Dean, and Jonathan Zinman. 2006. "Optimizing loan contracting and marketing strategies using field experimentation." Prepared for the 2006 Microcredit Summit.

Karlan, Dean, and Jonathan Zinman. 2008. "Credit elasticities in less-developed economies: Implications for microfinance." *American Economic Review* 98(3): 1040–1068.

Karlan, Dean, and Jonathan Zinman. 2009a. "Expanding microenterprise credit access: Using randomized supply decisions to estimate the impacts in Manila." Yale University, Dartmouth College, and Innovatior.s for Poverty Action (IPA) Working Paper.

Karlan, Dean, and Jonathan Zinman. 2009b. "Observing unobservables: Identifying information asymmetries with a consumer credit field experiment." *Econometrica,* forthcoming.

Karlan, Dean, and Jonathan Zinman. 2010. "Expanding credit access: Using randomized supply decisions to estimate the impacts." *Review of Financial Studies*, forthcoming.

Kennedy, Peter. 2004. *Guide to Econometrics*, 5th ed. Oxford: Blackwell Publishers.

Kerr, Steven. 1975. "On the folly of rewarding A, while hoping for B." *Academy of Management Journal* 18: 769–863.

Kevane, Michael, and Bruce Wydick. 2001. "Microenterprise lending to female entrepreneurs: Sacrificing economic growth for poverty reduction?" *World Development* 29(7) (July): 1225–1236.

Khandker, Shahidur R. 1998. *Fighting Poverty with Microcredit*. Oxford: Oxford University Press.

Khandker, Shahidur R. 2005. "Micro-finance and poverty: Evidence using panel data from Bangladesh." *World Bank Economic Review* 19: 263–286.

Khandker, Shahidur R., Baqui Khalily, and Zahed Kahn. 1995. "Grameen Bank: Performance and sustainability." World Bank Discussion Paper 306, Washington, DC.

King, Elizabeth, and Anne Hill. 1993. *Women's Education in Developing Countries: Barriers, Benefits and Policies*. Baltimore: Johns Hopkins University Press.

Kinsley, Michael, ed. 2008. *Creative Capitalism: A Conversation with Bill Gates, Warren Buffett, and Other Economic Leaders*. New York: Simon & Schuster.

Kirkpatrick, Colin, and Samuel Munzele Maimbo. 2002. "The implications of the evolving microfinance agenda for regulatory and supervisory policy." *Development Policy Review* 20(3): 293–304.

Klasen, Stephan, and Claudia Wink. 2001. "A turning point in gender bias mortality? An update on the number of missing women." University of Munich Working Paper.

Klonner, Stephan, and Ashok Rai. 2008. "Adverse selection in credit markets: Evidence from a policy experiment." Frankfurt University and Williams College Working Paper, September.

Kochar, Anjini. 1996. "Empirical analysis of models of household savings using cross-sectional LSMS Data." Draft, Stanford University, January.

Kochar, Anjini. 1997. "An empirical investigation of rationing constraints in rural credit markets in India." *Journal of Development Economics* 53: 339–371.

Krugman, Paul R. 1994. *Rethinking International Trade*. Cambridge. MA: MIT Press.

Labie, Marc. 1998. "Assessment of microfinance institutions sustainability: What have we learned from the Corposol-Finasol case?" Presentation at the Second Annual Seminar on New Development Finance. Goethe University of Frankfurt, 21–25 September. Typescript. Université de Mons-Hainaut, Belgium.

Labie, Marc. 2001. "Corporate governance in microfinance organizations: A long and winding road." *Management Decision* 39(4): 296–301.

Labie, Marc. 2003. "Corporate governance in the non-profit sector: A framework for microfinance organizations." 19th EGOS Colloquium. Copenhagen Business School, Warocque Research Center.

Labie, Marc, and Roy Mersland. 2010. "Corporate governance in microfinance." In Beatriz Armendáriz and Marc Labie, eds., *The Handbook of Microfinance*. London: World Scientific Publishing, forthcoming.

Ladman, Jerry, and Gonzalo Afcha. 1990. "Group lending: Why it failed in Bolivia." *Savings and Development* 14(4): 353–368.

Laffont, Jean Jacques. 2003. "Collusion and group lending with adverse selection." *Journal of Development Economics* 70: 329–348.

Laffont, Jean Jacques, and T. T. N'Guessan. 2000. "Group lending with adverse selection." *European Economic Review* 44: 773–784.

Laffont, Jean-Jacques, and Patrick Rey. 2003. "Moral hazard, collusion and group lending." IDEI Working Paper 122.

Laibson, David. 1997. "Golden eggs and hyperbolic discounting." *Quarterly Journal of Economics* 112(2): 443–477.

Ledgerwood, Joanna. 1999. *Microfinance Handbook: An Institutional and Financial Perspective*. Washington, DC: World Bank.

Ledgerwood, Joanna, and Victoria White. 2006. *Transforming Microfinance Institutions: Providing Full Financial Services to the Poor*. Washington, D.C.: International Bank for Reconstruction and Development/World Bank.

Levenson, Alec, and Timothy Besley. 1996. "The anatomy of an informal financial market: Rosca participation in Taiwan." *Journal of Development Economics* 51: 45–68.

Levine, Ross. 2005. "Finance and growth: Theory and evidence." In Philippe Aghion and Steven N. Durlauf, eds., *Handbook of Economic Growth*. Amsterdam: Elsevier Science.

Littlefield, Elizabeth, Jonathan Morduch, and Syed Hashemi. 2003. "Is microfinance an effective strategy to meet the Millenium Development Goals?" Washington, DC: CGAP, Focus Note 24. Washington, DC: The World Bank.

Lucas, Robert E., Jr. 1990. "Why doesn't capital flow from rich to poor countries?" *American Economic Review Papers and Proceedings* 80(2) (May): 92–96.

Madajewicz, Malgosia. 2004. "Joint liability versus individual liability in credit contracts." Columbia University Working Paper.

Madajewicz, Malgosia. 2005. "Can microcredit reduce poverty? The effect of the loan contract on loan size." In Patrick Bolton and Howard Rosenthal, eds., *Credit Markets for the Poor*. New York: Russell Sage.

Magnoni, Barbara. 2008. "Smart subsidy case study: Pro Mujer Nicaragua." EA Consultants Report.

Malkin, Elizabeth. 2008. "Microfinance's success sets off a debate in Mexico." *New York Times*. April 5, C1.

Manos, Ronny, and Jacob Yaron. 2008. "Measuring the performance of microfinance providers: An assessment of past and present practices." *International Journal of Financial Services Management* 3(2): 171–187.

Marshall, Alfred. 1890. *Principles of Economics*. London and New York: Macmillan and Co.

Martens, Bertin. 2002. "The role of evaluation in foreign aid programmes." In Bertin Martens, Uwe Mummert, Peter Murrell, and Paul Seabright, eds., *The Institutional Economics of Foreign Aid*. Cambridge: Cambridge University Press.

Mas, Ignacio. 2009. "The economics of branchless banking." *Innovations* 4(2): 57–75.

Mas, Ignacio, and Kabir Kumar. 2008. "Banking on mobiles: Why? How? For whom?" CGAP Focus Note 48 (June). Washington, DC: The World Bank.

Matin, Imran. n.d. "Dimensions and dynamics of MFI competition in Bangladesh." CGAP Note Book 1, Washington, DC. Available at www.cgap.org.

Matin, Imran. 1997. "Repayment performance of Grameen Bank borrowers: The 'unzipped' state." *Savings and Development* 21(4): 451–473.

Matin, Imran, and David Hulme. 2003. "Programmes for the poorest: Learning from the IGVGD programme in Bangladesh." *World Development* 31(3): 647–665.

Mayoux, Linda. 1999. "Questioning virtuous spirals: Microfinance and women's empowerment in Africa." *Journal of International Development* 11: 957–984.

McCord, Michael. 2001. "Health care microinsurance—Case studies from Uganda, Tanzania, India and Cambodia." *Small Enterprise Development* 12(1) (March): 1–15.

McIntosh, Craig. 2008. "Estimating treatment effects from spatial policy experiments: An application to Ugandan microfinance." *Review of Economics and Statistics* 90(1): 15–28.

McIntosh, Craig, Alain de Janvry, and Elizabeth Sadoulet. 2006. "How rising competition among microfinance institutions affects incumbent lenders." *Economic Journal* 115(506): 987–1004.

McIntosh, Craig, and Bruce Wydick. 2005. "Competition and microfinance." *Journal of Development Economics* 78(2) (December): 271–298.

McKee, Katharine. 2005. "Prerequisites for intermediating savings." In Madeline Hirschland, ed., *Savings Services for the Poor: An Operational Guide*. Bloomfield, CT: Kumarian Press. 27–42.

McKenzie, David, and Christopher Woodruff. 2006. "Do entry costs provide an empirical basis for poverty traps? Evidence from Mexican microenterprises." *Economic Development and Cultural Change* 55(1): 3–42.

McKenzie, David, and Christopher Woodruff. 2008. "Experimental evidence on returns to capital and access to finance in Mexico." *World Bank Economic Review* 22(3): 457–482.

McKernan, Signe-Mary. 2002. "The impact of microcredit programs on self-employment profits: Do noncredit program aspects matter?" *Review of Economics and Statistics* 84(1) (February): 93–115.

McKinnon, Ronald. 1973. *Money and Capital in Economic Development.* Washington, DC: The Brookings Institution.

Mersland, Roy, and R. Øystein Strøm. 2009. "Performance and governance in microfinance institutions." *Journal of Banking and Finance* 33(4) (April): 662–669.

Meyer, Richard. 2002. "Microfinance, poverty alleviation, and improving food security: Implications for India." In Rattan Lal, ed., *Food Security and Environmental Quality.* Boca Raton, FL: CRC Press.

MFI Solutions. 2008. "The implications of increased commercialization of the microfinance industry: What can we learn from the discussions that followed the Compartamos IPO?" Lancaster, PA: MFI Solutions.

The MicroBanking Bulletin. 2002. "Additional tables for all MFIs and financially self-sufficient MFIs." *The MicroBanking Bulletin* 8 (November): 58–85. Available at www.mixmbb.org.

The MicroBanking Bulletin. 2003. "Additional tables for all MFIs and financially self-sufficient MFIs." *The MicroBanking Bulletin* 9 (July): 61–76. Available at www.mixmbb.org.

The MicroBanking Bulletin. 2008. "2007 annual MFI benchmarks." *The MicroBanking Bulletin* 17 (Autumn): 35–41. Available at www.mixmbb.org.

MicroCapital. 2007. "Microfinance Funds Universe." http://www.microcapital.org/microfinance-funds-universe/.

Microcredit Summit. 2003. "State of the Microcredit Summit Campaign Report 2002." Available at www.microcreditsummit.org/pubs/reports/socr02_en.pdf.

Microcredit Summit Campaign. 2000. "Empowering women with microcredit: Microcredit Summit Campaign Report 2000." *Countdown 2005* 3(2–3) (July/August): 16–31.

MicroRate Survey. 2002. "Adjusted comparison table." June. Available at www.microrate.com.

Migot-Adholla, Shem, Peter Hazell, Benoit Blarel, and Frank Place. 1991. "Indigenous land rights systems in sub-Saharan Africa: A constraint on productivity?" *World Bank Economic Review* 5(1) (January): 155–175.

Miguel, Edward. 2005. "Poverty and witch killing." *Review of Economic Studies* 72(4): 1153–1172.

Miranda, Mario. 1991. "Area-yield crop insurance reconsidered." *American Journal of Agricultural Economics* 73(2): 233–242.

Mirrlees, James A. 1971. "An exploration in the theory of optimum income taxation." *Review of Economic Studies* 38(2): 175–208.

Mirrlees, James A. 1974. "Notes of welfare economics, information and uncertainty." In M. Balch, D. McFadden, and S. Wu, eds., *Essays in Equilibrium Behavior under Uncertainty.* Amsterdam: North-Holland.

Mirrlees, James A. 1976. "The optimal structure of incentives and authority within an organisation." *Bell Journal of Economics* 7: 105–131.

Montgomery, Richard. 1996. "Disciplining or protecting the poor? Avoiding the social costs of peer pressure in micro-credit schemes." *Journal of International Development* 8(2) (March–April): 289–305.

Morduch, Jonathan. 1994. "Poverty and vulnerability." *American Economic Review (AEA Papers and Proceedings)* 84 (May): 221–225.

Morduch, Jonathan. 1998. "Does microfinance really help the poor? New evidence on flagship programs in Bangladesh." Draft, MacArthur Foundation project on inequality working paper, Princeton University.

Morduch, Jonathan. 1999a. "Between the market and state: Can informal insurance patch the safety net?" *World Bank Research Observer* 14(2): 187–207.

Morduch, Jonathan. 1999b. "The microfinance promise." *Journal of Economic Literature* 37 (December): 1569–1614.

Morduch, Jonathan. 1999c. "The role of subsidies in microfinance: Evidence from the Grameen Bank." *Journal of Development Economics* 60 (October): 229–248.

Morduch, Jonathan. 2000. "The microfinance schism." *World Development* 28(4) (April): 617–629.

Morduch, Jonathan. 2001. "Babies and banks: Did rapid financial expansion help drive the historic fertility decline in Bangladesh?" Draft, New York University.

Morduch, Jonathan. 2004. "Consumption smoothing across space: Testing theories of risk-sharing in the ICRISAT study region of South India." In Steven Dercon, ed., *Insurance Against Poverty*. Oxford: Oxford University Press.

Morduch, Jonathan. 2006. "Micro-insurance: The next revolution?" In Abhijit Banerjee, Roland Benabou, and Dilip Mookherjee, eds., *Understanding Poverty*. New York: Oxford University Press.

Morduch, Jonathan. 2007. "Smart subsidy." In Bernd Balkenhol, ed., *Microfinance and Public Policy*. London: Palgrave/Macmillan, 72–85.

Morduch, Jonathan, and Stuart Rutherford. 2003. "Microfinance: Analytical issues for India." In Priya Basu, ed., *India's Financial Sector: Issues, Challenges and Policy Options*. New York: Oxford University Press.

Mosley, Paul. 1996a. "Indosia: BKK, KURK, and the BRI Unit Desa Institutions." In David Hulme and Paul Mosley, eds., *Finance Against Poverty*. London: Routledge.

Mosley, Paul. 1996b. "Metamorphosis from NGO to commercial bank: The case of BancoSol in Bolivia." In David Hulme and Paul Mosley, eds., *Finance Against Poverty*. London: Routledge.

National Bank for Agriculture and Rural Development [NABARD]. 2007. "Snapshot of SHG-Bank Linkage in India-March 2007." NABARD report, Delhi.

Otero, Maria, and Michael Chu. 2002. "Governance and ownership of microfinance institutions." In Deborah Drake and Elisabeth Rhyne, eds., *The Commercialization of Microfinance*. Bloomfield, CT: Kumarian Press.

Otero, Maria, Elisabeth Rhyne, and Mary Houghton. 1994. *The New World of Microenterprise Finance: Building Healthy Institutions for the Poor*. Bloomfield, CT: Kumarian Press.

Park, Albert, and Changqing Ren. 2001. "Microfinance with Chinese characteristics." *World Development* 29(1): 39–62.

Park, Hun Myoung. 2008. "Hypothesis testing and statistical power of a test." Technical Working Paper. The University Information Technology Services (UITS) Center for Statistical and Mathematical Computing, Indiana University.

Patten, Richard, and Jay Rosengard. 1991. *Progress with Profits: The Development of Rural Banking in Indonesia.* San Francisco: International Center for Economic Growth/HIID.

Paulson, Anna, and Robert Townsend. 2004. "Entrepreneurship and financial constraints in Thailand." *Journal of Corporate Finance* 10(2) (March): 229–262.

Pauly, Mark. 1968. "The economics of moral hazard: Comment." *American Economic Review* 58(3): 531–537.

Pearl, Daniel, and Michael Phillips. 2001. "Grameen Bank, which pioneered loans for the poor, has hit a repayment snag." *Wall Street Journal*, November 27, 2001, p. 1.

Pitt, Mark. 1999. "Reply to Jonathan Morduch's 'Does microfinance really help the poor? New evidence from flagship programs in Bangladesh.'" Typescript, Department of Economics, Brown University.

Pitt, Mark, and Shahidur Khandker. 1998. "The impact of group-based credit programs on poor households in Bangladesh: Does the gender of participants matter?" *Journal of Political Economy* 106(5): 958–996.

Pitt, Mark, Shahidur Khandker, Signe-Mary McKernan, and M. Abdul Latif. 1999. "Credit programs for the poor and reproductive behavior in low income countries: Are the reported causal relationships the result of heterogeneity bias?" *Demography* 36(1) (February): 1–22.

Pitt, Mark, Shahidur Khandker, and Jennifer Cartwright. 2006. "Empowering women with microfinance: Evidence from Bangladesh." *Economic Development and Cultural Change* 54(4) (July): 791–831.

Pitt, Mark, Mark Rosenzweig, and M. N. Hassan. 1990. "Productivity, health and inequality in the intrahousehold distribution of food in low income countries." *American Economic Review* 80(5): 1139–1156.

Platteau, Jean-Philippe. 2000. *Institutions, Social Norms, and Economic Development.* Amsterdam: Harwood Publishers.

Prinz, Michael. 2002. "German rural cooperatives, Friedrich-Wilhelm Raiffeisen and the organization of trust: 1850–1914." Typescript, Universitae Bielefeld, Germany.

Pritchett, Lant. 2002. "It pays to be ignorant: A simple political economy of rigorous program evaluation." *Journal of Policy Reform* 5(4) (December): 251–269.

Pronyk, Paul, James Hargreaves, and Jonathan Morduch. 2007. "Microfinance programs and better health: Prospects for sub-Saharan Africa."*Journal of the American Medical Association* 298(16) (October 24/31): 1925–1927.

Pulley, Robert. 1989. "Making the poor creditworthy: A case study of the integrated rural development program in India." World Bank Discussion Paper 58. Washington, DC: World Bank.

Radermacher, Ralf, Iddo Dror, and Gerry Noble. 2006. "Challenges and strategies to extend health insurance to the poor." In Craig Churchill, ed., *Protecting the Poor: A Microinsurance Compendium*. Geneva: Munich Re and ILO.

Rahman, Aminur. 1999. "Microcredit initiatives for equitable and sustainable development: Who pays?" *World Development* 26(12) (December): 67–82.

Rahman, Aminur. 2001. *Women and Microcredit in Rural Bangladesh: An Anthropological Study of Grameen Bank Lending*. Boulder, CO: Westview Press.

Rahman, Mizanur, and Julie Da Vanzo. 1998. "Influence of the Grameen Bank on contraceptive use in Bangladesh." Paper presented at the Conference on Microcredit and Fertility, Population Council, New York.

Rai, Ashok. 2002. "Targeting the poor using community information." *Journal of Development Economics* 69(1) (October): 71–84.

Rai, Ashok, and Tomas Sjöström. 2004. "Is Grameen lending effcient? Repayment incentives and insurance in village economies." *Review of Economic Studies* 71(1) (January): 217–234.

Rankin, Katherine. 2002. "Social capital, microfinance, and the politics of development." *Feminist Economics* 8(1): 1–24.

Ratha, Dilip, Sanket Mohapatra, K. M. Vijayalakshmi, and Zhimei Xu. 2008. "Revisions to remittance trends 2007." World Bank Migration and Development Brief 5.

Ravallion, Martin. 2009. "Should the randomistas rule?" *The Economists' Voice* 6(2): Article 6.

Rawls, John. 1971. *A Theory of Justice*. Cambridge, MA: Belknap Press, Harvard University Press.

Ray, Debraj. 1998. *Development Economics*. Princeton, NJ: Princeton University Press.

Reddy, Y. V. 1999. "Future of rural banking." Prof. G. Ram Reddy Third Endowment Lecture, Hyderabad, India, December 4.

Reed, Larry. 2006. "Commercialization: Overcoming the obstacles to accessing commercial funds while maintaining a commitment to reaching the poorest." In Sam Daley-Harris and Anna Awimbo, eds., *More Pathways Out of Poverty*. Bloomfield, CT: Kumarian Press.

Reserve Bank of India (RBI) 1954. *All-India Credit Survey*. Bombay: RBI.

Rhyne, Elisabeth. 1998. "The yin and yang of microfinance: Reaching the poor and sustainability." *The MicroBanking Bulletin* 2 (July): 6–8.

Rhyne, Elisabeth. 2001. *Mainstreaming Microfinance: How Lending to the Poor Began, Grew, and Came of Age in Bolivia*. Bloomfield, CT: Kumarian Press.

Richardson, Dave. 2003. "Going to the barricades with microsavings mobilization: A view of the real costs from the trenches." *MicroBanking Bulletin* 9 (July): 9–13.

Robert, Bruce L., Jr. 1979. "Agricultural credit cooperatives, rural development, and agrarian politics in Madras, 1893–1937." *Indian Economic and Social History Review* 16(2) (April–June): 163–184.

Robinson, Joan. 1933. *The Economics of Imperfect Competition*. London: Macmillan.

Robinson, Marguerite. 2001. *The Microfinance Revolution: Sustainable Banking for the Poor.* Washington, DC: The World Bank.

Rodrik, Dani. 1997. *Has Globalization Gone Too Far?* Washington, DC: Institute for International Economics.

Roodman, David, and Jonathan Morduch. 2009. "The impact of microcredit on the poor in Bangladesh: Revisiting the evidence." Center for Global Development Working Paper, Washington, DC.

Rose, Elaina. 1999. "Consumption smoothing and excess female mortality in rural India." *Review of Economics and Statistics* 81(1): 41–49.

Rosen, Harvey. 2002. *Public Finance*, 6th ed. New York: McGraw-Hill.

Rosenbaum, P., and D. Rubin. 1983. "The central role of the propensity score in observational studies for causal effects." *Biometrika* 70: 41–55.

Rosenberg, Richard. 1999. "Measuring microcredit delinquency: Ratios can be harmful to your health." Consultative Group to Assist the Poor, CGAP Occasional Paper No. 3, June. Available at www.cgap.org/docs/OccasionalPaper_03.pdf.

Rosenberg, Richard. 2007. "CGAP reflections on the Compartamos initial public offering: A case study on microfinance interest rates and profits." CGAP Focus Note 42. Washington, DC: Consultative Group to Assist the Poor.

Rosenberg, Richard. 2008. "Muhammad Yunus and Michael Chu debate commercialization." CGAP Microfinance Blog, October 14. Accessed November 24 2008. Available at http://microfinance.cgap.org/2008/10/14/muhammad-yunus-and-michael-chu-debate-commercialization/

Rosenberg, Richard, Adrian Gonzalez, and Sushma Narain. 2009. "The new moneylenders: Are the poor being exploited by high microcredit interest rates?" CGAP Occasional Paper 15 (February).

Rosenzweig, Mark R., and T. Paul Schultz. 1982. "Market opportunities, genetic endowments and intrafamily resource distribution: Child survival in rural India." *American Economic Review* 75(5): 723–746.

Roth, James. 1999. "Informal micro-finance schemes: The case of funeral insurance in South Africa." International Labour Organization Working Paper No. 22.

Rutherford, Stuart. 1997. "Informal financial services in Dhaka's slums." In Geoffrey Wood and Iffath Sharif, eds., *Who Needs Credit? Poverty and Finance in Bangladesh.* Dhaka: University Press Ltd.

Rutherford, Stuart. 2000. *The Poor and Their Money.* New Delhi: Oxford University Press.

Rutherford, Stuart. 2009. *The Pledge: ASA, Peasant Politics, and Microfinance in the Development of Bangladesh.* New York: Oxford University Press.

Sadoulet, Loïc. 2003. "The role of mutual insurance in group lending." Draft, ECARES/Free University of Brussels, March.

Sadoulet, Loïc, and Seth Carpenter. 2001. "Endogenous matching and risk heterogeneity: Evidence on microcredit group formation in Guatemala." Working paper, ECARES/Free University of Brussels.

Samphantharak, Krislert, and Robert M. Townsend. 2008. "Households as corporate firms: Constructing financial statements from integrated household surveys." UC-San Diego IRPS and University of Chicago Department of Economics Working Paper.

Schreiner, Mark. 1997. "A framework for the analysis of the performance and sustainability of subsidized microfinance organizations with application to BancoSol of Bolivia and Grameen Bank of Bangladesh." Unpublished Ph.D. diss., Rural Finance Group, Department of Agricultural, Environmental, and Development Economics, The Ohio State University, Columbus, OH.

Schreiner, Mark. 2003. "A cost-effectiveness analysis of the Grameen Bank of Bangladesh." *Development Policy Review* 21(3): 357–382.

Schreiner, Mark, and Jonathan Morduch. 2002. "Replicating microfinance in the United States: Opportunities and challenges." In Jim Carr and Zhong Yi Tong, eds., *Replicating Microfinance in the United States.* Baltimore: Woodrow Wilson Center/Johns Hopkins University Press.

Schreiner, Mark, and Jacob Yaron. 2001. *Development Finance Institutions: Measuring Their Subsidy.* Washington, DC: World Bank.

Schuler, Sidney, Syed Hashemi, and Ann Riley. 1997. "The influence of women's changing roles and status on Bangladesh's fertility transition: Evidence from a study of credit programs and contraceptive use." *World Development* 25(4): 563–575.

Schultz, T. Paul. 1990. "Testing the neoclassical model of family labor supply and fertility." *Journal of Human Resources* 25(4): 599–634.

Sebstad, Jennifer, and Gregory Chen. 1996. "Overview of studies on the impact of microenterprise credit." Report submitted to USAID Assessing the Impact of Microenterprise Services (AIMS), June.

Sen, Amartya. 1981. *Poverty and Famines: An Essay on Entitlements and Deprivation.* Oxford, UK: Oxford University Press.

Sen, Amartya. 1992. "Missing women." *British Medical Journal* 304: 586–587.

Servet, Jean-Michel. 2010. "Corporate responsibility versus social performances and financial inclusion." In Beatriz Armendáriz and Marc Labie, eds., *The Handbook of Microfinance.* London: World Scientific Publishing, forthcoming.

Sharma, Manohar, and Manfred Zeller. 1996. "Repayment performance in group-based credit programs in Bangladesh: An empirical analysis." Food Consumption and Nutrition Division, Discussion Paper 15, International Food Policy Research Institute, Washington, DC.

Shleifer, Andrei. 1985. "A theory of yardstick competition." *Rand Journal of Economics* 16(3) (Autumn): 319–327.

Siamwalla, Amar, Chirmsak Pinthong, Nipon Poapongsakorn, Ploenpit Satsanguan, Prayong Nettayarak, Wanrak Mingmaneenakin, and Yuavares Tubpun. 1990. "The Thai rural credit system and elements of a theory: Public subsidies, private information, and segmented markets." *World Bank Economic Review* 4(3): 271–296.

Silwal, Ani Rudra. 2003. "Repayment performance of Nepali village banks." Public Policy Honors Thesis, Swarthmore College, Swarthmore, PA, May.

Singh, Kareem. 1968. "Structure of interest rates on consumption loans in an Indian village." *Asian Economic Review* 10(4) (August): 471–475.

Skees, Jerry, Panos Varangis, Donald F. Larson, and Paul Siegel. 2004. "Can financial markets be tapped to help poor people cope with weather risks?" In Stefon Dercon, ed., *Insurance Against Poverty*. Oxford: Oxford University Press.

Skoufias, Emmanuel. 2001. "Is PROGRESA working? Summary of the results of an evaluation by International Food Policy Research Institute (IFPRI)." Food Consumption and Nutrition Division, Discussion Paper No. 118, Washington, DC.

Smith, Stephen. 2002. "Village banking and maternal and child health: Evidence from Ecuador and Honduras." *World Development* 30(4) (April): 707–723.

Snodgrass, Donald, and Jennifer Sebstad. 2002. "Clients in context: The impacts of microfinance in three countries: Synthesis report." MSI International, AIMS Project January, Washington, DC. Available at www.mip.org/pdfs/aims/AIMS_SynthesisReport.pdf.

Sobel, Joel. 2006. "For better or forever: Formal versus informal enforcement." *Journal of Labor Economics* 24(2): 271–297.

Steege, Jean. 1998. "The rise and fall of Corposol: Lessons learned from the challenges of managing growth." Microfinance Best Practices Working Paper. Available at www.mip.org/pdfs/mbp/corposol.pdf.

Steel, William F., and Ernest Aryeetey. 1994. "Informal savings collectors in Ghana: Can they intermediate?" *Finance and Development*. 19(2): 36–37.

Steel, William F., Ernest Aryeetey, Hemala Hettige, and Machiko Nissanke. 1997. "Informal financial markets under liberalization in four African countries." *World Development* 25(5): 817–830.

Stephens, Blaine. 2008. "MFI benchmark analysis: An industry still expanding, despite challenges." *The MicroBanking Bulletin* 17 (Autumn): 25–32. Available at www.mixmbb.org.

Stiglitz, Joseph E. 1974. "Incentives and risk sharing in sharecropping." *Review of Economic Studies* 41 (April): 219–256.

Stiglitz, Joseph E. 1990. "Peer monitoring and credit markets." *World Bank Economic Review* 4(3): 351–366.

Stiglitz, Joseph E., and Andrew Weiss. 1981. "Credit markets with imperfect information." *American Economic Review* 71: 393–410.

Strauss, John, and Kathleen Beegle. 1996. "Intrahousehold allocations: A review of theories, empirical evidence and policy issues." Typescript, Department of Agricultural Economics, Michigan State University.

Swain, Ranjula Bali, and Fan Yang Wallentin. 2007. "Does microfinance empower women? Evidence from self-help groups in India." Uppsala University, Department of Economics, Working Paper 2007: 24.

Tenenbaum, Shelly. 1993. *A Credit to Their Community: Jewish Loan Societies in the United States, 1880–1945*. Detroit: Wayne State University Press.

Thaler, Richard H. 1990. "Anomalies: Saving, fungibility and mental accounts." *Journal of Economic Perspectives* 4: 193–205.

Thaler, Richard H. 1994. "Psychology and savings policies." *American Economic Review (AEA Papers and Proceedings)*, May.

Thaler, Richard H., and Cass R. Sunstein. 2008. *Nudge: Improving Decisions about Health, Wealth, and Happiness.* New Haven: Yale University Press.

Thomas, Duncan. 1990. "Intrahousehold allocation: An inferential approach." *Journal of Human Resources* 25(4): 635–664.

Thomas, Duncan. 1994. "Like father like son, or, like mother like daughter: Parental education and child health." *Journal of Human Resources* 29(4): 950–988.

Todd, Helen. 1996. *Women at the Center: Grameen Bank Borrowers after One Decade.* Dhaka: University Press Ltd.

Townsend, Robert. 1997. "Microenterprise and macropolicy." In David Kreps and Kenneth F. Wallis, eds., *Advances in Economics and Econometrics: Theory and Applications,* vol. 2, Seventh World Congress (Econometrics Society Monograph). Cambridge: Cambridge University Press.

Townsend, Robert. 2000. "The impact of the crisis in Thailand." Typescript. University of Chicago.

Townsend, Robert, and Kinichi Ueda. 2006. "Financial deepening, inequality, and growth: A model-based quantitative evaluation." *Review of Economic Studies* 73(254): 251–293.

Townsend, Robert, and Jacob Yaron. 2001. "The credit risk contingency system of an Asian development bank." *Economic Perspectives* Q3: 31–48.

Udry, Christopher. 1996. "Gender, agricultural production, and the theory of the household." *Journal of Political Economy* 104(5): 1010–1046.

Udry, Christopher, and Santosh Anagol. 2006. "The return to capital in Ghana." *American Economic Review* 96(2): 388–393.

United Nations. 2000. *The World's Women 2000: Trends and Statistics.* New York: United Nations.

United Nations. 2003. "General assembly greenlights programme for the international year of microcredit 2005." United Nations Press Release. Available online at http://www.uncdf.org/english/microfinance/pubs/newsletter/pages/dec_2003/spotlight.php.

United Nations Advisors Group on Informal Financial Sector. 2008. *Key Messages.* New York: United Nations Capital Development Fund.

United Nations Development Program. 1996. *Human Development Report 1996.* New York: UNDP.

United Nations Development Program. 2006. *Evaluation of Gender Mainstreaming in UNDP.* New York: UNDP.

Valenzuela, Lisa. 2001. "Getting the recipe right: The experiences and challenges of commercial bank downscalers." USAID Microenterprise Best Practices Report.

Varghese, Adel. 2004. "Can moneylenders link with banks? Theory and evidence from Indian villages." Bush School of Government, Texas A & M University Working Paper.

Varghese, Adel. 2005. "Bank-moneylender linkage as an alternative to competition." *Oxford Economic Papers* 57(2): 315–335.

Varian, Hal. 1990. "Monitoring agents with other agents." *Journal of Institutional and Theoretical Economics* 146: 153–174.

Vermeersch, A. 1912. "Usury." *Catholic Encyclopedia*, vol. 15. Robert Appleton Company. Available at www.newadvent.org/cathen/15235c.htm.

von Pischke, J. D., Dale Adams, and Gordon Donald, eds. 1983. *Rural Financial Markets in Developing Countries: Their Use and Abuse.* Baltimore: World Bank/Johns Hopkins University Press.

Ward, Benjamin. 1958. "The firm in Illyria: Market syndicalism." *The American Economic Review* 48(4): 566–589.

Wenner, Mark. 1995. "Group credit: A means to improve information transfer and loan repayment performance." *Journal of Development Studies* 32: 263–281.

Woller, Gary. 2000. "Reassessing the financial viability of village banking: Past performance and future prospects." *MicroBanking Bulletin* 5 (September): 3–8.

Woller, Gary, and Mark Schreiner. 2003. "Poverty lending, financial self-sufficiency, and the six aspects of outreach." Working paper, Marriot School, Brigham Young University.

Women's World Banking. 2003. "What do microfinance customer value?" *What Works* 1(1). New York: Women's World Banking. Available at www.swwb.org.

Woodruff, Christopher. 2001. "Review of de Soto's The Mystery of Capital." *Journal of Economic Literature* 39(4) (December): 1215–1223.

Woolcock, Michael. 1998. *Social Theory, Development Policy, and Poverty Alleviation: A Comparative-Historical Analysis of Group-Based Banking in Developing Economies.* Ph.D. diss., Department of Sociology, Brown University.

World Bank. 1990. *World Development Report 1990.* New York: Oxford University Press.

World Bank. 2002a. "IFC invests in weather insurance in emerging markets." DevNews Media Center article. Available at www.worldbank.org.

World Bank. 2002b. *World Bank Indicators.* Washington, D.C.: World Bank

World Bank. 2007. *Finance for All? Policies and Pitfalls in Expanding Access.* World Bank Policy Research Report, August. Washington, DC: World Bank.

World Council of Credit Unions. 2007 and various years. *Statistical Report.* Available at www.woccu.org/memberserv/intlcusystem [Accessed March 2009.]

World Savings Banks Institute (WSBI). 2008. "WSBI position paper on the regulation of microfinance services." Brussels: WSBI.

Wright, Graham. 2000. *Microfinance Systems: Designing Quality Financial Services for the Poor.* London: Zed Books, and Dhaka: University Press Ltd.

Wright, Graham. 2001. "Dropouts and graduates: Lessons from Bangladesh." *Micro Banking Bulletin* 6 (April): 14–16.

Wright, Graham A. N., and Leonard Mutesasira. 2001. "The relative risks to the savings of poor people." MicroSave Briefing Note 6.

Wydick, Bruce. 1999. "Can social cohesion be harnessed to repair market failures? Evidence from group lending in Guatemala." *The Economic Journal* 109: 463–475.

Yaron, Jacob. 1992. "Assessing development financial institutions: A public interest analysis." World Bank Discussion Paper 174, Washington, DC.

Yunus, Muhammad. 1983. "Group-based savings and credit for the rural poor." Paper presented at the ILO-sponsored Inter-Country Workship on Group-Based Savings and Credit for the Rural Poor, Bogra, November 6–13. Dhaka: Grameen Bank.

Yunus, Muhammad, with Alan Jolis. 1999. *Banker to the Poor: Micro-Lending and the Battle against World Poverty.* New York: PublicAffairs.

Yunus, Muhammad. 2002. "Grameen Bank II: Designed to open new possibilities." Dhaka: Grameen Bank. Available at www.grameen-info.org/bank/bank2.html.

Yunus, Muhammad. 2006. Nobel Lecture. Oslo, Norway.

Yunus, Muhammad. 2008. *Creating a World Without Poverty: Social Business and the Future of Capitalism.* New York: Public Affairs.

Zeitinger, Claus-Peter. 1996. "Micro-lending in the Russian Federation." In J. Levitsky, ed., *Small Business in Transition Economies,* 85–94. London: IDTG Publishing. Reprinted in the *Quarterly Journal of International Agriculture* 42(2003): 371–383.

Zeller, Manfred, Meike Wollni, and Ahmed Abu Shaban. 2003. "Evaluating the poverty outreach of development programs: Results from case studies in Indonesia and Mexico." *Quarterly Journal of international Agriculture* 42(3): 371–383.

Abbreviations

ADA	Appui au Développement Autonome (Luxembourg)
ADEMI	Asociación para el Desarrollo de Microempresas, Inc. (Dominican Republic)
Adie	Association pour le droit à l'initiative économique (France)
ADMIC	Asesoría Dinamica a Microempresas (Mexico)
AIG	American International Group
IRDP	Integrated Rural Development Program (India)
ASA	Association for Social Advancement (Bangladesh)
ASCA	accumulating savings and credit association
BAAC	Bank for Agriculture and Agricultural Cooperatives (Thailand)
BASIX	Hyderabad-based microfinance institution promoting livelihoods (India)
BIDS	Bangladesh Institute of Development Studies
BRAC	Bangladesh Rural Advancement Committee (now known only as BRAC)
BRDB	Bangladesh Rural Development Board
BRI	Bank Rakyat Indonesia
CARE	Cooperative for Assistance and Relief Everywhere
CERISE	Comité d'Echange, de Réflexion et d'information sur les Systèmes d'Eparge-crédit (France)
CERMi	Centre for European Research in Microfinance (Belgium)
CGAP	The Consultative Group to Assist the Poor (Washington, DC)

Crédal	Crédit Alternatif (Brussels, Belgium)
CSR	Corporate Social Responsibility
EMN	European Microfinance Network
FAI	Financial Access Initiative
FFP	Fondos Financieros Privados
FINCA	The Foundation for International Community Assistance
FSS	Financial Self Sufficiency
GCAMF	Grameen Crédit Agricole Microfinance Foundation (France)
GDP	gross domestic product
GNP	gross national product
GPS	Grameen Pension Scheme
GTZ	Deutsche Gesellschaft für Technische Zusammenarbeit
GTC	Grameen Trust Chiapas (Mexico)
IBRD	International Bank for Reconstruction and Development (World Bank)
IDPM	Institute for Development Policy and Management (University of Manchester)
IFAD	International Fund for Agriculture and Development (Rome)
IMAGE	Intervention for Microfinance and Gender Equity (South Africa)
IPA	Innovations for Poverty Action
IPO	Initial Public Offering
IRDP	Integrated Rural Development Program (India)
J-Pal	Abdul Latif Jameel Poverty Action Lab (MIT)
KUPEDES	General rural credit loan product (BRI, Indonesia)
LSMS	Living Standards Measurement Survey (World Bank)
MBB	*MicroBanking Bulletin*
MDGs	Millennium Development Goals
MFC	The Microfinance Center (Eastern Europe and Newly Independent States)
MFI	microfinance institution

NGO	nongovernmental organization
OSS	Operational Self Sufficiency
PKSF	Palli Karma-Sahayak Foundation (Bangladesh)
PPP	Purchasing Power Parity
PRODEM	The Foundation for the Promotion and Development of Microenterprises (Bolivia)
PROGRESA	Programa de Educación, Salud y Alimentación (Mexico)
PROSHIKA	Training, Education, and Action (Bangladesh)
RBI	Reserve Bank of India
RCT	Randomized Controlled Trial
ROSCAs	rotating savings and credit associations
SEED	Supporting Enterprises for Economic Development saving product (Philippines)
SEWA	Self-Employed Women's Association (India)
SHG	Self Help Group
SIMPEDES	Simpanan Pedesaan saving product (BRI, Indonesia)
TABANAS	National savings product (BRI, Indonesia)
UNDP	United Nations Development Program
USAID	United States Agency for International Development
WSBI	World Savings Bank Institute (Brussels)

Name Index

Subject Index

Acceso FFP (Bolivia), 145
ACCION International, 18, 239–240, 280, 349–351
Accumulating savings and credit association (ASCA), 79–80
Actuar Bogotá (Colombia), 350
ADEMI (Dominican Republic), 160
ADMIC (Mexico), 267
Adverse selection, 8, 391n13, 405n16
  agency problem and, 41–45
  default and, 141 (*see also* Default)
  group lending and, 98, 101–108, 114, 128, 391nn13,15,18
  insurance and, 195–200
  intervention policies and, 31, 41–45, 49–53, 58–59, 387n13
  mitigating, 101–108
  numerical example of, 104–105
  regulation and, 260
  repayment burden and, 52–53
  risky types and, 51–52, 101–103
  safe types and, 51–52, 101–103
  savings and, 172, 186, 205, 397n14
  subsidies and, 331
Agency theory
  adverse selection and, 41–45
  Association of Social Advancement (ASA) and, 351, 367–368
  avoiding myopia and, 366
  Bank Rakyat Indonesia (BRI) and, 363–365
  commercialization and, 369–373
  Corposol and, 353–354
  discouraging deception and, 366–367
  fixed wages and, 352
  functional specialization and, 367–368
  high-powered vs. low-powered incentives and, 357–359

  intervention policies and, 39–48
  limited liability and, 40–41
  linking to local markets and, 54–57
  management practice and, 351–369
  Marshall and, 352
  Mirrlees and, 352
  multitask problem and, 353–356
  numerical example of, 45–48
  ownership and, 369–373
  participation constraint and, 352
  poverty reduction and, 353–356
  PRODEM and, 359–362
  PROGRESA/Oportunidades and, 367–368
  unmeasurable tasks and, 356–357
  yardstick competition and, 365, 407n18
Agriculture, 364
  alternative banking models and, 9–12, 384nn9,10
  Bank of Agriculture and Agricultural Cooperatives (BAAC) and, 30, 32, 120–121, 170, 263, 325–327, 384n9
  BRAC and, 22
  credit cooperatives and, 71, 80, 389nn12,14
  gender and, 216–217, 220, 226–227
  group lending and, 120, 152–153, 160
  impact measurement and, 285–286
  increased wages and, 9
  insurance and, 200
  intervention policies and, 30, 32
  moneylenders and, 32
  rainfall insurance and, 172, 199–201
  savings and, 170, 183
  sharecroppers and, 353, 406n9
  Small Farmer Credit Program (PCPA) and, 123

Shakti Foundation for Women
(Bangladesh), 172
Sharecroppers, 353, 406n9
Side payments, 105
SIMPEDES (Indonesia), 194
SKS program (India), 203, 336
Small Farmer Credit Program (PCPA,
Bolivia), 123
Social capital
gender and, 211, 232–233
group lending and, 115, 119–122, 128,
393n28
Solidarity groups
alternative banking models and, 138
gender and, 228–229, 399n19
group lending and, 97, 112, 114
impact measurement, 301
management practice and, 350–351
South Africa, 67
impact measurement and, 296–298
randomized control trials (RCTs) and,
296–298
rotating savings and credit associations
(ROSCAs) and, 75–77
savings and, 179–180, 183, 188
Sovereign debt problem, 141
Spandana (India), 299
Spillover, 285, 290, 301–302, 308, 315, 331
Sri Lanka, 53, 213–214
impact measurement and, 299–301
randomized control trials (RCTs) and,
299–301
tsunami of, 300
women and, 224–225
Standard & Poor's ratings, 19
State-owned development banks, 9–12
Statistics. See Impact measurement
Stigma, 157–158
Strong-arm strategies, 56
Subsidies, 4, 202
asset transfers and, 335
Association for Social Advancement
(ASA) and, 21
Bangladesh and, 20–21, 327–329
BRAC and, 334–337, 341
cheap credit issues and, 332
consultants industry and, 319
Corporate Social Responsibility (CSR)
and, 400n30
cost-benefit analysis of, 320–321,
325–341
counting, 322–325

credit plus plus services and, 339
cross-subsidization and, 23, 47, 58, 87,
102, 106, 197, 251–252, 338, 340, 373,
406n11
dependence index and, 321–325, 400n7
distribution and, 38–39
donor issues and, 320, 341
education and, 335–336
efficiency and, 332–333, 338–340
elasticity and, 322
enforcement rent and, 338
excessive, 405n5
exchange rate risk and, 323
financial self-sufficiency ratio (FSS)
and, 323
forms of, 323
Grameen Bank and, 322–329
impact measurement and, 319–320,
326–331, 334, 336
Income Generation for Vulnerable
Group Development (IGVGD)
program and, 334–336
Indonesia and, 20–21
information collection and, 319–320,
330–331
institutions/customer choice and,
333–334
interest rates and, 11, 318, 321–327,
330–338
loan guarantees and, 323
microcredit and, 318–319, 330
moving debates forward on, 330–331
rethinking, 17–23
skepticism of, 330–333
smart, 332–339
soft equity and, 323
soft loans and, 322–323
state-owned development banks and,
9–12
strategic long-term, 336–339
strategic short-term, 334–336
Targeting the Ultra Poor (TUP)
program and, 335–336
tax holidays and, 323
Thailand and, 325–327
USAID and, 239
very poor clients and, 334–336
women and, 328–329
Subsidy dependence index (SDI), 321,
323–325, 400n7
Sustainability
collateral and, 338